Das nächste Bitcoin

7 unbekannte Kryptowährungen mit enormen Gewinnpotentialen. So investieren Sie als Krypto-Einsteiger früh und ohne Vorkenntnisse in die besten digitalen Währungen der Zukunft

Julian Hirsch

Inhaltsverzeichnis

Vorwort

Im Schatten des dominierenden Bitcoins existieren Kryptowährungen, die technisch fortschrittlicher, innovativer und in sonstiger Hinsicht vielversprechender sind. Dieses Buch wird Sie in aller Ausführlichkeit über die allgemeine Funktionsweise von Kryptowährungen aufklären und auf Basis dieser Erklärungen veranschaulichen, wieso Bitcoin zum jetzigen Zeitpunkt die falsche Geldanlage ist. Im Vordergrund dieses Buches stehen 7 alternative Kryptowährungen, die mit Blick auf die Zukunft vielversprechender kaum sein könnten. Sie sind innovativ, teils elegant und schlank im System, oftmals handelt es sich um bahnbrechende Zukunftstechnologien – all das, was Bitcoin nicht ist.

Das Kernargument gegen Bitcoin ist keineswegs der hohe Kurswert und somit teure Ankaufspreis – nein, das ist aktuell kein Argument gegen auch nur irgendeine der Kryptowährungen! Denn wenn eine Kryptowährung als Zahlungsmittel akzeptiert werden wird, ist der heutige Kursverlauf nur ein Bruchteil dessen, was sie später einmal wert sein wird. Eine Investition lohnt sich also sogar bei hohen Kursverläufen, sofern Sie Ihr Geld über mehrere Jahre bis zu einem Jahrzehnt anlegen.

Der Bitcoin hat weitaus größere Probleme, die nicht nur Ihr angelegtes Kapital gefährden, sondern das Bestehen des ganzen Systems. Die Probleme sind substanziell, denn einerseits ist das System veraltet und andererseits befindet sich ein Großteil (96 %!) der Bitcoin-Einheiten im Besitz von Unternehmen und steht zur Nutzung prinzipiell nicht zur Verfügung. [1] Diese sowie weitere Probleme werden in Kapitel 1 ausführlich erläutert, mit Beispielen belegt und bewertet. Am Ende des ersten Kapitels werden Sie es verstehen: Andere Kryptowährungen bieten ein höheres Ertrags- und Zukunftspotenzial als Bitcoin.

Zahlreiche alternative Kryptowährungen haben das veraltete System des Bitcoins adaptiert und besser umgesetzt oder sogar durch komplett innovative und andersartige Ansätze übertroffen. Der Grund, weshalb Bitcoin trotzdem Rekorde um Rekorde bricht: Der Markt weiß nicht Bescheid. Sie werden nach dem Lesen dieses Buches Bescheid wissen, denn es erwarten Sie 7 faszinierende Kryptowährungen.

Die sieben Kryptowährungen in diesem Buch werden auf einer Skala von 1 bis 10 bewertet, wobei 10 das Beste ist. Darauf basierend erhalten Sie eine Einschätzung, wie viel Prozent Ihres Anlagebudgets Sie in jede der Kryptowährung investieren sollten. Auf Basis dieser prozentualen Einschätzungen ist es Ihnen möglich, ein Portfolio zusammenzustellen, in dem die einzelnen Kryptowährungen einem ihrer Qualität entsprechenden Anteil aufweisen. Außerdem werden Hinweise dazu gegeben, wann eine Investition zurückgezogen werden sollte.

IOTA ist viel mehr als eine reine Kryptowährung – es ist ein auf diverse Branchen anwendbares Kommunikationsprotokoll, ist für den wichtigen Zukunftsbereich der Machine-to-Machine-Transaktionen nutzbar und könnte die Digitalisierung der deutschen oder sogar weltweiten Industrie entscheidend prägen. Die technische Basis unterscheidet sich dabei weitreichend von der anderer Kryptowährungen – Sie lernen das faszinierende Konzept hinter IOTA in Kapitel 2 kennen!

Dash ist nach dem Krypto-Hype 2017 in der Liste der bekanntesten Kryptowährungen weit herabgerutscht, aber die grandiose Technik und die vollständige Anonymität bei Transaktionen sind nach wie vor überzeugende Alleinstellungsmerkmale. Was anderen Kryptowährungen nicht in dem Maße gelungen ist wie

Dash, aber für das Zukunftspotenzial einer Währung entscheidend ist: Die Kryptowährung wird in einem Land bereits von mehreren Bevölkerungsschichten akzeptiert. In welchem Land und wieso dies der Fall ist – mehr dazu in Kapitel 3!

Dann gibt es da noch Kryptowährungen wie *NEM*, die die Konzepte mehrerer Kryptowährungen aufgreifen und in sich vereinen. Eine hohe Chancengleichheit zwischen den Teilnehmern des NEM-Netzwerks und die technische Konzeption fördern eine rege Nutzung der Währung, was deren Akzeptanz als Zahlungsmittel begünstigt. Noch dazu bietet NEM Spielräume, Zahlungen an bestimmte Bedingungen zu knüpfen, was die Sicherheit und das Management von Transaktionen optimiert – Kapitel 4 verrät Ihnen Näheres!

Die angesprochenen Merkmale der genannten Währungen sind nur einige Merkmale unter vielen! Sammeln Sie in den Kapiteln 2 bis 8 dieses Buches die faszinierendsten und wichtigsten Informationen über die sieben Kryptowährungen IOTA, Dash, NEM, MaidSafeCoin, Binance Coin, Tron und Tether.

1
Knowhow zum Einstieg

„Investiere niemals in ein Business, das du nicht verstehst."

– Warren Buffet
(*1930; US-amerikanischer Großinvestor)

Am Anfang einer jeden **guten** Investitionsentscheidung steht das Knowhow. Ohne Wissen über das Produkt, in das ein Anleger Geld investiert, sind die Chancen auf Erfolg an Glück gebunden. Folglich steigen die Risiken für den Verlust des Geldes. Mit Wissen stellt sich die Sachlage ganz anders dar: Der Anleger ist imstande, die Chancen und Risiken eines Investments vernünftig abzuwägen, indem er das Produkt und dessen Umfeld genau analysiert.

Die Herausforderungen bei einer Investition in das **Produkt Kryptowährungen** bestehen vor allem darin, dass sich Anleger mit einer schwer einzuordnenden Geldanlage beschäftigen müssen: Kryptowährungen sind nicht als Geld anerkannt. Die

Kursverläufe erinnern aufgrund der **hohen Schwankungen** mehr an die Aktien eines jungen Unternehmens als an Kurse stabiler Währungen. Noch dazu sind Kryptowährungen eine Geldanlage mit hohem **technischem Schwerpunkt**, denn Algorithmen und Formeln sind bei der Funktionsweise einer Kryptowährung maßgeblich.

Auch wenn das alles anspruchsvoll und nach Studieninhalten klingen mag, ist die Geldanlage in Kryptowährungen dennoch kein Hexenwerk. Denn es reichen bereits Grundlagenkenntnisse der Technik und Mathematik von Kryptowährungen aus, um sich von allen anderen Anlegern abheben und rationale Investitionsentscheidungen treffen zu können. Alles an Inhalten, was wichtig ist, um Kryptowährungen zu verstehen und sinnvoll darin zu investieren, vermittelt Ihnen dieses Einstiegskapitel.

Definition und Arten von Kryptowährungen

„Der Oberbegriff Kryptowährung steht für digitale Zahlungsmittel mit einer umfassenden Verschlüsselung. Die zugehörigen Zahlungssysteme sind Gegenentwürfe zu gewöhnlichem haptischem Geld und können ausnahmslos über das Internet gekauft werden." [2] Für die Teilnahme an einer Kryptowährung bzw. die Inhaberschaft von Währungseinheiten ist es erforderlich, ein Wallet zu haben. Das Wallet ist eine digitale Geldbörse, in der die Währungseinheiten eines Teilnehmers gespeichert sind. Es ist somit vergleichbar mit dem Konto und dem Kontostand bei einer Bank.

Durch die umfassende Verschlüsselung von Kryptowährungen ist es möglich, „bargeldlosen Zahlungsverkehr ohne die Abhängigkeit, Aufsicht oder Mitwirkung von Banken und Behörden zu ermöglichen." [3] Dieses Konzept eines **Zahlungsverkehrs ohne eine überwachende zentrale Instanz** wird als *Dezentralität* bezeichnet. Im weiteren Verlauf dieses Buches werden Sie merken, dass nicht alle Kryptowährungen dezentral organisiert sind und durchaus Merkmale einer Zentralisierung aufweisen. Dies trifft allerdings auf die wenigsten Kryptowährungen zu und soll bei den populärsten dieser Kryptowährungen abgeschafft werden (siehe Kapitel 2 | IOTA), sodass die Dezentralität auch hier sichergestellt werden wird. Mit der Dezentralität gehen anonyme oder pseudonyme Transaktionen einher. Außerdem können Währungen mit einem dezentralen Charakter **nicht durch Geldpolitik reguliert** werden, wie es bei Währungen wie dem Euro oder US-Dollar der Fall ist.

Um Sicherheit gegen Manipulationen zu gewährleisten, liegen den Kryptowährungen verschiedene Systeme zugrunde. Das bekannteste dieser Systeme ist die Blockchain. Erfasst und beschrieben werden mit ihr die einzelnen Transaktionen. Veränderungen werden auf verschiedenen Computern gespeichert und sind so schwer manipulierbar. [3]

Abgrenzung von Währungen wie dem Euro und US-Dollar

Der wichtige Aspekt der Dezentralisierung bei Kryptowährungen tritt insbesondere dann zutage, wenn man sie mit den herkömmlichen Währungen – *Fiatgeld* genannt – vergleicht. Fiatgeld ist beispielsweise der 20-Euro-Schein in Ihrem Portemonnaie. Das Bargeld, das Sie mit sich tragen, und ebenso die Landeswährungen sind Fiatgeld. Zentrales Merkmal von Fiatgeld ist, dass es ...

I. **keinerlei Fundamentalwert besitzt**: Wenn man von heute auf morgen den Euro für wertlos erklären würde, wäre er es auch. Er besteht weder aus wertvollem Material noch ist er mit etwas besichert. Demgegenüber steht beispielsweise Gold: Dieses hat aufgrund seiner weltweiten Knappheit und seines in vielen Kulturen hohen Status einen Fundamentalwert. Daher ist es unmöglich, Gold wie bei Währungen und Bargeld einfach den Wert abzuerkennen.

II. **nicht über den Zahlungszweck hinaus nutzbar ist**: Geld dient lediglich der Zahlung. Würde es seinen Wert verlieren, hätte es keinen sonstigen Nutzen und wäre unter diesem Blickpunkt ebenfalls wertlos. Anders verhält es sich mit Gegenständen und Nahrungsmitteln, weil diese zur Produktion, zum Konsum oder zu anderen ihren Eigenschaften entsprechenden Zwecken genutzt werden können.

Gäbe es nicht die Zentralbanken, die das alleinige Recht zur Emission von Bargeld haben und sich Mühe geben, die Wertstabilität einer Währung aufrechtzuerhalten, dann würde das Fiatgeld als Zahlungsmittel nicht funktionieren, weil sich Staaten oder Institutionen beliebig viel Geld drucken könnten. Das Zahlungsmittel wäre außer Kontrolle und für jede Person in beliebigen Mengen zugänglich. Die **Zentralbanken gewährleisten eine kontrollierte Emission des Fiatgeldes und regulieren damit dessen Wert.** „Der Marktwert von Fiatgeld basiert ausschließlich auf Zukunftserwartungen und kann bei einem Wegfall der monetären Funktion auf null fallen." [Berentsen, Schär; S. 21]

Wussten Sie schon?

Wie sich der Wert des Geldes verändern kann, zeigen vor allem Inflationen. Unter Inflation ist die Abnahme des Geldwertes zu verstehen. Dadurch, dass mehr Geld in Umlauf ist, steigt der Preis der Güter. Wenn ein Gut vor einem Jahr noch 1,20 € gekostet hat und nun 1,30 € kostet, dann kann dies auf die Inflation zurückzuführen sein. Dasselbe Gut muss für mehr Einheiten einer Währung gekauft werden, weil der Wert der Währung gesunken ist. Eine geringe jährliche Inflationsrate von bis zu 2 % ist als Zeichen des Wirtschaftswachstums von Zentralbanken gewollt, doch bei einer mangelhaften Finanzpolitik kann es dazu kommen, dass die Inflationsrate bedrohlich hoch ansteigt. Bestes Beispiel ist Venezuela: U. a. durch die Planwirtschaft und den Einbruch der Erdölpreise lag die Inflationsrate dort im Jahre 2018 bei ca. 130.000 %! Dies bedeutet, dass eine Einheit der venezolanischen Währung innerhalb eines Jahres um 130.000 % an Wert verloren hat. Das Land befindet sich in Armut und aufgrund der hohen Inflation besteht keine Aussicht auf eine Stabilisierung der wirtschaftlichen Lage.

Neben dem Fiatgeld ist das *Giralgeld* ein weiterer guter Begriff zur Abgrenzung der Kryptowährungen. Unter Giralgeld fällt beispielsweise das Geld, das ein Großteil der Bürger auf seinem Konto parkt. Es handelt sich hierbei um die registerbasierte Virtualisierung von Ansprüchen auf physische (Bar-)Geldeinheiten. [Berentsen, Schär; S. 50] Solange sich ein Bürger das Geld nicht auszahlen lässt und es bar in der Hand hält, handelt es sich nur um einen Registereintrag, der dem Bürger verspricht, dass er sich das Geld bei der Bank holen oder es für Transaktionen nutzen kann. Die Kontrolle über das Register für Giralgeld stellt die Bank als zentrale Instanz sicher.

Wie sich bei einem **Vergleich des Fiat- und Giralgeldes mit den Kryptowährungen** zeigt, gehören die Kryptowährungen zwar in die Kategorie des Fiatgeldes, sind jedoch von den anderen Währungen deutlich abzugrenzen.

Zunächst einmal sei festgehalten, dass bei der Haltung von Kryptowährungen kein Anspruch auf die Auszahlung physischer (Bar-)Geldeinheiten besteht, sodass Kryptowährungen nicht als Giralgeld kategorisiert werden können. Außerdem fehlt die zentrale kontrollierende Instanz bei den dezentralisierten Kryptowährungen.

Wie das Fiatgeld haben **Kryptowährungen keinen fundamentalen Wert**. Der Wert von Kryptowährungen leitet sich hauptsächlich aus den Zukunftserwartungen und dem Vertrauen in die Technologie ab. Was allerdings das Argument des fehlenden Fundamentalwerts relativiert und den Kryptowährungen im Vergleich zum Fiatgeld Besonderheitsmerkmale verschafft, sind deren Limitierung und die vielfältigen Anwendungsbereiche. Die meisten Kryptowährungen weisen eine **begrenzte Anzahl an Einheiten** auf, was künftig einen Fundamentalwert fördern könnte. Die weitere Besonderheit von Kryptowährungen im Vergleich zum Fiatgeld ist die fehlende staatliche Akzeptanz als Zahlungsmittel. Dies macht Kryptowährungen nach aktuellem Stand zu einem freiwilligen Zahlungsmittel, das weltweit wenige Zahlungspartner akzeptieren, und zu einem Spekulationsobjekt, das wegen erhoffter Gewinne angekauft und verkauft wird. Die **vielfältigen Anwendungsbereiche** für Kryptowährungen ergeben sich aus der Nutzung der damit verbundenen Technologien für beispielsweise das Vertragsmanagement oder die Kommunikation zwischen Maschinen.

Bitcoin und Altcoins

Die am häufigsten genutzte Kategorisierung für Kryptowährungen ist die in zwei Arten: Bitcoin und *Altcoins*. Hierbei dient Altcoins als Abkürzung für „Alternative Coins"; also die Alternativen zum Bitcoin. Tim Schreder kommentiert diese Unterteilung der Kryptowährungen in seinem Buch *Das neue Geld – Bitcoin, Kryptowährungen und Blockchain verständlich erklärt* (2018) äußerst treffend: „Es unterstreicht noch einmal, wie dominant Bitcoin lange Zeit war beziehungsweise immer noch ist, wenn man alle anderen Coins einfach unter einem Sammelbegriff zusammenfasst." [Schreder; S.68]

Tatsächlich dominiert der Bitcoin nach wie vor den Markt für Kryptowährungen, wie sich besonders konkret in einem Vergleich der Marktkapitalisierungen verschiedener Coins zeigt (Stand: 10.03.2021):

Kryptowährung	Marktkapitalisierung (in Euro)
Bitcoin	886.032.086.885
Ethereum	177.847.369.659
Binance Coin	37.463.980.218
Cardano	31.402.021.896
Tether	31.173.625.352
Polkadot	29.801.844.240
Ripple	17.791.903.220
Uniswap	13.897.775.016
Litecoin	11.387.049.072
Chainlink	10.601.182.436

Quelle: https://coinmarketcap.com/de/ [4]

Abgesehen von der einseitigen und wenig aufschlussreichen Kategorisierung nach Bitcoin und Altcoins gibt es viele andere Möglichkeiten, Kryptowährungen zu unterteilen. Hierzu gehören z. B. technische Aspekte. Kryptowährungen könnten nach der Art und Weise, wie neue Einheiten gewonnen werden, unterteilt werden. Dadurch ließe sich, falls Anleger Kryptowährungen mit einem bestimmten Konsensmechanismus (siehe 1.3.3) bevorzugen, das Feld der für ein Investment in Frage kommenden Kryptowährungen eingrenzen. Welche Möglichkeiten bestehen, Kryptowährungen nach technischen und anderen Kriterien zu unterteilen, lernen Sie in den folgenden Unterkapiteln dieses Buches kennen. Die verschiedenen Kriterien und näheren Eigenschaften von Kryptowährungen werden Ihnen eine Hilfe dabei sein, Kryptowährungen für Ihre

Investments unter möglichst differenzierten Anlageentscheidungen zu bestimmen.

Technische Grundlagen: Wie funktionieren Kryptowährungen?

Die technische Grundlage, mit der Kryptowährungen überhaupt
entstehen, ist das *Mining* (Deutsch: Bergbau). Man wählte diese
Bezeichnung, weil das Errechnen neuer Einheiten von Kryptowährungen mit dem Schürfen von Gold oder Rohstoffen verglichen wurde. Im Gegensatz zum Bergbau erledigen im Mining
von Kryptowährungen nicht die Menschen die meiste Arbeit,
sondern die Computer.

Kernaufgabe der Computer ist es, einzelne Blöcke aus der *Blockchain* (Deutsch: Blockkette) zu errechnen. In diesen Blöcken
sind Informationen über Transaktionen eingespeichert. Jeder **er-
rechnete Block** wird **mit einer gewissen Menge an Einheiten
der Kryptowährung belohnt.** Wie viele Einheiten einer Kryptowährung es zur Belohnung gibt, variiert von Kryptowährung zu
Kryptowährung und hängt von der Menge der zurzeit im Umlauf
befindlichen Einheiten der jeweiligen Kryptowährung ab.

Die **Blockchain** erhält das System und die Kernideen einer
Kryptowährung, wie z. B. die dezentrale Organisation und die
Fälschungssicherheit, am Leben. Sie dient als eine **Datenbank, in
der alle neu errechneten Blöcke und getätigten Transaktionen
gespeichert** werden. Kommt ein neuer Block hinzu oder wird
mit einer bereits errechneten Einheit der Kryptowährung eine
Transaktion (z. B. Kauf eines Artikels) getätigt, so erfolgt eine Ak-
tualisierung der Blockchain.

Weil alle Personen, die Kryptowährungen errechnen, auch mit
diesen bezahlen oder sie anderweitig nutzen, entstehen durch

ihre Handlungen Änderungen an der Blockchain und es bildet sich ein **Netzwerk aus mehreren Nutzern.** Dieses Netzwerk macht die **Blockchain fälschungssicher.** Man bezeichnet dieses Netzwerk auch als *Peer-to-Peer-Netzwerk* (Deutsch: Gleichrangiger-zu-Gleichrangiger-Netzwerk). Alle Teilnehmer dieses Netzwerks haben dieselben Rechte. Diese Parität wird durch einen *Konsensmechanismus* (siehe 1.3.3) gewährleistet. Dieser Mechanismus ist ein Algorithmus, der sicherstellt, dass jedem Teilnehmer des Netzwerks dieselbe Kopie der Blockchain vorliegt.

Neben der Fälschungssicherheit im Peer-to-Peer-Netzwerk trägt der Konsensmechanismus dazu bei, dass sich die Blockchain dezentral organisieren lässt und keine Kontrollinstanz erforderlich ist. Kontrollinstanzen sind bei staatlich anerkanntem Geld ein Muss. Sie bemühen sich um Fälschungssicherheit, betreiben eine der wirtschaftlichen Situation angepasste Geldpolitik und wachen darüber, ob das Geld für legale oder illegale Zwecke eingesetzt wird. In einem Peer-to-Peer-Netzwerk sind diese Kontrollinstanzen nicht erforderlich, weil das System die Fälschungssicherheit gewährleistet.

Erzeugung eines Blocks

Wenn im Netzwerk einer der Miner einen neuen Block errechnet, erhält er eine bestimmte Anzahl an Währungseinheiten. Die Schwierigkeitsstufe, mit der neue Blöcke errechnet werden können, variiert mit 1) der jeweiligen Kryptowährung und 2) der Frage, wie viele Währungseinheiten einer Kryptowährung sich bereits im Umlauf befinden.

Zur näheren Erklärung dieser zwei Punkte: Grundsätzlich steigt die Schwierigkeitsstufe zum Errechnen eines Blocks, die sogenannte *Mining Difficulty*, in bestimmten Stufen an. Die **Steigerung**

der Mining Difficulty soll dazu führen, dass eine Kryptowährung nicht zu schnell berechnet wird und sämtliche Währungseinheiten zu schnell in Umlauf geraten. Dies gilt jedoch nicht für alle Kryptowährungen. Hier kommen wir wieder zum Konsensmechanismus: Dieser definiert näher, wie neue Einheiten einer Kryptowährung erzeugt und Transaktionen bestätigt werden. Jede Kryptowährung hat ausschließlich einen Konsensmechanismus, der bestimmte Vor- und Nachteile mit sich bringt.

Vom Grundsatz her muss bei der Erzeugung eines Blocks **immer ein mathematisches Rätsel gelöst** werden. Oft wird hierbei von einer Rechenaufgabe gesprochen. Zwar ist das Rätsel mathematischer Natur und es wird Rechenarbeit verrichtet, aber das Rechnen hat den geringsten Anteil. Hauptsächlich wird geraten, um auf die Lösung zu kommen. Hierbei muss eine *Nonce* (**Num**ber **on**ly used **on**ce; Deutsch: nur einmal genutzte Zahl) erraten werden. [5] Um diese Nonce zu erhalten, rechnet man über das *Reverse Engineering* (Deutsch: Rückrechnen) einen schwer lösbaren kryptographischen *Algorithmus* rückwärts. [Hosp; S. 68]

Ein Algorithmus ist ein „Lösungsverfahren in Form einer Verfahrensanweisung, die in einer wohldefinierten Abfolge von Schritten zur Problemlösung führt." [6] Dieses Verfahren ist bei den Kryptowährungen – abhängig vom Konsensmechanismus – mal mehr und mal weniger schwer gestaltet. In jedem Fall besagt die **klar definierte und unfehlbare Verfahrensanweisung**, wie beim „Ratespiel" zur Erzeugung eines neuen Blocks vorzugehen ist. Wurde die jeweilige Nonce erraten, dann ist sie zu den bekannten Werten eines zu erstellenden Blocks neu hinzuzufügen. Alle Werte werden zu einer Hashfunktion zusammengefügt, deren Hash entweder dem Target Hash entsprechen oder darunter liegen muss. Ist dies der Fall, dann ist das Rätsel erfolgreich gelöst und ein neuer Block erzeugt. [5]

Alles in allem gibt es also **folgende Abläufe zur Erzeugung eines neuen Blocks**:

1. Ermittlung einer Nonce durch die Lösung eines verschlüsselten Algorithmus;
2. Hinzufügen der Nonce zum Block, der errechnet werden soll;
3. Hashing der Nonce und aller anderen Werte im Block;
4. Test des Hashes, ob er dem Target Hash entspricht oder darunter liegt;
5. Und – falls das angestrebte Ergebnis nicht erreicht ist – die Wiederholung des Verfahrens.

Durchführung einer Transaktion

Kerscher beschreibt in seinem *Handbuch der digitalen Währungen* (2018) die Transaktion zwischen zwei Nutzern wie folgt: Wenn eine Person A einer Person B ein Guthaben überweisen möchte, fertigt sie hierfür einen **speziellen Block** an. Dieser Block enthält die **Daten der Transaktion** (z. B. Betrag, der überwiesen werden soll, sowie Empfänger) und wird mit einem *Private Key* (Deutsch: privater Schlüssel) signiert. Zudem muss der *Public Key* der Person B angegeben werden, um die Transaktion richtig zu adressieren. Alle Teilnehmer des Netzwerks erhalten diesen Block zugesandt. Damit die Transaktion stattfinden kann, müssen wie bereits beim Mining **alle Teilnehmer des Netzwerks den Block prüfen und ihn für korrekt befinden**. Nur dann wird die Transaktion als gültig bestätigt. Anschließend wird der Block an die Blockchain angehängt. Mit diesem letzten Schritt, dem **Anhängen des Blocks an die Blockchain**, ist das Guthaben von Person A an Person B übertragen. [Kerscher; S. 67]; [7]

Person B wiederum braucht ihren Public Key und den Private Key, um die Zahlungen zu empfangen. Außerdem, als Ergänzung zu Kerschers Erklärung, sind für eine Transaktion die Wallet-Adressen notwendig. Das Wallet (Deutsch: Brieftasche) ist der Ort, an dem die Einheiten einer Währung lagern. Verglichen mit einer Transaktion von Fiatgeld über das Online-Banking, könnte man das Wallet wie folgt erklären:

- Die Wallet-Adresse ist vergleichbar mit der IBAN, die man bei einer Überweisung angeben muss, um den Empfänger des Geldes zu definieren.
- Bei einer Überweisung über das Online-Banking werden zudem TANs benötigt. Die vielen verschiedenen TANs sind mit dem Private Key vergleichbar, der für die Veranlassung einer Überweisung bei Kryptowährungen notwendig ist.
- Mit dem Private Key und Public Key nehmen Personen das überwiesene Geld an und sehen ihre Kontostände ein; also gewissermaßen so wie die Nutzung einer PIN zum Geldabheben oder für andere Funktionen bei Banken.

Die Tatsache, dass der **Private und Public Key als Schlüssel** zur Anwendung kommen – man spricht von einem *Schlüsselpaarsystem* – und mathematisch eng miteinander verbunden sind, trägt dazu bei, dass **fälschungssichere Signaturen** erstellt werden können. Für die Funktion der Blockchain ist dieses Konzept essenziell.

Wussten Sie schon?

Public Keys und Wallet-Adressen dürfen an andere Teilnehmer des Netzwerks herausgegeben werden. Sie müssen es sogar, um Transaktionen durchführen und die Blöcke prüfen zu können. Was jedoch nie in die Hände einer anderen Person gelangen darf, sind die Private Keys. Jeden Private Key, den Teilnehmer

---

des Netzwerks haben, gilt es offline auf Hardware aufzube-
wahren und in einer verschlüsselten Datei zu speichern. Denn
sollte jemand den Private Key kennen, dann wird er in Kombination mit dem ohnehin meist bekannten Public Key den Zugriff auf die Währungseinheiten des betreffenden Teilnehmers
erhalten.

Verschiedene Konsensmechanismen

Um die Existenz einer Kryptowährung sicherzustellen, muss als
Konsens eine **Übereinstimmung der Nutzer über die Inhalte
der Blockchain** bestehen. Die verschiedenen hierfür geschaffenen Konsensmechanismen bringen spezifische Eigenschaften
mit sich, die die Sicherheit und Wirtschaftlichkeit einer Blockchain beeinflussen. [Kerscher; S. 68f] Gleichzeitig definieren
die einzelnen Konsensmechanismen, wie neue Einheiten einer
Kryptowährung geschaffen werden. Bei einigen Konsensmechanismen, wie z. B. dem *Proof-of-Work* bei Bitcoins, reicht die Errechnung eines Blocks aus. Andere Konsensmechanismen, die
bei anderen Kryptowährungen zum Einsatz kommen, verlangen
eventuell noch weitere Schritte.

Wichtig ist das nachfolgende Wissen für Sie als Anleger,
damit Sie die Kryptowährungen Ihrer Wahl in Bezug auf den
Konsensmechanismus beurteilen können. Denn jeder Konsensmechanismus hat seine eigenen Vor- und Nachteile. Zu Beginn
dieses Kapitels wurde ein Zitat von Warren Buffet gebracht. Nun
kommt ein weiteres: *„Warum investierst Du Dein Vermögen nicht
in ein Unternehmen, das Du magst? Schon Mae West sagte: 'Zuviel
von einer guten Sache kann wundervoll sein.'"* Auch Sie können
sich entscheiden, in eine Kryptowährung zu investieren, deren
Konsensmechanismus Sie für vernünftig halten. Wenn Sie sich
auf bestimmte Konsensmechanismen festlegen, die die Währung
Ihrer Wahl haben soll, dann grenzen Sie die Kryptowährungen,

die Sie zur Geldanlage auswählen können, weiter ein, was Ihnen die Entscheidungsfindung erleichtert.

Die meisten Kryptowährungen nutzen einen der folgenden fünf Konsensmechanismen: [Kerscher; S. 69ff]

- Proof-of-Work (PoW);
- Proof-of-Stake (PoS);
- Proof-of-Activity (PoA);
- Proof-of-Capacity (PoC);
- und Proof-of-Importance (PoI).

Proof-of-Work (PoW)

Der Mechanismus *Proof-of-Work* (Deutsch: Arbeitsbeweis) ist der am weitesten verbreitete bei Kryptowährungen. Auch bei den Bitcoins kommt dieser Konsensmechanismus zum Einsatz. Bei der Erzeugung eines Blocks müssen die Teilnehmer im Netzwerk wie gewohnt eine Aufgabe lösen, wobei eine *Rechenarbeit* („Work" für „Arbeit") anfällt. Der Nutzer eines Netzwerks, der einen Block zuerst errechnet hat, erhält als Belohnung die errechneten Einheiten gutgeschrieben.

Ein Beweis dafür, ob der Nutzer den Block richtig errechnet hat, wird eingeholt, indem ein *Hashwert* aus der Lösung der Aufgabe und dem Inhalt des errechneten Blocks generiert wird. Dieser Hashwert wird anderen Nutzern bzw. Rechnern im Netzwerk zur Prüfung übermittelt. Falls im Zuge dieser Prüfung eine Gültigkeit des Hashwertes erkannt wird, ist der PoW erbracht und der Block wird an die Blockchain angehängt.

Die **Anzahl an Einheiten einer Kryptowährung ist beim PoW begrenzt.** Was das zur Folge hat? Nun: Sollte es dazu kommen, dass der Schwierigkeitsgrad beim Ermitteln der Hashwerte gering ist und viele Nutzer minen, dann würden alle Einheiten einer Kryptowährung schnell errechnet sein. Ziel der Gründer von Kryptowährungen ist aber, alle Einheiten einer Kryptowährung über Jahre hinweg auszuschütten. Um dieses Ziel zu erreichen, hat die dem Netzwerk zugrunde liegende Software im PoW eine dynamische **Mining Difficulty**. Diese **passt sich der zur Verfügung stehenden Rechenkapazität im Netzwerk an.** [Kerscher; S.69f]

Bei der Kryptowährung Bitcoin beispielsweise passt sich der Schwierigkeitsgrad alle 2.016 Blöcke an. [Kerscher; S. 70f] Durch diese Anpassungen steigen die Anforderungen an das Netzwerk. Die benötigten Rechenleistungen im Zusammenhang mit Kryptowährungen gibt man mit Hashes an.

Wert	Erklärung
1 H/s (ein Hash pro Sekunde)	eine Hash-Berechnung pro Sekunde
1 KH/s (ein Kilohash pro Sekunde)	1.000 H/s
1 MH/s (ein Megahash pro Sekunde)	1.000 KH/s
1 GH/s (ein Gigahash pro Sekunde)	1.000 MH/s
1 TH/s (ein Terahash pro Sekunde)	1.000 GH/s
1 PH/s (ein Petahash pro Sekunde)	1.000 TH/s

Quelle: Kerscher, S. 72

Mit steigenden Anforderungen an die Rechenleistungen **steigt der Stromverbrauch.** Zwar hat das Mining mit seinem Ressourcenverbrauch dazu beigetragen, dass Hardware geschaffen wurde, die den Strom sparsamer verbraucht, doch hinterlassen die Auswirkungen des Minings bei Kryptowährungen mit dem PoW-Konsensmechanismus eine **denkbar negative Umweltbilanz**. Die gestiegenen erforderlichen Rechenleistungen haben auch dazu beigetragen, dass das Solo-Mining – also das Mining einzelner Personen an ihren Rechnern – unrentabel wurde. Dementsprechend minen heutzutage bei den bekannten Kryptowährungen fast ausschließlich große Unternehmen und Mining-Pools neue Einheiten.

Obwohl die Sicherheit des PoW-Mechanismus groß ist, gibt es Risiken, wenngleich diese von Experten als nahe null eingestuft werden. Angriffe auf das System sind trotz des Peer-to-Peer-Prinzips möglich. Der hohe Aufwand an Rechenleistung und damit verbundener Energie macht diese allerdings sehr unwahrscheinlich. Ein Beispiel zur **erfolgreichen Durchführung eines Angriffs** ist die **Übernahme von 51 % der Rechenkapazität im Netzwerk**: Würde eine Partei 51 % der Rechenleistung in einem Netzwerk durch ihre Hardware stellen, dann könnte sie die Kontrolle über alle Transaktionsbestätigungen übernehmen. Dieses Szenario ist bei bekannten Kryptowährungen, deren Errechnung schon weit fortgeschritten ist, wie z. B. Bitcoin, vollkommen abwegig.

Vorteile des PoW:
+ Bereits von Grund auf ist eine hohe Sicherheit im Netzwerk gegeben, weil alle Nutzer im Netzwerk gleichrangig sind und Transaktionen bestätigen müssen.
+ Bei bekannten Währungen besteht zudem eine hohe Sicherheit durch die geringe Erfolgsaussicht und mangelnde Lukrativität von Angriffen.
+ Die Kryptowährung ist dezentral organisiert, was ein hohes Maß an Anonymität bei den Transaktionen gewährleistet.

Nachteile des PoW:
- Es verbleibt eine sehr geringe Wahrscheinlichkeit für einen erfolgreichen Angriff durch die Übernahme von 51 % der Rechenleistung innerhalb eines Netzwerks.
- Das Mining verbraucht zunehmend Energie, wenn die Errechnung einer Kryptowährung voranschreitet.

Proof-of-Stake (PoS)

Im *Proof-of-Stake* (Deutsch: Beteiligungsnachweis) ist weniger Rechenleistung als beim PoW zur Gewinnung neuer Blöcke erforderlich. Bei diesem Konsensmechanismus wird nicht der Miner belohnt, der am schnellsten einen Block errechnet, sondern es werden die **Personen gelost, die rechnen dürfen**. Die Person bzw. die Maschine, die einen neuen Block durch Rechenleistung verifizieren kann, ist in diesem Mechanismus der *Validierer*.

Jede Person, die Währungseinheiten besitzt, kann als Validierer ausgewählt werden. Die Chancen auf die Wahl einer Person nehmen zu, je mehr Einheiten einer Kryptowährung sie besitzt und je länger diese Einheiten gehalten werden. Wurde ein Validierer gewählt und hat er durch Erbringung von Rechenleistung und Investition von Zeit die Blöcke validiert, so erhält er als Belohnung Transaktionsgebühren. Demnach erhält er nicht wie im PoW neue Coins, sondern eine Art **Verzinsung für die angelegten Einheiten**. [8] Da es bei diesem Konsensmechanismus nicht um das Schürfen oder Errechnen neuer Blöcke geht, gibt es den abgrenzenden Begriff *Minting* (aus dem Englischen von „mint"; Deutsch: prägen). [Kerscher; S. 77] Man könnte diesen Begriff so erklären, dass man durch die Haltedauer der Währungseinheiten, für die man als Validierer ausgewählt wird und eine Verzinsung erhält, das Bestehen der Kryptowährung prägt und so zu deren Erhalt beiträgt.

Vorteile des PoS:

+ Es ist eine geringere Rechenleistung als beim PoW erforderlich, um neue Coins zu generieren.

+ Aufgrund der geringeren benötigten Rechenleistung wird auch weniger Energie zur Erzeugung und Aufrechterhaltung von Währungseinheiten der Kryptowährung verbraucht, was umweltfreundlicher ist.

+ Im Gegensatz zum PoW besteht nicht die Gefahr eines 51-%-Angriffs.

Nachteile des PoS:

− Es kann zum sogenannten *Nothing-at-Stake-Problem* kommen: Wenn beim Errechnen zwei Ketten innerhalb einer Blockchain miteinander konkurrieren, könnten sich Validierer dafür entscheiden, auf beiden Ketten gleichzeitig zu validieren, um die Sicherheit zu steigern, dass ihre Kette die „richtige" ist. Es wäre unter den Validierern niemals möglich, einen Konsens über die Blockchain zu erzielen.

Proof-of-Activity (PoA)

Der *Proof-of-Activity* (Deutsch: Aktivitätsbeweis) ist eine **Kombination aus PoW und PoS**. Dementsprechend bezeichnet man ihn in Fachkreisen auch als hybriden Konsensmechanismus. Zunächst wird nach dem Konsensmechanismus PoW ein **Block errechnet**. Nachdem der Block an das Netzwerk gesendet wurde, ist eine **Verifizierung durch die Aktivität der Nutzer** erforderlich. Im Gegensatz zur automatisierten Verifizierung im PoW muss beim PoA „eine bestimmte Anzahl an Nutzern mit Guthaben in ihrem Wallet den Block durch ihren privaten Schlüssel bestätig[en]". [Kerscher; S.78]

Die genaueren technischen Details zum PoA entsprechen aufgrund seiner hybriden Form den vorigen Inhalten, in denen die Mechanismen PoW und PoS erklärt wurden. PoA wurde geschaffen, um eine besonders hohe Integrität und Vertrauenswürdigkeit des Netzwerks zu gewährleisten. Dabei kombiniert er einen Großteil der Vor- und Nachteile des PoW und PoS in einem. Wirklich gewinnen tut dabei keine Seite – weder die der Vorteile noch die der Nachteile –, sodass es sich insgesamt um einen zwar **sichereren, dafür aber aufwändigeren Mechanismus** handelt.

Vorteile des PoA:

+ Die Sicherheit fällt höher als beim PoW und PoS aus. Szenarien wie ein 51%-Angriff und das Nothing-at-Stake-Problem sind nicht denkbar.

+ Es gibt zwei Möglichkeiten, sich Einheiten zu verdienen: über das Errechnen von Blöcken und über das Validieren errechneter Blöcke.

+ Sowohl Nutzer mit Rechenkapazität als auch „normale" Anwender sind zur Nutzung der Kryptowährung animiert. [Kerscher; S. 78]

Nachteile des PoA:

− Im ersten Teil der Konsensfindung kommt genau das Verfahren zum Einsatz, das aufgrund des hohen Stromverbrauchs kritisiert wird: das PoW. [9]

Proof-of-Capacity (PoC)

Beim *Proof-of-Capacity* (Deutsch: Kapazitätsbeweis) setzen die Netzwerkteilnehmer ihren **Speicherplatz** ein. Daher rühren der Name „Kapazitätsbeweis" sowie die weiteren Synonyme *Proof-of-Space* und *Proof-of-Storage*. Im Netzwerk wird der von Teilnehmern zur Verfügung gestellte Speicher genutzt, um aus Hashes Graphen plotten zu lassen. [10] Zur genaueren Erklärung des Plottens: Auf der Festplatte wird eine Liste aller möglichen Nonce-Werte gespeichert. Jede Nonce hat 8.192 Hashes, die von 0 bis 8.191 nummeriert sind. Alle Hashes werden zu Scoops gepaart, was dann insgesamt 4.096 Scoops ergibt. [11] Der Netzwerkteilnehmer weist im nächsten Schritt seinen Speicherplatz nach, indem er die geplotteten Hashes überprüfen lässt. Bei Übereinstimmung ist der Nachweis der eingesetzten Kapazität erfolgreich. [10]

Wie in den anderen drei Konsensmechanismen sind **die Netzwerkteilnehmer im Vorteil, die einen höheren Einsatz einbringen.** Die Höhe des erbrachten Einsatzes wird anhand der *Deadlines* bemessen. Unter den Deadlines sind Fristen zu verstehen, innerhalb derer ein Block überprüft wird. Je kürzer die Frist, was durch möglichst viel Speicherplatz ermöglicht wird, umso eher wird ein Netzwerkteilnehmer schneller als die anderen Teilnehmer sein und die Belohnung für den Block für sich beanspruchen können. [11]

Die großen Nachteile des PoC sind die im Vergleich zu den anderen drei Konsensmechanismen **erhöhte Anfälligkeit für Hackerangriffe** sowie die Tatsache, dass die wenigsten Kryptowährungen diesen Konsensmechanismus nutzen. Beides geht wohl Hand in Hand, denn wären die Voraussetzungen für eine hohe Sicherheit des Netzwerks besser, dann würden auch mehr Kryptowährungen diesen Konsensmechanismus nutzen.

Vorteile des PoC:
+ Hohe Chancengleichheit innerhalb des Netzwerks, denn das Kaufen von Speicherplatz ist günstiger als der Erwerb leistungsfähiger Rechner (notwendig beim PoW; Anm.) oder der Besitz einer großen Menge der Kryptowährung (notwendig beim PoS; Anm.).
+ Durch die hohe Chancengleichheit wird eine zahlreiche Teilnahme von Personen im Netzwerk gefördert, was wiederum die dezentrale Verteilung begünstigt. [10]
+ Die Energieeffizienz ist um Längen besser als beim PoW und PoA.

+ Nach dem Mining können die Daten gelöscht werden, sodass die Festplatte wieder für private Zwecke genutzt werden kann.

Nachteile des PoC:

- Eine Anfälligkeit für Malware-Attacken besteht.
- Wenig verbreitet unter den verschiedenen Kryptowährungen.
- Würden mehr Kryptowährungen vom PoC Gebrauch machen, so würde es wahrscheinlich zu einem Wettrüsten unter den Netzwerkteilnehmern kommen, was die Nachfrage nach Festplatten mit hoher Kapazität erhöhen und die Chancengleichheit im Netzwerk reduzieren würde. Zu beobachten war dieses Wettrüsten bereits beim PoW anhand der Nachfrage nach Grafikkarten.

Proof-of-Importance (PoI)

Der *Proof-of-Importance* (Deutsch: *Wichtigkeitsbeweis*) **ähnelt von der Funktionsweise dem PoS.** Auch beim PoI müssen die Nutzer einen bestimmten Betrag in ihrem Wallet haben, um als Node tätig sein zu können. Neben diesem Betrag ist für eine ausreichende „Wichtigkeit" der Nutzer aber auch ausschlaggebend, **wie viele Nettotransfers sie in den letzten 30 Tagen getätigt haben.** Dabei haben aktuellere Transaktionen ein stärkeres Gewicht. Somit ergibt sich die Wahrscheinlichkeit, als Node zur Bestätigung von Blöcken gewählt zu werden und neue Währungseinheiten zu erhalten, aus der Menge an gehaltenen Coins und der Häufigkeit von Transaktionen. [Kerscher; S. 79]

In einem dezentralen System ist das Vertrauen in die Nodes entscheidend. Dabei gilt, dass **grundsätzlich diejenigen Nodes vertrauenswürdig** sind, die eine hohe Vernetzung zu anderen Teilnehmern des Netzwerks aufweisen und bereits an vielen

Transaktionen beteiligt waren. Dahingehend ist der Konsensmechanismus des PoI vorteilhaft, weil hier die Nodes am meisten Transaktionen bestätigen, die selbst am aktivsten sind und somit ihre hohe „Wichtigkeit" zur Aufrechterhaltung des Netzwerks bereits unter Beweis gestellt haben. [Hosp; S. 65]

Die Tatsache, dass im Gegensatz zum PoS auch die Transaktionshäufigkeit in die Bewertung der Knotenpunkte des Netzwerks einfließt, **animiert zur aktiven Nutzung der Kryptowährung.** Szenarien wie eine lange Haltedauer von Währungseinheiten, wie es bei den Bitcoins der Fall ist (mehr dazu in 1.4), sind hier nicht vorstellbar. Dies begünstigt die Tauglichkeit einer Währung zur alltäglichen Nutzung.

Vorteile des PoI:
+ Der Konsensmechanismus PoI fördert eine Chancengleichheit im Netzwerk. Es bestehen nämlich zwei Wege, um Geld zu verdienen.
+ Lange Haltedauern von Währungseinheiten sind quasi ausgeschlossen, denn wer Kryptowährungen aktiv nutzt und damit Transaktionen abwickelt, kann am meisten verdienen.
+ Die Generierung der Blöcke verläuft schneller und einfacher, was einen geringen Energieverbrauch zur Aufrechterhaltung des Netzwerks zur Folge hat.

Nachteil des PoI:
– Die Ansprüche an das Bewertungssystem, mit dem Nutzer beim PoI als Node ausgewählt werden, sind hoch. Es darf nicht zu kompliziert und nicht zu einfach sein, weil es den Nutzern ansonsten zu leichtfallen würde, durch das Erstellen von Fake-Accounts ein vorgetäuschtes Netzwerk und somit ein Machtmonopol aufzubauen. [12]

15 wichtige Fachbegriffe aus Technik, Investment und Geldpolitik

Hier erhalten Sie wichtige Begriffe aus den Bereichen Technik, Investment und Geldpolitik vorgestellt, die der Vertiefung der bisherigen Inhalte und dem besseren Verständnis der Folgeinhalte dieses Kapitels dienen. Durch die Kenntnis technischer Fachbegriffe erlangen Sie die Möglichkeit, die Funktionsweise von Kryptowährungen noch besser nachzuvollziehen. Die Fachbegriffe aus dem Investmentbereich unterstützen Sie dabei, Investitionsentscheidungen überlegter und somit mit geringerem Risiko zu treffen. Letztlich sind die Fachbegriffe aus der Geldpolitik insbesondere deswegen relevant, um die Zukunftsfähigkeit von Kryptowährungen einschätzen zu können.

Technik

Fork (Hard Fork / Soft Fork)

Fork bedeutet auf Deutsch „Gabel". Dieser Begriff wurde gewählt, weil Forks bei Kryptowährungen eine „Ab-Gabelung" beschreiben. Hierbei spaltet sich ein Teil einer Kryptowährung vom anderen Teil derselben Kryptowährung ab. *Hard Forks* sind solche, bei denen aus einer Währung zwei verschiedene Währungen werden. Bei *Soft Forks* hingegen bleibt die Währung bestehen, stattdessen finden Änderungen innerhalb des Netzwerks statt. Man könnte Soft Forks daher mit Updates vergleichen. [Schreder; S. 81ff]

Fork ist ein bekannter Begriff aus der Softwareentwicklung. Er beschreibt den Fall, dass eine neue Version einer Software geschaffen wird, die sich vom bisherigen Quellcode unterscheidet. Die Gründe für Forks in der Softwareentwicklung sind vielfältig:

- Test von Funktionen;
- Implementierung neuer Funktionen;

23

- Entwicklung der Software in eine komplett neue Richtung;
- oder Entwicklung der Software zu einem eigenständigen Produkt bzw. einer eigenständigen Variante.

In der Blockchain von Kryptowährungen treten diese Veränderungen durch Abspaltungen von dem bisherigen Systemprotokoll ein. [13] Das ideale Beispiel hierfür bildet der Bitcoin-Fork vom 1. August 2017. Dabei spaltete sich ein Teil des Bitcoin-Netzwerks ab, weil es eine Streitigkeit über die Blockgröße gab. Der eine Teil war für eine Erhöhung der Blockgröße, der andere dagegen. Für den Hard Fork programmierten die Netzwerkteilnehmer die Währung so um, dass eine gesteigerte Blockgröße möglich war. Diese neue Währung, die dabei entstand, ist eine der aktuell populärsten: Bitcoin-Cash.

Hinweis!

Bei der Nutzung eines Online-Wallets bei einem Drittanbieter ist Vorsicht im Hinblick auf Forks gegeben: Am Tag des Forks könnte es passieren, dass der Anbieter des Wallets die Private Keys nicht mehr unterstützt oder sogar löscht. Dann wäre das ganze Geld des Anlegers verloren! Der Anbieter wäre im Recht, denn er könnte es argumentativ so darlegen, dass es sich beim Fork um eine normale Weiterentwicklung der Kryptowährung oder deren Update handelt. Daher bietet es sich immer an, die Private Keys zu Währungseinheiten auf lokalen Datenträgern und somit bei sich selbst zu speichern – dies kann auch als Ergänzung zum Wallet beim Online-Anbieter erfolgen. So sind die Keys gegen Datenverlust doppelt geschützt.

Interessant ist wohl die Frage, was mit dem eigenen Geld passiert, wenn sich ein Teil des Netzwerks bei einer Kryptowährung von dem anderen Teil abspaltet: *Hat der Anleger dann doppelt so viel Geld oder werden seine Währungseinheiten einfach auf gut Glück einer der beiden Währungen zugeordnet?* Tatsächlich verdoppelt sich das Vermögen des Anlegers. Beim Bitcoin-Fork von 2017 beispielsweise erhielt jeder dieselbe Menge an Währungseinheiten sowie die zugehörigen Private Keys in beiden Netzwerken. [Schreder; S. 81ff] Ganz so lukrativ, wie es sich anhört, ist der Deal aber nicht wirklich. Denn es ist wahrscheinlich, dass entweder beide Kryptowährungen durch die Abspaltung an Wert verlieren oder die eine Kryptowährung deutlich an Wert verliert, während die andere minimal Wert verliert. Jedenfalls kommt es im Zuge der Abspaltung meist zum Endergebnis, dass die Einheiten von Kryptowährungen, die man insgesamt hat, genauso viel oder weniger Geld wert sind als die Einheiten zuvor. Stattdessen stehen beim Fork Anleger, Nutzer sowie Miner der Kryptowährungen vor einer entscheidenden Frage: Welche der beiden Kryptowährungen unterstütze ich? Langfristig und auch kurzfristig kann es sein, dass sich eine der beiden Kryptowährungen durchsetzt, während die andere komplett von der Bildfläche verschwindet oder nur noch eine untergeordnete Rolle spielt.

Jeder Fork – ob Hard oder Soft Fork – hat bestimmte Beweggründe. Wer Geld in eine Kryptowährung anlegt, die sich abspaltet, oder nach der Abspaltung einer Kryptowährung in eine der beiden entstandenen Währungen investieren möchte, sollte sich genau Gedanken darüber machen, ob eine Währung und – falls ja – welche der Währungen vom Fork profitiert. Einige Forks können beispielsweise durch technologischen Fortschritt motiviert sein. Grundsätzlich ist technologischer Fortschritt zu begrüßen. Demnach könnte es sich lohnen, den Teil der Kryptowährung zu unterstützen, der den fortschrittlichen Weg geht. Unterm Strich entscheidet der Individualfall: Genau über den Fork informieren, gut überlegen und mit Köpfchen spekulieren.

Eine Soft Fork meint Updates des Systems, die bestimmte Änderungen herbeiführen. Meist sind diese Änderungen nur für

Knotenpunkte – also *Nodes* – im System wichtig. Gewöhnliche Nutzer können die Kryptowährung sogar weiterhin in der älteren Version nutzen, zumindest bei den meisten Soft Forks. Ein Beispiel für eine Soft Fork ist die Überarbeitung der Signatur-Validierung: Bei BIP 66 für Bitcoin kam es durch diese Maßnahme zu einer gesteigerten Sicherheit, weil die Echtheitsprüfung bei Transaktionen verbessert wurde. Ein ohnehin schon sicheres System wurde somit noch sicherer.

Mining Pool

Bei Kryptowährungen wie Bitcoin, bei denen schon eine große Menge an Währungseinheiten errechnet ist, ist es aufgrund der vielen Rechenzentren und der starken Konkurrenz für Miner mit einem Budget, das weniger als fünfstellig ist, nicht mehr lohnend, ins Mining einzusteigen. Selbst, wenn die Rechner zur Rechenarbeit lange laufen, bestehen keine Aussichten, einen Block früher als die Konkurrenten zu errechnen und als Belohnung Coins zu erhalten. Zur Lösung dieses Problems haben die „kleineren Miner" die Chance, sich an *Mining Pools* (Deutsch: Schürfgemeinschaft) zu beteiligen.

In den Mining Pools wird die Rechenleistung aller Pool-Teilnehmer gebündelt, was aufgrund der höheren Gesamt-Rechenleistung die Chance auf das Errechnen eines Blocks und den Erhalt der Belohnung erhöht. Alle Miner, die in einem Mining Pool sind, erhalten ihren Anteil am Erfolg, der sich nach der investierten Rechenleistung richtet. Eine Person, die in einem Pool mehr Rechenleistung investiert, erhält auch einen höheren Anteil als die Personen, die weniger Rechenleistung investieren. Leer geht allerdings kein Miner aus, weswegen sich die Mining Pools für die meisten Miner mehr lohnen als das Mining ohne Pool. Tatsächlich sind für den Großteil der errechneten Blöcke bei der Währung Bitcoin zurzeit die Mining Pools verantwortlich.

Node

Ein *Node* (Deutsch: Knoten) ist der Knotenpunkt innerhalb eines Systems. Relevant sind darunter vor allem die *Full Nodes*. Auf ihren Systemen ist die gesamte Blockchain gespeichert. Sie tragen außerdem durch die Erfüllung verschiedener Aufgaben dazu bei, dass das System am Laufen gehalten wird. Alle Aufgaben der Nodes lassen sich im Grunde genommen so zusammenfassen, dass sie dem Abgleich der Transaktionen mit den Konsensregeln dienen. [14] Etwas seltener, weil nur in einigen Kryptowährungen auffindbar, sind die *Master Nodes*. Sie haben zum einen die Rechte und Pflichten der Full Nodes, zum anderen erweiterte Rechte und Pflichten. So können sie u. a. befugt sein, bestimmte Transaktionen beschleunigt umzusetzen oder die Anonymität bei Transaktionen zu steigern.

> ### *Beispiel*
>
> Die Kryptowährung *Dash* (siehe Kapitel 3) ist bekannt dafür, nicht komplett dezentralisiert organisiert zu sein. Es existiert eine „Dachgesellschaft" aus *Master Nodes*. Diese haben bei Abstimmungen über Änderungen im Netzwerk Stimmanteile und außerdem Anspruch auf Gewinnbeteiligungen. Durch diese Organisation ist die Kryptowährung ein Stück weit mit den Aktien eines Unternehmens vergleichbar. Das macht die Kryptowährung Dash zwar spannend, raubt ihr aber den demokratischen und dezentralisierten Gedanken, der den Kryptowährungen eigentlich zugrunde liegt.

Open Source

„Open Source" bedeutet wortwörtlich aus dem Englischen ins Deutsche übersetzt „Freie Quelle". Das „frei" bezieht sich auf die freie Verfügbarkeit des Quellcodes. Es existieren auch die Bezeichnungen „freie Software" und „offene Software". Die Software darf in diesem Fall von jeder Person heruntergeladen, kopiert und verteilt werden. Ob ein Entgelt für die Nutzung und Verbreitung der Software veranschlagt wird oder es kostenlos ist, ist dabei unerheblich. Falls eine Gebühr verlangt wird, so dient sie nicht dem Profit, sondern der Kostendeckung des Anbieters. Alles in allem existieren folgende Kernmerkmale für eine Open-Source-Software:

- Lizenz der Software ist frei verfügbar;
- nicht-kommerzielle Einstellung des Anbieters;
- hoher Grad an Zusammenarbeit bei der Programmentwicklung;
- und starke räumliche Verteilung der Entwickler. [15]

Durch diese Eigenschaften werden vorteilhafte Voraussetzungen dafür geschaffen, dass die Software weiterentwickelt und optimiert wird. Dieses Konzept machen sich die Entwickler von Kryptowährungen zunutze. Die Quellcodes von Kryptowährungen, die Open Source sind, können von jeder Person bearbeitet und optimiert werden. Ob eine Übernahme ins Netzwerk erfolgt, ist eine Frage dessen, wie viele Netzwerkteilnehmer den Änderungen zustimmen. Falls es zu keinem Konsens kommt, dann sind Hard Forks wie bei Bitcoin und Bitcoin Cash möglich.

Initial Coin Offering (ICO)

Beim *Initial Coin Offering* (zu Deutsch: Initiatives Münz-Angebot) wird eine bestimmte Menge von Einheiten einer Kryptowährung, wobei es auch die komplette Menge sein kann, an Anleger verkauft. Im Gegensatz zur Vorgehensweise bei anderen Kryptowährungen wird ein Teil der Einheiten oder sämtliche Einheiten nicht errechnet, sondern ist vorab vorhanden.

Auf Basis dieses Wissens lässt sich die Bezeichnung „Initial Coin Offering" auch besser verstehen: Auf Initiative der Entwickler der Währung werden Währungseinheiten in Umlauf gebracht. Die Einheiten müssen nicht selbstständig von den Anlegern bzw. Nutzern errechnet werden. Das Initial Coin Offering kann nützlich sein, um Gelder zu erhalten, die man für Entwicklungsschritte der Kryptowährung benötigt.

Nach dem Offering wird bei den meisten Kryptowährungen mit ICO ansonsten alles so gehandhabt wie bei anderen Kryptowährungen: Blockchain und anonyme sowie dezentrale Abwicklung der Transaktionen.

Investment

Marktkapitalisierung

Unter der Marktkapitalisierung ist der Wert eines Unternehmens, einer Kryptowährung oder einer anderen Sache zu verstehen. Während bei der Analyse von Aktien die Marktkapitalisierung komplizierter geregelt ist, verhält es sich bei Kryptowährungen ganz simpel: Man nimmt den Kurswert für eine Währungseinheit, also einen Coin, und multipliziert diesen mit der Anzahl aller erhältlichen Coins einer Währung. So entsteht die Marktkapitalisierung. Anhand der Marktkapitalisierung wird beurteilt, wie wertvoll eine Währung ist. Bei der Marktkapitalisierung liegt der Bitcoin auf Platz 1. Die Marktkapitalisierung ist als Kennzahl wichtig, denn ansonsten hätte der geringe Kurswert einiger Kryptowährungen ein hohes Täuschungspotenzial: Nur weil der Kurswert einer Währung im Vergleich zu einer anderen wesentlich geringer ist, heißt es nicht, dass sie eine geringere Marktkapitalisierung hat. Denn wenn die Währung mit dem geringeren Kurswert eine höhere Anzahl an Währungseinheiten hat, dann kann sie insgesamt trotzdem wertvoller sein. Somit ist die Marktkapitalisierung die wichtigste Kategorie, anhand derer Kryptowährungen in Rankings platziert werden.

Allzeithoch

Das Allzeithoch ist ein Zeichen von Stärke. Die meisten Kryptowährungen hatten ihr Allzeithoch Ende 2017 und Anfang 2018, als der generelle Hype auf dem Markt alle Kryptowährungen erfasste und der Bitcoin sozusagen als Zugpferd die Kurse aller anderen Kryptowährungen mit sich zog. Genaueres werden Sie bei den Analysen der Kurshistorien in den Kapiteln zu den sieben Kryptowährungen erfahren.

Mit dem Allzeithoch ist der höchste Wert eines Coins gemeint, den es jemals in der Geschichte dieses Coins gab. Insbesondere die Kryptowährungen, die nach 2017 bzw. 2018 ihr Allzeithoch übertroffen haben oder sich diesem angenähert haben, sind gewissermaßen krisenfest und beständig. Denn sie haben nach stark rücklaufenden Kursen wieder zu alter Stärke zurückgefunden.

Bärenmarkt/Bullenmarkt

Wenn auf einem Markt über einen längeren Zeitraum die Kurse sinken, dann liegt ein Bärenmarkt vor. An der Börse bezeichnet man einen solchen Zeitraum auch Baisse. Das Gegenteil des Bärenmarkts ist der Bullenmarkt bzw. die Hausse. Es geht hierbei stets um einen allgemeinen Trend, sodass davon oftmals sogar Währungen erfasst werden, bei denen die Kursverläufe eigentlich gegensätzlich laufen müssten, weil z. B. während des Bärenmarkts besondere Erfolge der Entwickler-Teams verbucht werden. Der bekannteste Bullenmarkt bei Kryptowährungen fand ab Mitte bis Ende 2017 statt, der Bärenmarkt in den darauffolgenden Monaten.

Dividende

Der Begriff *Dividende* stammt aus dem Aktienmarkt. Anleger werden mal mehr, mal weniger – die Höhe der Dividendenzahlungen hängt von der Aktie und dem jeweiligen Unternehmen ab – am Gewinn des Unternehmens, an dem sie Aktien halten, beteiligt. Diese Dividendenzahlungen sind ein passives Einkommen. Einige Kryptowährungen, z. B. jene mit einem Proof-of-Stake-Konsensmechanismus, bieten in Ähnlichkeit zu Dividendenzahlungen die Möglichkeit, eine Verzinsung des eigenen Guthabens in den Wallets zu erhalten. Wie dies funktioniert, variiert mit den Kryptowährungen und wird in den Kapiteln 2-8 dieses Buches gut veranschaulicht. Dies ist zusätzlich zu dem bloßen Kauf von Kryptowährungen und deren Kurssteigerungen eine weitere Option, um Geld zu verdienen.

Stop Loss

Das Stop-Loss-Limit bzw. die Stop-Loss-Grenze dient dazu, Verluste bei Investitionen zu minimieren. Anleger sehen sich bei der Investition in verschiedene Anlageprodukte, darunter auch Kryptowährungen, mit Risiken und Chancen konfrontiert. Manchmal entwickelt sich daraus sogar ein Verhalten der Anleger, das dem von Spielern im Casino gleicht: Man kommt mit dem Verlust des Geldes nicht klar oder will diesen nicht wahrhaben, sodass man die Investition beibehält oder Geld in ein anderes Produkt investiert, bis man den Verlust ausgeglichen oder Gewinn eingefahren hat. Dabei kann man jedoch alles verlieren. Daher sollen feste Grenzen eingeführt werden. Diese sind vor der Investition zu definieren, um emotionalen Reaktionen auf Kursverläufe vorzubeugen. Für gewöhnlich ist diese Grenze, der *Stop Loss*, präzise definiert: „Ab einem Kurswert XY verkaufe ich, weil mir der Kursverlust zu riskant wird." Eine alternative Möglichkeit haben vor allem professionelle Anleger. Diese lassen sich nicht von den aktuellen Kurswerten irritieren, sondern beobachten ganz genau die Hintergründe der Kursverluste: „Ist das alles nur Marktstimmung und in Wirklichkeit ist das Unternehmen bzw. die Kryptowährung eine sichere Geldanlage?" In diesem Fall wäre sogar bei Kursverlusten ein Zukauf von Unternehmensaktien bzw. Währungseinheiten denkbar.

CFDs (Contracts for Difference)

Nicht näher wird in diesem Buch auf die *CFDs* eingegangen. Grund dafür ist, dass es sich um eine Methode der Geldanlage handelt, die hochspekulativ ist. Dies widerspricht dem langfristigen und möglichst risikoarmen Investieren in Kryptowährungen, wie es in diesem Ratgeber im Vordergrund steht. Was die CFDs (zu Deutsch: *Differenzkontrakte*) so spekulativ macht, sind die einsetzbaren Hebel. Man setzt nur einen Teil des eigenen Geldes ein, aber erhöht durch den gewählten Hebel den Einsatz: Wenn beispielsweise 10 € mit einem Hebel von 10 eingesetzt werden, dann ist es so, als würde man 100 € einsetzen. Bei einem Kursgewinn profitiert man mehr, als wenn man die 10 € ohne Hebel eingesetzt hätte. Allerdings verliert man auch entsprechend mehr bei einem Kursverlust. Die Investition in Kryptowährungen über CFDs ist auf einigen wenigen Börsen, u. a. *Etoro*, möglich. Hohe Gewinnchancen stehen hohen Verlustrisiken gegenüber. Da Kryptowährungen in der Wertentwicklung schon ohne CFDs unberechenbar genug sind, sollten Sie sich stets an die langfristige Geldanlage in physische Coins halten. Falls Sie doch in CFDs investieren, dann sollten Sie besonders darauf achten, Stop-Loss-Grenzen anzuwenden.

Portfolio

Das *Portfolio* meint im Investment eine Ansammlung verschiedener Geldanlagen. So gibt es das Wertpapier-Portfolio als Bezeichnung für eine Ansammlung mehrerer Wertpapiere. Ebenso sind Portfolios aus Kryptowährungen möglich. Der Vorteil bei einem Portfolio besteht darin, dass in mehrere Währungen investiert wird. Dadurch streuen Sie das Risiko: Denn wenn eine Kryptowährung sich negativ entwickelt, haben Sie noch andere

Kryptowährungen im Portfolio, die die Verluste ausgleichen. Dieses Prinzip der *Risikostreuung* ist vor allem bei langfristigen Investitionen ein Grundsatz, nach dem das das eigene Geld angelegt werden sollte. So minimieren Sie die Risiken, Ihr Geld zu verlieren.

Geldpolitik

<u>Deflation</u>

Die *Deflation* ist als Begriff ausschlaggebend, wenn es um das Zukunftspotenzial von Kryptowährungen geht. Ein Großteil der Kryptowährungen ist mengenmäßig begrenzt, wie z. B. Bitcoin. Man stelle sich nun vor, die Kryptowährung Bitcoin würde tatsächlich ein gesetzlich akzeptiertes und häufig genutztes Zahlungsmittel werden: Was würde geschehen, wenn die verfügbaren Einheiten der Kryptowährung im Umlauf wären und der Wohlstand der Menschen wachsen würde? Bei wachsendem Wohlstand wären mehr Einheiten einer Kryptowährung notwendig. Doch diese wären nicht verfügbar. Die einzig logische Folge wäre, dass der Wert der Währungseinheiten steigen würde, indem die Preise für die Waren sinken.

Bei einer Deflation sinkt das Preisniveau der Waren. Grundsätzlich sind Deflationen negative Zeichen in der Volkswirtschaft. Sie signalisieren nämlich, dass der verfügbaren Gütermenge eine zu geringe Nachfrage in der Bevölkerung gegenübersteht. Dies bedeutet, dass die Preise sinken müssen, um die Kaufkraft der Bevölkerung zu steigern. Allerdings ergeben sich für die Unternehmen dadurch Nachteile, weil der Gewinn sinkt. Eine Deflation ist innerhalb einer Volkswirtschaft das Zeichen eines Rückgangs der wirtschaftlichen Leistung. [16] Das Ziel der Zentralbanken und Politik ist deswegen immer eine Inflationsrate von rund 2 %. Sie stellt ein wirtschaftliches Wachstum in gesundem Rahmen sicher

– so zumindest die globale Annahme im Rahmen der Finanzpolitik. Bei der Inflation nimmt das allgemeine Preisniveau zu. Dies zeigt, dass eine hohe Nachfrage und Kaufkraft herrschen. Gründe hierfür sind in der Regel Wohlstand, eine geringe Arbeitslosigkeit und ein Wachstum der Wirtschaft.

Die mit den Kryptowährungen einhergehende Deflation ist allerdings durch die Währung an sich verursacht und muss nicht zwingend ein Abbild der wirtschaftlichen Leistung sein; will meinen: Es ist den Kryptowährungen langfristig vorherbestimmt, an Wert zu gewinnen, indem das allgemeine Preisniveau sinkt. Anders kann bei mengenmäßig begrenzten Kryptowährungen kein wirtschaftliches Wachstum erreicht werden. Demnach würde nicht die Deflation an sich, sondern die Höhe der Deflation darüber entscheiden, wie es um die Wirtschaftsleistung steht. Fürs Erste ist eine Deflation kein negatives Kriterium. Bei genauerem Blick kann es allerdings dazu kommen, dass die Deflation künstlich erhöht wird, indem Spekulanten größere Mengen der Währungseinheiten horten und so die Knappheit der Währung verstärken. Dadurch steigt der Wert der Währung stärker an und die Deflation erhöht sich. [17] An dieser Stelle wird deutlich, worin das Problem der Kryptowährungen als staatlich genehmigtes Geld bestünde: Es könnte viel stärker mit dem Geld spekuliert werden, als es aktuell der Fall ist, weil 1) eine Knappheit der Geldeinheiten bestünde und 2) keine regulierende Instanz wie der Staat oder die Zentralbanken einschreiten könnte.

Lösungen für dieses Problem lassen sich aber auch finden: Updates der Kryptowährungen, Änderungen der Blockchains, die Koexistenz mehrerer Kryptowährungen, um die Knappheit einer Währung durch andere Währungen zu kompensieren sowie weitere Maßnahmen wären denkbar. Somit ist die Deflation kein K.o.-Kriterium für das Zukunftspotenzial der mengenmäßig begrenzten Kryptowährungen, aber ein potenzielles Problem, das eventuell einige Anleger unter den Lesern in ihre Anlageentscheidungen einbeziehen möchten.

Liquidität

Die *Liquidität* (zu Deutsch: Zahlungsfähigkeit) dient der Bewertung dessen, wie hoch die Zahlungsfähigkeit einer Person, eines Unternehmens oder einer anderen Einrichtung ist. Alles, das einen Kontostand hat, kann dahingehend bewertet werden, wie liquide bzw. zahlungsfähig es ist. Sollte der Kontostand hoch sein, dann ist von einer hohen Zahlungsfähigkeit auszugehen. Gleichzeitig sollten die laufenden Kosten geringer als der Kontostand und der Kontostandzuwachs sein, damit die Liquidität keine Momentaufnahme, sondern möglichst dauerhaft gegeben ist. Bedeutend ist dieser Begriff im Zusammenhang mit dem Budget von den in Verbindung mit Kryptowährungen stehenden Unternehmen und Unternehmern: Je liquider diese sind, umso besser können sie die eigenen Kryptowährungen vermarkten und zu deren Wachstum beitragen. Ein Beispiel für diesen Sachverhalt ist die Kryptowährung *Dash* (siehe Kapitel 3), die zeitweise im Rahmen eines speziellen Konzepts einen eigenen YouTube-Kanal betrieb, in dem eine bekannte Moderatorin die Währung erklärte. Zu begreifen ist also, dass hinter Kryptowährungen wirtschaftliche Akteure oder Unternehmen stehen, deren Liquidität einer von mehreren Faktoren ist, die das Zukunftspotenzial der Kryptowährungen beeinflussen können – zumindest, solange die jeweilige Währung noch nicht so bekannt und „selbstvermarktend" ist wie der Bitcoin.

(Finanz-)Marktregulierung

Die *Regulierung von Märkten* ist eine Maßnahme von Regierungen, um in das Wirtschaftsgeschehen einzugreifen und dieses zu lenken. Ein Beispiel für entsprechende Eingriffe ist die Auferlegung von Pflichten an Unternehmen, die an der Börse notiert sind. Diese müssen in der Rechnungslegung und Bilanzierung gewisse Vorschriften erfüllen, die klar definiert sind und von der *BaFin* (Bundesanstalt für Finanzdienstleistungsaufsicht) überprüft werden. Die Regeln können Unternehmen auf der einen Seite zwar die Aktivitäten erschweren und zusätzliche Kosten verursachen, doch sie sorgen auf der anderen Seite für Klarheit, sodass Unternehmen sich nicht in rechtliche Grauzonen befinden wie z. T. bei nicht regulierten Märkten. Letzteres ist häufig ein Problem bei dem Markt für Kryptowährungen, für den es an Regulierungen in den meisten Staaten mangelt. Nun gibt es zwei Szenarien: Entweder die Regulierungen innerhalb eines Staates verbessern die Rahmenbedingungen für im Kryptowährungsmarkt aktive Unternehmen oder sie verschlechtern die Rahmenbedingungen. So oder so beeinflussen die Regulierungen der Kursverlauf von Kryptowährungen immens. Ein Beispiel dafür, welche Konsequenzen das Durchgreifen eines Staates gegen Krypto-Börsen haben kann, liefert das Kapitel 6 über den *Binance Coin*.

Die „Probleme" mit den Bitcoins (oder: Wieso es für Investitionen jetzt zu spät ist ...)

Aufs Einfachste heruntergebrochen: 49.294,56 € Kurswert pro Bitcoin (Stand: 19.03.2021). Damit begründen viele Personen, wieso die Investition in Bitcoins zu spät sei. Der Wert sei mittlerweile so hoch, dass sich ein Einstieg nicht mehr lohnen würde. Aber genau das ist die falsche Argumentation. Denn der Wert allein in einem seit nicht mal zwei Jahrzehnten existierenden Krypto-Markt hat eine verschwindend geringe Aussagekraft. Natürlich sind die Kursverläufe vom Bitcoin schwindelerregend und verursachen bei einigen Anlegern eine hohe Verlustangst. Dies trifft aber auf jede Kryptowährung zu und ist kein spezielles Contra-Argument gegen Bitcoin. Viel wichtiger als die hohen Kursverläufe ist Folgendes: Wenn sich auch nur eine Kryptowährung als offizielles Zahlung-

smittel in irgendeiner Form etabliert – etwa durch eine gesetzliche
Anerkennung oder die häufige Nutzung in Bevölkerung und Unternehmen –, dann sind Kurswerte wie 49.294,56 € pro Bitcoin
nur ein Lacher. Mit dem Moment des endgültigen Durchbruchs
wird eine Kryptowährung einen Wert erreichen, der heute noch
unvorstellbar ist, sodass sich Investitionen zum heutigen Zeitpunkt definitiv bezahlt machen werden. Das Problem, weswegen
eine Investition in Bitcoin zu spät kommt, besteht also keineswegs
im Kurswert. Die Probleme, weswegen es für eine Investition in
Bitcoin zu spät ist, sind wesentlich tiefgreifender und gravierender.
Dass sie vom Markt nicht begriffen werden, verschlimmert den
Tatsachenbestand umso mehr.

Ungleiche Verteilung der Bitcoin-Einheiten

Ein Blick darauf, wie eine x-beliebige Währung genutzt wird, of-
fenbart das allergrößte Problem des Bitcoin: Mit der steigenden
Nachfrage wird die Währung immer häufiger genutzt. Eine ange-
messene Aufteilung unter den Personen, die die Währung nutzen,
gewinnt dann an Bedeutung. Doch wie will man die Bitcoins auf-
eilen, die zu 96 % im Besitz von Mining-Pools und -Unternehmen
sind? [1] Das gilt es zu begreifen: **Pools und Unternehmen, aber
nicht die aktiven Nutzer, die mit den Einheiten handeln möcht-
en, besitzen fast die kompletten Währungseinheiten!** Dadurch,
dass nur 4 % Bitcoin-Einheiten zur Nutzung bereitstehen, wird
eine noch größere Knappheit erzeugt, als eigentlich besteht. Denn
96 % der Einheiten werden aus Prinzip – jetzt und vermutlich auch
in Zukunft – von den Mining-Pools und Unternehmen gehalten.

Der Preis wird also durch eine Knappheit von 4 % aller möglichen
Einheiten nach oben getrieben. Nun stellen Sie sich vor, was passiert, wenn **ein beträchtlicher Anteil der zurückgehaltenen 96 %
von Bitcoin plötzlich auf den Markt geschmissen** wird: Die eben
noch so wertvollen Bitcoin-Einheiten **verlieren rapide an Wert!**
Die Mining-Pools und -Unternehmen geraten in Panik und folgen

der Marktstimmung, verkaufen schnell weitere Einheiten und treiben die Kurse noch weiter nach unten. So wird in einem eigentlich deflationären System tatsächlich eine Hyperinflation zur Realität, weil aus zuvor nur 4 % der verfügbaren Währungen plötzlich über 50 % und irgendwann sogar an die 100 % werden.

Um das bis hierhin Erklärte noch leichter verstehen zu können, sei dieser Sachverhalt anhand eines Beispiels am Mietwohnungsmarkt demonstriert. Wichtiger Hinweis vorab: Der Sachverhalt wird überspitzt demonstriert, um es besser verständlich zu machen. Es entspricht in Bezug auf den Markt an Mietwohnungen nicht den real umsetzbaren Bedingungen.

Beispiel

Man nehme eine Gruppe von fünf Investoren, die ihr reichhaltiges Kapital bündelt und 80 % der Wohnungen in einer Stadt aufkauft. Es besteht ohnehin schon eine Knappheit an Wohnraum in der betreffenden Stadt. Die Investoren entscheiden – weil sie wie die Mining-Pools und -Unternehmen im Bitcoin-Netzwerk nur an der Wertsteigerung der Immobilien bzw. Mietsteigerung interessiert sind – die 80 % Wohnungen dem Markt vorzuenthalten. Die Bevölkerung ist geschockt. Alle Bürger müssen von einem Tag auf den anderen mit 20 % der bisherigen Wohnungen klarkommen. Was passiert? Das Wettbieten um den heiß begehrten Wohnraum beginnt und die Mietpreise steigen enorm an. Zahlreiche Leute bleiben obdachlos – im Bitcoin-Netzwerk sind sie stattdessen währungslos, wobei das Prinzip dasselbe ist. Ein halbes Jahr später geben die Investoren plötzlich die ganzen Wohnungen zum Kauf und zur Miete auf den Markt: Die Folge sind stark sinkende Preise. So wird es auch im Bitcoin-Netzwerk der Fall sein, falls sich nichts ändert. Doch die

> Preise sinken nicht einfach nur auf das vorige Niveau. Weil sich aufgrund der Wohnungsknappheit viele WGs gegründet haben oder Personen ins Umland gezogen sind, sinken die Preise auf einen Tiefststand. So wird es wohl auch im Bitcoin-Netzwerk der Fall sein. Denn die Leute werden auf andere Kryptowährungen wechseln. Dies ist sogar bereits mehrmals erfolgt, wie die Vorstellungen der einzelnen Kryptowährungen in den Folgekapiteln zeigen werden.

Diese Problematik bei Bitcoin, die aus der **künstlich verstärkten und dadurch verzerrten Knappheit der Bitcoins** resultiert, ist mit Blick auf die Zukunft das allergrößte Problem, dessen sich allerdings die wenigsten Nutzer und Investoren bewusst sind. Es wird vielleicht jahrelang oder jahrzehntelang gut laufen – bis irgendwann die vorenthaltenen Massen an Bitcoin-Einheiten in Umlauf gebracht werden und die Kurse massiv zu sinken beginnen. Dieses Problem haben nahezu alle Kryptowährungen, die bereits bekannt und mengenmäßig begrenzt sind. Vor allem aus diesem Grund ist es wichtig, einen Blick auf weniger bekannte Kryptowährungen zu werfen.

Merken Sie sich: Der richtige und nicht zu späte Zeitpunkt für eine Investition in mengenmäßig begrenzte Kryptowährungen ist zum einen immer dann gegeben, wenn die Währungseinheiten gleichmäßig unter den Netzwerkteilnehmern verteilt sind und nicht zwecks Spekulation in hohen Mengen vorenthalten werden. Zum anderen sind weitere Kriterien zu berücksichtigen, um die es in den folgenden Zeilen natürlich noch gehen wird. Die ungleiche Verteilung der Währungseinheiten ist allerdings für das Bitcoin-Netzwerk ein grundsätzliches K.o.-Kriterium, solange sich an dieser Verteilung nichts ändert.

Umweltkriterium

Die Sparkasse führte ein Interview mit Uwe Burkert, dem Chefvolkswirt der Landesbank Baden-Württemberg, durch. Ein Randthema war die Klimafreundlichkeit von Bitcoin. Eine Angabe, die Uwe Burkert nannte, schockiert unter ökologischem Blickpunkt regelrecht: Die **Erderwärmung könnte durch das Mining von Kryptowährungen in den kommenden 30 Jahren um 2 °C zunehmen.** [18]

Ein wichtiger Aspekt, der Bitcoin in die Karten spielt, ist die Tatsache, dass sich die Kryptowährung trotz dieses klimatischen Problems nicht sanktionieren lässt. Sie ist dezentralisiert. Weder das Abschalten des Internets noch das Einkassieren der Server durch die Regierung kann Bitcoin stoppen, denn es müsste entweder das gesamte Internet auf der Welt abgeschaltet oder alle Server aller Netzwerkteilnehmer auf dem Globus einkassiert werden – nicht vorstellbar.

Dennoch wird eine Kryptowährung, die langfristig das Klima gefährdet, sich nicht durchsetzen können, sodass der eben erwähnte Vorteil der Dezentralisierung keine Rolle spielt. Im Zweifelsfall wird die **Gesellschaft sich gegen eine Nutzung von Bitcoin entscheiden** und zu einer der energiefreundlicheren Varianten wechseln. Heutzutage herrschen Zeiten, in denen nicht nur einzelne weltweit bekannte Gruppen von Aktivisten (Stichwort: *Fridays for Future*) an das ökologische Verantwortungsbewusstsein mahnen. Auch die Regierungen sind sich ihrer Verantwortung gegenüber dem Planeten bewusst und nutzen ihre Möglichkeiten, um die Gesellschaft zu erreichen und für das Thema zu sensibilisieren.

Vor einem Jahrzehnt war es anders. Doch spätestens seit *Fridays for Future* hat die Klimadebatte derart an Aufwind und Dynamik gewonnen, dass sie die Zukunft von Bitcoin bedroht. Sie fragen sich, wieso Bitcoin dann nicht schon längst in dem Programm von Fridays for Future oder den Klimapaketen der Regierung steht? Die Antwort ist einfach: Sowohl Aktivisten als auch die Regierung haben aktuell wichtigere Programmpunkte zu bewältigen, was übrigens viel über die (noch nicht vorhandene) Relevanz von Bitcoin aussagt. Die Währung mag also groß erscheinen und die Kursverläufe mögen beeindrucken, aber letzten Endes ist Bitcoin nichts anderes als ein veraltetes System, das andere Kryptowährungen längst übertrumpft haben.

Fazit

Nach diesem Kapitel sind Sie in der Lage, in ein Business zu investieren, das Sie verstehen. Somit schließt sich der Kreis zwischen dem eröffnenden Zitat dieses Kapitels und Ihrer vollendeten Entwicklung zum qualifizierten Anleger. Bitte erweitern Sie Ihr Wissen regelmäßig, indem Sie sich wöchentlich an drei bis fünf Tagen Zeitfenster reservieren, in denen Sie sich weiter über die Technik der Kryptowährungen und News aus der Welt der Kryptowährungen informieren. Seien Sie immer up-to-date, denn es ändern sich regelmäßig Kleinigkeiten bei den Kryptowährungen.

Nach diesem Kapitel wissen Sie Bescheid, wie Kryptowährungen funktionieren. Dies vereinfacht Ihnen Ihre Investitionsentscheidungen, denn Sie sind beispielsweise in der Lage, Kryptowährungen mit dem PoW-Konsensmechanismus per se aus Ihren Investitionsentscheidungen auszuschließen, wenn Ihnen der hohe Energieverbrauch nicht zusagt. Unter dem Blickpunkt des immer wichtiger werdenden Umweltschutzes und des Klimawandels wäre dieser Gedanke bei einer langfristigen Geldanlage schlüssig. Sie haben nun das Knowhow, um verschiedene Kryptowährungen anhand mehrerer Kriterien zu beurteilen. Tun Sie dies differenziert, notieren Sie die Pro- und Contra-Argumente und legen Sie sich auf Investitionen fest, hinter denen Sie stehen und die

Sie verantworten können. Handeln Sie möglichst rational, denn unter emotionaler Einwirkung besteht tendenziell das höhere Risiko für Fehlinvestitionen.

Nun, da Sie das kleine Einmaleins des Anlegers kennen und mit dem Business vertraut sind, ist es Zeit, sich den einzelnen Kryptowährungen zu widmen. Bei einigen der Kryptowährungen werden Sie sehen, dass es immer etwas Neues zu lernen gibt. Die Kryptowährung IOTA beispielsweise wird Ihr Wissen aus diesem Kapitel völlig über den Haufen werfen, denn eine Blockchain suchen Sie dort vergebens ...

2

Ökosystem und Kryptowährung zugleich: IOTA

*I*OTA [19] ist unter dem Blickpunkt der Digitalisierung eine äußerst interessante Kryptowährung. Die Nutzung und die Ansätze der Kryptowährung gehen weit über die Zahlung hinaus. IOTA eröffnet in zahlreichen Branchen innovative Möglichkeiten, wozu u. a. die Mobilitäts- und Versicherungsbranche gehören. Schon der Name IOTA (Kurzversion für: Internet of Things Alliance) verdeutlicht, dass es bei IOTA darum geht, **Systeme, Menschen und weitere Komponenten miteinander zu verbinden**. Die Investition in IOTA ist daher nicht nur eine Investition in eine Währung, sondern gewissermaßen eine Investition in eine bestimmte Zukunftsvision.

Allgemeines

IOTA wurde im Jahre 2015 von David Sønstebø, Sergey Ivancheglo, Dominik Schiener und Serguei Popov in Berlin gegründet. Eine **Non-Profit-Organisation mit dem Namen IOTA-Stiftung und Sitz in Berlin** entwickelt die Technologie weiter, finanziert diese und hält sie als Open-Source-Software für sämtliche Entwickler lizenzfrei. Die Finanzierungshilfen durch die Non-Profit-Organisation sind auch für private Entwickler erhältlich. Hierfür wurde der *Fonds für die Entwicklung des Ökosystems* geschaffen. Durch die Gelder aus diesem Fonds können Entwickler die Umsetzung ihrer Ideen finanzieren. Bedingung hierfür ist, dass die Ideen als Innovationen dazu beitragen, dass das IOTA-Ökosystem profitiert bzw. gestärkt wird.

Das IOTA-Ökosystem umfasst die Kryptowährung als eine Komponente, die dem Zahlungsverkehr dient. Allerdings ist die Kryptowährung nicht für Zahlungen zwischen Menschen vorgesehen, sondern für Zahlungen zwischen Maschinen. Es handelt sich also um eine **reine Machine-to-Machine-Währung**. Wenn Personen mit ihrem Fahrzeug fürs Tanken bezahlen möchten, müssen sie selbst keine Transaktion veranlassen. In dem Anwendungsbereich der Währung ist vorgesehen, dass die Maschine „Fahrzeug" mit der Maschine „automatisierte Stromtankstelle" kommuniziert und die Bezahlung auf diese Weise abgewickelt wird. [Schreder; S. 79] Dies mag jetzt noch surreal klingen, ist mit Blick in die Zukunft aufgrund der voranschreitenden Digitalisierung jedoch ein nicht unwahrscheinliches Szenario.

Neben dem Bereich Mobilität, der abgesehen von autonomen Transaktionen zwischen Fahrzeugen und Maschinen auch nutzungsabhängige Versicherungen umfasst, ist die Anwendung von IOTA auf viele weitere Bereiche bzw. Branchen ausgedehnt:

- Sozialer Einfluss
- Mobilität
- Smart Cities
- Welthandel
- Digitale Identität

Die Entwickler von IOTA schaffen insgesamt ein umfassendes Ökosystem, das sich u. a. mit Zielen wie der **Nachhaltigen Verwendung von Ressourcen**, der **Bereitstellung hochaktueller Transport- und Infrastrukturdaten** sowie der **Optimierung von Lieferketten** im globalen Handel befasst.

Geschichte und Intention hinter IOTA

Bereits jetzt dürfte klar sein: IOTA ist mehr als eine Kryptowährung. Es ist ein digitales Projekt, das sich gesellschaftlichen, wirtschaftlichen, ökologischen und weiteren Aspekten widmet und in diesen Bereichen Optimierungen anstrebt. Doch wie konnte es so weit kommen? Wie konnte sich eine Kryptowährung entwickeln, die gleichzeitig weit mehr als eben eine Kryptowährung ist?

Die Erklärung ist ganz einfach: Die Entwickler wollten ein Kommunikationsprotokoll schaffen, das **für die Zukunft einen sicheren Austausch von Daten** gewährleistet. Mit Blick auf die Zukunft spielte schon vor der Gründung 2015 und umso mehr zum jetzigen Zeitpunkt das Internet of Things (IoT) eine zentrale Rolle.

Wussten Sie schon?

Das IoT (**I**nternet **o**f **T**hings; deutsches Kürzel: IdD für **I**nternet **d**er **D**inge) ist ein Sammelbegriff „für die Vernetzung von Gegenständen des Alltags oder von Maschinen im industriellen Umfeld per Internet [...]. Geräte bekommen eine eindeutige Identität (Adresse) im Netzwerk und werden mit künstlicher Intelligenz ausgestattet. Dadurch sind sie in der Lage, über das Internet zu kommunizieren und Aufgaben voll automatisiert auszuführen. Die intelligenten Geräte werden oft auch als Smart Devices bezeichnet."Abgesehen von der

---

automatisierten Kommunikation der Geräte untereinander umfasst das IoT eine erleichterte Bedienung durch den Nutzer: Wenn die Geräte nicht untereinander kommunizieren, so sind sie durch die Vernetzung miteinander für die Anwender immerhin leichter zu steuern. Beispielsweise können über ein Endgerät wie das Smartphone sämtliche anderen Geräte daheim, im Büro oder in der Industrie gesteuert werden. [20]

Durch die Offenheit für die Community wuchs das Kommunikationsprotokoll IOTA in mehrere Branchen hinein. Mittlerweile ist es aufgrund der großen Community, dem Entwicklungsfonds und den Investitionen durch Investoren sowie Kooperationen mit Unternehmen ein breites Ökosystem geworden, das in mehreren Branchen mit ausgereiften Konzepten präsent ist.

Zu dem Veröffentlichungszeitpunkt 2016 war die begrenzte Menge von 2.779.530.283.277.761 IOTA bzw. 2.779.530.283 *MIOTA* (1 MIOTA = 1 Mega-IOTA = 1.000.000 IOTA; Anm.) geschaffen. Damals wurden sämtliche Coins im Rahmen eines *Initial Coin Offerings* an Investoren herausgegeben. [Kerscher; S. 199] Heute wird mit dieser festen Menge an Coins gehandelt. Es muss also **keine Rechenarbeit mehr erfolgen, um neue Coins zu errechnen**, was das System sparsam macht. Rechenleistung ist allein bei Transaktionen zu erbringen, wobei vom Proof-of-Work als Konsensmechanismus Gebrauch gemacht wird. Die notwendige Rechenleistung liegt dabei weit unter der des Bitcoin-Netzwerks.

Mit ihrem Konzept der Machine-to-Machine-Kommunikation erregte die Währung IOTA **Aufmerksamkeit bei Risikokapitalgesellschaften** und vollzog im Juni 2017 den Sprung auf Platz 1 der wertvollsten Kryptowährungen an der Handelsbörse Bitfinex. Grund für diesen ersten Platz war u. a. eine Investition der Gesellschaft *Outlier Ventures* in Höhe eines siebenstelligen Betrags. Als Gründe für die Investition nannte Outlier Ventures das hohe Zukunftspotenzial von IOTA. Die Gesellschaft sprach davon, eine „langfristige strategische Investition[en]" tätigen zu wollen und den hohen Kursschwankungen auf Handelsplätzen keine Beachtung zu schenken. Als Gründe für das Zukunftspotenzial von IOTA nannte Jamie Burke, der CEO von *Outlier Ventures*, insbesondere die **Blockless Blockchain**, die ein besonderes technisches Merkmal von IOTA ist und im Gegensatz zu Bitcoin das **System ökologischer macht und gebührenfreie Transaktionen ermöglicht.** [21] Abgesehen hiervon stellt die Einfachheit des Werteaustauschmechanismus im IOTA-Netzwerk eine vielversprechende Zukunft in Aussicht.

Nach der millionenschweren Beteiligung von *Outlier Ventures* an IOTA erlangte das System schnell an Popularität, was mutmaßlich der Schlüssel zum **Abschluss erfolgreicher Kooperationen** und bekannter **Umstiege von Bitcoin-Nutzern auf IOTA** war:

- Das Unternehmen *SatoshiPay* für die Abwicklung von Mikrozahlungen beschließt im Juli 2017, das Bitcoin-Netzwerk als Abwicklungsnetzwerk zu verlassen und die laut eigener Aussage „überlegene" Technologie von IOTA zu nutzen. [22]
- Der gemeinnützige Charakter zeigt sich im August 2017, als IOTA der Organisation *REFUNITE* die eigene Technologie zur Verfügung stellt, um die Verfolgung von Flüchtlingsfamilien vor und nach Konflikten zu optimieren. Dadurch solle die Zusammenführung der Familien erleichtert werden. [23]
- Im November 2017 schließen *Sopra Steria* und IOTA eine Partnerschaft ab, bei der die beiden Partner gegenseitig von dem Knowhow in Puncto „Sicherer Datenaustausch im Internet der Dinge" profitieren. Die zwischen den Systemen der beiden Partner geschaffenen Synergien sollen den sicheren Datenaustausch verbessern. [24]

Tatsächlich war das Jahr 2017 trotz eines Sicherheitsbugs, der behoben wurde, ein äußerst erfolgreiches für IOTA. Neben der Anerkennung als Stiftung im November 2017 gab der größte Fintech-Hub in Singapur, *LATTICE80*, sogar bekannt, **in Singapur ein IOTA-Innovationslabor** zu eröffnen.

Die Folgejahre nach 2017 brachten IOTA bis heute zahlreiche neue nationale sowie internationale Partnerschaften ein. Das IOTA-Ökosystem wurde ausgeweitet und optimiert. Sicherheitslücken wurden geschlossen. Aktuell (Stand: März 2021) ist das Kommunikationsprotokoll IOTA mit Partnern wie *Bosch*, *Volkswagen* und *Deutsche Telekom* populär aufgestellt. [25]

Technische Merkmale

Die größte technische Auffälligkeit beim IOTA-Netzwerk ist, dass das System **nicht auf einer Blockchain basiert, sondern auf der DAG-Technologie** (DAG steht für „Directed Acyclic Graph"; Anm.). [Schreder; S. 78] Umgangssprachlich bezeichnet man einen solchen Graphen als *Tangle*. Wie genau die mathematische Konzeption dieses Tangles ist, würde den Rahmen dieses Kapitels sprengen und nicht zielführend sein. Die wichtigsten Aspekte der DAG-Technologie werden in dieser Liste und der darauffolgenden Grafik ersichtlich:

- Jeder Benutzer, der eine Transaktion tätigen will, muss zunächst zwei Transaktionen validieren. Als Gegenleistung muss er für seine eigene Transaktion keine Gebühren zahlen. Hierdurch erklärt sich, wieso das **IOTA-Netzwerk gebührenfrei** ist.
- Zur Durchführung einer Transaktion muss jeder Nutzer außerdem eine Rechenaufgabe vollführen, was somit dem Konsensmechanismus PoW entspricht. Allerdings ist die zu erbringende Rechenleistung weitaus geringer als bei Bitcoin und anderen Altcoins mit PoW.

- Weiter muss jede Transaktion nicht nur durch einen Nutzer validiert werden, sondern durch mehrere. Erst wenn sich eine bestimmte Menge an Validierungen akkumuliert, kann eine Transaktion erfolgen.

- Diese bisher erläuterte Technologie sichert das Netzwerk einerseits durch die mehrfach erforderlichen Validierungen und andererseits durch das PoW vor fehlerhaften Transaktionen ab.

- Außerdem trägt die Technologie zu einer **beliebigen Skalierbarkeit des Netzwerks** bei. Denn je mehr Akteure im IOTA-Netzwerk sind, umso größer ist der Nutzen: Transaktionen werden mit zunehmender Nutzerzahl schneller validiert und schneller getätigt.

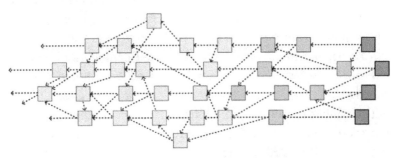

Abbildung 1: Kommunikationsprotokoll

Anmerkung zur Grafik: Die Grafik zeigt die einzelnen Transaktionen in Form von Quadraten. Die grauen Quadrate sind ohne Validierung, die roten Quadrate haben zu wenige Validierungen und die grünen Quadrate stellen die bereits getätigten Transaktionen mit ausreichend Validierungen dar. Die Striche mit Pfeilen geben an, wie viele Validierungen die einzelnen Akteure bei ihrer Transaktion durchführen.

Im Rahmen dieser Technologie, die auch *Distributed-Ledger-Technologie* („Distributed Ledger" für „verteilte Kassenbücher", weil die Transaktionen bei jedem Akteur innerhalb des Netzwerks gespeichert werden; Anm.) genannt wird, gibt es bei IOTA einen *Koordinator* (Deutsch: Koordinator) als **zentrale Instanz.** Dieser Koordinator ist u. a. dafür verantwortlich, regelmäßig Meilensteine zu veröffentlichen, die alle bis zu einem bestimmten Zeitpunkt getätigten Transaktionen umfassen. Durch die zentrale Instanz in Form des Koordinators ist bei IOTA keine Dezentralisierung wie beispielsweise bei Bitcoin oder Ethereum gegeben. Dies stellt eine Schwachstelle des Systems dar, weil der Koordinator das Vertrauen missbrauchen könnte. Daher ist es ein **selbst erklärtes Ziel des IOTA-Netzwerks, auf lange Sicht den Koordinator abzuschaffen** und durch eine andere, dezentrale Version zu ersetzen. [26]

Neben dieser Technologie ist unter technischem Blickpunkt interessant, wie Nutzer von IOTA Gebrauch machen können, um z. B. Geräte untereinander kommunizieren zu lassen. Hierfür existiert das Open-Source-Framework *IOTA Access.* Über dieses kann jede Person **Zugriffskontrollsysteme für ihre intelligenten Geräte erstellen.** Über diese Systeme lassen sich Zugriffsrechte an andere Personen verteilen, Zahlungen von Maschine zu Maschine veranlassen, Geräte untereinander vernetzen und kontrollieren sowie zahlreiche weitere Funktionen nutzen. Die Durchführung der Aufgaben, die durch Nutzer über IOTA Access veranlasst wird, ist sowohl auf private Anwender als auch große Einrichtungen ausgelegt. [27]

Wie aber funktioniert dieses Framework rein technisch betrachtet?

In einem Blogbeitrag auf der IOTA-Website mit Namen *Smart Access To IoT Devices* erklären die Autoren den Vorgang anhand mehrerer Beispiele. Hierbei wird anhand des Managements von Zugriffsrechten erläutert, wie ein Vater die Rechte definieren könnte, um seiner Tochter ein Auto zu leihen:

1. Es wird das Objekt definiert, z. B.: (*Objekt == Fahrzeug*)
2. Für dieses Objekt muss ein Anliegen definiert werden. Im Falle des Verleihs des Autos könnte dieses Anliegen lauten: (*Betreff == Fahrzeug.Besitzer.Tochter*)

3. Dann könnte das Zugriffsrecht bzw. der Befehl, dass sich das Auto für die Tochter öffnen und nutzbar werden soll, wie folgt formuliert sein: *(Aktion == d)*

4. Hierfür müssen aber unter Umständen Bedingungen gegeben sein, wie etwa eine vorliegende Versicherung auf den Namen der Tochter: *(Eigentümer.Tochter.ist.versichert == wahr)*

5. Ferner ist es möglich, die Leihe des Autos auf einen bestimmten Zeitraum zu beschränken, wenn der Vater das Auto in bestimmten Zeiträumen selbst braucht: *(0900 ≤ localTime) && (localTime ≥ 2000)* [27]

So funktioniert das Management der Zugriffsrechte. Ähnlich gestalten sich Befehle zur Zahlung und für weitere Anwendungsbereiche. Über IOTA Access lässt sich **nutzerfreundlich eine automatisierte Kommunikation von Geräten untereinander einrichten.**

Historie: Kursverläufe der letzten Jahre

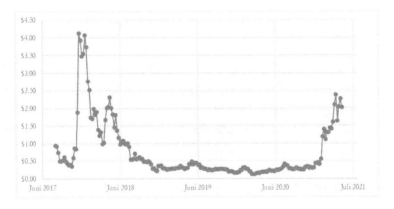

Abbildung 2: Chart IOTA [28]

Der Chart zeigt den Kursverlauf einer Einheit MIOTA in US-Dollar seit der Veröffentlichung der Währung. Bis im Jahre 2016 die Veröffentlichung der Währung erfolgte, gab es demnach keinen

Wert. Seitdem gibt es in der Historie des Kursverlaufs fünf auffällige Zeiträume:

- 2016 bis 19.12.2017 (Veröffentlichung und Hype)
- 19.12.2017 bis 07.04.2018 (Bärenmarkt)
- 07.04.2018 bis 05.05.2018 (Aufschwung durch Marktstimmung)
- 05.05.2018 bis 01.02.2021 (Abschwung mit ruhiger Folgephase)
- 01.02.2021 bis 13.03.2021 (Aufstieg wegen steigendem Vertrauen und Innovationen)

Veröffentlichung und Hype

Seit Veröffentlichung bis zum **19.12.2017** legte der Kurs einen steilen Anstieg auf sein **Allzeithoch mit 5,25 US-Dollar** pro Einheit MIOTA hin. Dieser Anstieg lässt sich mit den in der Geschichte unter 2.1.1 erwähnten Erfolgen (mehrere Kooperationen, Investitionen, Partnerschaften; Anm.) sowie dem generellen Hype um Kryptowährungen zu dieser Zeit erklären.

Bärenmarkt

Der auf das Allzeithoch vom 19.12.2017 bis zum **07.04.2018** auf **ca. 0,98 US-Dollar** pro Einheit MIOTA folgende Kursverlust der Währung ist nichts anderes als ein Bärenmarkt gewesen. Der **Bärenmarkt war eine Folge der Überbewertung nahezu aller Kryptowährungen gegen Ende 2017.**

Aufschwung durch Marktstimmung

Vom 7.04.2018 an ging es bis zum **5.05.2018** mit dem Kurs aufwärts auf **2,39 US-Dollar** pro Einheit MIOTA. Der Anstieg machte sich ebenso bei anderen Kryptowährungen bemerkbar, hat außer der Marktstimmung keine ersichtlichen Gründe und unterstreicht die hohe Volatilität, die die Kurse von Kryptowährungen auszeichnet.

Abschwung mit ruhiger Folgephase

Von 5.05.2018 bis zum **1.02.2021** sank der Wert einer Einheit MIOTA auf ungefähr **0,41 US-Dollar**. In diesem fast dreijährigen Zeitraum war der Wert bereits früh, nämlich am 15.12.2018, auf einem niedrigen Wert von 0,22 US-Dollar. Von diesem Zeitpunkt an schwankte der Kurs regelmäßig in einem Rahmen von 0,12 US-Dollar bis zu den besagten 0,41 US-Dollar am 1.02.2021 pro Einheit MIOTA. In diesem Zeitraum war es generell ruhig um die Kryptowährungen geworden und Anhaltspunkte für einen Hype gab es nicht, sodass sich größere Interpretationen für diesen Zeitraum erübrigen.

Aufstieg wegen steigendem Vertrauen und Innovationen

Die Zeitspanne vom 1.02.2021 bis jetzt (Stand: 13.03.2021) steht für einen **neuen Aufschwung vieler Kryptowährungen,** was sich auch im Kursverlauf bei IOTA bemerkbar macht. Der Preis steht nun bei **1,36 US-Dollar** pro Einheit MIOTA. In der Größenordnung oberhalb eines US-Dollars verweilt der Kursverlauf bereits seit ungefähr Mitte Februar. Die aktuelle Steigerung ist einerseits auf die Marktstimmung durch die Corona-Pandemie und das generelle Anlegerverhalten zurückzuführen. Beispielsweise haben vermehrte Investitionen von Elon Musk und anderen millionensowie milliardenschweren Investoren dazu beigetragen, dass das **Vertrauen der Anleger in Kryptowährungen stieg.** Andererseits hat IOTA selbst einige Änderungen durchgeführt, die auf dem Markt gut ankommen: Das neue Smart-Contract-Protokoll sowie Upgrades und Optimierungen des Systems tragen maßgeblich zum Aufwind im Chart bei. [29]; [30]

Kritikansätze und Besonderheiten von IOTA

Die Kritikansätze der Kryptowährung IOTA ergeben sich aus ihren Besonderheiten im Vergleich zu den anderen Kryptowährungen, da diese Währung sich technisch und ideell stark von den anderen Kryptowährungen unterscheidet. Welch ein hoher Besonderheitsgrad IOTA in Expertenkreisen attestiert wird, zeigt sich anhand eines Interviews der *Börse Stuttgart* mit dem Kryptowährungsexperten Markus Miller. Unter dem Titel *Krypto Update: IOTA – Nonplusultra oder Shitcoin?* wird im Video auf YouTube zunächst auf den Zwiespalt unter Anlegern verwiesen. So schieden sich bei einer Bewertung der Währung durch Anleger die Geister. Die Befürworter würden die **Chancen von IOTA im Multimilliarden-Markt IoT loben**, während den Kritikern die **zentrale Instanz in Form des Koordinators ein Dorn im Auge** sei. Nach Abwägung der Vor- und Nachteile überwiegen nach Ansicht des Experten Markus Miller die Chancen. [31] Doch von welchen Vor- und Nachteilen sprechen wir hier im Klartext?

Vorteile

Einer der zentralen Vorteile der Kryptowährung IOTA besteht darin, dass sie einen **Multimilliarden-Markt zum Ziel** hat: Das IoT wird künftig immer wichtiger werden. IOTA, das sich **für diesen Markt frühzeitig vielversprechend und mit einer ausgefeilten Technologie positioniert** hat, gewann in seiner Historie und gewinnt auch heute noch zahlreiche Kooperationen in diesem Bereich. Vor allem bei der Kommunikation von Maschinen in der Industrie ergeben sich große Chancen für IOTA, zu einer deutschlandweit und global relevanten Standard-Lösung zu werden. Wird allein dieses Potenzial wahrgenommen, dann steht IOTA eine glorreiche Zukunft bevor.

Beispiel

Im Interview der *Börse Stuttgart* mit Markus Miller fällt eine besonders interessante Argumentation: Miller verweist darauf, dass die 30 wertvollsten im DAX gelisteten Unternehmen eine geringere Marktkapitalisierung aufweisen als in den USA das Unternehmen *Apple* allein. IOTA sei für die deutsche Industrie ein technologisch interessantes Projekt, das insbesondere unter dem Blickpunkt der bereits jetzt vorhandenen Kooperationen mit Unternehmen weltweit die Chancen hätte, als deutsches Tech-Unternehmen künftig eine global immense Rolle zu spielen. Dann wären die knapp 900 Millionen US-Dollar Marktkapitalisierung von IOTA (Stand des Interviews: Februar 2020) nur ein kleiner Bruchteil dessen, was IOTA erreichen könnte. [31]

Eine günstige Voraussetzung, weswegen sich IOTA mehr für den Einsatz in der Industrie empfiehlt als die Technologien anderer Kryptowährungen, ist die **Tangle-Technologie**. Sie ist unter vielen Befürwortern von IOTA ein zentrales Argument, weil sie weitaus geringere Stromkosten erfordert als Blockchains mit dem PoW-Konsensmechanismus und zusätzlich **Mikrozahlungen sowie gebührenfreie Transaktionen ermöglicht**. Außerdem ist die Technologie hoch skalierbar und bringt einen schnelleren Konsens mit sich, denn mit einer steigenden Anzahl an Nutzern im System steigt auch die Geschwindigkeit der Transaktionen. [Kerscher; S.200]

Abgesehen von diesen zentralen Vorteilen hat IOTA durch die Anerkennung als Non-Profit-Stiftung einen weiteren Vorteil: Die Möglichkeit, Kapital in Form von Coins einzubringen, um Weiterentwicklungen zu finanzieren, erlaubt Innovationen wie Anfang 2021, die das Steigen des Kursverlaufs begünstigen.

Nachteile

Die Tatsache, dass IOTA mit dem IoT in einem Multimilliarden-Markt tätig ist, birgt neben den hohen Chancen auch hohe
Risiken. Das Geschäftsfeld ist herausfordernd, weil es umkämpft
ist und künftig wahrscheinlich noch stärker umkämpft sein wird.

Die **Zentralität durch den Koordinator** ist zwar ein Kritikpunkt, doch die sukzessiven und bereits weit vorangeschrittenen
Bemühungen IOTAs zur Abschaffung des Koordinators relativier-
en diesen Kritikpunkt. Es ist zu beobachten und zu beurteilen, ob
IOTA den Weg hin zu einer Dezentralisierung komplett und erfolgreich beschreiten wird.

Zuletzt sind Sicherheitslücken bei IOTA nicht zu leugnen. Ein
wesentlicher Teil dieser Sicherheitslücken wurde bereits beseitigt,
aber ein Teil ist noch verblieben. Beispielsweise führt die Tangle-Technologie dazu, dass das Risiko der Übernahme des Netzwerks nicht bei 51 % wie bei Bitcoin, sondern bei 34 % liegt. Der
Koordinator macht dieses Risiko wett. Dementsprechend wird
auch bei der Dezentralisierung ohne einen Koordinator eine Er-
satzlösung gefunden werden müssen, die das Risiko einer Netzw-
erk-Übernahme verhindert.

Fazit

Bezüglich all der Nachteile muss IOTA hoch angerechnet werden,
dass die Kryptowährung erst seit 2016 veröffentlicht ist. Für diesen
kurzen Zeitraum hat sie die Risiken früh erkannt und beseitigt, ehe
es zu substanziellen Schäden kommen konnte. Der einzige signi-
fikante Diebstahl von Währungseinheiten erfolgte 2019 durch ein
fehlerhaftes Verhalten von Nutzern, die ihre Tokens in einem On-
line-Wallet verwalteten, das gehackt wurde. IOTA selbst hat Lück-
en rechtzeitig beseitigt und wurde nie gehackt. Fehler und Defizite
– unter die Defizite fällt auch der Koordinator – werden rechtzeit-

ig erkannt, offen kommuniziert und lösungsorientiert angegangen. Somit verbleibt der Eindruck einer technisch sicheren Währung, die in Form der Tangle-Technologie und der Positionierung im IoT enorme Chancen hat, an Wert, Bekanntheit und Bedeutung in zahlreichen Branchen – vor allem in der Industrie – zu gewinnen. Aufgrund des im Verhältnis zu den enormen Perspektiven aktuell günstigen Preises pro Einheit MIOTA sowie die bereits vorhandenen Partner und Kooperationen erscheint eine Investition in IOTA als äußerst sinnvoll.

> ➤ **Bewertung: 8 von 10**
> ➤ **Anlageempfehlung: zwischen 20 und 60 % des vorgesehenen Anlage-Budgets**
> ➤ **Investition zurückziehen bei: Verdrängung von IOTA durch Konkurrenz im Industrie-Sektor**

3

Reine Kryptowährung: Dash

So innovativ IOTA auch war, so sehr „Back-to-the-Roots"
führt Sie die Kryptowährung *Dash* [32]. Die Entwickler
dieser Kryptowährung **bauen auf dem System vom Bitcoin
auf** und machen daraus kein Geheimnis. Dash entstand, weil das
Bitcoin-Netzwerk viel Energie verbraucht und nicht anonym, sondern nur pseudonym ist. Diese Defizite wurden behoben und es
entstand Dash. Weil der Gründer der Kryptowährung, Evan Duffield, früher selbst im Bitcoin-Netzwerk tätig war, wusste er genau,
was er tat. Es entstand ein regelrechter Siegeszug von Dash, der die
Kryptowährung zwischenzeitlich zu einem ernsten Konkurrenten
von Bitcoin machte. Heute (Stand: März 2021) befindet sich Dash
nicht mal unter den Top 40 der wertvollsten Kryptowährungen.
Wenn man betrachtet, wie viele **erfolgreiche Kooperationen und
überzeugende Weiterentwicklungen** Dash vorzuweisen hat, ist
diese Platzierung nicht nachvollziehbar. Es ergibt sich bei einem
genauen Check der Kryptowährung berechtigt die Vermutung,
dass das letzte Lied noch nicht gesungen ist und Dash einen Wied-
eraufstieg erfahren könnte.

Allgemeines

Dash wurde mit dem Bestreben geschaffen, eine bessere Alternative zum Bitcoin zu sein. Blickt man rein objektiv auf die Features, die die Kryptowährung hat, und die Performance im Netzwerk, so ist Dash zweifellos besser. Ein **schlankes technisches System mit einem cleveren Algorithmus** sorgt für ein deutlich energieeffizienteres PoW, als es bei Bitcoin gegeben ist. Noch dazu haben Nutzer die Option, Ihre **Transaktionen besonders schnell und/ oder vollständig anonym zu tätigen**. Diese beiden Optionen gibt es bei Bitcoin nicht. Die Vorzüge und Features von Dash haben jedoch ihren Preis: Ein dezentrales System ist aufgrund der Master Nodes, die eine Dachgesellschaft innerhalb des Netzwerks bilden, nicht mehr gegeben.

Geschichte und Intention hinter Dash

Die Kryptowährung Dash ging 2014 an den Start. Damals trug sie noch den Namen *XCoin*. Veröffentlicht wurde sie von **Evan Duffield**, einem US-amerikanischen Software-Entwickler. Duffield selbst ist der Schlüssel, um einen Großteil des Konzepts hinter Dash zu verstehen. Seine **Spezialität als Software-Entwickler beruhte darauf, bestehende Systeme zu verbessern**. Als er 2010 mit der Welt der Kryptowährungen in Berührung kam und am System von Bitcoin arbeitete, war er fasziniert. Bis 2014 sammelte er Kenntnisse über Bitcoin, die Blockchain und weitere technische Aspekte in Verbindung mit den Kryptowährungen. [33]

Als er genug Kenntnisse hatte, entschloss er sich, das zu tun, was er als Software-Entwickler bei großen Firmen schon jahrelang getan hatte: das System verbessern. Weil dies bei Bitcoin nicht möglich war, schuf er eine neue Kryptowährung, nämlich XCoin. Trotz anfänglicher Fehler, die er korrigierte, waren von vornherein zwei wesentliche Neuerungen im Vergleich zu Bitcoin enthalten:

- InstantSpeed
- PrivateSend
- X11-Algorithmus

Mehr Informationen zu diesen Neuerungen gibt es im nächsten Abschnitt über die technischen Merkmale. Bereits im Februar 2014, ein Jahr nach der Veröffentlichung, wurde der Name der Währung in *Darkcoin* geändert. Mutmaßlicher Grund für die Namensänderung war die Tatsache, dass das System die **vollständig anonyme Tätigung von Transaktionen** ermöglichte. Dieser – sozusagen – Schleier über den Transaktionen hielt die **Identität der Nutzer noch geheimer als in pseudonymen Systemen wie Bitcoin**. Somit war der Darkcoin geboren.

Als Berichte über illegale Transaktionen mit Darkcoin laut wurden, er in Verbindung mit dem Darknet gebracht wurde und das Feature DarkSend (heute: PrivateSend) ebenfalls nichts Legales vermuten ließ, erfolgte eine **erneute Namensänderung. Im März 2015** wurde aus Darkcoin die Kryptowährung **Dash** (kommt von *Digital Cash*; Deutsch: *digitales Geld*). So konnte die Verbindung der Kryptowährung zum Darknet weniger offensichtlich gemacht werden, zumal Dash vom Entwickler Evan Duffield nicht als eine Währung fürs Darknet oder illegale Transaktionen vorgesehen war. Er wollte, eigenen Aussagen nach, nur eine vollständige Anonymität bei Transaktionen gewährleisten. Dass Dash zwischenzeitlich zur Trendwährung für illegale Transaktionen wurde, war nicht vorgesehen.

Im Jahr **2017**, als die Kursexplosion der Kryptowährungen begann, **erlangte auch Dash große Popularität**. Einerseits war die steigende Bekanntheit der Kryptowährungen mit dem Zugpferd Bitcoin ein Vorteil, andererseits erkannte die Öffentlichkeit die Besonderheiten von Dash. Ab Juni 2016 bis Juni 2017 **berichtete beispielsweise die Moderatorin und Journalistin Amanda B. Johnson**

auf YouTube regelmäßig unter dem Titel *Dash: Detailed* über die Kryptowährung. Als Folge der Sendung stieg die Popularität von Dash weiter an. [Koenig; S. 95] Nach dem Ende der Sendung im Juni 2017 war Dash bereits bekannt genug, um zeitweise sogar ein noch stärkeres Kurswachstum als Bitcoin hinzulegen. [34] Das mittlerweile große Entwicklerteam von Dash nutzte den Aufwind und **schloss Partnerschaften mit Größen wie *Amazon* und *Hotels.com*.** Abgesehen hiervon wurde mit dem *Evolution Wallet* eine äußerst nutzerfreundliche Geldbörse für Dash-Tokens eingeführt. [Koenig; S.99 f]

Heute ist Dash eine Währung, die nach starken Kursverlusten im Anschluss an den Krypto-Hype Ende 2017 weit aus dem Ranking der besten Kryptowährungen herausgerutscht ist. Hinter den Kulissen allerdings tut sich vieles: Beispielsweise ist **Dash in Venezuela die beliebteste Kryptowährung mit einer hohen Akzeptanz in der Bevölkerung.** Durch die Herabwertung der Landeswährung Bolivar ist Dash ein wichtiges Zahlungsmittel geworden, um trotz Hyperinflation handeln und bezahlen zu können. [35] Um dies zu erreichen, mühte sich Dash sogar, das eigene System umzukrempeln. Nicht nur Personen mit Internet sollten Transaktionen abwickeln können, sondern auch Personen ohne weitreichende technische Möglichkeiten. Es entstand daher die **Funktion *Dash-Text*.** Fortan war es möglich, ohne Internet und stattdessen über SMS-Zahlungen mit Dash abzuwickeln.

Technische Merkmale

Weil Dash auf dem **PoW-Konsensmechanismus** basiert, ist die Anzahl der verfügbaren Einheiten je nach Quelle auf ca. 18 Millionen [Koenig; S.95 ff.], 18,9 Millionen [Kerscher; S.90] oder eine ähnliche Größenordnung begrenzt. Wie viele Einheiten der Kryptowährung genau vorhanden sind, lässt sich bei Dash im Gegensatz zu Bitcoin nicht präzise bestimmen, was daran liegt, dass die Menge der neu geschaffenen Coins – *Block Reward* genannt –

bei Dash mit jedem Block neu berechnet wird und ein Stück weit flexibel ist. Ebenso wird die Mining Difficulty mit jedem Block neu festgelegt. Die **Steuerung des Block Rewards und der Mining Difficulty dienen dem Zweck, das Mining attraktiv zu halten**: Wenn es eine Phase gibt, in der weniger Miner am Werk sind, wird der Block Reward höher angesetzt, um neue Miner anzulocken und das Mining attraktiv zu machen. Andersherum sinkt der Block Reward in Phasen, in denen viele Miner die Währung errechnen.

Wie Sie bereits bestens wissen, kommt beim Errechnen der Blöcke ein Algorithmus zum Einsatz. Der angewendete **X11-Algorithmus** ist ein besonderes technisches Merkmal von Dash, denn er ist einerseits **energieeffizienter als der Algorithmus namens SHA-256 bei Bitcoin**, andererseits ist die Konstruktion *dedizierter Hardware* nahezu unmöglich. [36]

Wussten Sie schon?

Dedizierte Hardware ist physische Ausstattung für Rechner, die auf die Ausführung einer speziellen Aufgabe ausgerichtet ist. Beim SHA-256-Algorithmus bei den Bitcoins war es möglich, spezielle Hardware zu konstruieren, die die Anwendung des SHA-256-Algorithmus besonders gut beherrscht. Dies optimierte das Mining und verhalf Anwendern dedizierter Hardware zu Vorteilen beim Mining. Der Einsatz dedizierter Hardware kann die Entstehung eines Monopols innerhalb des Bitcoin-Netzwerks erleichtern, denn Mining-Pools oder -Unternehmen, die zum einen eine enorme Rechenleistung bündeln und zum anderen dedizierte Hardware nutzen, haben starke Vorteile im Vergleich zu anderen Minern.

Wieso es bei Dash nicht möglich ist, eine dedizierte Hardware zu konstruieren und sich damit Mining-Vorteile zu verschaffen? In Dashs System wird im Gegensatz zu dem Bitcoins nicht eine spezielle

Aufgabe durchgeführt, sondern es werden 11 verschiedene und aneinander gekettete Algorithmen und somit verschiedene Aufgaben durchgeführt; daher der Name X11-Algorithmus. Eine dedizierte Hardware für 11 verschiedene Algorithmen kann nur unter besonders hohen – in diesem Fall nicht lukrativen – Kosten geschaffen werden. Erstaunlich ist, dass die Ausführung der 11 Hash-Algorithmen bei Dash energieeffizienter als die des SHA-256-Algorithmus bei Bitcoin ist. Aufgrund der Vorteile des X11-Algorithmus kann man die These unterstreichen, dass **Dash tatsächlich eine Weiterentwicklung und Optimierung des Bitcoin-Systems** ist.

Ein weiteres technisches Merkmal ist die Teilnehmer-Struktur im Netzwerk. Die Entwickler von Dash empfanden die langwierigen Entscheidungsfindungen in einem komplett dezentralisierten Netzwerk als problematisch. Aus diesem Grund schufen die Entwickler „eine Art Dachgesellschaft, die sich um die Weiterentwicklung der Kryptowährung kümmert." [Schreder; S.75] Diese **Dachgesellschaft** wird durch die Master Nodes repräsentiert, wobei der Begriff Master Nodes im einleitenden Kapitel in einer Box erklärt wurde. Um **Master Node zu werden und Entscheidungsgewalt zu erhalten**, muss man über **1.000 Dash-Coins** verfügen. Die Rechenleistung ist nicht relevant, es wird rein nach dem Vermögen gegangen. [Koenig; S. 98] Die Master Nodes genießen u. a. folgende Rechte und haben u. a. folgende Möglichkeiten:

- 45-prozentige Beteiligung an den Block Rewards von Minern (die restlichen 45 % gehen an die Miner und 10 % verbleiben zur Bezahlung von Entwicklern oder Designern im Netzwerk; Anm.) [Koenig; S. 96];
- Durchführung der Features InstantSpeed und PrivateSend (siehe 3.3.1);
- und Stimmanteile bei der Abstimmung über Änderungen im Netzwerk und beim Einsatz des Budgets. [Schreder; S. 75]

64

Die Features InstantSpeed und PrivateSend sind technische Besonderheiten, die über die Master Nodes abgewickelt werden. Sie ermöglichen eine schnellere Durchführung von Transaktionen bzw. komplett anonyme Zahlungen im Dash-Netzwerk. Für die Nutzung der Features fallen zusätzliche Gebühren an, die die Master Nodes erhalten.

Historie: Kursverläufe der letzten Jahre

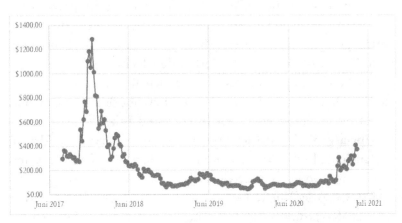

Quelle: https://www.btc-echo.de/kurs/dash/ [37]

- 2014 bis 20.12.2017 (Veröffentlichung und Hype)
- 20.12.2017 bis 07.04.2018 (Bärenmarkt)
- 07.04.2018 bis 04.05.2018 (Aufschwung durch Marktstimmung)
- 04.05.2018 bis 16.12.2018 (Beispielloser Fall des Kurses)
- 16.12.2018 bis 28.06.2019 (Nutzung in Venezuela beschert Gewinne)
- 28.06.2019 bis 12.02.2020 (Gerüchte, Skandale und deren Widerlegung)
- 12.02.2020 bis 28.01.2021 (Ruhige Folgephase)
- 28.01.2021 bis 03.04.2021 (Aufstieg wegen steigendem Vertrauen und passiven Verdienstmöglichkeiten)

65

<u>Veröffentlichung und Hype, Bärenmarkt und Aufschwung durch Marktstimmung</u>

Nach der Veröffentlichung 2014 entwickelte sich der Kurs von Dash zunächst unauffällig. Ab 2016 allerdings, noch bevor es im Jahre 2017 den Krypto-Hype unter Anlegern gab, ging es mit der Bekanntheit und dem Ruf von Dash steil bergauf. Hierzu trugen u. a. die technischen Besonderheiten von Dash bei, wobei allem voran die Anonymität bei Transaktionen positiv aufgefasst wurde. Bedingt durch die Besonderheiten von Dash erweckte die Kryptowährung mit ihren schnell steigenden Kursen Aufmerksamkeit. **Berichterstattungen wie die von Amanda B. Johnson auf YouTube** unter dem Titel *Dash: Detailed* **förderten den Kursanstieg von Dash**, sodass die Währung besser als diverse andere Kryptowährungen performte. Dash stieg nach Ethereum zum zweitgrößten Altcoin auf; insgesamt war Dash also **nach Bitcoin und Ethereum die Kryptowährung mit der drittgrößten Marktkapitalisierung.** [Hileman & Rauchs; S. 14 ff] Natürlich profitierte Dash gegen Ende des Jahres 2017 massiv von dem generellen Hype um Kryptowährungen, was erklärt, wieso der Kursverlauf von Ende 2017 bis Mai 2018 dem der anderen Kryptowährungen ähnelte: Zunächst gab es den Bärenmarkt vom 20.12.2017 bis zum 07.04.2018, ehe es zu Aufschwung durch Marktstimmung vom 07.04.2018 bis zum 04.05.2018 kam. Bis hierhin ist im Kursverlauf also vieles ähnlich wie bei der Kryptowährung IOTA. Doch danach sind die Kursverläufe von Dash wesentlich feiner.

<u>Beispielloser Fall des Kurses</u>

Was sich ab dem 04.05.2018 bis zum 16.12.2018 ereignete, ist ein beispielloser Fall des Kurses. **Von 488,28 US-Dollar am 04.05.2018 ging es hinunter auf 63,15 US-Dollar am 16.12.2018.** Nur knapp über ein halbes Jahr war vergangen und schon war die Kryptowährung Dash aus dem Ranking der besten Kryptowährungen tief nach unten gesackt und von der Landkarte weitestgehend verschwunden. Dies steht im Gegensatz zum Kursverlauf von IOTA und anderen Kryptowährungen. *Was ist der Grund dafür, dass andere Kryptowährungen einen weniger radikalen Kursverlust als die Kryptowährung Dash hatten?* Ein eindeutiger Grund lässt sich nicht herausfiltern, jedoch ist die Mutmaßung naheliegend, dass es Dash in diesem Zeitraum nach dem Hype, in dem jede Kryptowährung vorsichtig betrachtet wurde und eine deutliche Korrektur der Kurse erfolgte, wegen der Anonymität am meisten erwischte und die Skepsis aufgrund möglicher Verwendung im Darknet am höchsten ausfiel. Zudem wurde der Markt durch neue Kryptowährungen bzw. die steigende Popularität älterer Kryptowährungen breiter, was ein weiterer Faktor sein könnte.

Nutzung in Venezuela beschert Gewinne

Die **Kursgewinne zwischen dem 16.12.2018 und dem 28.06.2019 von 63,15 US-Dollar auf 169,51 US-Dollar** lassen sich allein dadurch erklären, dass Dash in Venezuela (siehe 3.1.1) eine hohe Akzeptanz erlangte. [35] Wieso die Kurse trotz der hohen Akzeptanz schwankten und nicht stärker wuchsen, ist anhand dieser Venezuela-Erklärung ebenfalls gut nachvollziehbar und plausibel: Um stärkere Kursgewinne zu verursachen, reichte die Akzeptanz in einem wirtschaftlich am Boden liegendem Land nicht aus. Die Gelder, die bewegt wurden, waren gering und dienten der Bevölkerung zur Versorgung mit dem Nötigsten. Daher stieg der Kurs nur auf knapp über 100 US-Dollar. Nichtsdestotrotz zeigte sich in dieser Zeitspanne, dass die **Entwickler von Dash imstande waren, ein Bedürfnis zu erkennen, darauf mit maßgeschneiderten Lösungen zu reagieren und Dash zu Kursgewinnen und häufigerer Nutzung zu verhelfen.** Dies zeugt von einer marktwirtschaftlichen Orientierung und einer ausgeprägten Fähigkeit, selbst in schwierigen Phasen Lösungen zu finden, um der Kryptowährung wieder Auftrieb zu verleihen.

Gerüchte, Skandale und deren Widerlegung

Wieder war bei Dash in einem sechsmonatigen Zeitraum vieles los. Ab dem 28.06.2019 bis zum **12.02.2020** ging es für Dash von 169,51 US-Dollar zwar **runter auf 133,80 US-Dollar**, doch in Anbetracht der Tatsache, dass der Kurs zwischenzeitlich (am 26.12.2019) bei 39,94 US-Dollar lag, ist der Wert von 133,80 US-Dollar als Erfolg zu betrachten. Was geschah in dieser Zeitspanne, in der der Kurswert ...

- anfangs 169,51 US-Dollar durch die Akzeptanz in Venezuela;
- dann 39,94 US-Dollar;
- und schließlich wieder 133,80 US-Dollar pro Coin betrug?

Bis **Dezember 2019** hielten sich Gerüchte hartnäckig, dass es **durch einen der Master Nodes zu einem Betrug kommen könnte.** Dabei war die Rede von einem sogenannten *Exit Scam*: Dieser aus der Wirtschaft stammende Begriff bezeichnet einen Fall, bei dem sich ein Unternehmen oder eine Person mit den Kundengeldern aus dem Staub macht, ohne die Dienstleistung oder Vereinbarung einzuhalten. Es hieß, dass einer der Master Nodes planen würde, die Kundengelder zu veruntreuen und dann das Netzwerk zu verlassen. Dieses Gerücht, hielt sich hartnäckig über Monate hinweg und schwebte als dunkle Wolke über der guten Arbeit, die das Entwicklerteam von Dash die ganze Zeit vollzog. Das **funktionierende Geschäft in Venezuela wurde nämlich derweil auf weitere lateinamerikanische Staaten erweitert und es wurden Kooperationen mit *Burger King* und dem Zahlungsdienstleister *ATAR* geschlossen.** Auch die Nutzungshäufigkeit von Dash stieg. [38] Als das **Gerücht über den Exit-Scam widerlegt** wurde, konnte Dash vom 26.12.2019 bis 12.02.2020 erfolgreich ins neue Jahr starten und **Kurszuwächse mit geringen Schwankungen** verbuchen.

Ruhige Folgephase

Vom 12.02.2020 bis zum 28.01.2021 ereignete sich relativ wenig in der Kurshistorie. Von den 133,80 US-Dollar zu Beginn der Zeitspanne fiel der Kurs auf 103,06 US-Dollar am 28.01.2021. Diese Kursverläufe sind rein zufällig; unter Umständen werden die Corona-Krise und das Streben der Anleger nach etwas sichereren Anlagemöglichkeiten dazu geführt haben, dass der Kurs um 30 US-Dollar fiel. Was positiv zu beurteilen ist, ist die Tatsache, dass es nach vielen Phasen von Schwankungen und dem schädigenden *Exit-Scam*-Gerücht unter dem Strich zu einer Stabilisierung des Kurses kam.

Aufstieg wegen steigendem Vertrauen und passiven Verdienstmöglichkeiten

Innerhalb der Folgemonate vom 12. Februar 2021 bis zum jetzigen Zeitpunkt (Stand: 03.04.2021) legte Dash einen **Kurszuwachs auf 242,98 US-Dollar** hin. Zum Vergleich: Bei IOTA stieg der Kurs in einem ähnlichen Zeitraum ebenfalls, was auf das steigende Vertrauen der Anleger in Kryptowährungen allgemein sowie die Innovationen IOTAs zurückzuführen ist. Auch Dash profitiert von dem steigenden Vertrauen der Anleger minimal, jedoch viel stärker von den **passiven Verdienstmöglichkeiten, die das Netzwerk den Master Nodes bietet**. In Dashs Netzwerk ist es möglich, als Master Node durch das Stacking passives Einkommen zu erwirtschaften. Diese lukrative Verdienstmöglichkeit bescherte Dash Kurszuwächse. Ebenfalls ein Faktor für die Kurszuwächse ist wahrscheinlich der Ausbau der Kooperationen. Das **Entwicklerteam setzt die jahrelange Arbeit an neuen Kooperationen auch Anfang 2021 fort**. [39]

Kritikansätze und Besonderheiten bei Dash

Wenn man die Kurshistorie von Dash ein weiteres Mal rekapituliert, wird auffallen, dass die Entwickler eine ausgezeichnete Arbeit an der Kryptowährung vollzogen haben. Dennoch ging es für die Kryptowährung von Platz 3 der Kryptowährungen mit der höchsten Marktkapitalisierung im Ranking unglaublich weit nach unten. Bei einem derart beispiellosen Kursverlust könnte man meinen, es müssten klare Fehler gemacht worden sein. Allerdings war genau das nicht der Fall, wie sich in der Kurshistorie feststellen lässt. Stattdessen musste Dash immer wieder aufs Neue gegen eine stark negative Berichterstattung (Stichworte: Verwicklung in illegale Transaktionen & Exit-Scam), negative Marktstimmungen und das geringe Wissen der Anleger ankämpfen. Viele der Anleger folgten dem Trend des Marktes und warfen verstärkt einen Blick auf die anderen Kryptowährungen. Anders lässt es sich nicht erklären, dass Dash derart an Wert eingebüßt hat. Denn eigentlich gibt es an der Währung und deren Management kaum etwas auszusetzen.

Vorteile

Die Vorteile von Dash beginnen bereits bei der Technik. Mit den technischen Besonderheiten InstantSpeed, PrivateSend und dem X11-Algorithmus sind den Dash-Entwicklern **mehrere Optimierungen im Vergleich zum Bitcoin-Netzwerk** gelungen. Diese Optimierungen fördern zugleich genau die Eigenschaften von Kryptowährungen, die von Befürwortern der Kryptowährungen als maßgeblich angesehen werden:

- Schnelle Transaktionen;
- vollkommene Anonymität anstelle von Pseudonymität;
- und Chancengleichheit im Netzwerk.

Die schnellen Transaktionen sind dank des Features Instant Send möglich, bei dem sich **Währungseinheiten innerhalb weniger Sekunden an jeden Ort der Welt verschicken** lassen. In diesem Punkt können nur wenige Kryptowährungen mithalten. Dank des frei wählbaren Features Private Send ist die Anonymität sichergestellt. [Schreder; S. 74 f] Dieses **Alleinstellungsmerkmal der vollständigen Anonymität** – ein Großteil der Kryptowährungen ist nämlich nur pseudonym – haben ansonsten nur noch Kryptowährungen wie ZCash, Monero und eine geringe Anzahl weiterer. Die Anonymität entspricht dem Idealbild vieler Kryptowährungsbefürworter. Zuletzt wäre da noch die **Chancengleichheit im Netzwerk** zu nennen, die durch den X11-Algorithmus ermöglicht wird, weil die Herstellung dedizierter Hardware nicht möglich bzw. mit einem enormen und nicht lukrativen Aufwand verbunden ist. Somit sinkt das Risiko feindlicher Übernahmen des Netzwerks beträchtlich.

Aus dem X11-Algorithmus ergibt sich noch ein weiterer Vorzug des Dash-Netzwerks, nämlich die **Energieeffizienz.** Zwar macht der Algorithmus die Probleme des PoW, das grundsätzlich nicht umweltfreundlich ist, nicht wett, aber immerhin ist das Problem des Energieverzehrs gemindert. Somit ist Dash mit Hinblick auf die Zukunft wesentlich umweltfreundlicher als andere Kryptowährungen mit dem PoW als Konsensmechanismus.

Besonders und vorteilhaft ist bei Dash, dass **10 % der Block Rewards in die *Treasury* fließen, woraufhin sie fürs Marketing und die Entwicklung zur Verfügung stehen.** [Koenig; S. 96] Dadurch hat die Kryptowährung eine finanzielle Reserve, die Bitcoin und eine Reihe anderer Kryptowährungen nicht haben. Folglich ist es kein Wunder, dass Marketingaktionen wie die YouTube-Sendung *Dash Detailed* mit Amanda B. Johnson fruchteten und sich positiv in der Kursentwicklung und Popularität von Dash bemerkbar machten. Auch die Expansion von Dash durch zahlreiche Kooperationen wird zum Teil aus der Treasury finanziert. Ähnlich hat auch die in Kapitel 2 vorgestellte Kryptowährung IOTA ein eigenes Budget für die Weiterentwicklung. Wie sich anhand von Dash bestätigt, scheinen diese Budgets zur Innovation den Kryptowährungen grundsätzlich gut zu tun. Voraussetzung hierfür ist, dass sie von einem kompetenten Entwicklerteam verwaltet und genutzt werden, womit der nächste Vorteil von Dash zur Sprache kommt: das Entwicklerteam.

Das Team, das bereits zu Beginn durch den Gründer und seine Helfer kompetent besetzt war, wuchs im Laufe der Geschichte. Aktuell ist das Entwicklerteam von Dash der Grund, weswegen die Kryptowährung nicht längst von der Bildfläche verschwunden ist. In Zeiten, in denen es für den Kursverlauf bergab ging und die negativen Berichte um den Exit-Scam kursierten, setzte das **Entwicklerteam** die Expansion in Lateinamerika unbeirrt fort und **demonstrierte Zielstrebigkeit, Krisenfestigkeit sowie – einmal mehr – Kompetenz.**

Wussten Sie schon?

In der Analyse von Unternehmen gibt es die Kennzahl *KBV* (*Kurs-Buchwert-Verhältnis*). Dabei wird beurteilt, wie das Verhältnis des Aktienkurses zum Buchwert des Unternehmens ist. In den Buchwert des Unternehmens fließen vor allem die Werte des Inventars ein, das ein Unternehmen besitzt. Ein Manko bei dieser Kennzahl wurde bereits von Analysten erkannt: Das KBV und auch sonst keine Kennzahl bezieht den Wert des Personals für ein Unternehmen ein. Dabei haben oftmals die Unternehmen, die das beste Personal in ihren Reihen haben, einen riesigen Vorteil gegenüber Konkurrenten aus derselben Branche. Wenn Sie bei Kryptowährungen in Ihre Anlageentscheidungen auch die Qualitäten der Entwicklerteams einbeziehen, dann agieren Sie analytisch sehr detailliert und wesentlich professioneller als mutmaßlich über 90 % der anderen Anleger.

Wo die Rede von dem Entwicklerteam von Dash ist und die Box auf ein fortschrittliches Merkmal in der Analyse von Kryptowährungen hinwies: Bei Dash ist das Entwicklerteam das Zünglein an der Waage! Phasenweise macht es den Eindruck, als seien dort Vorstandschefs aus Konzernen mit jahrzehntelangen Erfahrungen am Werkeln, die jede Krise eindrucksvoll kommunizieren und lösen. Das Entwicklerteam erscheint als ein großer Vorteil von Dash. Insbesondere das **Aufgreifen der Bedürfnisse von Dash-Nutzern und das Entwickeln akkurater Lösungen beeindrucken regelrecht.** Dieses Aufgreifen der Bedürfnisse wurde am Beispiel Venezuelas deutlich, als speziell für diesen Markt die Möglichkeit von Transaktionen per SMS entwickelt wurde. Von dieser Entwicklung profitieren natürlich die Nutzer weltweit ebenfalls, aber angestoßen wurde die Idee zu dieser Entwicklung durch ein aufmerksames Beobachten der Situation in Venezuela und die Schaffung einer entsprechenden Innovation.

Zuletzt sind zwei bisher noch nicht angesprochene Vorteile von Dash zu nennen: zum einen die **geringen Gebühren**, zum anderen die **Skalierbarkeit des Systems.** Das Versenden von Geld kostet bei normalen Transaktionen ohne die Inanspruchnahme der freiwilligen Features rund 0,1 Cent, was im Vergleich mit Kreditkarten- und Überweisungsgebühren beim Giralgeld quasi nichts ist. Generell sind die Transaktionsgebühren nicht nennenswert und werden auch bei einer Vergrößerung des Netzwerks nicht signifikant anwachsen. Apropos Vergrößerung des Netzwerks: Das Netzwerk ist beliebig skalierbar und lässt sich an hohe Nutzerzahlen sowie häufige Transaktionen anpassen, wie Sidem (Name eines Mitarbeiters der *Dash Embassy*; Anm.) in einem Vortrag bzw. Interview auf YouTube erwähnt. [40] Dies ist bei vielen Kryptowährungen, so auch beim Branchenprimus Bitcoin, nicht der Fall. Dort wird es ohne Änderungen bei einer steigenden Anzahl an Nutzern und Transaktionen zu einem immer langsamer arbeitenden Netzwerk kommen, weil die Bestätigung von Transaktionen länger dauern wird. Die einzigen Lösungsansätze bestehen in Forks und Reduktionen der Daten durch Anbindung eines zweiten Netzwerks. Beides hat Vor- und Nachteile. Dash hingegen ist **durch das System mit den Master Nodes imstande, bis zu einer 200-fachen Blockgröße, wie sie aktuell vorhanden ist, zu skalieren.** [40] Dies verschafft Raum für ein enormes Datenvolumen und ermöglicht auch bei sehr vielen Nutzern eine schnelle Abwicklung der Transaktionen.

Nachteile

Bei den Nachteilen von Dash geht es darum, das Haar in der Suppe zu finden. Einen offensichtlichen Nachteil gibt es immerhin: die Zentralisierung durch die Master Nodes. Diese **Zentralisierung widerspricht auf der einen Seite dem Grundgedanken der Kryptowährungen**, auf der anderen Seite dient sie der problemlosen Skalierung des Netzwerks und vereinfacht die Entscheidungsfindung zwischen den Nutzern. Außerdem ist es Master Nodes durch das Stacking möglich, passiv Geld zu verdienen, was die Attraktivität des Netzwerks definitiv steigert. Unterm Strich lässt sich sagen, dass ein Nachteil noch nie entspannter betrachtet werden konnte als in diesem Fall. Denn es ist nahezu sicher – wie anhand der aktuellen Nutzerzahlen des Dash-Netzwerks deutlich wird –, dass sich trotzdem ausreichend Nutzer finden werden, die die Vorzüge dieser moderaten Zentralisierung zu schätzen wissen. Positiv ist außerdem, dass jede Person die Chance hat, Master Node zu werden, und die Master Nodes sich gegenseitig kontrollieren.

Weiter geht es mit einem weniger offensichtlichen Nachteil von Dash: *Tainted Coins*. Auf Deutsch bedeutet dieser Begriff „**verdorbene Münzen**" und er verweist auf bestimmte **Coins im Netzwerk, die mit illegalen Transaktionen in Verbindung stehen**. Aufgrund der Transparenz des Netzwerks kann die Geschichte eines Coins nachverfolgt werden. Ein Coin, der gestohlen wurde oder mit dem für ein illegales Gut bezahlt wurde, ist weniger wertvoll als ein „reiner" Coin. [Hosp; S. 152 f] Grund hierfür ist die Annahme, dass ein Großteil der Nutzer im Netzwerk aus moral-

ischen Gründen keinen mit illegalen Aktivitäten in Verbindung
stehenden Coin besitzen möchte.

> **Hinweis!**
>
> Was tun, wenn ein Tainted Coin gekauft wurde? Ein Lösung-
> sansatz besteht darin, ihn mit reinen Coins zu vermischen.
> Bei Transaktionen, die mehrere Coins als Zahlbetrag umfas-
> sen, kann ein Tainted Coin beispielsweise sieben reinen Coins
> beigemischt werden. Je häufiger dies getan wird, desto geringer
> wird der Taintedness-Grad des jeweiligen Coins, weil die
> Transaktionshistorie länger ist und mehr legale Transaktionen
> umfasst. [Hosp; S. 153]

Zu guter Letzt kommt der Nachteil zur Sprache, den man weder
den Entwicklern noch dem Netzwerk oder dem Konzept vorw-
erfen kann: die **immer wieder erfolgten Kursverluste**. Der Wert
von Dash nahm mehr als andere Kryptowährungen ab. Tatsächlich wird die herausragende Arbeit des Dash-Entwicklerteams
nicht schuld daran gewesen sein, sondern das Drumherum: generelle Marktstimmung, Negativberichte und die Entscheidungen
der Anleger speziell in Bezug auf Dash. Ein erheblicher Teil der
Kursverluste war – vor allem in ihrem Ausmaß – unberechtigt. Die
Tatsache, dass Dash sich trotzdem weiterentwickelt hat, relativiert den Nachteil der Kursverluste. Vielmehr entsteht daraus ein
Vorteil, weil eine aktuell extrem unterbewertete Kryptowährung
gefühlt zum Spottpreis erhältlich ist.

Fazit

Die Kryptowährung Dash hat in den ersten knapp 3,5 Jahren seit
Veröffentlichung eine Erfolgsgeschichte hingelegt, die vollkommen berechtigt war. Sowohl das Konzept als auch dessen Umsetzung und Weiterentwicklung stimmten absolut und tun dies nach wie

vor. Leider waren die Kursverläufe insbesondere seit Mitte 2018 bis Anfang 2020 ungünstig, obwohl sich die Marktstimmung gegen Dash teilweise nicht mal erklären ließ. Daher spiegelt sich die solide Arbeit des Entwicklerteams nicht vernünftig im Kurs wider. Dash wurde Anfang 2020 zeitweise häufiger als *Litecoin* genutzt, lag er in der Marktkapitalisierung trotzdem deutlich dahinter zurück. Am Beispiel von Dash lässt sich gut veranschaulichen, dass den Berichterstattungen der Medien und den Entscheidungen der Anleger nicht immer zu trauen ist. Während die Kurse sanken, arbeitete man bei Dash diszipliniert und gut, was auch in Zukunft zu erwarten ist. Auch wenn die Gefahr verbleibt, dass ein herausragendes und hochqualitatives Projekt mit Top-Entwicklern im Hintergrund allein von der Marktstimmung und den Anlegern zugrunde gerichtet wird, bietet sich eine Investition in Dash an. Die aktuell deutliche Unterbewertung der Kryptowährung könnte bei einer Kurskorrektur bereits in einigen Monaten beachtliche Gewinne bescheren. Die vielen Kooperationen und die hohe Akzeptanz von Dash in zahlreichen Staaten auf dem Globus animieren zu Optimismus.

➢ **Bewertung: 6 von 10**
➢ **Anlageempfehlung: zwischen 10 und 30 % des vorgesehenen Anlage-Budgets**
➢ **Investition zurückziehen bei: Kursverlusten, die länger als ein Jahr anhalten und die keine Gegenmaßnahmen durch das Entwicklerteam erfahren**

4

Plattform: NEM;
Kryptowährung: XEM

EM, NEM, XYM, Symbol, NEM NSI1 ... Das **Ökosystem von NEM** [41] – unter dem Namen NEM ist die Kryptowährung am bekanntesten – erfordert einiges an Erklärung. Tatsächlich befindet sich NEM zurzeit (Stand: April 2021) in einer Phase der Innovation und Veränderung. Das ohnehin schon innovative System, die zugehörige Kryptowährung und alle Funktionen werden zurzeit noch weiter ausgebaut. Herausgekommen ist **Mitte März das System Symbol mit der Kryptowährung XYM**. Wie bei IOTA ist NEM von vornherein nicht auf ein neues System zum Zahlungsverkehr beschränkt gewesen. Die Entwickler von NEM setzten sich eine **Revolution des Vertrags-, Vermögens, und Transaktionsmanagements** zum Ziel. Dies kann in Form von NEM und der Kryptowährung XEM gelingen. Nun zünden die Entwickler mit Symbol und der Kryptowährung XYM die nächste Stufe. Es handelt sich nicht um eine reine Kryptowährung, sondern um Infrastrukturen und Ökosysteme, von denen Unternehmen flexibel Gebrauch machen können. Mit NEM ins digitale Zeitalter? Eine Erörterung.

Allgemeines

Die **Kryptowährung XEM** entstand 2015 in Japan. Sie ist **Teil der Krypto-Plattform NEM**, die neben der Währung an sich weitere Features vereint. [42] Neben den Entwicklern aus Japan arbeiten weitere Entwickler aus dem gesamten asiatischen Raum an der Entwicklung der Kryptowährung. Anreiz zur Schaffung der Kryptowährung war das *New Economy Movement* (NEM). Obwohl es falsch ist, wird die Kryptowährung des Öfteren als NEM bezeichnet.

Das New Economy Movement ist eine **ideologische Bewegung**, die sich eine **nachhaltige und gerechte Wirtschaftsordnung im digitalen Zeitalter** zum Ziel gesetzt hat. Die Krypto-Plattform NEM mit ihren Funktionen soll zum Erreichen dieses Ziels beitragen. Weil das Ziel der Bewegung anspruchsvoll ist, wurde NEM passend zum Ziel hochinnovativ gestaltet. Die Funktionen gehen weit über die eines bloßen Bezahlmittels hinaus. Obwohl dies so ähnlich wie die Funktions- und Anwendungsvielfalt von IOTA (siehe Kapitel 2) klingt, sind die Funktionen und Anwendungsbereiche für NEM doch gänzlich andere. Dementsprechend setzen die Entwickler von NEM an anderen Stellen als IOTA innovative Merkmale. Im Gegensatz zu IOTA basiert die Kryptowährung auf einer Blockchain, wie sie bereits von anderen Kryptowährungen bekannt ist, jedoch weist die **Blockchain eine abgewandelte Form** auf. Es existieren bereits Zusammenarbeiten mit Finanzinstituten und Privatunternehmen in Japan. Dank Anwendungsvielfalt und Innovativität bringt sich das Konzept NEM mit der Kryptowährung XEM und seinen neuesten Schöpfungen Symbol und XYM fürs digitale Zeitalter vielversprechend in Stellung.

Geschichte und Intention hinter NEM

Um die Kryptowährung mit allem, was dazugehört, nachvollziehen zu können, ist zuallererst ein Blick auf das *New Economy Movement* (Deutsch: *Bewegung der Neuen Wirtschaft*) hilfreich. Der Begriff *New Economy* ist nicht neu, gelangte er doch bereits um die Jahrtausendwende herum zu Berühmtheit, als das Internet, zugehörige Dienstleister und die Anfänge der Digitalisierung in aller Munde waren. Die neue digitale Wirtschaft wurde „gehypt", sodass viele Anleger ihr Geld in Unternehmen wie Amazon, Deutsche Telekom und weitere investierten. Es entstand eine Blase, die schließlich platzte, und Anleger auf dem Aktienmarkt verloren einen erheblichen Teil ihrer Investitionen. *Ist dies ein schlechtes Vorzeichen für das New Economy Movement mit der Kryptowährung XEM?*

Nein, denn die Bewegung hinter NEM besteht nicht aus einer Reihe an Anlegern, die in möglichst viele verschiedene Aktien bzw. sonstige Anlageprodukte investieren. NEM ist eine **Bewegung, die einzig und allein von Entwicklern initiiert wurde und ein einziges Produkt umfasst.** Dass rund um dieses eine Produkt eine Blase entsteht, ist weit weniger wahrscheinlich als die New-Economy-Blase an der Börse um die Jahrtausendwende herum. Die Entwickler, die sich zusammengetan haben, haben eine Lösung geschaffen, die die Wirtschaft für das digitale Zeitalter möglichst gut ausstatten soll. Ziel war von vornherein, **einerseits ein neues Zahlungsverkehrssystem zu schaffen, andererseits das Vertragswesen zu optimieren.** Wie das erreicht werden sollte – darüber gab es bereits zu Beginn der Währung verschiedene Überlegungen.

Eine der Überlegungen war, die Währung als einen Hard Fork von *Nxt* zu erstellen. [Kerscher; S. 182] Diese Idee kam nicht von irgendwo her, denn die Kryptowährung Nxt ähnelte in vielerlei Hinsicht dem Konzept, das für XEM vorgesehen war:

- Bitcoin-Quellcode als Grundlage;
- Neuprogrammierung des Bitcoin-Quellcodes und Erweiterung um diverse Zusatzfunktionen;
- Integrierung von Features für Abstimmungen, Chats, Börse für den dezentralen Handel von Unternehmens- und Projektanteilen;
- sowie anders als bei Bitcoin der Konsensmechanismus Proof-of-Stake. [Kerscher; S. 158 f]

Letzten Endes wurde die Idee eines Hard Forks von Nxt nicht umgesetzt, weil durch die Entwicklung eines komplett neuen Ökosystems noch weitreichendere Innovationen eingeführt werden sollten, die den Wünschen und Bedürfnissen der Community treffender entsprachen. **Im Bitcointalk-Forum** *UtopianFuture* **begann am 19. Januar 2014 der Aufruf zur Teilnahme der Nutzer an der Entwicklung von NEM.** [Kerscher; S. 182] Mit der Teilnahme zahlreicher Nutzer wuchs das New Economy Movement und alle Features und Funktionen, die XEM bekam, spiegeln die Ziele und Ansprüche dieser vielen Nutzer wider.

Die **Veröffentlichung von NEM erfolgte am 31. März 2015 in einem Zwei-Komponenten-System**: Zum einen gab es den Server mit der NEM-Infrastruktur (*NEM Infrastructure Server*; NIS), zum anderen die für die Interaktion mit dem Netzwerk verwendete Software. Aktuell heißt diese Software *NanoWallet*. Sie läuft über jeden Webbrowser, was eine hohe Kompatibilität garantiert. Über diese Software werden Transaktionen abgewickelt und Informationen über Erzeugnisse innerhalb des Netzwerks ausgetauscht. [Kerscher; S. 182]

Besonderheiten von NEM sind von Anfang an die weiteren Anwendungsmöglichkeiten gewesen, die über den reinen Zahlungszweck hinausgehen. So griffen die Entwickler die *Smart Contracts* von Ethereum auf und schufen die sogenannten *Smart Assets* (Deutsch: intelligente Vermögenswerte), die auf den Smart Contracts basieren. [Miller; S.9] Was **Smart Contracts und Smart Assets** besonders macht, ist die **Hinterlegung von Regeln, unter denen bei Trigger-Events bestimmte Aktionen elektronisch und vollautomatisch ausgeführt werden** [43]. NEM war und ist die erste Kryptowährung bzw. Krypto-Plattform, die Möglichkeiten für Smart Assets in diesem Umfang erschuf. Sie bietet neuartige und komfortable Ansätze, das Vertrags-, Transaktions- und Vermögensmanagement zu automatisieren bzw. zu optimieren.

Beispiel

Das Vertrags-, Vermögens- und Transaktionsmanagement lässt sich bei NEM durch die Multisignaturen optimieren. Experte Markus Miller schreibt in seinem kurzen Infomaterial *Krypto-X: Diese 3 Kryptowährungen explodieren in 2021* (2021): „Multisignaturen ermöglichen Zahlungen, die an bestimmte Vertragsbedingungen gekoppelt werden. Zahlungsfreigaben werden dabei erst nach einer bestimmten Mindestanzahl von digitalen Unterzeichnern ausgeführt. Diese Einsatzmöglichkeiten sind besonders für Unternehmen interessant, um Auszahlungen oder auch Lieferungen kostengünstig automatisiert und rechtssicher ausführen zu lassen." [Miller; S. 9] Dies ähnelt ein Stück weit dem System von IOTA, das beispielsweise erst die Nutzung einer Maschine gestattet, sobald eine bestimmte Anzahl an Bedingungen erfüllt ist. Nur ist IOTA für die Kommunikation zwischen Maschinen vorgesehen, während die Anwendung von NEM für Menschen gedacht ist.

Diese Funktionen haben dem Netzwerk NEM zahlreiche Kooperationen eingebracht. **Im asiatischen Raum wird die Kryptowährung von vielen Finanzinstituten und privaten Unternehmen genutzt.** Die Blockchain-Software NEMs wird in Form einer kommerziellen Blockchain, die den Namen *Mijin* trägt, getestet. [Kerscher; S. 183] Aufgrund der Nutzung und regelmäßig neuer Kooperationen sind die Bekanntheit und der Kursverlauf der zugehörigen Kryptowährung XEM im Laufe der letzten Jahre stetig gestiegen, sodass XEM zwischenzeitlich zu den wertvollsten 10 Kryptowährungen der Welt gehörte.

Im Verlaufe der steigenden Popularität NEMs gab es eine einzige negative Nachricht, die direkt zu einem Skandal wurde: In der Nacht vom 25. auf den 26. Januar 2018 wurden XEM-Coins im Wert von 400 bis 500 Millionen US-Dollar von der japanischen Börse *Coincheck* gestohlen. Als Reaktion kündigte die Börse an, den Nutzern den Schaden zu ersetzen, während die Entwickler von XEM die Coins markierten und somit unbenutzbar machten. [44] Wie es möglich war, diese Coins zu markieren und somit den Diebstahl unwirksam zu machen, wird anhand der faszinierenden technischen Merkmale im nächsten Abschnitt 4.1.2 erklärt. Fakt ist, dass andere Kryptowährungen solche **Möglichkeiten zur Kennzeichnung gestohlener Coins** in dieser Form nicht bieten. An dieser Stelle sei auch betont, dass der Hack nicht im NEM-Netzwerk stattfand, sondern an einer Börse. Das **NEM-Netzwerk wurde bisher kein einziges Mal gehackt und gilt als hochsicher.**

Interessant ist es, abschließend die **zwei verschiedenen Produkte von NEM** zu betrachten. Das eine ist die Version von 2015 und wird unter der Bezeichnung NEM NIS1 geführt. Die zugehörige Kryptowährung ist XEM. Dann gibt es noch die **zweite Version der NEM-Blockchain, nämlich das am 17. März 2021 gestartete Symbol**, dessen zugehörige Kryptowährung auf den Namen XYM hört und ebenfalls handelbar ist. [45]

Durch die zusätzliche Veröffentlichung von Symbol ist NEM zu einem **zweikettigen Ökosystem** geworden. Anwendern steht es frei, sich für eines der beiden Systeme zu entscheiden. In jedem Fall ist **Symbol funktionsreicher, vielfältiger und technisch qualitativer konzipiert.** Allem voran Unternehmen profitieren von diversen neuen Funktionen, die in Erweiterung zu NEM NIS1 ein umfassenderes Vertrags-, Vermögens- und Transaktionsmanagement möglich machen. [46]

Technische Merkmale

Bei den technischen Merkmalen gilt es zwischen dem NEM NIS1 und dem jüngst veröffentlichten Symbol zu unterscheiden. Ehe ein ausführlicher Vergleich durchgeführt wird, sei zunächst betont, wie viel individuellen Spielraum das System den Anwendern bietet. Eventuell haben Sie mal von Baukastensystemen für Websites gehört: Anbieter wie *WIX* und *Jimdo* werben damit, dass man bei ihnen eine Website ohne jegliche Vorerfahrungen erstellen kann. Dafür zieht man einzelne Bausteine an die gewünschten Stellen und verfasst darin Texte, bebildert diese Bausteine oder vollzieht andere Schritte, für die die Anbieter die technischen Möglichkeiten bieten. Aufs Einfachste heruntergebrochen, sind **NEM NIS1 und Symbol ebenfalls Baukastensysteme; allerdings auf einem um Längen (!) höheren Niveau mit schier unbegrenzten Spielräumen in der Anwendung.** Beispielsweise ist es in NEMs Systemen möglich, eigene private Blockchains zu konfigurieren. Sogar die Entwicklung eigener Kryptowährungen ist möglich. [47] All diese Möglichkeiten sind vor allem für Unternehmen relevant, die eigene sichere Datenbanken und Arbeitsprozesse erschaffen wollen. Aufgrund der hohen technischen Anforderungen bei der Nutzung des Systems und der individuellen Arbeit innerhalb des Systems ist **NEM für professionelle Anwender wie z. B. IT-Experten geeignet** oder für Personen und Unternehmen, die Profis für sich arbeiten lassen.

Ein Vergleich der beiden Systeme NEM NIS1 und Symbol wird auf der offiziellen Website von NEM präsentiert, aufgeteilt auf die drei Bereiche: Funktionen, Protokoll und APIs.

Funktionen

NEM NIS1	Symbol from NEM
Multisig-Konten	Mehrstufige Multisig-Konten
Kontobeschränkungen	Erweiterte Kontobes-chränkungen
Mosaikbeschränkungen	Mosaikbeschränkungen
----	Kettenübergreifende Transak-tionen
----	Metadaten- Steuerelemente
----	Integrierte hybride öffentli-che/private Blockchain
Mosaike	Mosaike
Namespaces	Namespaces
Plug-ins	Plug-ins

Quelle: https://nem.io/platforms/ [48]

Mosaike sind **besondere Smart Assets, die sich nicht ändern.** [49] Ein Beispiel hierfür könnten Immobilien oder Aktien sein. Sie unterliegen im Gegensatz zu Transaktionsbedingungen (diese sind ein potenziell wandelbares Smart Asset; Anm.) keinen Änderungen. Eine Immobilie ist und bleibt eine Immobilie, sie wird sich nicht ändern. Beide Systeme bieten die Möglichkeit, solche Assets zu integrieren und **wahlweise bestimmte Beschränkungen (z. B. für den Zugriff auf diese) zu programmieren.** Genau diese Mosaikfunktion ist es übrigens, die es den Entwicklern bei dem Diebstahl von XEM-Coins von der Börse Coincheck ermöglichte, die Coins zu markieren. [44]

Was die **Multisignatures** sind, die oben in der Tabelle erwähnt werden, wurde bereits in 4.1.1 anhand eines Beispiels erklärt. Symbol bietet den Vorteil, dass sich die Multisignature-Konten mehrstufig aufsetzen lassen, was z. B. zur Folge hat, dass sich **Konditionen im Vertrags-, Vermögens- und Transaktionsmanagement differenzierter festlegen** lassen. In Symbol sind drei Features enthalten, die NEM NS1 nicht bietet:

- Kettenübergreifende Transaktionen, die es ermöglichen, den Wert von XYM (zur Erinnerung: dies ist die eigene Währung im System Symbol) auf andere Blockchains, wie etwa die von Bitcoin, zu übertragen [50];
- Metadaten-Steuerelemente, die z. B. dazu dienen können, das Einhalten von Validierungsregeln sicherzustellen;
- und integrierte hybride öffentliche/private Blockchain; dies meint das erwähnte Feature, eigene Blockchains erstellen zu verwalten zu können.

Zuletzt sei aus dem obigen Vergleich auf die **Namespaces** und **Plugins** eingegangen. Beide sind sowohl in NEM NS1 als auch bei Symbol vorhanden. Namespaces sind Adressen, die dem Nachweis von Berechtigungen dienen. Sie werden anstatt der gewöhnlichen Adressen verwendet, die in der Regel die einzelnen Nutzer und Unternehmen repräsentieren. Den **Adressen lassen sich Vermögenswerte, Rechte und weitere Komponenten zuweisen.** [51] Plugins sind Erweiterungen, um die das Netzwerk ergänzt werden kann, um bestimmte Funktionen einfacher implementieren zu können.

Beispiel

Um alles bis hierhin bestmöglich zu verstehen, soll hier eine Transaktion beispielhaft beschrieben werden: Alexandra und Ingo sind Nutzer, die miteinander handeln möchten.Ihren Namen sind im NEM-Netzwerk Adressen zugeordnet. Alexandra ist eine Angestellte des Unternehmens *Feenstaub*,

---

die eine Berechtigung benötigt, Gelder und Bonuspunkte der Firma zu überweisen. Diese Berechtigung erhält sie in Form eines Namespaces, der unter bestimmten Bedingungen gilt. Dank der Berechtigung kann sie Geld und Bonuspunkte zu Ingo überweisen, falls im Rahmen der Transaktion bestimmte Bedingungen erfüllt sind. Ingo hat gerade seinen hundertsten Kauf beim Unternehmen Feenstaub abgeschlossen und soll dafür als Belohnung 10 Bonuspunkte erhalten. Weil laut hinterlegten Regeln im System die Überweisung erlaubt ist und der Namespace gilt, darf Alexandra die Transaktion veranlassen. Die Bonuspunkte, die sie überweist, sind das Mosaik im System. Falls im Unternehmen die Ausschüttung von Bonuspunkten an die Zustimmung mehrerer Personen geknüpft ist, wäre eine Überweisung allein durch Alexandra nicht möglich. In diesem Szenario könnte das Unternehmen Multisignaturen hinterlegen, bei denen zunächst Alexandra und dann zwei weitere Mitarbeiter aus anderen Abteilungen der Überweisung zustimmen müssen, ehe die Bonuspunkte an Ingo ausgeschüttet werden.

PROTOKOLL	
POI (Proof-of-Importance)	POS+ (Modifizierter Proof-of-Stake)
---	Kassenbon
---	Merkle State Transition Proof
P2P Transaktionen	Aggregierte P2P- Transaktionen
Feste Gebühren	Anpassbare Gebühren
Keine Inflation	Anpassbare Inflation
API's	
In Java codiert	In C++ codiert

Quelle: https://nem.io/platforms/ [48]

NEM NIS1 basiert auf einer **Blockchain mit einem POI-Konsensmechanismus** (siehe Kapitel 1.2.3). Wie Sie aus dem ersten Kapitel wissen, animiert dieser Konsensmechanismus im Gegensatz zum Proof-of-Stake zur **aktiven Nutzung einer Kryptowährung.** Die Entwickler trafen bereits früh Vorkehrungen dafür, dass die Währung nicht nur zu spekulativen bzw. profitorientierten Zielen gehalten wird, sondern in der Anwendung Relevanz erlangt. Demgegenüber steht der **modifizierte POS-Konsensmechanismus – auch *POS*+ genannt –**, der bei NEMs **Symbol** Anwendung findet. Modifiziertes POS deshalb, weil das Vermögen des Nutzers als Entscheidungsgrundlage für die Beauftragung mit Aufgaben im Netzwerk genommen wird, die Aktivität der Nutzer in Form von Transaktionen der eigenen Coins jedoch ebenfalls einberechnet wird. Somit ähnelt das POS+ von Symbol in gewisser Hinsicht dem POI.

Weitere Unterschiede beim Aspekt Protokoll äußern sich bei Symbol darin, dass es den **Erhalt von Kassenbons bei Zahlungen** ermöglicht und den *Merkle State Transition Proof* nutzt. Letzterer ist ein Verfahren, das innerhalb der Blockchain eine **höhere Sicherheit und Skalierbarkeit** begünstigt. Ferner bietet Symbol die Option, aggregierte Transaktionen durchzuführen. Hierbei werden mehrere Transaktionen in einer Transaktion gebündelt und ausgeführt.

Zuletzt sei kurz auf die APIs beider Systeme eingegangen. Ein API (*Application Programming Interface*; Deutsch: Programmierschnittstelle) ist ein Programmteil, der dazu dient, andere Programme an NEM NIS1 bzw. Symbol anzubinden. NEM NIS1 arbeitet mit Java, während Symbol C++ verwendet. Die Sprachen Java und C++ unterscheiden sich u. a. dahingehend, als dass C++ höhere Leistungen begünstigt.

Historie: Kursverläufe der letzten Jahre

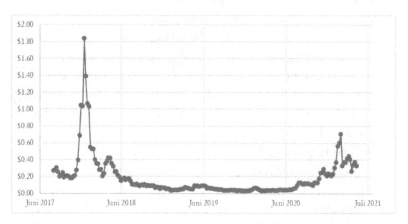

Quelle: https://www.btc-echo.de/kurs/nem/ [52]

Da Sie bereits mit einigen Mustern von Kursverläufen vertraut sind, können wir in diesem Kapitel die Erklärungen zum Kursverlauf von XEM kürzer halten. Tatsächlich zeigen sich im Kursverlauf von XEM nur **zwei Auffälligkeiten**; nämlich der bis ins Jahr 2018 und somit länger als bei anderen Kryptowährungen anhaltende Hype sowie der jüngste Kursverlust von März bis April 2021:

- 2015 bis 07.01.2018 (Veröffentlichung und Hype)
- 07.01.2018 bis 04.04.2018 (durch Diebstahl bei Coincheck befeuerter Bärenmarkt)
- 04.04.2018 bis 06.05.2018 (Aufschwung durch Marktstimmung)
- 06.05.2018 bis 31.08.2020 (Abschwung mit ruhiger Folgephase)
- 31.08.2020 bis 05.03.2021 (Aufstieg wegen steigenden Vertrauens und Innovationen)
- 05.03.2021 bis 06.04.2021 (Kursverlust durch Fork zu Symbol bzw. XYM)

Wie bei zahlreichen anderen Kryptowährungen ließ sich zu Zeiten des Hypes um Kryptowährungen Ende 2017 ein immenser Kursanstieg beobachten. Dieser **Anstieg hielt bei XEM im Gegensatz zu den anderen Kryptowährungen über das Jahr 2017 hinaus bis zum 07.01.2018 an.** Dieser Tag bescherte der Kryptowährung ein **Allzeithoch von 1,87 US-Dollar** pro Coin.

Interessant ist an dieser Stelle die Frage, ob der Kurs von XEM sich noch länger oben gehalten hätte. Denn auffällig ist, dass Bitcoin und der Großteil der Altcoins bereits 2017 in den Bärenmarkt eintraten und stark fallende Kurse verzeichneten. Der XEM-Kurs stieg jedoch bis ins Jahr 2018. Nun könnte man die These aufstellen, dass der Bärenmarkt bei XEM zeitversetzt eintrat und sich ab 2018 einstellte. Allerdings ist auffällig, dass im Januar 2018 der Diebstahl bei Coincheck stattfand. Zwar hat dies nichts mit der Sicherheit des NEM- und somit XEM-Netzwerks zu tun, doch reagierten die **Anleger aufgrund ihrer Unwissenheit** darüber, wer oder was gehackt wurde, wohl vorschnell und ließen den **Kurs von XEM aufgrund des Fehlers von Coincheck rapide sinken.** Die Tatsache, dass der XEM-Kurs verlor, ging im allgemeinen Bärenmarkt unter. Allerdings ist die Vermutung nicht unberechtigt, dass XEM aufgrund des geringen Preises pro Coin sich ohne den Fehler der Coincheck-Börse noch ein paar Wochen oder Monate länger oben gehalten hätte und einer der wertvollsten Altcoins geworden wäre. Da die Dinge gegensätzlich liefen, blieb zeitweise lediglich ein Platz unter den Top 10 der wertvollsten Kryptowährungen.

Ansonsten zeigt sich beim Kursverlauf von XEM bis zum 05.03.2021 ein ähnliches Muster wie bei allen anderen Kryptowährungen. **Auffällig: Ab dem 05.03.2021 zeigt sich ein Kursverlust**, bei dem der Kurs vom zwischenzeitlichen Hoch von 0,7 US-Dollar pro Coin auf 0,4 US-Dollar pro Coin zum 06.04.2021 sinkt. Der **Grund für diesen Kursverlust ist der Hard Fork**, bei dem Daten und somit auch **Währungseinheiten vom**

NEM NIS1 auf Symbol migriert wurden. Dieser Fork bescherte den Nutzern zunächst die doppelte Menge an Coins, ging aber natürlicherweise mit einem Wertverlust von Coins in der alten Währung – also in diesem Fall XEM – einher.

Hinweis!

Der Sachverhalt, dass Nutzer nach einem Hard Fork dieselbe Menge an Coins im neuen Netzwerk erhalten wie im alten Netzwerk und dass sich die Kurswerte dadurch verändern, wurde bereits in Kapitel 1.3 erläutert. Der Kursverlust bei XEM stellt somit keine Auffälligkeit dar. Das, was XEM an Wert verloren hat, hat XYM ungefähr an Wert gewonnen [53]. Fürs Erste ist es eine Nullsummenrechnung. Insofern ist der jetzige Kursverlust nicht kritisch zu beurteilen.

Kritikansätze und Besonderheiten bei NEM

Kritikansätze und Besonderheiten von NEM zu schildern, ist aufgrund der beiden Währungen und der weitreichenden Funktionalitäten des Ökosystems komplex. Im Folgenden wird bestmöglich zwischen NEM, Symbol, XEM und XYM differenziert. Bitte behalten Sie vor Augen, dass in der Kürze keine Vor- und Nachteile zusammengestellt werden können, die den vier Komponenten des NEM-Ökosystems inhaltlich angemessen gerecht werden. Die folgenden Absätze gewährleisten allerdings, dass Sie inhaltlich besser als mindestens 90 % der Anleger informiert sind. Weitere Entscheidungshilfen zur Geldanlage entnehmen Sie bitte dem Fazit oder erschließen Sie sich aus den vorangegangenen detaillierten Berichten über die Geschichte und die technischen Merkmale der Kryptowährung.

Vorteile

Unabhängig davon, ob vom POI-Konsensmechanismus aus NEM NIS1 oder POS+-Konsensmechanismus aus Symbol die Rede ist: Bei NEM sind die **Nutzer dazu animiert, die jeweilige Kryptowährung aktiv zu nutzen.** Lange Haltezeiten der Währungseinheiten wie im reinen POS sind höchst unwahrscheinlich, weil nicht lukrativ. **Zudem verursacht die Blockchain keinen hohen Energieverbrauch,** wie er beim Schürfen der Währungseinheiten bei Bitcoin oder anderen Währungen mit dem PoW-Konsensmechanismus gegeben ist. Weil NEM eine der wenigen Kryptowährungen ist, die den PoI verwenden, und die einzige Kryptowährung mit einem PoS+ ist, ergibt sich in diesem Punkt ein echtes Alleinstellungsmerkmal, das positiv zu bewerten ist.

Ein weiterer Vorteil von NEM besteht darin, dass es ein **umfassendes System** ist, das eben nicht nur dem Zahlungsverkehr dient. Dies kann grundsätzlich auf alle Kryptwährungen zutreffen, denn auch die Blockchain vom Bitcoin und die Blockchain von Dash lassen sich für weitere Verwendungszwecke nutzen. Allerdings unterscheidet sich NEM von anderen Kryptowährungen darin, dass **von vornherein ein entsprechendes Ökosystem mit einer vielfältigen Anwendbarkeit geschaffen wurde.** Dieses Ökosystem verfügt aktuell – dies ist ein weiterer Vorteil – im asiatischen Raum über ein hohes Ansehen und zahlreiche Kooperationen.

Bei seinen vielfältigen Anwendungsbereichen haben sich die Entwickler von NEM ebenso wie die von IOTA einen Bereich ausgesucht, der in der Zukunft zunehmend relevant sein wird. **Unternehmen** investieren große Budgets in die Digitalisierung ihrer Arbeitsprozesse und in die IT-Sicherheit. Anstatt teure Tools zu kaufen, besteht die Option, **möglichst viele Prozesse mithilfe der sicheren Systeme NEM NIS1 oder Symbol zu digitalisieren.** Diese Perspektive für den Einsatz in Unternehmen als Ersatz oder Ergänzung zu kostenpflichtigen Programmen eröffnet NEM die Chance auf eine häufige Nutzung. Dabei müssen IOTA und NEM gar nicht in Konkurrenz zueinander treten. Eine Koexistenz beider Kryptowährungen bzw. Netzwerke ist absolut denkbar, weil beide Kryptowährungen/ Netzwerke ihre Besonderheiten haben und es unter den Unternehmen reichhaltig Zielgruppen gibt, die sich die Nutzung von IOTA und NEM gewissermaßen untereinander aufteilen können. NEM ist neben IOTA eine der Kryptowährungen, die anderen Kryptowährungen starke Konkurrenz machen können, aber **denen selbst keine Kryptowährung einfach so Konkurrenz machen kann**. Je etablierter NEM auf dem Markt sein und je häufiger es genutzt werden wird, umso wahrscheinlicher ist es, dass das gesamte Angebot aus dem NEM-Netzwerk nicht zu verdrängen sein wird.

Abschließend seien kurz die Vorteile angesprochen, die sich aus den technischen Merkmalen des NEM-Netzwerks ergeben: Die **Währung sowie das gesamte Ökosystem sind skalierbar**. Energieeffizienz und trotzdem hohe Leistung gehen aufgrund der cleveren technischen Konzeption Hand in Hand. **Chancengleichheit und der dezentrale Grundgedanke** hinter den Kryptowährungen werden mit dem PoI bzw. PoS+ als Konsensmechanismen gewahrt. Die Option, die jeder Nutzer hat, nämlich die **Durchführung von Transaktionen an bestimmte Nutzer des Netzwerks zu delegieren**, verhindert, dass nur die Nutzer mit dem größten Vermögen und der höchsten Aktivität innerhalb des Netzwerks profitieren. Man bezeichnet diese Funktion als *Delegated Harvesting*, was zur Chancengleichheit beiträgt. [54]

Nachteile

Das NEM-Ökosystem hat keine ersichtlichen Nachteile, die nicht auch der Konsensmechanismus PoI hätte (siehe 1.2.3). Dementsprechend muss im NEM-System **beim Bewertungssystem des PoI, mit dem der Node ausgewählt wird**, lediglich darauf geachtet werden, dass es einen **optimalen Schwierigkeitsgrad der Nachvollziehbarkeit** hat, um einerseits das Erstellen eines Fake-Netzwerks zu verhindern und andererseits eine ausreichende Transparenz sicherzustellen. [17] Diese Herausforderung meisterten die Entwickler vor allem bei der neuen Kryptowährung XYM hervorragend, indem sie das ursprüngliche PoI optimierten und in ein PoS+ umwandelten. Im Rahmen dieses PoS+ ist aufgrund der neuen und differenzierteren Auflagen einerseits eine höhere Sicherheit gegen das Erstellen von Fake-Accounts gewährleistet, andererseits verbleibt eine ausreichende Transparenz innerhalb des Netzwerks. So **kommt der Nachteil des PoI bei NEM kaum zu tragen.**

Es verbleiben zwei Nachteile, die der Rede wert sind und das gesamte Netzwerk NEM bzw. Symbol betreffen. Zum einen ist die **erschwerte Anwendbarkeit** als Nachteil anzuführen, denn die **Nutzung aller Features gelingt in der Regel nur Personen mit IT-Fähigkeiten oder viel Lernbereitschaft.** Somit scheint es eine Währung rein für Unternehmen, Institutionen und technisch versierte Privatanwender zu sein. [55] Zum anderen ist der Nachteil beim NEM, dass sich das Netzwerk **in einer von der Konkurrenz umkämpften Branche** bewegt. Mehr noch als bei IOTA, das immerhin auf die Machine-to-Machine-Kommunikation spezialisiert ist, ist bei NEM davon auszugehen, dass zwar keine anderen Kryptowährungen, dafür aber Unternehmen, die auf die Digitalisierung anderer Unternehmen spezialisiert sind, Konkurrenten sein werden.

Fazit

Außerhalb von Asien verfügt das Netzwerk NEM über eine geringere Popularität und wird seltener genutzt. Dies ist per se kein schlechtes Zeichen. Bereits Großkonzerne wie die *Alibaba Group* aus China haben vorgemacht, dass es für eine hohe Marktkapitalisierung und unternehmerischen Erfolg keiner globalen Positionierung als Marktführer bedarf. Asien ist ein großer Kontinent mit noch größerer Bevölkerung und reichlich wirtschaftlichen Perspektiven. In vielen Bereichen sind die Unternehmen Asiens technologische Vorreiter. Allein eine häufige Nutzung und zunehmende Akzeptanz von NEM bzw. Symbol im asiatischen Raum könnte für massive Anlageerfolge bei Investition in die Kryptowährungen genügen. Beobachten Sie als Anleger daher vor allem die Entwicklungen im asiatischen Raum. Je länger namhafte Kooperationen, wie die bereits vorhandenen mit Universitäten und staatlichen Institutionen, anhalten und je mehr Kooperationen hinzukommen, umso besser ist es für die Kursprognose. Letzten Endes bieten NEM und Symbol mit ihren Kryptowährungen sowie sonstigen Funktionen vielfältige Möglichkeiten und sind fast schon vergleichbar mit dem enormen Potenzial IOTAs. Eine Tatsache allerdings schmälert die Aussichten für NEM sowie Symbol und lässt die Prognose etwas schlechter als für IOTA ausfallen: Während IOTA auf die Machine-to-Machine-Kommunikation ausgerichtet ist, hat NEM eine derartige Spezialisierung nicht. Dies nimmt dem Profil etwas Schärfe und birgt eine gewisse Gefahr der Verdrängung durch Unternehmen. Unter den Kryptowährungen ist NEM etwas wahrlich Besonderes, aber ob das Konzept sich auch gegen Unternehmen als Konkurrenten durchsetzen kann, die anderen Unternehmen bei der Digitalisierung der Arbeitsprozesse helfen, steht in den Sternen. Sie als Anleger sind aufgerufen, selbst eine Prognose diesbezüglich aufzustellen.

- ➢ **Bewertung: 6 von 10**
- ➢ **Anlageempfehlung: zwischen 10 und 20 % des vorgesehenen Anlage-Budgets**
- ➢ **Investition zurückziehen bei: ein Jahr oder länger konstant rückläufiger Menge bzw. Abbruch von Kooperationen (vor allem in Asien auf Entwicklung der Kooperationen achten)**

5

Netzwerk: MaidSafe; Kryptowährung: MaidSafeCoin (MAID)

Sie haben zwei Kryptowährungen bzw. Systeme kennengelernt, die wichtige Anliegen der Digitalisierung aufgreifen: IOTA als Machine-to-Machine-Kommunikationsprotokoll, beispielsweise für die Industrie 4.0, und NEM als Schlüssel zur Digitalisierung der Prozesse in Unternehmen. Außerdem wurde Dash vorgestellt; eine klassische Kryptowährung mit dem Hauptziel, als Zahlungsmittel zu dienen. Nun bringt der *MaidSafeCoin* [56] komplett andere Ansätze mit sich und sorgt für eine weitere Überraschung in diesem Buch: Dem MaidSafeCoin liegt ein System mit dem Namen *MaidSafe* zugrunde, das die **Dezentralisierung des Internets** anstrebt. Politische Hintergründe sind dabei eine Motivation. Über ein Projekt, das die Art und Weise, wie Menschen das Internet nutzen, revolutionieren könnte ...

Allgemeines

Die Entwickler von MaidSafe greifen **aktuelle und wahrschein-liche künftige Probleme des Internets** auf, um mit dem Maid-Safe-Netzwerk Lösungen für diese Probleme zu bieten. Unter die Probleme fallen mehrere Aspekte, die politischer Natur sind.

Einer dieser Aspekte ist die **Kontrolle über private Daten.** In seinem Buch *Das digitale Debakel* (2015) äußerst sich Andrew Keen allgemein äußerst kritisch über das Internet und bezieht sich in einem Teil des Buches speziell auf die Tatsache, dass das Konsumverhalten von Nutzern systematisch ausgespäht wird. Er fordert staatliche Regulierungen, um die Kontrolle zurückzuge-winnen. [57]

Mit dieser Aussage ist Keen nicht allein. Auch **Sir Tim Bern-ers-Lee, der als Erfinder des Internets bekannt ist,** sieht Prob-leme bei der Kontrolle der privaten Daten. Seine Aussage dazu: *„Das derzeitige Geschäftsmodell vieler Webseiten lautet: kostenloser Inhalt im Austausch gegen persönliche Daten. Viele stimmen dem zu, indem sie lange und verwirrende AGB akzeptieren, aber eigentlich ist es den meisten egal, welche Daten über sie gesammelt werden, wenn nur der Inhalt kostenlos bleibt. Wir verlieren dabei aber einen Punkt aus den Augen. Unsere Daten werden in Containern gespeichert und wir verlieren die Kontrolle darüber."* [58]

Doch Berners-Lee geht noch weiter, indem er die **Folgen des Sam-melns von Daten bis in die Politik** erläutert: *„Firmen und Regi-erungen können jeden unserer Schritte nachvollziehen und Gesetze erlassen, die auf unserem Recht auf Privatsphäre herumtrampeln. In repressiven Regimen ist es leicht zu sehen, welcher Schaden entstehen kann, denn dort werden Blogger verhaftet oder getötet und politische Gegner können beobachtet werden."* [58]

Eine Lösung? Berners-Lee nennt hierzu einen wohl dosierten Gebrauch persönlicher Daten in Unternehmen. [58] Wie die Unternehmen dazu gebracht werden sollen, lässt er hingegen offen.

Zugegebenermaßen sind Lösungen für die Nutzung persönlicher Daten von Internetnutzern in Unternehmen alles andere als einfach zu finden; sie sind sogar schwer vorstellbar. Ansätze wie die **DSGVO (Datenschutzgrundverordnung)** sollten zu einem größeren Schutz der Nutzerdaten beitragen, haben aber stattdessen in vielen Fällen die **Nutzung des Internets verkompliziert** oder Unternehmen sogar Schlupflöcher geboten, noch mehr Daten von den Nutzern einzuholen.

Beispiel...

Facebook fragte die Nutzer im Rahmen der neuen Datenschutzregeln ab, ob sie eine Gesichtserkennung zulassen würden. Eine Gesichtserkennung wurde vor der DSGVO von Facebook noch nicht durchgeführt. Den Umstand des neuen Gesetzes nutzte Facebook, um bei Gelegenheit noch mehr Daten von den Nutzern zu gewinnen, indem diese zustimmten. [59] Da es viele Menschen gibt, die sich ohne Achtsamkeit durch die Fragen zu Cookies und Co. klicken oder allem von vornherein zustimmen, ist es nicht unwahrscheinlich, dass Facebook mit seinem Schachzug erfolgreich war, sodass viele Nutzer unwissentlich der Gesichtserkennung zustimmten und Facebook mehr Daten als vor Erlass der DSGVO von den Nutzern gewann.

Ein weiterer wichtiger Punkt, den Berners-Lee erwähnt, ist: *„Ich habe mir das Netz als eine offene Plattform vorgestellt, die es jedem*

*von überall ermöglichen sollte, Informationen zu teilen, Chancen zu
nutzen und miteinander zu arbeiten, ganz gleich, welche geographis-
chen und kulturellen Grenzen bestehen mögen."* [58]

Macht man sich nun Gedanken darüber, wie es **heutzutage um die
internationale und interkulturelle Kommunikation sowie Bereitstellung von Informationen** steht, dann ist es offenkundig, dass
hier **größte Defizite** bestehen. Regelmäßig werden in Staaten bestimmte Inhalte gesperrt oder deren Nutzung wird eingeschränkt.
Dies schränkt den interkulturellen und internationalen Austausch
ein.

Abgesehen von all diesen Aspekten gibt es noch das Risiko von
Cyber-Attacken gegen Unternehmen und Privatpersonen. *Bitkom*,
der Digitalverband Deutschlands, nennt zahlreiche Bedrohungen,
die bestehen:

- Schadsoftware
- Schäden durch webbasierte Software
- infizierte Websites und mobile Apps
- Botnetze
- Denial-of-Service-Attacken
- Spam
- Phishing
- Viren-Baukästen
- physischer Verlust
- Datenverlust [60]

Schon allein die Menge der Bedrohungen ist alarmierend. Anti-
viren-Software ist in vielen Fällen für die Privatnutzer nicht mal
ausreichend. Denn ebenso wie sich die Software weiterentwickelt,
entwickeln sich auch die Hacker und Cyber-Kriminellen weiter,
die mittlerweile Schadsoftware auf Basis künstlicher Intelligenz
(KI) nutzen, was den Schutz vor Attacken erschwert. Das Risiko

von Cyber-Angriffen ist insbesondere für Krypto-Börsen groß. Mehrmals bereits kam es vor, dass Börsen gehackt wurden und Personen ihre Coins verloren.

An dieser Stelle kommt das Netzwerk MaidSafe (auch: *Safe Network*) zum Einsatz: Es soll das Internet dezentralisieren und damit all die genannten Probleme lösen. Durch verschlüsselte Datenübertragung sei der Datenschutz der Nutzer gewährleistet. Die dezentrale Serverstruktur trage dazu bei, dass Veränderungen im Netzwerk nur durch einen Konsens unter allen Nutzern getroffen werden könnten. Es sei unmöglich, das Safe Network abzuschalten oder zu zensieren. Die zugehörige Kryptowährung MaidSafeCoin (kurz: MAID) sei skalierbar und könne daher an ein beliebig großes Netzwerk angepasst werden.

Geschichte und Intention hinter MaidSafeCoin

Das Entwicklerteam von MaidSafe ist **in Schottland ansässig**, wo die ganze Geschichte mit der Gründung durch David Irvine begann. Irvine, selbst ein renommierter und international bekannter IT-Spezialist, hat ein Team um sich herum gebildet, das seine Vorstellung eines funktionierenden und „verbindenden" Internets widerspiegelt. Im **Entwickler-Team** vereint sind **Personen verschiedener Nationalitäten und Kulturen**. Der genaue Wortlaut auf der Website von MaidSafe zur Zusammensetzung des Teams ist: *„Obwohl wir in Ayr, Schottland, ansässig sind, haben wir Talente aus vielen verschiedenen Kulturen und Ländern angezogen, die die Benutzer widerspiegeln, denen wir dienen. Trotz dieser Vielfalt teilen wir alle eine Mission: den Wunsch, Sicherheit und Privatsphäre für alle zu bieten."* [61]

Dieses Zitat ermöglicht den direkten Themenwechsel von der Zusammensetzung des Teams zu den **Zielen des MaidSafe-Netzwerks**: Die **Privatsphäre, Sicherheit und Freiheit der Nutzer**

gewährleisten. Genau dies sind die Aspekte, die bereits in 5.1 als aktuelle und künftige Probleme des World Wide Webs vorgestellt wurden. Laut Interpretation der Aussagen der Entwickler geht MaidSafe bei der Lösung dieser Probleme äußerst differenziert vor; Beispiel: Datenschutz: Es gehe nicht darum, Geheimnisse oder Dinge zu verbergen, die nicht verborgen gehören. Stattdessen sei das Ziel, den **Nutzern die Fähigkeit zu geben**, über das Teilen verschiedener Gedanken, Botschaften und Aktionen mit anderen Nutzern innerhalb eines Netzwerks **selbst zu entscheiden.** [61] Das Bestreben, den Nutzern im umfassenden und schwer kontrollierbaren Internet die Kontrolle über sich selbst und die eigenen Daten zu geben, war letztlich der Antrieb zur Schaffung des MaidSafe-Netzwerks.

Über die gesamte Geschichte des MaidSafe-Netzwerks existieren keine relevanten Informationen, da das Netzwerk hauptsächlich auf die privaten Nutzer abzielt. Kooperationen mit Unternehmen lassen sich nicht finden, ebenso sind Skandale sowie besondere Erfolge nicht gegeben. Dies liegt nicht zuletzt daran, dass das Netzwerk noch nicht online ist. Zurzeit findet eine **Entwicklung des Netzwerks** statt. An der Entwicklung der Open-Source-Software dürfen sich auch **Personen aus aller Welt beteiligen.** Zusätzlich stellt das Team Personen fest an, sofern diese gewisse Qualifikationen vorzuweisen haben. Reichlich Kapital zur Realisierung der eigenen Vision scheint also vorhanden zu sein.

Die aktuell erhältliche Kryptowährung MaidSafeCoin ist nichts anderes als eine „Überbrückungswährung"; gemeint ist, dass mit Online-Schaltung des Netzwerks die erworbenen MaidSafeCoins in die eigentlich im Netzwerk vorgesehenen SafeCoins im Verhältnis 1:1 eingetauscht werden können. Mehr dazu im folgenden Unterkapitel 5.1.2.

Technische Merkmale

Das **dezentrale Internet des MaidSafe-Netzwerks ist über einen Browser nutzbar,** der kostenlos auf der Website von MaidSafe heruntergeladen und genutzt werden kann. Bis hierhin ist also alles so, wie wenn Sie z. B. *Mozilla Firefox* oder *Google Chrome* downloaden, installieren, starten und darin surfen würden. Spannend ist der Blick hinter die Kulissen: Wo werden die Daten gespeichert, wenn Personen das Internet nutzen?

Bei Mozilla Firefox und Google Chrome werden Daten auf den Datenträgern der Nutzer gespeichert und sind abrufbar. Diese Daten erhalten Unternehmen beim Besuch der Nutzer auf ihren Websites, wenn die Nutzer dem Datentracking zustimmen. Dies ist für ein einschränkungsfreies Web-Erlebnis auf vielen Internetseiten notwendig. Wenn jemand den MaidSafe-Browser nutzt, kann dagegen **niemand die persönlichen Daten des Nutzers auslesen.** Grund hierfür sind die **Verschlüsselung und das Splitting der Daten:**

- Jede Datei wird in einzelne Teile zerlegt.
- Diese Teile werden mit anderen Teilen derselben Datei vermischt.
- Alle Teile werden verschlüsselt.
- Danach erfolgt ein Splitting der Teile innerhalb des Netzwerks.
- Die einzelnen Teile einer Datei werden automatisiert innerhalb des Netzwerks zwischen verschiedenen Computern verschoben. [62]

Um eine Datei zu hacken, müssten Sie also zum richtigen Zeitpunkt wissen, auf welche Teile diese Datei gesplittet und mit welchen Teilen diese Datei vermischt wurde. Sie müssten alle Computer mit den jeweiligen Teilen kontrollieren und Zugriff auf alle Dateien erlangen. Dies ist sehr unrealistisch, weswegen definitiv nur die Dateien, von denen Sie es sich wünschen, für alle Personen sichtbar ins Netzwerk gelangen. Alles, was für Sie privat ist und nicht an andere Personen gelangen soll, bleibt stets verschlüsselt, nicht einsehbar und nicht durch Hacker einnehmbar. Ganz anders ist es hingegen in anderen Browsern mit zentralisierten Server-Strukturen.

Die Basis für die Funktionsweise des MaidSafe-Netzwerks bildet die Serverstruktur. **Das Netzwerk funktioniert nach dem PoC-Konsensmechanismus.** Hierbei stellen die Knotenpunkte des Netzwerks Speicherkapazität und Rechenleistung zur Verfügung. Je mehr von beidem ein Knoten zur Verfügung stellt, umso besser ist es für diesen, denn sein Service (man nennt diesen Service der Zurverfügungstellung von Speicherkapazität und Rechenleistung *Vault*; Anm.) wird mit SafeCoins belohnt. **SafeCoins sind das Honorar für die Dienste beim Betrieb des Netzwerks.** Jeder Nutzer, der eine Vault-Software downloadet und seine Bereitschaft zur Erbringung des Vault-Services ausdrückt, kann Knotenpunkt werden und SafeCoins verdienen.

> ### Hinweis!
>
> Es sei an dieser Stelle nochmals betont, dass die gespeicherten Dateien verschlüsselt sind. Keiner der Knotenpunkte hat im Rahmen seines Vault-Services die Möglichkeit, die verschlüsselten und in verschiedenen Datenpaketen auf mehrere Knotenpunkte verteilten Dateien einzusehen. Zwar speichert er die Dateien bei sich, ein Zugriff auf diese ist jedoch nicht möglich. Somit ist die Sicherheit innerhalb des Netzwerks gewährleistet und eine Manipulation der Dateien ausgeschlossen.

Das **Netzwerk ist selbstverwaltend und kann auf Änderungen in Echtzeit reagieren.** Dies trägt zu einem geringen Arbeitsaufwand für die Entwickler und einem hohen Zuverlässigkeitsgrad für die Nutzer bei. Es kommt keine Blockchain zum Einsatz, was das Netzwerk zu einer **Plattform** macht: Je mehr Nutzer gegeben sind, umso größer ist der Nutzen des Netzwerks. Es ist **beliebig skalierbar**, was für die Zukunftsfähigkeit essenziell ist.

Sobald das Netzwerk online ist, können die heute auf Krypto-Börsen erhältlichen MaidSafeCoins im Wert 1:1 in SafeCoins umgetauscht werden. Die **SafeCoins** sind nicht als generelles Zahlungsmittel weltweit vorgesehen, sondern dafür gedacht, **Netzwerkdienste zu bezahlen.** [63] Beim Kauf von MaidSafeCoins wird also eine Wette bzw. Prognose darauf abgeschlossen, dass das Netzwerk online gehen und genutzt werden wird. Veröffentlicht wurden die MaidSafeCoins im April 2014 in einer Stückzahl von 452 Millionen. Die maximale Menge der künftig im MaidSafe-Netzwerk erhältlichen SafeCoins soll 4,3 Milliarden betragen. [Kerscher; 179 f]

Historie: Kursverläufe der letzten Jahre

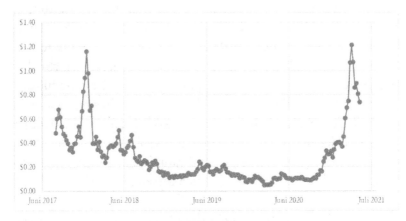

Quelle: https://www.btc-echo.de/kurs/maidsafecoin/ [64]

Im April 2014 veröffentlicht, war es zunächst einige Monate still um die Kryptowährung MaidSafeCoin. Ungefähr ab dem 27. Januar 2015 begannen die Kurse anzusteigen. Das **Muster des Kursverlaufs ist bis Anfang 2021 vergleichbar mit dem vieler anderer Kryptowährungen:**

- April 2014 bis 03.01.2018 (Veröffentlichung und Hype; 1,16 US-Dollar pro Coin auf dem bis dahin höchsten Hoch)
- 03.01.2018 bis 29.03.2018 (Bärenmarkt mit Kursverlust bis 0,23 US-Dollar pro Coin)
- 29.03.2018 bis 25.07.2018 (Aufschwung durch Marktstimmung)
- 25.07.2018 bis Oktober 2020 (Abschwung mit ruhiger Folgephase)
- Oktober 2020 bis 15.04.2021 (Aufstieg wegen steigender Bekanntheit mit Allzeithoch von 1,37 US-Dollar pro Coin)

Kleinere Abweichungen von mehreren Monaten bei den Kursverlaufsmustern sind im Vergleich zu anderen Kryptowährungen gegeben. Beispielsweise dauerte der Aufschwung durch Marktstimmung zwischen dem 29.03.2018 und 25.07.2018 bis zu drei Monate länger als bei anderen Kryptowährungen, die viel schneller wieder Kursverluste verbuchten. Eine besondere Ursache für den beim MaidSafeCoin lange anhaltenden Aufschwung lässt sich nicht finden; wahrscheinlich ist der Grund dafür, dass Anleger aufgrund des sehr geringen Preises pro Coin vermehrt in MaidSafeCoin investierten. Doch irgendwann betraf der generelle Abschwung auf dem Krypto-Markt auch diesen Kursverlauf.

Nun (Stand: 15.04.2021) erlebt der MaidSafeCoin einen starken Kursanstieg. Im Gegensatz zum Großteil der Kryptowährungen hat der MaidSafeCoin **im Frühjahr 2021, am 12. April 2021, ein neues Allzeithoch von 1,37 US-Dollar pro Coin** erreicht. Dies klingt zwar nach einer spektakulären positiven Entwicklung, ist jedoch mit Hinblick auf den geringen Preis des Coins mit Vorsicht zu betrachten. Nichtsdestotrotz merkt man in breiten Teilen der Krypto-Welt, dass der **MaidSafeCoin sowie das MaidSafe-Netzwerk immer bekannter** werden. Somit verbirgt sich hinter den seit Oktober 2020 stark steigenden Kursen sicher auch die Zuversicht der Anleger, dass das Konzept des MaidSafe-Netzwerks ein hohes Zukunftspotenzial hat.

Kritikansätze und Besonderheiten von MaidSafeCoin

Dem MaidSafe-Netzwerk liegt eine **völlig innovative, aber leider noch gar nicht erprobte Idee** zugrunde. Gründer Irvine und sein Entwickler-Team erkannten mehrere Probleme, die das Internet heutzutage hat und in der Zukunft mit der allerhöchsten Wahrscheinlichkeit nach wie vor haben wird. Sie schufen eine Lösung – und das, obwohl eine Lösung denkbar schwierig zu finden ist, weil das Internet bereits etabliert, auf dem gesamten Globus genutzt und durch die Staaten regulierbar ist! Diese **Lösungsfindung und die Qualitäten des MaidSafe-Netzwerks sind dem Entwickler-Team hoch anzurechnen**, aber wann wird das Netzwerk online geschaltet und wird es ausreichend Nutzer haben, um wachsen zu können und an Bedeutung zu erlangen? Es sind die Ungewissheiten, die am MaidSafe-Netzwerk und dem MaidSafeCoin zweifeln lassen.

Vorteile

Ein offensichtlicher Vorteil des MaidSafe-Netzwerks ist dessen **Alleinstellungsmerkmal;** nämlich, dass es zur **Dezentralisierung des Internets** vorgesehen ist. Die **einfache Nutzung**, bei der nur ein Download des Browsers erforderlich ist, spricht für das Netzwerk. Über allem steht aber die Frage danach, wie stark die Nachfrage sein wird: Empfinden die Nutzer ein dezentralisiertes Internet als notwendig oder sind sie mit der Nutzung ihrer Daten einverstanden, sodass der Datenschutz in ihren Augen zweitrangig oder sogar noch unwichtiger ist? Bei der Antwort auf diese Frage lässt sich nur mutmaßen. Trotzdem ist es berechtigt zu glauben, dass es immer einen Anteil an Nutzern geben wird, die dem Schutz ihrer Daten ein verstärktes Augenmerk widmen. Diese Nutzer werden im MaidSafe-Netzwerk eine einfach anwendbare Lösung zu ihrem Datenschutz finden.

Noch viel größer und wahrscheinlicher sind die Potenziale des MaidSafe-Netzwerks nicht in der Nutzung zum Datenschutz, sondern für einen **unbeschränkten Zugang zu den Inhalten des Internets**; allem voran in Staaten, in denen Inhalte zensiert werden. In der Volksrepublik China beispielsweise sind viele Nachrichtenseiten aus den USA und einige aus Europa gesperrt. Außerdem ist die Informationswebsite *Wikipedia* nicht zugängig. Soziale Medien aus den USA sind ebenfalls zum Teil zugriffsbeschränkt. Auch die Türkei machte in der jüngeren Vergangenheit regelmäßig durch Zensuren auf sich aufmerksam. Falls das MaidSafe-Netzwerk bereits in wenigen Staaten wie den genannten populär und anstelle anderer Browser genutzt wird, um die Zensuren zu umgehen, ist es sehr wahrscheinlich, dass der Wert der MaidSafeCoins und später SafeCoins zunehmen wird. Zu berücksichtigen ist hierbei, dass Staaten wie China und die Türkei eine große Bevölkerung haben. **Allein schon eine häufige und verbreitete Nutzung des Maid-Safe-Netzwerks in China wäre ein Meilenstein für die Entwickler von MaidSafe.**

Apropos Entwickler: Die **multikulturelle Zusammensetzung des Entwickler-Teams** von MaidSafe hat den potenziellen Vorteil, dass sich die Nutzer aus verschiedenen Orten der Welt besser mit dem Projekt identifizieren können und dem Projekt mehr Vertrauen schenken. Dieser Vorteil ist zwar vorerst gering zu gewichten, bringt dem MaidSafe-Netzwerk allerdings ein paar Bonuspunkte in der gesamten Bewertung ein. Für den Fortschritt des Projekts MaidSafe ist außerdem der Fleiß des Entwickler-Teams zu berücksichtigen. In einem Check auf dem YouTube-Channel *My Digital Strategist* erfolgte eine Prüfung der Aktivität des Entwickler-Teams auf GitHub, wobei sich zeigte, dass **regelmäßige Updates und Arbeiten an dem Projekt** stattfinden. [65] Auch ein Blick in das Forum der Community, wo sich Nutzer (es müssen keine Entwickler sein; Anm.) beteiligen und verschiedene Versionen des Netzwerks testen, beweist ein **hohes Aktivitätslevel aller Beteiligten.** [66]

Bisher sind drei Vorteile geklärt:

1. Keine Kryptowährung und kein mit einer Kryptowährung in Verbindung stehendes System hat das spezielle Alleinstellungsmerkmal von MaidSafe, nämlich die Dezentralisierung des Internets. Somit ist das MaidSafe-Netzwerk grundsätzlich ohne Konkurrenz; „grundsätzlich", weil natürlich jederzeit ein konkurrierendes System geschaffen werden könnte und es Systeme mit ähnlichen Ambitionen (z. B. TRON; siehe Kapitel 7) gibt.
2. Außerdem ist das Entwickler-Team durch seine multikulturelle Zusammensetzung und bis dato kontinuierliche Arbeit mit David Irvine als sehr erfahrenem Gründer ein positives Zeichen. Vor allem im Hinblick auf die globalen Ziele des MaidSafe-Netzwerks ist die Zusammensetzung des Teams förderlich.
3. Die Nutzung des MaidSafe-Netzwerks ist einfach. Sowohl das Surfen über den einfach zu downloadenden Browser als auch das Verdienen von SafeCoins über die Vault-Software erfordern keine komplexen technischen Kenntnisse.

Der dritte Aspekt aus der Aufzählung sollte vertieft werden, da er die technischen Merkmale des MaidSafe-Netzwerks betrifft. Wie bereits erwähnt, ist das Netzwerk beliebig skalierbar, weil es auf die Blockchain verzichtet. Je mehr Nutzer im Netzwerk sind, umso stärker werden Nutzen und Leistung des Netzwerks. Diese Eigenschaft ist einer Plattform ähnlich. Einen **plattformähnlichen Aufbau** hat auch das Netzwerk von NEM und XEM (siehe Kapitel 4). Bereits aus der *Platform Economy* wurde am Beispiel von Unternehmen wie *Amazon*, *Uber* und *Airbnb* deutlich, wie vorteilhaft die hohe Skalierbarkeit ist und wie sehr die **Bekanntheit und der Wert der Plattformen mit jedem zusätzlichen Nutzer ansteigen** kann.

Eine Dezentralisierung und Sicherheit des Netzwerks sind trotz der fehlenden Blockchain durch die vielen verschiedenen Knotenpunkte gesichert. Die Knotenpunkte stellen innerhalb des Netzwerks Speicherplatz zur Verfügung, womit sie sich im Rahmen des Proof-of-Capacity-Konsensmechanismus SafeCoins verdienen. Wenn Sie an Kapitel 1.2.3 zurückdenken, so werden sie sich an die Vor- und Nachteile des PoC erinnern. Einer der Nachteile war die höhere Anfälligkeit für Hackerattacken im Vergleich zu anderen Konsensmechanismen. Dieser Nachteil ist im MaidSafe-Netzwerk gemindert, weil dieses im Gegensatz zu anderen Kryptowährungen mit PoC die Dateneinheiten vorher in Teile zerlegt, auf verschiedene Computer aufteilt und ständig zwischen den Computern verschiebt. Somit gelten für MaidSafe die **Vorteile des PoCs, erweitert um den Vorteil einer höheren Sicherheit**.

Nachteile

Das MaidSafe-Netzwerk ist **noch nicht online**. Genau hiermit beginnt eine Menge an **Fragen und Unklarheiten**, die die Zukunft des Netzwerks ungewiss machen. Was, wenn die Entwickler plötzlich keine Lust mehr haben? Kein Problem, dann gibt es immer noch genug andere Entwickler, die sich um das Projekt kümmern, da es Open Source ist.

Wie sieht es jedoch aus, wenn nicht ausreichend Personen das Netzwerk nutzen? Bedenken, dass das Netzwerk bzw. irgendeine der vielen Kryptowährungen im Laufe der Zeit unattraktiv wird, gibt es viele. Beim MaidSafe-Netzwerk sind diese Bedenken jedoch größer, da das **Netzwerk nur zur Dezentralisierung des Internets gedacht ist und die SafeCoins lediglich darin als Bezahlmittel nutzbar sein werden.** Es gibt keine Blockchain, deren Technologie sich auch zum Vertragsmanagement und für andere Zwecke nutzen ließe. Das MaidSafe-Netzwerk mit der zugehörigen Kryptowährung ist eine Insellösung, wenngleich eine unter dem Blickpunkt der Probleme des Internets attraktive Insellösung.

Damit das MaidSafe-Netzwerk attraktiv bleibt, arbeiten die Entwickler an Lösungen, um bis zur Online-Schaltung mehr Nutzer zu gewinnen. Es werden grundsätzlich viele Wege geboten, um sich am Projekt beteiligen zu können: testen, Codes schreiben und verbessern, Vorschläge einbringen und promoten. [67] Die vielen Perspektiven zur Beteiligung am Projekt sind als positiv zu bewerten, lösen aber nicht das Problem der unvorhersehbaren Zukunft des Netzwerks.

Fazit

Zweifel sind bei der Geldanlage in MaidSafeCoins berechtigt. So innovativ und grundsätzlich positiv die Idee hinter dem Netzwerk ist, mindestens genauso sehr steht dessen Zukunft in den Sternen. Da trifft es sich hervorragend, dass der **aktuelle Preis pro MaidSafeCoin äußerst gering** ist! Es spricht aufgrund des geringen Kurses nichts dagegen, dem eigenen Portfolio an Kryptowährungen mit einer Investition in den MaidSafeCoin ein bisschen Risiko beizumischen. Nicht vergessen: Ein hohes Risiko birgt die Chance auf eine hohe Rendite.

Zum jetzigen Zeitpunkt ist die Investition in den MaidSafeCoin spekulativ. Dass der MaidSafeCoin auf seinem Allzeithoch ist, macht sie noch spekulativer. Es gibt zwei mögliche Strategien, zu investieren: Entweder Sie investieren jetzt langfristig oder Sie warten, bis der MaidSafeCoin an Wert verloren hat, und investieren zum späteren Zeitpunkt, um beim nächsten Kursanstieg einen noch höheren Gewinn aus Ihrer Investition mitzunehmen.

Letzten Endes gibt es beim MaidSafeCoin noch geringere Sicherheiten als bei anderen Kryptowährungen, doch das MaidSafe-Netzwerk und dessen Potenzial zur Lösung elementarer Probleme im Internet sind **zu interessant, um den MaidSafeCoin einfach zu ignorieren.** Bei dem geringen Preis und hohen Risiko sollten Sie nur einen geringen Anteil Ihres Budgets investieren, der bei Verlust nicht schmerzt. Wird das MaidSafe-Netzwerk tatsächlich populär, so wird aus dem geringen Anteil Ihres Investitionsbudgets voraussichtlich ein äußerst großer Gewinn resultieren. Komplett unwahrscheinlich ist dies nicht, denn schon eine Nutzung des Netzwerks in wenigen Staaten würde voraussichtlich zu einem immensen Wertanstieg des MaidSafeCoins beitragen.

> - **Bewertung: 4 von 10**
> - **Anlageempfehlung: zwischen 3 und 5 % des vorgesehenen Anlage-Budgets**
> - **Investition zurückziehen bei: ausbleibender Veröffentlichung des Netzwerks oder geringen Nutzerzahlen nach der Veröffentlichung**

6

Krypto-Börse: Binance; Kryptowährung: Binance Coin (BNB)

Hier geht es zunächst um eine Börse: „Kryptos ganz einfach kaufen & verkaufen – Tritt der weltweit größten Krypto Börse bei" lautet der Aufruf [68]. Die 2017 in Hongkong gegründete **Krypto-Börse Binance mit jetzigem Sitz in Malta hat eine eigene Kryptowährung veröffentlicht.** Diese heißt *Binance Coin* (kurz: *BNB*) und dient der Zahlung verschiedenster Gebühren an der Börse. [Kerscher; S. 188] Somit ist das Schicksal des Binance Coins abhängig von der Entwicklung der Krypto-Börse. Bleibt diese groß oder wächst sogar, so wird der Binance Coin voraussichtlich immer gefragt sein.

Allgemeines

2017 wurde die Krypto-Börse *Binance* von **Changpeng Zhao** gegründet. Er hatte zuvor mehrere Jahre Erfahrungen im Markt für Kryptowährungen gesammelt. Davor hatte er **studiert und war beruflich im Zusammenhang mit Wertpapier-Börsen aktiv.** So schuf er u. a. Hochfrequenz-Systeme, die Börsenmaklern den Handel mit Wertpapieren vereinfachten. Technisch hat er also zahlreiche Vorerfahrungen und Kompetenzen vorzuweisen. Der Erfolg von Binance als Krypto-Börse festigt den Eindruck seines Knowhows.

Bis heute befindet sich die Börse Binance unter der Leitung von Changpeng Zhao, wenngleich sich der Sitz der Börse geändert hat: Weil der Markt für Kryptowährungen in China zunehmend staatlich reguliert wurde und drohte, seinen ursprünglichen Zweck – Dezentralisierung und Anonymität – zu verlieren, **wechselte Binance den Unternehmenssitz und zog nach Malta.** In Malta sind durch mehrere „krypto-freundliche" Gesetzesentwürfe Rahmenbedingungen geschaffen worden, die Unternehmen aus dem Bereich der Kryptowährungen mehr Sicherheit bieten. Die Rahmenbedingungen enthalten **gesetzliche Richtlinien für ...**

- erstmalige Angebote neuer Coins;
- Börsengeschäfte;
- und die Führung von Protokollen in Unternehmen. [69]

In China gibt es ebenfalls Regulierungen und Richtlinien, jedoch sind diese für die Verbreitung und das Zukunftspotenzial von Kryptowährungen destruktiv. Malta hingegen hat **konstruktive Rahmenbedingungen** geschaffen, die die Verbraucher schützen und den Unternehmen sowie Kryptowährungen eine gute Chance bieten, sich weiterzuentwickeln. Während Krypto-Börsen in anderen Staaten das Problem haben, sich aufgrund fehlender verbindlicher Richtlinien bzw. Gesetze in rechtlichen Grauzonen zu bewegen, hat Binance in Malta den Vorteil, sich an klaren Regelwerken orientieren und dadurch unternehmerisch schneller vorankommen zu können. [69] Es dürfte also wenig verwundern, dass Binance **zurzeit die größte reine Krypto-Börse mit dem vielfältigsten Angebot und dem größten Handelsvolumen ist:**

Börse	24h-Handelsvolumen (08.05.2021; 9:20 Uhr)	Wöchentliche Besuche	Märkte	Coins
Binance	47.979.389.854 €	27.657.536	1.214	358
Huobi Global	15.620.158.910 €	1.342.816	963	326
Coinbase Pro	5.430.382.334 €	3.577.326	197	63
Kraken	2.404.439.374 €	2.938.774	285	62

Quelle: https://coinmarketcap.com/de/rankings/exchanges/ [70] (die Tabelle wurde gekürzt und leicht abgewandelt; Anm.)

Ein mehr als dreimal so großes Handelsvolumen wie bei *Huobi Global* veranschaulicht den enormen Vorsprung der Krypto-Börse Binance. Die wesentlich höhere Besucherzahl ist ein ebenfalls relevantes Kriterium, denn je höher die Besucherzahlen ausfallen, umso bekannter ist die Börse. Es ist einleuchtend, dass viele Personen bei der Frage nach einer Krypto-Börse – falls sie denn überhaupt eine Börse kennen – als erstes den Namen Binance parat haben. Es ist **DIE Krypto-Börse, wovon der Binance Coin profitiert ...**

Geschichte und Intention hinter dem Binance Coin

Der Binance Coin wurde in erster Linie geschaffen, um die Börse Binance zu stärken. Er ist primär für die **Nutzung zu verschiedenen Zwecken innerhalb der Börse** vorgesehen. Zum einen betrifft dies die Zahlung verschiedener Gebühren, wozu beispielsweise die Listungs-, Börsen- und Handelsgebühr gehören. Zum anderen ist der Coin für IEO-Investitionen über die Plattform Binance nutzbar. [71] Diese Investitionen sind sozusagen Fundraising-Verfahren, bei denen Coins einer neuen Kryptowährung an Investoren und Privatanleger herausgegeben werden. Über dieses Verfahren wurde auch der Binance Coin selbst herausgegeben. Anstatt die Coins zu minen oder anderweitig zu errechnen, sind diese bereits im Voraus produziert und werden an die Anleger verteilt. Konzepte wie die Blockchain sowie die Grundgedanken der Dezentralität und Anonymität bleiben je nach Kryptowährung dennoch bestehen.

Durch **mehrere Partnerschaften** ist es Binance gelungen, den Coin zudem **außerhalb der eigenen Börse für weitere Zwecke nutzbar zu machen**. In den Bereichen Zahlung, Reisen, Unterhaltung, Service und Finanzen gibt es u. a. folgende Angebote:

- Erstellung von Smart Contracts bei *MyWish* (für Erklärung der Smart Contracts: siehe 4.1.1)
- Erwerb von Clouds und Webservern bei *CenterServ*
- Buchung von Unterkünften über *Travala.com*
- Aufnahme von Darlehen bei *Nexo*
- Kauf virtueller Geschenke bei *Gifto*
- Kauf von Smartphones von *HTC* [72]

Bis hierhin stellen wir fest, dass der Binance Coin vor allem dazu geschaffen wurde, die Krypto-Börse Binance zu stärken. Im Verlaufe der Jahre seit seiner Herausgabe 2017 wurden allerdings Partnerschaften geschlossen, die Besitzern von Binance Coins mehrere Verwendungszwecke ermöglichen. Diese Verwendungszwecke (z. B. Buchung von Hotels und Kauf von Smartphones) sind zwar stark auf bestimmte Partner begrenzt, jedoch attraktive zusätzliche Perspektiven für die Anwendung des Binance Coin, auf denen aufgebaut werden kann.

Zweifelsohne ist das **Besondere hinter dem Binance Coin dessen Verbindung zur Börse Binance**. Im Gegensatz zu den meisten anderen Coins hat der Binance Coin also eine Absicherung: Seine Nutzung und Bekanntheit ist daran gebunden, wie sich die Krypto-Börse Binance entwickelt. Binance wiederum dient zum Handel und Tausch von Kryptowährungen und ist die größte reine Krypto-Börse. Sofern nicht alle Kryptowährungen von der Bildfläche verschwinden werden, wird es für den Binance Coin **wohl immer eine Existenzgrundlage** geben.

Um die **Popularität und Attraktivität des Binance Coins zu fördern**, hatten die Entwickler beschlossen, bei der Begleichung von Handels- und Transaktionsgebühren mit Binance Coin **Rabatte** zu geben. Wenn eine Zahlung nicht mit herkömmlichen Währungen wie Euro und US-Dollar, sondern stattdessen mit Binance Coin erfolgte, erhielten Nutzer folgende Rabatte:

- 1. Nutzungsjahr (2017): 50 % Rabatt auf alle Gebühren
- 2. Nutzungsjahr (2018): 25 % Rabatt auf alle Gebühren
- 3. Nutzungsjahr (2019): 12,5 % Rabatt auf alle Gebühren
- 4. Nutzungsjahr (2020): 6,75 % Rabatt auf alle Gebühren
- ab dem 5. Nutzungsjahr (2021): keine Rabatte mehr [Kerscher; S. 188]

Die Rabatte trugen in der Tat zu einer höheren Attraktivität des Binance Coins bei, was sich in seinen Kursverläufen (mehr dazu unter 6.2) bemerkbar machte, jedoch ein bestimmtes Problem mit sich bringt: Mit dem Sinken der Rabatte bis hin zu keinen Rabatten ab 2021 nimmt die Attraktivität des Binance Coins ab, sodass der Preis des Binance Coins sinken müsste. Weil die Entwickler dieses Problem voraussahen, schufen sie zusammen mit dem Rabattkonzept auch eine Art **„Rückkauf- und Vernichtungskonzept"** für Binance Coins: Von den insgesamt herausgegebenen 200 Millionen Binance Coins sollen bis zu 100 Millionen Coins, also die Hälfte, zurückgekauft und vernichtet werden (Stichwort: *BNB-Burning*). [Kerscher; S. 188 f] Dies soll den aufgrund der sinkenden Rabatte zu erwartenden Wertverlust der Binance Coins minimieren oder verhindern und **auf lange Sicht den Wert der Coins steigern.**

Wie lassen sich all die Erkenntnisse zur Geschichte und Intention beim Binance Coin zusammenfassen? Zuallererst soll der Binance Coin das ohnehin erfolgreiche und weltweit bekannte Binance-Ökosystem antreiben. Die Rabatte als Lockmittel und das BNB-Burning zur Verhinderung des Wertverlustes nach Abschaffen der Rabatte haben bis hierhin gefruchtet und den Binance Coin (Stand: Mai 2021) zur Kryptowährung mit der fünftgrößten Marktkapitalisierung gemacht. Weitere Verwendungszwecke sind aufgrund der Partnerschaften mit Finanzdienstleistern und weiteren Unternehmen möglich, doch das Herzstück und der Hauptnutzen des Binance Coins sind die Stärkung des Binance-Ökosystems. Dies sichert den Binance Coin zugleich ab, denn er ist in seiner Weiterentwicklung nicht auf sich allein gestellt, sondern profitiert von der Größe und Bekanntheit der Krypto-Börse Binance, die aus dem Krypto-Markt kaum wegzudenken ist.

Technische Merkmale

Der Binance Coin wurde **auf der Ethereum-Plattform herausgegeben**. Neben der Kryptowährung Ether gibt es Ethereum, das eine Software-Plattform ist und Entwicklern verschiedene Möglichkeiten bietet. Zu diesen Möglichkeiten gehören die Smart Contracts, die Ethereum einen enormen Popularitätsschub verliehen. Außerdem können Entwickler auf der Ethereum-Plattform eigene Anwendungen und Kryptowährungen entwickeln. Hierzu dient die *Ethereum Virtual Machine* (*EVM*) als Hilfestellung. Dabei wird die speziell für Ethereum entwickelte Programmiersprache *Solidity* genutzt. [Kerscher; S. 92 f] Mit diesen Möglichkeiten entwickelten die Techniker der Krypto-Börse Binance die eigene Währung Binance Coin, wobei sie keine eigene Blockchain erstellen mussten, sondern die bereits vorhandene von der Ethereum-Plattform nutzten. So war es anfangs, 2017. **Heute** hat der Binance Coin **eine andere Blockchain, die dennoch eng an die**

Ethereum-Plattform angelehnt und mit allen Anwendungen der Plattform kompatibel ist.

Die *Binance Smart Chain* (*BSC*) ist eine eigens entwickelte Blockchain, die ohne den rechenintensiven und unökologischen Konsensmechanismus PoW auskommt. Durch das Verfahren **Proof of Stake** werden die Personen gewählt, die Transaktionen bestätigen können. Neue Einheiten müssen, wie schon erwähnt, nicht mehr berechnet werden, da alle Währungseinheiten bereits im Umlauf sind. Es geht bei dem PoS der Binance Smart Chain also rein um die **Validierung von Transaktionen**, für die die Validierer mit Coins belohnt werden.

Die Verwendung des PoS anstelle des PoW ist nicht der größte Vorteil, den die Binance Smart Chain gegenüber der Ethereum-Blockchain hat. Vielmehr ist der herausstechende Vorteil der Binance Smart Chain in der **Schnelligkeit und den geringeren Kosten gegenüber der Ethereum-Blockchain** zu finden; beide Vorteile – Geschwindigkeit und Kosten – sind dem Konsensmechanismus und einer generellen technischen Optimierung durch die Binance-Entwickler zu verdanken. Noch dazu ist die Binance Smart Chain mit der Ethereum-Plattform hochkompatibel. Durch die bereits erwähnte Ethereum Virtual Machine zur Herstellung eigener Anwendungen und die Open-Source-Eigenschaft des Projekts Ethereum konnten die Binance-Entwickler eine direkte Anbindung ans Ökosystem von Ethereum schaffen. Die **für Ethereum geschriebenen Apps sind auch auf der Binance Smart Chain nutzbar und laufen dort sogar schneller und reibungsloser.** Weil das Ethereum-Netzwerk wegen der hohen Bekanntheit und des aufwändigen PoW-Konsensmechanismus immer stärker ausgelastet wurde, wurde die Binance Smart Chain in den ersten Monaten des Jahres 2021 bei vielen Nutzern zu einer bevorzugten Alternative. Zwar bleibt Ethereum aufgrund seiner Marktvorteile nach wie vor der Platzhirsch, doch die technischen Innovationen der Binance Smart Chain und die aufkommende Konkurrenz für Ethereum sind real. [73]; [74]; [75]

Historie: Kursverläufe der letzten Jahre

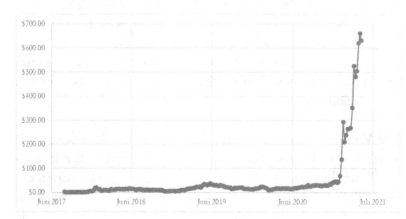

Quelle: https://www.btc-echo.de/kurs/binance-coin/ [76]

Der Hype in den letzten Monaten des Jahres 2017 und Anfang 2018, von dem nahezu alle Kryptowährungen betroffen waren, ging an dem Binance Coin fast unbemerkt vorbei. So entsteht eine **recht übersichtliche und erst zu Beginn des Jahres 2021 an Fahrt aufnehmende Kurshistorie**:

- 2017 bis 31.01.2021 (mühsamer Weg zur Popularität)
- 31.01.2021 bis 19.02.2021 (rapider Kursanstieg aufgrund Binance Smart Chain)
- 19.02.2021 bis 25.03.2021 (Kursverlust durch Marktstimmung)
- 25.03.2021 bis 08.05.2021 (starker Kurszuwachs mit Allzeithoch dank Popularitätsschub, Binance Smart Chain und Marktstimmung)

Der Grund, weswegen der Binance Coin von seiner Veröffentlichung 2017 bis 2021 einen unspektakulären Kursverlauf hat, liegt wohl darin, dass er vom generellen Krypto-Hype 2017/2018 nicht erfasst wurde: kein Hype = also keine Motivation für Anleger sowie Nutzer, sich nach neuen Kryptowährungen umzuschauen. Mit der Zeit, vor allem durch die Nutzung im Binance-Ökosystem, wurde der Binance Coin bekannter und gewann an Wert. Womöglich sorgten auch die **Rabatte für BNB-Nutzer an der Krypto-Börse** für einen leichten Kursgewinn der Währung, denn schon 2020 entwickelte sich der Kurswert leicht positiv.

Ab **Anfang 2021** kam der **Durchbruch**: Der Binance Coin gewann aufgrund der in kürzester Zeit entwickelten **Binance Smart Chain** eine höhere Anzahl an Nutzern für sich, was allein schon Erklärung genug wäre. Noch dazu partizipierten Anleger an den Kursgewinnen der Währung, was die Währung durch die Marktstimmung noch rasanter an Wert zulegen ließ. Das Ergebnis war ein **zwischenzeitliches Allzeithoch von 333,36 US-Dollar pro Coin am 19. Februar 2021.** Die Aktivität der euphorisierten Anleger hatte auch ihre Nachteile, nämlich eine Überbewertung, die nach Kurskorrekturen zu einem starken Kursverlust führte, sodass ein Coin nach dem zwischenzeitlichen Allzeithoch vom 19. Februar 2021 schließlich am 25. März 2021 bei 234,14 US-Dollar notierte. Damit war die, im Vergleich zu anderen Kryptowährungen, einmalige Rallye im ersten Quartal 2021 jedoch noch nicht vorbei ...

Weil der Binance Coin durch seinen schnell und stark gestiegenen Kurswert eine höhere Bekanntheit erlangte, legten immer mehr Anleger Geld an und der **Kurs wurde durch die Marktstimmung auf ein neues Allzeithoch am 03. Mai 2021 in Höhe von 677,47 US-Dollar pro Coin (!) getrieben.** Auch die fortschreitenden Innovationen der Bitcoin Smart Chain verbreiteten sich als Neuigkeit und befeuerten den Kurs durch einen Anstieg an Nutzern im Binance-Ökosystem nochmals. Nach der Rallye Anfang 2021 belegt die Kryptowährung ganz plötzlich und unerwartet – da zu Beginn des Jahres nicht absehbar – den **vierten Platz unter den Kryptowährungen mit der höchsten Marktkapitalisierung**. (Stand: Mai 2021)

Besonderheiten und Kritikansätze beim Binance Coin

Durch seine Anbindung an die Krypto-Börse Binance ergeben sich für den Binance Coin gleich mehrere Besonderheiten und Vorteile. Diese verleihen ihm einerseits eine besondere Art der **Stabilität**, wie sie bei anderen Kryptowährungen nicht anzutreffen ist. Andererseits bedingt die Anbindung an die Krypto-Börse, dass der Binance Coin sogar in Phasen, in denen die Kurse der meisten Kryptowährungen sinken, zum Teil gebraucht wird. Wie das sein kann? Aus einem interessanten Grund, der einen genaueren Blick erfordert ...

Vorteile

Stellen Sie sich folgendes Negativszenario vor: Es herrscht ein Bärenmarkt. Die Marktstimmung, staatliche Regulierungen oder Angriffe auf die Netzwerke verleiten die Anleger dazu, ihre Währungseinheiten möglichst schnell zu verkaufen. Sie akzeptieren sogar geringere Verkaufspreise, nur um ihre Coins schnell loszuwerden. *Welche Argumente gäbe es nun dafür, dass der Binance Coin von diesem Bärenmarkt weniger stark betroffen ist und sein Kurs nicht allzu stark sinkt?* Die Anbindung an die Börse ist der Grund für eine bessere Prognose, denn **für Bärenmärkte an der Krypto-Börse Binance gilt Folgendes:**

1. Fallen die Kurse, dann verkaufen die Anleger Ihre Währungseinheiten.
2. Um einen Verkauf zu tätigen, müssen die Anleger Transaktionen abwickeln. Diese Transaktionen ziehen Gebühren nach sich.
3. Zur Zahlung der Gebühren wird entweder reales Geld oder der Binance Coin verwendet. Letzterer ist günstiger als reales Geld und wird deswegen wohl von den Anlegern bevorzugt zur Zahlung genutzt werden.
4. Die Nutzung des Binance Coins verhindert nicht zwingend, dass sein Kurs ebenfalls fällt, solange ein Bärenmarkt herrscht. Jedoch hat er nach wie vor einen Nutzen und könnte dadurch geringer im Wert sinken als die anderen Kryptowährungen.

Hinweis!

Wie schon mehrmals angemerkt, agieren Anleger auf dem Markt für Kryptowährungen im Großen und Ganzen irrational. Die Wertentwicklungen der Kryptowährungen entbehren teilweise jeglicher Logik, wie u. a. am Beispiel von Dash (siehe Kapitel 3) und *TRON* (siehe Kapitel 7) deutlich wird. Daher ist zum jetzigen Zeitpunkt (Stand: Mai 2021) davon auszugehen, dass der Binance Coin von einem Bärenmarkt miterfasst werden würde. Blickt man hingegen mehrere Jahre in die Zukunft, so ist davon auszugehen, dass aufgrund der steigenden Popularität, des Zukunftspotenzials und der Vielseitigkeit der Kryptowährungen immer mehr informierte Anleger mit finanzwirtschaftlichem Hintergrund in Kryptowährungen investieren werden. Sobald dies eintritt, wird der Binance Coin nach der in der Auflistung erklärten Logik in Bärenmärkten stabiler sein. Denn keiner qualifizierten Person entgeht die Absicherung des Binance Coins durch dessen Anbindung an die Krypto-Börse.

Die Entwickler haben mit dem Binance Coin demnach eine Kryptowährung geschaffen, die bessere Kursprognosen als der Markt haben wird, falls die Kurse fallen, die allgemeine Marktstimmung sich gegen die Kryptowährungen richtet und Panik auf den Märkten herrscht.

Außerdem wird der **Nutzen des Binance-Ökosystems konstant erweitert**: Aufgrund der Entwicklung der **Binance Smart Chain mit einwandfreier Kompatibilität zum Ethereum-Netzwerk** ist ein Anreiz geschaffen worden, von dem Ethereum-Netzwerk auf das Binance-Ökosystem umzusteigen. Auf der Ethereum-Plattform entwickelte dezentrale Apps sind auf der Binance Smart Chain problemlos nutzbar.

Die Binance Smart Chain selbst ist eine hochentwickelte Blockchain, die wesentlich umweltfreundlicher ist als andere Blockchains. Eine **hohe Geschwindigkeit bei der Abwicklung von Transaktionen** und die **geringen Transaktionsgebühren** haben im Jahr 2021 für den enormen Kurszuwachs des Binance Coins gesorgt und werden auch in naher Zukunft zentrale Vorteile bleiben.

Eine gewisse Attraktivität des Binance Coins für Nutzer leitet sich auch aus den vielfältigen Aufbewahrungsmöglichkeiten ab. Wie auf der Webseite https://www.binance.com/de/bnb#storeBnbSection von Binance aufgeführt ist, eignen sich 15 sichere Wallets zur Aufbewahrung von Währungseinheiten des Binance Coins. [77] Beim Klick auf die jeweiligen Wallets werden Nutzer direkt zu den Anbietern weitergeleitet, bei denen sie sich näher informieren können. Auf diesem Wege wird deutlich, wie hoch die **generelle Nutzerfreundlichkeit** ist: Nahezu alles, was es über den Binance Coin und dessen Nutzung zu wissen gibt, finden Nutzer auf der Website von Binance übersichtlich und einfach aufgeführt. Für erstmalige Nutzer von Kryptowährungen ist es durchaus hilfreich, eine simple Website-Gestaltung vorzufinden. Über diesen Vorzug könnte der Binance Coin noch viele Anfänger für sich begeistern und dadurch an Bekanntheit und Wert gewinnen. So hat jedenfalls die Börse Binance zahlreiche Anleger und Trader für sich gewonnen.

Nachteile

Nahezu jeder der Vorteile des Binance Coins ist mit Vorsicht zu genießen. Wo die Absicherung des Binance Coins durch seine Anbindung an die Börse als erster Vorteil genannt wurde: Diese **Absicherung gilt nur unter der Voraussetzung, dass der Binance Coin seine Attraktivität zur Zahlung von Gebühren behält.** Wegen der seit diesem Jahr nicht mehr vorhandenen Rabatte für Zahlungen der Gebühren mit dem Binance Coin ist schwer abzusehen, ob die Nutzungszahlen des Binance Coins zurückgehen oder nicht. Ein leichter Rückgang an Nutzungszahlen ist denkbar, ein starker jedoch nicht, weil viele der Nutzer noch Rücklagen an Binance Coins haben, die sie wohl nutzen werden, um die Transaktionsgebühren zu zahlen. Immerhin mindert das BNB-Burning den Effekt, dass sich eventuell sinkende Nutzerzahlen des Binance Coins allzu stark im Kursverlauf der Kryptowährung niederschlagen.

Außerdem **differenzierter zu beurteilen ist die Entwicklung der Binance Smart Chain**: Unter den Vorteilen wurden die Geschwindigkeits- und Kostenvorteile sowie die komplette Kompatibilität mit der Ethereum-Plattform angesprochen. Diese Vorteile gelten nach wie vor, bringen aber einen Nachteil mit sich: die **mangelnde Dezentralität**. Wer von der Binance Smart Chain Gebrauch machen möchte, muss dies über die Krypto-Börse oder die sogenannte Binance-Bridge tun – beides ist zentralisiert. Möchte Binance über seine Blockchain Auszahlungen an bestimmte Nutzer stoppen, dann ist es problemlos machbar. Dies hat zwar den Vorteil, dass im Gegensatz zu anderen Blockchains gestohlene Währungseinheiten unbenutzbar gemacht werden können, ist aber das komplette Gegenteil der eigentlich bevorzugten Dezentralisierung.

Zuletzt hat die Anbindung an die Krypto-Börse den offenkundigen Nachteil, dass **Skandale und Hacks gegen die Börse sich nachteilig auf den Kurswert des Binance Coins auswirken können.** In Anbetracht der Tatsache, dass Negativschlagzeilen in der Geschichte der Börse Binance bereits mehrfach auftraten [78]; [79], ist es nicht unwahrscheinlich, dass es erneut Negativschlagzeilen geben wird, die den Kursverlauf des Binance Coins negativ beeinflussen. Diesbezüglich kann man von Glück reden, dass die Börse Binance aufgrund ihrer Größe und der enormen Liquidität nahezu jede realistische Krise sehr gut meistern kann.

Fazit

Hardliner unter den Krypto-Investoren, die Aspekte wie die Dezentralität höher als alles andere bewerten, werden den Binance Coin und die Binance Smart Chain nicht nutzen. Demzufolge entfällt eine potenzielle Gruppe an Nutzern. Weil der Markt für Kryptowährungen immer größer wird, machen die Hardliner aber einen immer geringeren Anteil an den Nutzern von Kryptowährungen aus. Dementsprechend ist die **mangelnde Dezentralität nicht einmal ansatzweise ein K.-o.-Kriterium für den Binance Coin und die Binance Smart Chain.** Beide haben ihre Daseinsberechtigung und erfahren zurecht Zuspruch. Aufgrund ihrer Energieeffizienz und des geringen Kostenfaktors werden sie auch noch in den nächsten Jahren im Mittelpunkt des Krypto-Markts stehen.

Die **Größe und die finanzielle Stabilität der Krypto-Börse Binance fördern die Entwicklung des Binance Coins immens.** Treten Defizite zutage, so bestehen die finanziellen Mittel, um Innovationen vorzunehmen und diese sofort massenwirksam zu vermarkten, um die Zielgruppe für den Binance Coin oder die eigene Blockchain zu begeistern.

Das einzige Problem besteht zurzeit in dem **hohen Kurswert des Binance Coins.** Nach zwei spektakulären Kursgewinnen, die mit jeweils neuen Allzeithochs einhergingen, ist der Wert eines Coins im Vergleich zum Jahr 2020 zurzeit (Stand: Mai 2020) bemerkenswert hoch. Es könnte **jederzeit zu einer Kurskorrektur** kommen, durch die der Preis pro Coin deutlich fällt. Genau diese Korrektur sollten Sie als Anleger abwarten, ehe Sie Ihr Geld möglichst langfristig in den Binance Coin anlegen. Wahrscheinlich wird es weiterhin starke Schwankungen geben, aber bei einer Investition nach der Korrektur haben Sie den Vorteil, dass sich die Verluste aus der Kurskorrektur nicht auf ihr Portfolio auswirken.

> ➢ **Bewertung: 7 von 10**
> ➢ **Anlageempfehlung: zwischen 15 und 50 % des vorgesehenen Anlage-Budgets; erst nach Kurskorrektur anlegen**
> ➢ **Investition zurückziehen bei: finanzieller Schieflage der Krypto-Börse Binance**

7

Ökosystem: TRON; Kryptowährung: TRONIX (TRX)

*T*RON [80] ist ein auf einer Blockchain basierendes System, das ursprünglich als eine **Plattform zum Teilen multimedialer Inhalte** gedacht war. Die zugehörige Kryptowährung heißt TRONIX und hat das Kürzel *TRX*. Künstler und Medienschaffende sollen im TRON-Netzwerk ihre Dokumente, Filme, Musikdateien und sonstige Werke veröffentlichen können – ein heutzutage sehr wichtiges Geschäftsfeld, wie die hohen Nutzerzahlen bei Streaming-Diensten zeigen. Allerdings hat TRON im Laufe der Zeit aufgestockt und sich mit dem MaidSafeCoin vergleichbare Ziele gesetzt: die Dezentralisierung des Internets.

Allgemeines

Laut einer Statistik von *Statista* **nutzten in Deutschland im Jahr 2020 knapp 14 % der Bevölkerung täglich Videostreaming-Dienste** wie *Netflix* und *Amazon Prime Video*. Insgesamt 23 % der Bevölkerung machten einmal oder mehrmals pro Woche Gebrauch von verschiedenen Videostreaming-Diensten. [81] Abgesehen hiervon gibt es noch einen bedeutenden Anteil an Nutzern von Musikstreaming-Diensten in der Bevölkerung. Es streamt also definitiv mehr als ein Fünftel der deutschen Bevölkerung. Ursprünglich war das Ziel bei TRON, ein weltweites Entertainmentsystem zu schaffen. [Kerscher; S. 217] Durch die Veröffentlichung ihrer Inhalte im **TRON-Netzwerk** sollten **Künstler und Medienschaffende nicht nur ihre Inhalte publizieren, sondern auch mit den Nutzern besser kommunizieren können.** An dieser Stelle lohnt sich ein schneller Vergleich mit den bisher bekannten Streaming-Diensten:

- Bei den bisherigen Streaming-Diensten können Personen ihre Werke veröffentlichen, jedoch nicht direkt mit den Nutzern kommunizieren. Dies ist im TRON-Netzwerk komplett anders.

- Die Künstler und Streaming-Dienste haben Abmachungen, im Rahmen derer die Streaming-Dienste am Gewinn teilhaben. Schlimmstenfalls sind die Erträge der Künstler wesentlich geringer als die der Streaming-Dienste. Im TRON-Netzwerk gibt es diese Problematik nicht, weil das TRON-Netzwerk von den Künstlern für das Teilen von Inhalten kein Geld verlangt.

- Stellen Künstler ihre Inhalte den Nutzern gegen ein Entgelt zur Verfügung, so fallen **keine Transaktionsgebühren** an, was es den Künstlern möglich macht, die **Preise für die Nutzer geringer als bei den Streaming-Diensten** anzusetzen und dennoch denselben oder sogar einen größeren Profit einzufahren. Bei der Nutzung von Streaming-Diensten sorgen die hohen Gebühren der Streaming-Dienste eventuell dafür, dass die Preise für Medien höher angesetzt werden, was wiederum die Preise für die Nutzer erhöht.

Hinweis!

YouTube und vergleichbare Video-Plattformen wie *Vimeo* sind keine klassischen Streaming-Dienste, sondern Soziale Medien, weil Inhalte hier kostenlos ausgetauscht werden und eine Kommunikation zwischen Künstlern und Nutzern möglich ist.

Wie sich zeigt, widmen sich die Entwickler von TRON einem wesentlichen Problempunkt der heutigen Zeit, denn Streaming-Dienste wie *Netflix* und *Spotify* kassieren hohe Provisionen von den Künstlern, wenn Nutzer Inhalte der Künstler aufrufen und hören, lesen oder schauen. Der Ansatz der Entwickler hat somit das Potenzial, die Preise für die Verbraucher sogar zu senken. Auf jeden Fall würden die Produzenten weniger Provisionen an die Zwischenhändler (das sind die Streaming-Dienste; Anm.) zahlen. [82]

Mittlerweile soll TRON **weit mehr als das angestrebte Content-Entertainment-System** werden. Es ist die Rede von der Dezentralisierung des Internets. Hierbei werden dieselben Probleme aufgegriffen, die bereits im Unterkapitel 5.1 für den MaidSafeCoin erläutert wurden. In Form des TRON-Netzwerks wird eine blockchainbasierte Lösung für die Probleme geboten. Dabei ist eine sechsphasige Roadmap festgelegt, die zuletzt sogar die Dezentralisierung der Gaming-Industrie anstrebt. [83] Aufgrund der fehlenden Spezialisierung und gezielten Ausrichtung auf die Dezentralisierung des Internets ist TRON vorerst nicht als direkter Konkurrent von MaidSafeCoin anzusehen und MaidSafeCoin behält sein in Kapitel 5 erklärtes Alleinstellungsmerkmal.

Geschichte und Intention hinter TRON

Gegründet wurde TRON im September 2017 von Justin Sun. Hierzulande unbekannt, ist Justin Sun in China hingegen bereits als ein **junger Visionär** bekannt. So war er beispielsweise in Fernsehsendungen zu sehen, war zudem der erste Student an der Eliteuniversität des *Alibaba*-Gründers Jack Ma (Alibaba ist ungefähr das chinesische Pendant zu Amazon und hat eine Marktkapitalisierung von über 500 Milliarden Euro; Anm.) und bezahlte laut *Bloomberg* 4,57 Millionen US-Dollar für ein gemeinsames Essen mit dem berühmten US-Investor und -Börsenguru Warren Buffett.

Was lehren diese Infos? **Justin Sun** ist bekannt, durch seinen Studienabschluss wohl sehr kompetent und offensichtlich wohlhabend, wenn er derart teure „Mahlzeiten" bezahlen kann. Sowohl die Bekanntheit und das Vermögen als auch insbesondere die Kompetenz sind **vorteilhafte Eigenschaften, um ein ambitioniertes Projekt wie TRON voranzutreiben.**

Die ursprüngliche Intention Suns und seiner Entwickler, ein **Content-Entertainment-System** zu schaffen, stellte eine **vielversprechende Nische** dar. Nun ist die erweiterte Intention, das Internet zu dezentralisieren und damit den Nutzern die Kontrolle über ihre Privatsphäre wiederzugeben, ambitionierter. Trotz der hohen Ambitionen erscheint dieser Schritt der Entwickler plausibel, denn **TRON verfügt über alle Mittel, um die Dezentralisierung des Internets erfolgreich umzusetzen:**

- Solide Finanzen und reichlich Kapital zur Expansion;
- Kompetenz an der Spitze durch Justin Sun und das gesamte Team;
- Vertrauensfaktor und großes Marketing-Potenzial durch Justin Sun als Gesicht hinter TRON;
- sowie bereits mehrere Partner, um die Expansion erfolgreich umzusetzen.

Um näher auf einige dieser Punkte einzugehen, sei u. a. zur Kompetenz des Teams erwähnt: Sun arbeitet zurzeit an der globalen Expansion von TRON. In Singapur gegründet, hat TRON mittlerweile einen doppelten Hauptsitz in Singapur und San Francisco und richtet weitere Auslandsbüros ein. Dabei werden Entwickler, Buchhalter und andere qualifizierte Personen in der ganzen Welt gesucht. Die Konditionen und Aussichten für die Mitarbeiter sind für ein derart junges Projekt äußerst lukrativ; es wird mit internationalen Geschäftsreisen und neuesten Technologien gelockt. [84]

Wirklich interessant ist auch ein Blick auf die **Kernpartner**, die TRON mittlerweile für sich gewinnen konnte: alles bekannte Namen. *Samsung* und *Opera* als weltweit bekannte Unternehmen sind dabei. *BitTorrent* ist zumindest branchenintern sehr bekannt. Regelmäßig gibt es Gerüchte, dass sogar Alibaba Partner werden könnte. [85] Eine Partnerschaft mit dem milliardenschweren börsennotierten Konzern Alibaba wäre ein Trumpf für TRON, der die Bekanntheit noch stärker erhöhen würde. Bei der Akquise von Partnern wird offenkundig eine ausgezeichnete Arbeit verrichtet.

Technische Merkmale

Ursprünglich basierte die TRON-Blockchain auf Ethereum, doch **am 25. Juni 2018 wurde eine eigene Blockchain geschaffen.** Im Rahmen dieser Blockchain kommt der **delegierte PoS als Konsensmechanismus** zum Einsatz. Der PoS dient dabei nicht der Erzeugung neuer Währungseinheiten, sondern dem Vollzug von Transaktionen. Alle vorhandenen Währungseinheiten sind nämlich bereits herausgegeben, 100 Milliarden sind es an der Zahl. [Kerscher; S. 176]

Hinweis!

Weil alle Währungseinheiten von TRONIX herausgegeben sind, ist der erstmalige Erwerb von Coins niemals anonym. Die Coins müssen beim ersten Mal an einer Börse gekauft werden, was mit einem Identitätsnachweis und der Nutzung eines Bankkontos einhergeht. Einmal erworben, können jedoch alle Transaktionen mit TRONIX innerhalb des Netzwerks anonym getätigt werden.

Die Währungseinheiten wurden zum einen an Privatanleger herausgegeben, zum anderen an die *TRON Foundation* unter der Leitung von Gründer und CEO Justin Sun. Außerdem fand ein *Initial Coin Offering* statt. Der Konsensmechanismus delegiertes PoS dient dazu, die Transaktionen abzuwickeln. Im Rahmen des Mechanismus gibt es bei TRON die ...

1. **Besitzer, die freiwillig ihre Coins einfrieren**, um dafür **Stimmrechte** zu erhalten, mit denen sie darüber abstimmen dürfen, welche Nutzer Super-Repräsentanten werden.
2. besagten **Super-Repräsentanten, die per Abstimmung das Recht erhalten, Blöcke zu erstellen und dadurch Transaktionen zu validieren**. Als Belohnung für diese Arbeit erhalten sie Coins. [82]

Die Struktur des Netzwerks soll dazu beitragen, dass im TRON-Netzwerk **bis zu 2.000 (!) Transaktionen pro Sekunde** abgewickelt werden können – zum Vergleich: Bitcoin kommt auf 3-6 Transaktionen pro Sekunde und Ethereum auf 25. [86] Die enorme Geschwindigkeit des Netzwerks ist wichtig, um bei zunehmendem Wachstum einen flotten und für die Nutzer zufriedenstellenden Ablauf der Transaktionen sicherzustellen.

Es verwundert kaum, dass mehrere technische Merkmale von Ethereum übernommen wurden, so vor allem die Smart Contracts (für Erläuterung der Smart Contracts: siehe 4.1.1). Diese machen Kreditkartenzahlungen und Vertragsmanagement möglich. Während die **Smart Contracts** im Netzwerk von Ethereum Transaktionsgebühren nach sich ziehen, sind sie **im Netzwerk von TRON kostenfrei**, was auf den Konsensmechanismus bei TRON zurückzuführen ist.

Ein weiteres nennenswertes Feature im TRON-Netzwerk sind die **dApps**. Hierbei handelt es sich um **dezentralisierte Anwendungen, die User selbst erstellen können** und die ebenfalls aus dem Ethereum-Netzwerk bekannt sind. Nach Erstellung können Künstler über diese Apps beispielsweise zu selbst festgelegten Konditionen ihre Inhalte anbieten. Alternativ besteht die Möglichkeit, bereits vorhandene Apps zur Distribution der eigenen Inhalte gebührenfrei zu verwenden.

Historie: Kursverläufe der letzten Jahre

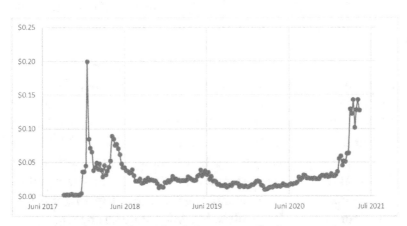

Quelle: https://www.btc-echo.de/kurs/tron/ [87]

Da bereits aus den letzten Kapiteln Hintergrundwissen zu den Kurshistorien der Kryptowährungen vorhanden ist, ist der Großteil der Kurshistorie der Währung TRX selbsterklärend. Die Kryptowährung wurde gewissermaßen **mitten in den Hype hineingeboren und profitierte aufgrund ihres geringen Preises von zeitweise unter einem Cent besonders stark davon:** Da ein Coin günstiger war als bei den anderen gehypten Kryptowährungen, kauften die Anleger viel TRX ein. Es folgten der Bärenmarkt mit starkem Kursverlust, ein minimaler Aufschwung durch die Markstimmung, dann eine ruhige Folgephase und schließlich der Kursgewinn Anfang 2021. Konkret handelt es sich dabei um folgende Zeiträume:

- September 2017 bis 05.01.2018 (Veröffentlichung und Hype)
- 05.01.2018 bis 02.04.2018 (Bärenmarkt)
- 02.04.2018 bis 30.04.2018 (Aufschwung durch Markstimmung)
- 30.04.2018 bis 29.01.2021 (Abschwung mit ruhiger Folgephase)
- 29.01.2021 bis 07.05.2021 (Aufstieg durch steigende Bekanntheit und Innovationen)

Das **Allzeithoch der Kryptowährung rührt vom 05. Januar 2018** und beträgt knapp **0,23 US-Dollar pro Coin.** Den nach dem Hype aus 2017/2018 niedrigsten Kurswert erreichte TRX am 14. März 2020 mit 0,0098 US-Dollar. Nach einem satten Anstieg im Jahr 2021 liegt der Wert eines TRX zurzeit (Stand: Mai 2021) bei ca. 0,16 US-Dollar, was ungefähr 13 Euro-Cent entspricht. Mit diesem aktuellen Kurswert nimmt TRX aufgrund seiner hohen Gesamtanzahl an Coins einen **Rang unter den Top 15 der Kryptowährungen mit der größten Marktkapitalisierung** ein.

Nichtsdestotrotz ist die Entwicklung des TRX-Kurses ein eindrucksvoll trauriges Beispiel dafür, wie wenig sich einige Anleger über Entwicklungen einzelner – vor allem weniger bekannter – Kryptowährungen informieren. Die Anlageentscheidungen sind teilweise irrational und folgen sehr stark der allgemeinen Marktstimmung. Schon allein die Tatsache, dass die Ankündigung der Partnerschaft mit Samsung Anfang 2020 den Kursverlauf kaum positiv beeinflusste, stattdessen kurz danach ein geringer Kursverlust zu beobachten war, wirft Fragen über die Aktivitäten der Anleger auf. Situationen wie Anfang 2020 sind wiederum für informierte und rationale Anleger umso mehr eine Chance, um zurzeit und auch in zukünftigen Phasen eines nicht nachvollziehbar geringen Kurswertes Einheiten der Währung nachzukaufen.

Besonderheiten und Kritikansätze bei TRON

Eine Besonderheit im Netzwerk von TRON ist die **hohe Toleranz gegenüber anderen Währungen.** Es gibt eine Tauschbörse, in der verschiedene Kryptowährungen umgetauscht werden können. Darüber hinaus ist TRON wie der Binance Coin ein **Konkurrent für Ethereum,** wobei Smart Contracts, die dezentralisierten Apps und eine höhere Geschwindigkeit des Netzwerks zentrale Vorteile gegenüber Ethereum sind. Das aggressive Marketing bringt TRON **namhafte Partnerschaften** ein und fördert das Wachstum des Netzwerks. Besser könnten die Aussichten für eine gute Zukunft kaum sein, oder?

Vorteile

Partnerschaften mit Marken wie Samsung und der Kauf von Bit-Torrent gelingen nicht einfach so aus dem Stegreif. Es braucht die richtigen Personen, das richtige Projekt und das richtige Marketing – all dies scheint TRON zu haben. Wie bei den Kryptowährungen MaidSafeCoin und IOTA kann man nur loben, dass ein Problemfeld der Zukunft erkannt wurde und entsprechende Lösungen geboten werden. So stellt die Schaffung eines für Künstler und

Nutzer vorteilhaften Ökosystems **Lösungen für die Probleme und Beseitigung der Barrieren diverser Streaming-Dienste** dar. Aber TRON hat sich weiterentwickelt und nimmt anhand seiner Roadmap weitreichendere Ziele ins Visier, wie u. a. Aktivitäten in der Gaming-Industrie. Weil TRON mittlerweile nicht mehr auf ein Ziel, nämlich das dezentrale Entertainment-System, beschränkt ist, kommt es für mehr Anwendungsbereiche in Frage und kann zu einer Lösung für mehrere Probleme der Gegenwart sowie Zukunft werden. Eine **ausgezeichnete Öffentlichkeitsarbeit von Justin Sun, gewissermaßen dem „Steve Jobs" von TRON**, stellt die Weichen für die Verbreitung von TRON. Die namhaften Partnerschaften sind ein Zeichen dessen, welche Zusammenarbeiten künftig noch zu erwarten sind. Die Prognose einer glorreichen Zukunft von TRON ist auf Basis des gelungenen Marketings und Vertriebs nicht unberechtigt.

Wussten Sie schon?

Justin Sun hat mit *Peiwo* eine Anwendung entwickelt, die mittlerweile über zehn Millionen Nutzer miteinander verbindet. Hier können Personen gemeinsam Online-Spiele spielen und Livestreams gucken. Aufgrund der enthaltenen Entertainment-Inhalte könnte Sun zur Ausweitung des TRON-Netzwerks einfach Peiwo und TRON miteinander verbinden. [85] Sun kann also zum Teil in Eigenregie das TRON-Netzwerk vergrößern. Von diesem klugen Kopf ist in der Zukunft viel zu erwarten, TRON könnte dabei der Ausgangspunkt sein.

Mit bis zu 2.000 Transaktionen pro Sekunde ist das **TRON-Netzwerk pfeilschnell.** Geschwindigkeit ist, wie bereits am Binance Coin deutlich wurde, ein entscheidendes Argument für Nutzer, um eine Kryptowährung zu verwenden. Auch **in Puncto Smart Contracts und dezentralisierte Apps hat TRON Gemeinsamkeiten mit dem Binance Coin**: Beides ist im TRON-Netzwerk möglich.

Der größere Vorzug im Vergleich zum Binance Coin besteht in dem **stärkeren Ausmaß der Dezentralisierung.** Wie der Binance Coin ist TRON nicht vollends dezentralisiert. Während beim Binance Coin die Krypto-Börse Binance jedoch die volle Kontrolle über die Abwicklung von Zahlungen hat, sind bei TRON immerhin die Nutzer aufgrund des delegierten PoS als Konsensmechanismus an der Macht. Aktionen wie das Einfrieren von Transaktionen sind bei TRON durch keine zentrale Stelle wie im Binance-Ökosystem umsetzbar, sondern eine Frage der Nutzer, die gemeinsam einen Konsens zu treffen haben.

Ein Mindestmaß an Dezentralität, die Entwicklung von dApps, ein Gaming- und Entertainmentsystem, das qualifizierte Personal mit Justin Sun als ehrgeizigem, millionenschwerem und kompetentem Studienabsolventen: Von dem erforderlichen Kapital über ein herausragendes Projekt bis hin zu den richtigen Mitarbeitern bündelt das Projekt TRON alles, was ein erfolgreiches Unternehmen braucht.

Nachteile

Wo soeben geschrieben wurde, dass das Projekt TRON alles Notwendige für ein erfolgreiches Unternehmen in sich bündelt: Gerade **die Größe des Projekts kann ein Nachteil sein.** Denn in nahezu jedem Bereich hat TRON Konkurrenz. Die Dezentralisierung des Internets ist das große Ziel der Entwickler des MaidSafeCoins. Smart Contracts und dezentralisierte Apps sind durch Ethereum bekannt geworden, aktuell ist Binance Coin als größter Konkurrent des Ethereum-Netzwerks in aller Munde. Schnelle und günstige Transaktionen sind mittlerweile bei diversen alternativen Kryptowährungen anzutreffen. Dieses Ausmaß an Konkurrenz lässt eines naheliegen: TRON hat dann **die besten Chancen, groß und bekannt zu werden, wenn das Gesamtkonzept gelingt.**

Auch ohne eine derart erfolgreiche Umsetzung seiner Roadmap wird TRON natürlich Zukunftsaussichten haben, doch die Konkurrenz wird die Wachstumsmöglichkeiten stets einschränken. Zudem ist der langfristige Zeithorizont der Roadmap bis in die 2030er Jahre hinein ein Nachteil, denn die Konkurrenz schläft währenddessen nicht und könnte an TRON vorbeiziehen.

Durch das delegierte PoS ist die **Dezentralität bei TRON eingeschränkt.** Diesen Nachteil werden einige Anleger und Nutzer kritisch sehen, aber für die breite Masse der Anwender wird er wohl eine untergeordnete Rolle spielen. Auch der Nachteil, dass **TRON in Teilen oder komplett ein Plagiat sein könnte** [85], dürfte als Nachteil kaum zum Tragen kommen. Eine ähnliche Debatte und einen daraus resultierenden Rechtsstreit gab es das Soziale Netzwerk Facebook betreffend: Es hieß, dass Gründer und CEO Mark Zuckerberg den Winklevoss-Brüdern die Idee gestohlen hätte. Es kam zu einer Entschädigungszahlung und der Rechtsstreit wurde beigelegt, ohne dass Facebook oder Mark Zuckerberg weitreichend geschädigt wurden. Falls TRON kein komplettes Plagiat ist, dann werden wohl auch Sun und TRON an der Debatte nicht zugrunde gehen.

Fazit

TRON ist ein faszinierendes Projekt, das in seiner Gesamtheit in der Welt der Kryptowährungen und deren Ökosystemen einmalig ist. In seine Bestandteile zerlegt, hat TRON allerdings Ähnlichkeiten zu anderen Ökosystemen, z. B. in Bezug auf Smart Contracts zu Ethereum und Binance Coin. Aufgrund der ausgeprägten Konkurrenz und der zusätzlich äußerst langfristigen Roadmap gehört TRON zu den risikoreicheren Investments unter den Kryptowährungen.

Trotzdem: Der **Fokus auf ein Content-Entertainmentsystem ist innovativ,** Justin Sun ist ehrgeizig und die **bisherigen Partner-**

schaften sind überzeugend, sodass sich die Aufnahme von TRON ins Portfolio lohnt. Potenzielle Genies wie Justin Sun hatten es in der Geschichte der letzten über 100 Jahre nie leicht: Es beginnt mit Nicola Tesla, der allein und verarmt in einem Hotelzimmer starb, und reicht bis Steve Jobs, dessen Karriere nach der Exmatrikulation von der Universität in einer Garage und mit sehr viel Ablehnung begann – Genies haben manchmal große, wenig verständliche Visionen und kämpfen gegen starke Widerstände. So ist es wohl aktuell auch bei Sun, der mit TRON ein riesiges und sogar für die Ökosysteme von Kryptowährungen untypisches Projekt aufbaut. Bis hierhin sieht alles sehr überzeugend aus, den Rest werden Sie als Anleger in den folgenden Jahren und Jahrzehnten beobachten können.

- ➤ **Bewertung: 5 von 10**
- ➤ **Anlageempfehlung: zwischen 5 und 15 % des vorgesehenen Anlage-Budgets**
- ➤ **Investition zurückziehen bei: Misserfolg in den entscheidenden Sparten (Content-Entertainment und später Gaming) sowie Verlust der Partnerschaften in Kombination mit anhaltenden Kursverlusten**

8

Bezahlsystem: Stellar; Kryptowährung: Lumens (XLM)

S o unscheinbar *Stellar* [88] erscheint, mindestens genauso besonders ist das Bezahlsystem mit seiner zugehörigen Kryptowährung *Lumens* (kurz: *XLM*). Das bescheidene Ziel von Stellar ist es, den **weltweiten Transfer von Geldern** zu ermöglichen. Dabei kommt ein **komplett eigenes Konsensprotokoll mit ausgeprägter Dezentralität und hoher Sicherheit zum Einsatz.** Zudem haben die Entwickler von Stellar auch eine soziale Komponente bedacht. Über ein Bezahlsystem mit einer Währung, das in seiner Unscheinbarkeit so viel Besonderes verbirgt ...

Allgemeines

Bei vielen der Kryptowährungen geht es um Alleinstellungsmerkmale. Bitcoin als Vorreiter der Branche braucht keine bzw. hat das Alleinstellungsmerkmal, den dezentralen Zahlungsverkehr überhaupt weltweit bekannt und einfach zugänglich gemacht zu haben. Ethereum erlangte Bekanntheit durch die Smart Contracts und andere dezentralisierte Anwendungen. Dann gibt es noch Kryptowährungen wie Dash mit Schwerpunkt auf der Anonymität der Transaktionen. Andere Kryptowährungen sind besonders innovativ, weil sie Teil ambitionierter Ökosysteme sind, wie es z. B. bei NEM und IOTA der Fall ist.

Stellar bewegt sich außerhalb dieses Rasters, weil es „nur" darum geht, den weltweiten Transfer von Geldern zu ermöglichen und die **zugehörige Kryptowährung Lumens lediglich eine „Umrechnungswährung"** ist; was bedeutet: Wenn jemand bei Stellar US-Dollar in Euro umtauscht, dann werden die Gebühren in Lumen (0,0001 Lumen sind die Gebühren für Transaktionen; Anm.) gezahlt, der Wert der Ausgangswährung wird in Lumen umgerechnet und von Lumen in die andere Währung umgerechnet. Dies ist für die Nutzer vorteilhaft, weil **Stellar einige Probleme beim internationalen Zahlungsverkehr löst und sogar soziale Nachteile beheben kann**. Wie dies gelingt, verrät ein Blick auf die Geschichte und die Intention hinter dem System Stellar ...

Geschichte und Intention hinter Stellar

Als *Unbanked* werden Personen bezeichnet, die keine eigenen Bankkonten haben. Die Gründe dafür, kein Bankkonto zu haben, können vielschichtig sein und von dem fehlenden Zugang zur Infrastruktur über ein unzureichendes Mindestguthaben für die Eröffnung eines Bankkontos bis hin zum Misstrauen gegenüber dem Bankensystem reichen. Die **Entwickler von Stellar haben diese Personengruppe berücksichtigt** und wollen mit ihrem Bezahlsystem nicht nur eine Zahlungsplattform für Unternehmen und Zahlungsdienstleister schaffen, sondern **auch einzelne Menschen weltweit verbinden**. [89] Zwar ist auch die Nutzung von Stellar an einige Bedingungen geknüpft, wie u. a. das Vorhandensein eines digitalen Endgeräts, doch ein Mindestguthaben und ein für Staaten sowie andere Instanzen nachverfolgbares eigenes Konto sind nicht erforderlich.

Mit dem Schwerpunkt auf der Abwicklung internationaler Zahlungen und dem Umtausch von Währungen ist Stellar eine **Hybridlösung,** die sich einerseits aus einem von den Kryptowährungen bekannten **Peer-to-Peer-Netzwerk** und andererseits einer **Dienstleistung für den elektronischen Zahlungsverkehr** zusammensetzt. [89] Im Gegensatz zu elektronischen Zahlungsdienstleistern wie PayPal ist die Anonymität und Sicherheit der große Vorteil.

Für die Anonymität und Sicherheit verantwortlich ist ein eigens entwickelter Konsensmechanismus. 2014, zum Zeitpunkt der Veröffentlichung von Stellar, gab es diesen Konsensmechanismus noch nicht. Stattdessen basierte Stellar auf dem Protokoll vom Projekt *Ripple*, das ebenfalls eine Kryptowährung ist. Weil sich das Protokoll als ungeeignet erwies, erfolgte im April 2015 eine Abspaltung von Ripple. [Kerscher; S. 215] Zum nun genutzten Konsensmechanismus erfahren Sie mehr unter dem folgenden Punkt 8.1.2.

Aufgrund des **Konzepts mit der sozialen Komponente,** das aufgrund der **geringen Transaktionsgebühren** gut umsetzbar ist, nutzen mittlerweile immer mehr Unternehmen und gemeinnützige Organisationen das Bezahlsystem von Stellar. Insbesondere in den Entwicklungsländern ist die Nachfrage hoch: Seit Dezember 2016 gibt es u. a. **Partnerschaften auf den Philippinen, in Indien und in Westafrika.** Seit Oktober 2017 arbeiten Stellar und das renommierte US-amerikanische Unternehmen *IBM* zusammen. Ziel der gemeinsamen Arbeit ist die **Erhöhung der Geschwindigkeit des globalen Zahlungsverkehrs.** [Kerscher; S. 215]

Aktuell (Stand: Mai 2021) befindet sich die Kryptowährung Stellar Lumens unter den Top 15 der Kryptowährungen mit der höchsten Marktkapitalisierung. Ähnlich wie Dash sind die Partnerschaften in den Entwicklungsländern ein ertragreiches

Geschäft, bei dem in den Folgemonaten und -jahren von einem erfolgreichen Ausbau auszugehen ist. Ein perfektes Beispiel hierfür sind Meldungen um einen **möglichen Deal mit der ukrainischen Regierung**: Demnach kämen Stellar und Lumen für eine *Zentralbank der digitalen Währungen* (*CBDC* für *Central Bank Digital Currency*) infrage. Wie sich der Deal weiterentwickelt, steht aber noch in den Sternen. [90]

Technische Merkmale

Zwei Aspekte sind unter den technischen Merkmalen einen gesonderten Blick wert: auf der einen Seite der Konsensmechanismus, auf der anderen Seite die Verwaltung des eigenen Vermögens und die Abwicklung von Transaktionen.

Der Konsensmechanismus hört auf den Namen *Stellar Consensus Protocol* (kurz: *SCP*). Bei diesem Protokoll **stimmen ausgewählte Knotenpunkte darüber ab, ob eine Transaktion für korrekt befunden und getätigt wird oder nicht**. Ein mögliches Problem bei dieser Vorgehensweise ist, dass es unehrliche, verräterische oder manipulierende Knotenpunkte geben könnte. Um dem entgegenzuwirken, müssen mehrere Knotenpunkte den Transaktionen zustimmen. Dabei kann der Nutzer selbst auswählen, wie viele und welche der Knotenpunkte seiner Transaktion zustimmen müssen. Die Annahme hierbei ist, dass sich mit der Zeit eine Menge vertrauenswürdiger Knotenpunkte herauskristallisiert, die das System gegen Abweichungen sowie Fehler sicherer machen. [89] Gespeichert werden alle Vermögensstände und Transaktionen in einem **Hauptbuch**, dessen **Übereinstimmung auf allen Servern** das Ziel des Konsensmechanismus ist, um das System fehlerfrei am Laufen zu halten.

Wenn Personen Transaktionen abwickeln möchten, dann muss zunächst Geld eingezahlt werden. Dies ist übrigens die einzige Herausforderung für die Unbanked, denn irgendwie müssen die

Personen ohne Bankkonto das Geld bei Stellar einzahlen. Sobald dies gelungen ist, brauchen sie jedoch kein Bankkonto mehr. Sie haben nun **Lumen auf ihrem digitalen Konto**. Aus diesen Lumen können die Personen einen *US-Dollar-Token* **erstellen, der fest an den Wert des US-Dollars gebunden ist**, oder einen anderen Währungs-Token. Diese Art der Transaktion ist vor allem bei weltweitem Handeln ein enormer Vorteil, weil in jeder beliebigen Währung gehandelt werden kann. [91]

Beispiel

Eine Person aus den Philippinen arbeitet im Ausland und möchte Geld nach Hause zu ihrer Familie schicken. Die Landeswährung in den Philippinen ist weniger wertstabil als der US-Dollar, in der diese Person ihren Lohn erhält. Die US-Dollar werden bei Stellar in einen US-Dollar-Token verwandelt, nachdem sie zuvor in Lumen umgerechnet wurden. Das US-Dollar-Token ist wertstabil und wird zur Familie geschickt, die ebenfalls Stellar nutzt. Die Familie kann das US-Dollar-Token so lange halten, bis sie bereit ist, Teile davon oder das komplette Token in die Landeswährung umzuwandeln, sich die Summe in der heimischen Währung auf ein Bankkonto zu überweisen und dann zu nutzen. Oder aber die Familie wandelt das US-Dollar-Token in eine andere Währung um und nutzt diese direkt zur Zahlung, sofern der Zahlungspartner ebenfalls Stellar oder andere Kryptowährungen akzeptiert.

Letzten Endes ist die Vorgehensweise bei Transaktionen und der Erstellung von Währungstokens nur dann vollends zu verstehen, wenn es selbst ausprobiert oder ausführlich in Videos erklärt wurde. Diese Möglichkeit besteht hier im Ratgeber nicht. Bedenken Sie daher, dass es für Sie als Anleger nicht wichtig ist, die Funktionsweise komplett zu verstehen, sondern allein das Wissen über die Funktionen bei Stellar relevant ist, um die Anlageentscheidungen zu treffen.

Historie: Kursverläufe der letzten Jahre

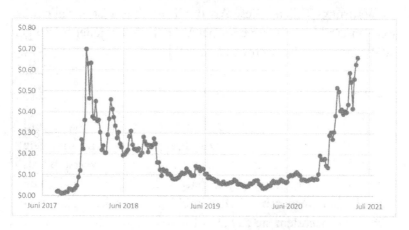

Quelle: https://www.btc-echo.de/kurs/stellar/ [92]

Nach dem Binance Coin ist Stellar das nächste eindrucksvoll ernüchternde Beispiel dafür, wie sehr die Anleger bei Kryptowährungen ihre Entscheidungen nach Lust und Laune zu treffen scheinen. Anders lässt sich nicht erklären, dass zum Zeitpunkt, als Stellar seine Partnerschaft mit IBM schloss und immer mehr internationale Zusammenarbeiten begann (Dezember 2018) der Kurs keinen gebührenden Gewinn verbuchte. Scheinbar ging die Information über die gute Arbeit im Stellar-Team an den meisten Anlegern vorbei, was letzten Endes den Kursverlauf gemäß der allgemeinen Marktstimmung erklärt. Auch ansonsten **richtet sich der Kursverlauf des Lumens nach dem allgemeinen Kursverlauf nahezu aller Kryptowährungen**:

- Hype Ende 2017/Anfang 2018 mit Allzeithoch von ca. 0,88 US-Dollar pro Coin am 03.01.2018.

- Bullenmarkt bis April 2018, zwischenzeitlich Aufschwung bis Ende April 2018 und darauf folgender Abschwung mit ruhiger Folgephase bis Ende 2020
- Aufwärtstrend von Ende 2020 bis Mai 2021 durch allgemeine Marktstimmung und steigende Bekanntheit; zwischenzeitlich höchster Wert am 13. April 2021 mit ca. 0,66 US-Dollar pro Coin

Besonderheiten und Kritikansätze bei Stellar

Viele der Vorteile von Dash (siehe Kapitel 3) gelten auch für das System Stellar mit der Kryptowährung Lumen. Durch die Akzeptanz in zahlreichen Entwicklungsländern und die häufige Nutzung hat sich Stellar bereits ein **außerordentlich solides Fundament für eine generelle Akzeptanz als Zahlungsmittel** erarbeitet.

Die Arbeit bei Stellar muss deswegen noch stärker gelobt werden als die bei Dash, weil Stellar **mehr internationale Partnerschaften als Dash** hat und die Grundidee der **Dezentralität akkurat umsetzt.** Hierzu trägt der eigene Konsensmechanismus bei, der – wenn überhaupt – den einzigen Nachteil von Stellar birgt: Zwar ist die Abwicklung der Transaktionen dezentral, doch wenn der Großteil der Knotenpunkte das System manipulieren möchte, dann ist die Durchführung der Transaktionen gefährdet. Wie unwahrscheinlich dieses Szenario jedoch ist, spiegelt sich darin wider, dass für eine erfolgreiche Manipulation der Transaktionen die durch Zufall bestimmten und sich nicht kennenden Knotenpunkte zum Großteil destruktive Absichten haben müssten. Dies ist unwahrscheinlich.

Alles in allem verbleibt ein vom Konsensmechanismus her **sicheres, energiesparsames und vertrauenswürdiges System**, das zahlreiche Partnerschaften hat, diese ausbaut und – das wäre ein Coup (!) – sogar Teil der Digitalisierungsstrategie einer europäischen Regierung werden könnte. Die Vorzeichen für Stellar stehen ausgezeichnet, weil die Partnerschaften zahlreich sind und Lumen mit einer Platzierung unter den Top 15 der Kryptowährungen mit der höchsten Marktkapitalisierung aktuell im Blickfeld der Anleger ist.

Wussten Sie schon?

Die *Corporate Social Responsibility* (kurz: *CSR*) ist bei Investitionen in Unternehmen ein relevantes Kriterium. Unternehmen sind verpflichtet, im Rahmen ihrer Jahresabschlussberichte Informationen dazu zu geben, wie sie ihrer sozialen Verantwortung (Stichworte: Arbeitsbedingungen, Umwelt) gerecht werden. Auch bei Kryptowährungen könnte dies früher oder später eine große Rolle spielen. Kommt es dazu, so ist davon auszugehen, dass Stellar von den Anlegern sozusagen als „DIE Fairtrade-Währung" unter den Kryptowährungen angesehen werden wird.

Fazit

Wie schon erwähnt, kann Stellar auf den ersten Blick unscheinbar wirken, weil es sich die Abwicklung von Zahlungen zum Ziel setzt. Da mag so manch eine Person, die nur einen kurzen Blick auf die Website von Stellar wirft, denken: „Schön, dafür kann man aber alle Kryptowährungen nutzen!" Doch wie **sozial und kreativ** (Stichwort: Erstellung von Tokens verschiedenster Währungen) Stellar diesem Zweck dient, ist **in der Landschaft der Kryptowährungen unvergleichlich**.

Noch dazu sind die vielen Partnerschaften und die rege Nutzung des Bezahldienstes in mehreren Entwicklungsländern ein Beleg dafür, dass das **Konzept von Stellar weltweit auf Zuspruch stößt**.

Die Überzeugung der ukrainischen Regierung ist in Form eines Vorvertrages sogar schriftlich niedergelegt. Stellar ließ sich in diesem Kapitel in Kürze erklären, aber um das System wirklich zu verstehen, ist dessen Nutzung am besten. So oder so dürfte am Ende eine Entscheidung für eine Geldanlage in diese Kryptowährung leichtfallen.

- ➤ **Bewertung: 9 von 10**
- ➤ **Anlageempfehlung: zwischen 40 und 60 % des vorgesehenen Anlage-Budgets**
- ➤ **Investition zurückziehen bei: Bekanntwerden unentdeckter Sicherheitslücken im hauseigenen Konsensmechanismus und zunehmendem Verlust der Partnerschaften**

Nachwort

Sie wissen nun, dass sich hinter den meisten Kryptowährungen mehr als ein bloßes Zahlungsmittel verbirgt. Den meisten Projekten liegt eine Idee zugrunde, die Probleme auf smarte und im digitalen Zeitalter gefragte Art und Weise zu lösen vermag. Ob für die Industrie, die Revolution des Internets, das Entertainment oder andere Bereiche: Kryptowährungen sind in ihrer Gesamtheit wahre Alleskönner!

Welches der beeindruckenden Projekte sich letzten Endes durchsetzt, steht in den Sternen. Der Beginn des Jahres 2021 hat eine faszinierende neue Etappe auf dem Weg der Kryptowährungen zur Bekanntheit und Anerkennung in breiten Schichten der Bevölkerung eingeläutet: Die Akzeptanz einiger Währungen in Staaten und Unternehmen nimmt teilweise rasant zu. Zugleich werden die Technologien immer ausgefeilter und massentauglicher. Kryptowährungen haben das Potenzial, einen noch nicht definierbaren, aber wesentlichen Teil der menschlichen Zukunft zu prägen. Investitionen zum jetzigen Zeitpunkt können Anlegern durch die langfristige Wertsteigerung ein Vermögen bescheren.

Doch Vermögenssteigerungen setzen Erfolg bei der Geldanlage voraus. Erfolg tritt nur in den seltensten Fällen durch Zufall ein. Um sich nicht auf den Zufall zu verlassen und kein hohes Risiko bei der Geldanlage einzugehen, ist Wissen über das Business notwendig. In diesem Sinne schließt dieser Ratgeber mit einem Zitat von Warren Buffett, mit dem er im ersten Kapitel seinen Anfang nahm: *„Investiere niemals in ein Business, das du nicht verstehst.“*

Lesen Sie und informieren Sie sich bitte über weitere und nicht nur diese 7 Kryptowährungen. Die hier vorgestellten Kryptowährungen sind außergewöhnlich, doch vielleicht gibt es irgendwo eine noch beeindruckendere und facettenreichere Währung, in die Sie investieren möchten? Tun Sie bitte eines aber nie: nach Lust und Laune investieren, wie es der Großteil der Anleger zu handhaben scheint. Anders als anhand der Launen der Anleger lassen sich die einander stark ähnelnden Kursverläufe der Kryptowährungen nicht erklären. Ein Anreiz für ein Experiment: Nehmen Sie die Kursverläufe der letzten 6 Jahre der wertvollsten 50 Kryptowährungen und legen Sie diese übereinander. Die Verläufe werden einander stark ähneln. Hierin zeigt sich, wie sehr die Marktstimmung die Krypto-Börsen prägt.

Irgendwann mit dem Fortschritt der Kryptowährungen werden jedoch Profi-Anleger die Bühne betreten, die jedes Unternehmen und jede Währung zwei bis drei volle Arbeitstage lang analysieren und darauf basierend rationale Entscheidungen treffen. Spätestens dann werden die Wertentwicklungen der Kryptowährungen nachvollziehbarer und zuverlässiger sein. Seien Sie zusammen mit den anderen Lesern dieses Ratgebers eine der ersten Personen, die den wahren Wert von Kryptowährungen analysiert, wie es in diesem Buch erläutert wurde. Dann werden Sie mit hoher Wahrscheinlichkeit langfristig sehr erfolgreiche Geldanlagen in Kryptowährungen tätigen.

Quellenverzeichnis

Literatur-Quellen:

Berentsen, A.; Schär, F.: *Bitcoin, Blockchain und Kryptoassets – Eine umfassende Einführung.* Norderstedt: BoD – Books on Demand, 2017.

Hileman, Dr. G.; Rauchs, M.: *GLOBAL CRYPTOCURRENCY BENCHMARKING STUDY.* Cambridge: Cambridge Centre for Alternative Finance, 2017.

Hosp, Dr. J.: *Kryptowährungen – Bitcoin, Ethereum, Blockchain, ICOs & Co. einfach erklärt.* München: FinanzBuch Verlag, 2018. 1. Auflage.

Kerscher, D.: *Handbuch der digitalen Währungen – Bitcoin, Litecoin und 150 weitere Kryptowährungen im Überblick.* Dingolfing: Kemacon UG, 2018. 2., aktualisierte und überarbeitete Auflage.

Koenig, A.: *Crypto Coins – Investieren in digitale Währungen.* München: FinanzBuch Verlag, 2018. 3. Auflage.

Miller, M.: *Krypto-X: Diese 3 Kryptowährungen explodieren in 2021.* Bonn: FID Verlag GmbH, 2021.

Schreder, T.: *Das neue Geld – Bitcoin, Kryptowährungen und Blockchain verständlich erklärt.* München: Piper Verlag GmbH, 2018.

Online-Quellen:

[1] Boerse.de, *Was gegen den Bitcoin spricht.* https://www.boerse. de/bitcoin/contra-bitcoin.

[2] chrissikraus; Schmitz, P.: Blockchain Insider, *Was ist eine Kryptowährung?* https://www.blockchain-insider.de/was-ist-eine-kryptowaehrung-a-860837/.

[3] Bendel, Prof. Dr. O.: Gabler Wirtschaftslexikon, *Kryptowährung.* https://wirtschaftslexikon.gabler.de/definition/kryptowaehrung-54160.

[4] CoinMarketCap, *Top 100 Kryptowährungen nach Börsenwert.* https://coinmarketcap.com/de/.

[5] Gruber, G.: futurezone, *Mining: So funktioniert das Schürfen nach Bitcoin* https://futurezone.at/digital-life/mining-so-funktioniert-das-schuerfen-nach-bitcoin/400002913.

[6] Siepermann, Dr. M.: Gabler Wirtschaftslexikon, *Algorithmus* https://wirtschaftslexikon.gabler.de/definition/algorithmus-27106.

[7] Bitpanda.com, *Was sind Public Keys, Private Keys und Wallet Adressen?.* https://www.bitpanda.com/academy/de/lektionen/was-sind-public-keys-private-keys-und-wallet-adressen/.

[8] chrissikraus; Schmitz, P.: Blockchain Insider, *Was ist Proof of Stake (PoS)?.* https://www.blockchain-insider.de/was-ist-proof-of-stake-pos-a-900657/.

[9] chrissikraus; Schmitz, P.: Blockchain Insider, *Was ist Proof of Activity (PoS)?.* https://www.blockchain-insider.de/was-ist-proof-of-activity-poa-a-954104/.

[10] chrissikraus; Schmitz, P.: Blockchain Insider, *Was ist Proof of Capacity (PoC)?*. https://www.blockchain-insider.de/was-ist-proof-of-capacity-poc-a-954183/.

[11] Hayes, A.: Investopedia, *Proof of Capacity (Cryptocurrency)*. https://www.investopedia.com/terms/p/proof-capacity cryptocurrency.asp#:~:text=Proof%20of%20capacity%20(PoC)%20 is,mining%20rights%20and%20validate%20transactions.

[12] Schiller, K.: Blockchainwelt, *Was ist Proof-of-Importance (POI) und wie funktioniert es?*. https://blockchainwelt.de/proof-of-importance-poi/.

[13] chrissikraus; Schmitz, P.: Blockchain Insider, *Was ist ein Fork?*. https://www.blockchain-insider.de/was-ist-ein-fork-a-857796/.

[14] Hauck, F.: Blockchain Center.net, *Node*. https://www.blockchaincenter.net/wiki/node/.

[15] Nüttgens, M.: Enzyklopädie der Wirtschaftsinformatik Online-Lexikon, *Open-Source-Software*. https://www.enzyklopaedie-der-wirtschaftsinformatik.de/lexikon/uebergreifendes/Kontext-und-Grundlagen/Markt/Open-Source-Software.

[16] Bundeszentrale für Politische Bildung, *Deflation*. https://www.bpb.de/nachschlagen/lexika/lexikon-der-wirtschaft/19113/deflation.

[17] Müller, T.: Focus Online MONEY, *Risiko Deflation – Die gefeierte Knappheit der Bitcoins ist zugleich ihre große Schwäche*. https://www.focus.de/finanzen/experten/mueller/risiko-deflation-die-gefeierte-knappheit-der-bitcoins-ist-zugleich-ihre-grosse-schwaeche_id_6661173.html.

[18] Sparkasse, *Bitte ein Bit?*. https://www.sparkasse.de/themen/geldanlage/bitcoin.html.

[19] IOTA, *Homepage*. https://www.iota.org/.

[20] Luber, S.; Litzel, N.: Bigdata Insider, *Definition – Was ist das Internet of Things?*. https://www.bigdata-insider.de/was-ist-das-internet-of-things-a-590806/.

[21] Aitken, R.: Forbes, *IOTA's Bitfinex Listing Surges To $1.5B Record-Breaking 'Crypto' Capitalization On Market Debut*. https://www.forbes.com/sites/rogeraitken/2017/06/15/iotas-bitfinex-listing-surges-to-1-5b-record-breaking-crypto-capitalization-on-market-debut/#2b02fb4975a5.

[22] Pollock, D.: Cointelegraph, *Micropayment Company Ditches "Outdated Bitcoin" For IoT Technology*. https://cointelegraph.com/news/micropayment-company-ditches-outdated-bitcoin-for-iot-technology.

[23] D'Anconia, F.: Cointelegraph, *IOTA Blockchain to Help Trace Families of Refugees During and After Conflicts*. https://cointelegraph.com/news/iota-blockchain-to-help-trace-families-of-refugees-during-and-after-conflicts.

[24] Sopra Steria, *Blockchain and the IoT: Sopra Steria partners with IOTA*. https://www.soprasteria.com/newsroom/press-releases/details/blockchain-and-the-iot-sopra-steria-partners-with-iota.

[25] Handelsblatt, *IOTA*. https://www.handelsblatt.com/themen/iota.

[26] IOTA, *Open Source Coordinator on Mainne*. https://blog.iota.org/open-source-coordinator-on-mainnet-386c3931907b/.

[27] IOTA, *Smart Access To IoT Devices.* https://www.iota.org/solutions/access.

[28] Eigene Darstellung, Daten BTC ECHO, *IOTA-Kurs.* https://www.btc-echo.de/kurs/iota/#chart.

[29] Emden, T.: IG, *IOTA Kurs steigt um 20 Prozent: Anleger aus dem Häuschen.* https://www.ig.com/de/nachrichten-und-trading-ideen/iota-kurs-steigt-um-20-prozent--anleger-aus-dem-haeusschen-210305#information-banner-dismiss.

[30] Emden, T.: IG, *IOTA Kurs: Tesla befeuert Rallye.* https://www.ig.com/de/nachrichten-und-trading-ideen/iota-kurs--tesla-befeuert-rallye-210209#information-banner-dismiss.

[31] Börse Stuttgart (YouTube-Kanal), *Krypto Update: IOTA – Nonplusultra oder Shitcoin?.* https://www.youtube.com/watch?v=eWifgPRg0uw.

[32] Dash, *Homepage.* https://www.dash.org/de/.

[33] bit2me ACADEMY, *Wer ist Evan Duffield? Der Schöpfer von DASH.* https://academy.bit2me.com/en/who-is-evan-duffield-dash-creator/.

[34] finanzen.net, *Vom Darkcoin zum Dash: Wer hinter der Kryptowährung steckt.* https://www.finanzen.net/nachricht/devisen/anonymitaet-pur-vom-darkcoin-zum-dash-wer-hinter-der-kryptowaehrung-steckt-6021729.

[35] Glüsing, J.: SPIEGEL, *Nichts zu essen, aber kostenlos Benzin.* https://www.spiegel.de/wirtschaft/soziales/venezuela-nichts-zu-essen-aber-kostenlos-benzin-das-plant-juan-guaido-a-1251621.html#ref=rss.

[36] CRYPTOLIST, *Was ist Dash?*. https://www.cryptolist.de/dash.

[37] BTC ECHO, *Dash-Kurs Chart*. https://www.btc-echo.de/kurs/dash/.

[38] Recksiek, M.: CRYPTOMONDAY, *Dash Kurs Explosion – Top 10, Venezuela, Burger King und der nicht vorhandene Exit Scam*. https://cryptomonday.de/dash-kurs-explosion-top-10-venezuela-burger-king-und-der-nicht-vorhandene-exit-scam/.

[39] Schiller, K: Blockchainwelt, *Dash Prognose 2021 – 2025: Vielversprechendes Investment?*. https://blockchainwelt.de/dash-prognose/.

[40] The Morpheus Tutorials (YouTube-Kanal), *Dash: eine Kryptowährung mit Zukunft - mit Sidem von der Dash Embassy*. https://www.youtube.com/watch?v=NMJbyp3yeTE.

[41] NEM, *Homepage*. https://nem.io/.

[42] COINHERO, *Was ist NEM? Eine Krypto-Plattform der nächsten Generation*. https://coin-hero.de/nem/.

[43] Mitschele, Prof. Dr. A.: Gabler Wirtschaftslexikon, *Smart Contract*. https://wirtschaftslexikon.gabler.de/definition/smart-contract-54213.

[44] Bergmann, C.: BitcoinBlog.de, *Größter Krypto-Hack aller Zeiten: Bitcoin nicht beteiligt*. https://bitcoinblog.de/2018/01/30/groesster-krypto-hack-aller-zeiten-bitcoin-nicht-beteiligt/.

[45] Symbol, *Homepage*. https://symbolplatform.com/.

[46] Shaw, D.: Symbol, *Symbol wurde gestartet.* https://symbol-platform.com/latest/symbol-has-launched/.

[47] IT TIMES, *NEM: Die Smart Asset Blockchain - Was hinter der Kryptowährung XEM und dem Slogan New Economy Movement steckt.* https://www.it-times.de/news/nem-die-smart-asset-blockchain-was-hinter-der-kryptowahrung-xem-und-dem-slogan-new-economy-movement-steckt-127429/.

[48] NEM, *UNSERE PLATTFORMEN – Wegweisende Technologie in einem leistungsstarken Ökosystem vereint.* https://nem.io/platforms/.

[49] Kenton, W.: Investopedia, *Smart Assets.* https://www.investopedia.com/terms/s/smart-assets-cryptocurrency.asp.

[50] DACH EOS, *Cross-chain Transaktionen & Massenadoption.* https://dach-eos.io/cross-chain-transaktionen-massenadaption/.

[51] BTC ACADEMY, *NEM.* https://www.btc-echo.de/academy/bibliothek/nem/.

[52] BTC ECHO, *NEM-Kurs Chart.* https://www.btc-echo.de/kurs/nem/.

[53] CoinMarketCap, *XYM-Kurs Chart.* https://coinmarketcap.com/de/currencies/symbol/.

[54] chrissikraus; Schmitz, P.: Blockchain Insider, *Was ist NEM?.* https://www.blockchain-insider.de/was-ist-nem-a-1000095/.

[55] Weidemann, T.: t3n, *Kryptowährungen jenseits von Bitcoin: Litecoin, Monero, Ripple.* https://t3n.de/magazin/kryptowaehrungen-jenseits-bitcoin-litecoin-monero-243888/.

[56] Safe Network, *Homepage*. https://safenetwork.tech/.

[57] ZEIT Online, Das digitale Debakel. https://www.zeit.de/angebote/buchtipp/keen/index.

[58] Olschewski, M.: Business Insider, *Der Erfinder des Internets erklärt, welche drei Probleme wir online endlich lösen müssen*. https://www.businessinsider.de/tech/der-erfinder-des-internets-erklaert-welche-drei-probleme-wir-online-endlich-loesen-muessen-2017-3/.

[59] Mansholt, M.: stern, *Wenn der Datenschutz zu Hause das Licht ausschaltet: Die absurden Folgen der DSGVO*. https://www.stern.de/digital/online/dsgvo--die-absurden-folgen-des-datenschutz-gesetzes-7999562.html.

[60] Krösmann, C.: *bitkom*, Die zehn größten Gefahren im Internet. https://www.bitkom.org/Presse/Presseinformation/Die-zehn-groessten-Gefahren-im-Internet.html.

[61] MaidSafe, *Who we are*. https://maidsafe.net/about_us/.

[62] MaidSafe, *How it works*. https://safenetwork.tech/how-it-works/.

[63] Safe Network, *Frequently Asked Questions*. https://safenetwork.tech/faq/#how-do-i-buy-safecoin.

[64] BTC ECHO, *MaidSafeCoin-Kurs Chart*. https://www.btc-echo.de/kurs/maidsafecoin/.

[65] My Digital Strategist (YouTube-Kanal), *MaidSafeCoin (MAID) Token Review: Should you invest or not?*. https://www.youtube.com/watch?v=BGN6D84lUlw.

[66] Safe Network Forum. https://safenetforum.org/.

[67] Safe Network, *It's the dawn of a new web. Help us create it.* https://safenetwork.tech/get-involved/#feedback.

[68] Binance, *Homepage.* https://www.binance.com/de.

[69] maltatoday, *Why world leader crypto exchange Binance moved to Malta.* https://www.maltatoday.com.mt/business/business_news/93170/why_world_leader_crypto_exchange_binance_moved_to_malta#.YJY2tLUzY2y.

[70] CoinMarketCap, *Die besten Spot-Börsen für Kryptowährung.* https://coinmarketcap.com/de/rankings/exchanges/.

[71] Coinhero, *Was ist der Binance Coin – eine virtuelle Währung oder steckt mehr dahinter?.* https://coin-hero.de/binance-coin/.

[72] Binance, *BNB.* https://www.binance.com/de/bnb#useBnbSection.

[73] Petereit, D.: t3n, *BNB entfesselt: Binance Coin steigt 20 Prozent an einem Tag.* https://t3n.de/news/bnb-entfesselt-binance-coin-20-1371980/.

[74] Petereit, D.: t3n, *Krypto-Konkurrenz: Die Binance Smart Chain setzt an, Ethereum zu überholen.* https://t3n.de/news/krypto-binance-smart-chain-ethereum-1358731/.

[75] t3n, *Was steckt hinter der Binance Smart Chain?.* https://t3n.de/news/steckt-binance-smart-chain-1370453/.

[76] BTC ECHO, *Binance Coin-Kurs Chart.* https://www.btc-echo.de/kurs/binance-coin/.

[77] Binance, *BNB*. https://www.binance.com/de/bnb#storeB-nbSection.

[78] Hunter, J. S.: Finance FWD, *Milliarden-Gewinne, Klagen und Hacks – die Binance-Story*. https://financefwd.com/de/die-bi-nance-story/.

[79] Horch, P.: BTC ECHO, *Binance Hack: Bitcoin-Börse verliert über 7.000 BTC* https://www.btc-echo.de/news/binance-hack-bitcoin-boerse-verliert-ueber-7-000-btc-71938/.

[80] TRON, *Homepage*. https://tron.network/index?lng=en.

[81] Statista, *Nutzungshäufigkeit von Mediatheken und Streamingdiensten in Deutschland im Jahr 2020*. https://de.statista.com/statistik/daten/studie/627483/umfrage/nutzungshaefigkeit-von-videostream-anbietern-in-deutschland/.

[82] CoinMarketCap, *TRON* https://coinmarketcap.com/de/currencies/tron/.

[83] Bitcoin2Go, *Tron Prognose 2021: Welches Potenzial steckt hinter TRX?*. https://bitcoin-2go.de/tron-prognose/.

[84] TRON, *About*. https://tron.network/about?lng=en.

[85] Trends der Zukunft, *TRON Coin (TRX): Das steckt hinter der Kryptowährung für das Web 4.0*. https://www.trendsderzukunft.de/tron-coin-trx-das-steckt-hinter-der-kryptowaehrung-fuer-das-web-4-0/.

[86] Coinhero, *Was ist Tron - eine virtuelle Währung oder steckt mehr dahinter?*. https://coin-hero.de/tron/.

[87] BTC ECHO, *TRON-Kurs Chart*. https://www.btc-echo.de/kurs/tron/.

[88] Stellar, *Homepage*. https://stellar.org/.

[89] Cryptolist, *Was ist Stellar?*. https://www.cryptolist.de/stellar.

[90] Steinadler, R.: Bitcoin Kurier, *Ukraine baut CBDC auf Basis von Stellar – XLM-Kurs explodiert*. https://bitcoin-kurier.de/ukraine-baut-cbdc-auf-basis-von-stellar-xlm-kurs-explodiert/.

[91] Stellar, *Intro to Stellar*. https://stellar.org/learn/intro-to-stellar.

[92] BTC ECHO, *Stellar-Kurs Chart*. https://www.btc-echo.de/kurs/stellar/.

CPSIA information can be obtained
at www.ICGtesting.com
Printed in the USA
BVHW010517271121
622603BV00002B/17

A Bethnal Green
MEMOIR

A Bethnal Green
MEMOIR

Recollections of Life
in the 1930s–1950s

DEREK HOUGHTON

To my granddaughter Averil,
who has brought a ray of sunshine into our lives.

First published 2009

The History Press
The Mill, Brimscombe Port
Stroud, Gloucestershire, GL5 2QG
www.thehistorypress.co.uk

British Library Cataloguing in Publication Data.
A catalogue record for this book is available from the British Library.

ISBN 978 0 7509 5126 5

Typesetting and origination by The History Press
Printed in Great Britain

CONTENTS

ACKNOWLEDGEMENTS

I am indebted to those who in the past suggested that I should write a book. To my wife Sheila; who was the source of encouragement, both in her advice and the long hours spent working on the manuscript. Carole Hamburger; who has been of tremendous help in reviewing and editing at each stage of writing. My sister Dawn, cousins Sheila, Brenda and Mavis; who furnished me with endless reminders of the past and provided photographs long since forgotten.

To write a book was a seed that has been lying dormant in the back of my mind for many years, ready to spring out. The prime reason for my writing is to record for my children, relatives, colleagues and friends how life really was in the East End's Bethnal Green.

Many have never comprehended the environment in which we grew up.

In the successful show and film *Fiddler on the Roof*, the main character, Tevye, played by Topol, looks up to heaven and speaks to God. 'I know it's no great shame to be poor, on the other hand, it's no great honour either.' Those words say a very great deal, especially to the likes of those like myself who grew up surrounded by poverty.

Finally I am eternally grateful to those families and the boys and girls that I grew up with in St Peter's Avenue, and the people of Bethnal Green of that era. Without them there would have been no story to tell.

I

OUR STREET

here was once a street in Bethnal Green. How I wish that street were still there rather than having been replaced by uninspiring drab architecture, devoid of character and without soul; to be able to return once in a while, to stand in the street where I grew up. To look at the houses and the people who had lived in them, and to bring back the memories of my boyhood. This community, gone forever, was once bound by a common element – poverty. Everyone in that street knew everyone else; there was a 'togetherness'. It was like a village. It was a togetherness that grew even stronger when Hitler's Luftwaffe released their bombs on the East End of London.

Our street, St Peter's Avenue, was included in the council's slum clearance proposals in the five years leading up to 1965. At the stroke of a pen, faceless officials sitting in the town hall's council chamber concluded that our street was to be demolished forever; its community spirit broken and its residents scattered to the four corners of Tower Hamlets, to dwell in cold, grey, concrete, monolithic jungles. The likelihood of seeing the people whom I grew up with ever again was slim.

Many of the streets that were to remain could not compare with St Peter's Avenue. It was bounded by Hackney Road to the north, which in 1587 was referred to as the highway from Shoreditch to Mare Street. Old Bethnal Green Road lay to the south, which in 1538 was named Cocks Lane. In 1642 it became Rogues Lane, and in 1717, Whores Lane. It finally became acceptable when it was named Old Bethnal Green Road. Warner Place lay to the west and Mansford Street to the east.

It was a street like many others in Bethnal Green, a street of terraced houses, and the larger houses at the top had at one time of their lives housed the gentry. The basements were kitchens and sculleries, while the top of the houses acted as servant's quarters. They had been very grand in their day.

Others graduated to even smaller houses, as you walked from Hackney Road. Two-thirds of the houses in the street were built in a uniform fashion of three upper rooms. The upper front room, with two large windows looking out on to the street, had two small balconies with a decorative wrought iron surround, large enough to

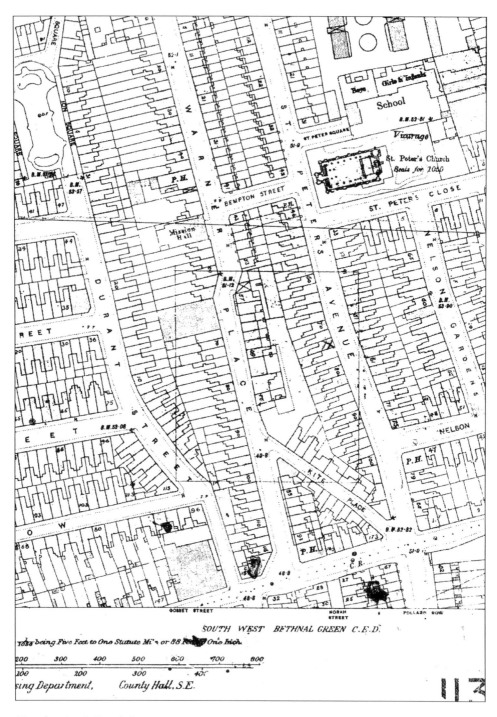

Map showing St Peter's Avenue.

accommodate your bottom and watch any parade that might be passing by! There were three rooms on the lower ground floor. These included a scullery, and a small garden, and yard with an outside toilet. The luxury of having a bathroom was totally unknown. No one owned their home, they were all rented. The very thought of buying your own house was never considered, it would have been like placing a millstone around your neck. Besides, very few were in a position to qualify for a mortgage even if they had wanted to. Unemployment was high, jobs were scarce, and we were in a depression.

There was something very special about our street; I could never quite put my finger on it, never really understanding why it felt so special, but it did. To my mind, it was a cut above the surrounding streets, as it was never scruffy or run down, nor did it have an air of poverty about it. What is it with a street that becomes part of you, that you feel it and breathe it?

Poverty was forever there. Getting through each day to see that there was a meal on the table to feed the family. Scheming and scratching to make ends meet, sharing the despair with neighbours in the same inescapable position as you. Poverty compelled you to take roads you did not want to travel down, having no option but to do so if it meant survival. Under these conditions, Bethnal Green was a perfect breeding ground for those who had higher aspirations. It was like the embryo for the criminal, the fighter, and for those seeking a better way of life, all trying to find a way out.

The 1930s was a decade of depression. Unemployment was at its peak, and there were many people in the East End who resorted to crime to make ends meet. Each week the local rag, *The Hackney Gazette*, would publish the court cases. The findings of the courts were much harsher then in meting out sentences and punishment to the guilty offenders. Robbery with violence was considered a very serious crime. On 21 July 1933, Frank Muir, aged twenty, was sentenced to four years penal servitude, plus eighteen strokes of the cat-of-nine-tails for robbing women with violence. The counterfeiting of £1 notes, half crowns, florins and shillings abounded. In November 1934, one man was found passing forged £1 notes at Clapton Dog Stadium and was sentenced to seven years penal servitude. In the same year, James Sims of 36 Nelson Street was found to be in possession of nine counterfeit florins and was sentenced to two years penal servitude. Counterfeiting had become quite rampant during those years.

To understand the circumstances and conditions, one has to look into the history of Bethnal Green. Poverty had been in and around Bethnal Green for a very long time; overcrowding was caused by poverty. Since the poor could not afford more spacious abodes they needed to stay close to their work. In the late 1880s the largest category of the population was 'comfortable' with a fairly good wage coming in. These were mainly craftsmen in the furniture trade. Bethnal Green had the highest percentage of poor and very poor, mostly labourers and people underemployed in the furniture and dress trades. The 'comfortable' artisans and clerks lived around Victoria Park.

In 1881, 872 out of a population of 129,000 people in Bethnal Green were Irish and 925 foreign-born. Foreign immigrants formed a minute percentage of the population. Mostly born in Germany, Poland, and Russia, they were the poor Jews who had fled the pogroms and whose concentration made them stand out more than their numbers merited. By 1899, Jews formed at least 95 per cent of the population south of Mare Street, and almost 80 per cent in Brick Lane. The ghetto, full of synagogues, backroom factories, and little grocery stores reeking of pickled herring, garlic sausage and onion bread, was occupied by alien people speaking a strange language. The smell of sweat, overcrowding, and high rents were associated with Jews, as victims and sometimes as perpetrators. Some Jews were middle class and invested in property which they rack rented. Anti-Jewish feeling, fuelled by the resentment of slum dwellers, expelled in the clearances, ignited against the landlords in 1898.

The liberal Jewish establishment of the United Synagogue, including Sir Samuel Montagu and the Rothschild's, understood the danger of the unarticulated alien. They opposed the sweating system and rack renting. It resulted in them founding the Four Per Cent Industrial Dwellings Company to provide homes for Jewish artisans. One benefit of the Jewish settlement that found agreement, acknowledged by their opponents, the missioners, was the declining incidence of drunkenness, and possibly because of that, the decline in infant mortality.

The distended numbers of Jews aggravated poverty and crowding. By 1901 there was an overall concentration in Bethnal Green of 170 people per acre. The number of houses reached 17,283 in 1881 and 17,354 in 1891; a density of twenty-three houses per acre, after which numbers seem to decrease, to 14,848 in 1901 and 13,649 in 1911. Most people (76 per cent in 1901 and 79 per cent in 1911) lived in tenements with fewer than five rooms, with nearly a third of those in just two rooms. In the 1880s there were old houses where the upper room, once used for weaving, had been portioned in two or three rooms for two families, with another family on each floor. Overcrowding was made worse by the loss of gardens to workshops and warehouses, although sanitation improved.

Mare Street, Hackney, *c.* 1912. This section is known as 'The Narroway'.

One of my earliest recollections of poverty which had a long lasting effect was the eviction of a husband and wife from their home because they were unable to pay their rent. Neighbours stood around their furniture, stacked at the curbside, in total silence with a feeling of helplessness at seeing the contents of their home put out on the street. The poor woman was sobbing her heart out, clutching at her children's hands, her children too young to understand their parents' plight. The neighbouring women standing around were sharing her misery and crying too. It was a profoundly unforgettable experience.

In its better days, one of St Peter's Street's most celebrated residents was Wilkie Collins, the nineteenth-century author best known for *The Women in White,* which many years later would be made into a musical by Andrew Lloyd Webber. He also wrote one of the first detective novels, *The Moonstone.* A very successful author, he was a great friend of Charles Dickens.

Further down the road at No. 70 resided Horatio Bottomley. In 1888 he founded the *Financial Times* and was its first chairman. In 1906 he established the patriotic journal *John Bull*, and he was also elected Liberal MP for the Borough of Hackney. Bottomley's politics earned him a reputation as a populist, but his financial strategies meant he was seen as a common swindler by many. He was later charged with fraud and mismanagement, and was sentenced to seven years imprisonment and expelled from Parliament. He died in penury in 1933.

It was commonplace for many of the homes to have two families living in them. Normally when a son or daughter married, they would move in with their parents and occupy the upper part of the house. If children came along, the house would accommodate six to seven people, if not more. The first floor landing was utilized as a kitchen, having a gas stove installed, and the only toilet for both families would be outside in the yard.

The women in our street generally wore a crossover apron, and in the summer months it was often the only outer garment worn. There were two elderly ladies down the street, very prim and proper who always wore mop caps, and seemed to belong to another age. Everyone knew them as the 'old maids'. Whenever you passed their house, you would find them cleaning, dusting and polishing. Most women took pride in their homes, both inside and out. Doorsteps were hand rubbed in either white or green hearthstone. Some steps looked decidedly smarter where red cardinal polish was applied, if they could afford it that is.

The pavement immediately outside the homes was washed and scrubbed with birch brooms. Door knockers, doorknobs, letter boxes, and foot gratings were polished. Some knockers and door handles were black, and like the foot grating, they would be polished with Zebo, a black graphite polish. Others were made of brass, and seldom would you see any brass door furniture tarnished. Many front doors were artificially grained to give the appearance of a more expensive type of wood. 'Japanning' and 'Graining' have since become a lost art; you rarely see this type of work anymore.

Just two or three years before the outbreak of the war, the name of our street was changed from St Peter's Street to St Peter's Avenue. Smart, white enameled street signs in black lettering, with the Borough of Bethnal Green lettered in red, were placed above the existing old street signs. It was almost like feeling we had 'arrived' and had been given class status!

I was too young at the time to give any thought as to why the name was changed, but later came to realise that we did after all have trees in our street, not very mature ones, but trees nevertheless! This had probably given us the entitlement of calling ourselves an 'Avenue'. It did make us feel rather elevated, particularly as we actually had greenery, which was most abundant in the grounds surrounding St Peter's Church. Most other streets were devoid of foliage of any description.

We had a cinema, The Hackney Grand Central. Its entrance was in Hackney Road, and on the corner stood a stone Grecian urn-style water fountain. No water spouted from it, but if you pressed a button on the mounted brass lion's head, water would pour from the mouth. Chained to the fountain was a galvanized iron mug from which we would drink. It had a dreadful metallic taste, I hated using it, but there was no other alternative. Pressing that button to release water to cup in your hands, or drink directly from its mouth, was a physical impossibility as it had a circular stone surround, with a small channel that gathered water before it ran away, and so prevented you from drinking directly from the spout. The channel was often blocked with people's paper debris, sometimes to the point of overflowing which left you standing in puddles of water to get a drink. We had no knowledge then of sanitation. How, or why, we never caught a disease from that horrible iron mug remains a scientific mystery!

Half-way down the road was St Peter's Church, with an adjacent church school of the same name. Further along we had 'our' public house, The Oxford Arms. We considered it 'our pub', it was used by the family at regular intervals and whenever relatives visited us. It had large rooms above that were used for functions, particularly weddings. You always knew when a wedding party was in progress by the amount of confetti lying outside the pub on the pavement, and the music and voices coming from above the pub.

Next door was Jones the dairy; both pub and dairy were later demolished by a bomb during the Blitz. Most of the dairies around the East End at that time were Welsh-owned. I recall a dairy in Gossett Street that actually had two cows in a small barn-like structure at the side of the dairy, something I had never seen before or since in the whole of London! At the bottom, on our side of the street, the end house formed an apex. One side of the house was in St Peter's Avenue and the other side in Kite Place. It was occupied by Mr Abrahams and his daughters; Mr Abrahams, bespectacled with a walrus moustache, was a cobbler whose front room-cum-workshop on the ground floor faced Pollards Row and Gossett Street. Whenever you passed Mr Abrahams' window, he would be there, boot nails in his mouth, working away at a boot on a last, always giving you a nod as you passed by. Near to Mr Abrahams was Mr Irons, the confectioners and newsagents. They had a cigarette machine at the side of the entrance door; it was a Kensitas machine which, for 2*d* would dispense a very slim packet of two cigarettes with a Swan Vesta match alongside each one. Kensitas cigarettes were unmistakable by their logo of a butler dressed in black tails holding out a tray. Mr Irons, a very obese grey-haired man, and his lame wife would stand behind their counters, the shop's shelves festooned with jars of sweets. His counters sagged under the weight of newspapers, magazines and comics: *The Daily Sketch, News Chronicle, Titbit's, Everybody's, Picture Post, Lilliput,* and many other papers and periodicals now long gone.

As a young boy, to walk into Mr Irons' shop was like walking into Aladdin's Cave. The colours of the confectionery in glass jars on the rows of shelves would bedazzle and excite the taste buds. To watch Mr Irons carefully weigh the sweets on his scales and empty them into a small white paper bag became a performance, though what you could buy with a halfpenny or a penny was very limited. I entered a raffle in their shop one day and completely forgot about it, returning for something or another a few days later, when Mr Irons informed me that I had won first prize. It was a model of the Queen Mary. How elated and happy I was to win such a wonderful thing, to go home and proudly display such a beautiful prize! It made my spirits soar. I often wonder what became of it.

Through the course of the week, from the early morning milk deliveries by the milkmen from the United or Express Dairies, with the chinking of milk bottles and a yodel, our street had its callers all day long, with rag and bone men and with pot and saucepan repairers. New saucepans were hardly ever purchased; the pot repairer plugged the holes, or you could buy a pot-menders' kit and repair them yourself. Then there was the knife and scissor sharpener, who honed your knives and scissors, sparks flying everywhere from the grindstone wheel he was pedaling away on; often there was the glazier, panes of glass strapped to his weary back, bent from his weighty load, his cry of 'Windows to mend' ringing out. We also had an occasional visit from the chimney sweep, a black-smudged face with his bundle of brushes carried over his shoulder. In the evenings you would hear the cries of 'dog winner' from the vendor selling the sheet of dog results from the London dog tracks. Some of the rag-and-bone men would come by horse and cart, a round-a-bout on the back of the cart painted in the patriotic colors of red, white and blue in Union Jack fashion. You handed him your old clothes, but if you had none, you would have to pay him a penny for a ride. If you had clothes to give him, you were given the ride and a goldfish in a glass bulbous bowl. On one visit from the rag and bone man, I benevolently gave away my Father's best grey flannel trousers for a goldfish and a ride on the roundabout! My Mother, having found out what I had done, went running around the streets to locate the rag and bone man to retrieve them. I gave her further anxiety by putting the goldfish to bed, laying that poor creature on top of some rice pudding in her bed for its supper!

On Sundays the street really came alive. In the mornings we had the Church Lads Brigade, marching through playing drums and bugle, occasionally followed later on by the Boy Scouts and Girl Guides from the Red Church (St James the Less). Later in the morning, we would have the Salvation Army station themselves outside our house forming a circle, singing hymns to the playing of concertinas and tambourines, a few prayers and a sermon or two thrown in for good measure, and a vendor selling winkles, whelks, shrimps and cockles. Winkles were always a favourite for an East End Sunday tea, accompanied by sticks of celery. Today, I can't even look at a winkle, but then hunger was always on the agenda and you ate literally anything that was put before you. Then there was the Muffin Man, who sold his muffins and crumpets, ringing his bell. A barrel organ would later appear, its music giving the street a very happy atmosphere. It is a great pity they are no longer heard around the streets. The Walls ice cream man would ride his tricycle through, the slogan was 'Stop me and buy one'. The ices were made from frosted

Bethnal Green Road, showing the 'Red Church'.

water ice inside a triangular carton, and as you demolished the ice, you would push it to the top of the carton, usually finishing up with a handful of colored water! Later in the afternoon a couple of fellows would come along, roll out a tap board and start to tap dance and sing. It was much later in life that I understood they were gay, known in the East End as 'Irons', Cockney slang for iron hoofs – poofs. We would all sit on the curbside and watch them perform. I loved it when Sundays arrived; it was one huge round of lively street entertainment, merriment and activity.

There were many families down the street who were extremely poor. They stood out, as they carried an air of poverty, their faces telling everything. Devoid of merriment, their body language gave the signs of futility, and their faces had a look of despair. It never entered my head to realise that we were also poor; we simply never gave it a thought. Fortunately we were not as badly off as many others, you just didn't know anything else; there was nothing to compare it with.

Sunday also meant regular visits to the market. The Flower Market in Columbia Road, just two streets away, would begin its day with the sleepy street coming to life. The whole morning would be spent moving in a continual throng from the Flower Market through to Petticoat Lane via Brick Lane. There is something about a market that has forever held its fascination; its atmosphere, colour, and its characters, the yelling, shouting, haggling and the banter from the vendors. The many tongues becoming a symphony, the crowds a moving canvas.

We would look at the flowers, plants, trees and shrubs, and listen to the shouts and cries from the sellers as we struggled through the crowds. If you were canny you would visit the market when it was close to closing down as prices would become rock bottom rather than the traders having to hold on to their stock. In Columbia Road there was a Gothic structure that always appeared incongruous compared to the rest of the area. I, like many others, must have passed it a million times without questioning why it was there, or how it came to be there.

Columbia Road Flower Market began in the nineteenth century, not as a flower market but a market of assorted stalls selling all kinds of different produce, spread along the full length of Columbia Road. In 1864 the benevolent Baroness Angela Burdett Coutts had the inspiration to build a market square within Columbia Road, to provide cheap food and fish from the then thriving East Coast ports. The plans included a large Gothic-style building with shops surrounding it, and flats above to provide affordable accommodation for the traders. After the church-like structure known as Columbia Market was erected, the enterprise failed and the traders returned to the street.

Leaving the Flower Market we would walk on through to the 'Shallorams', a strange name used only in our family. The name had baffled me for years, as indeed it bewildered the rest of the family, but it was a Yiddish word for something old and worn. 'Shallorams' was something we thought my Grandmother had made up. It was a street of second-hand clothing, practically the whole of the East End shopped there. You would find people tossing over bundles of shirts, some with evidence of soiling on the shirt tails that you attempted to ignore and pretend wasn't there! Vendors without stalls would have their garments in the curbside on a bed sheet or canvas. Here you would see people trying on hats, coats, and furs. Piles of clothing churned over, money exchanging hands, and prices being haggled.

Walking through to Club Row where the cats and dogs were sold, you could find every breed under the sun, sometimes even a monkey or two. Then, on to the Bird Market with the chirps and cheeps and whistles and an array of colours of the plumage of our feathered friends, all ready to be sold. Canaries, budgerigars, finches, parrots and a hundred other varieties of birds in small boxed cages hanging on the street walls.

Brick Lane would have its greengrocers' stalls and seafood stalls, the bagel lady, the jellied eel stall serving white porcelain bowls of jellied eels with hunks of white bread. The eels were embedded in a heap of transparent jelly, sprinkled with vinegar and peppered, with five or six pieces of eel to the bowl. The flesh was removed from the bones in the mouth, and the bones spat out onto the pavement and into the road. Indian seamen would come from the docks, mingling through the throngs of people and buy sewing machines to take back to their ships, and finally to India.

Then there was Cheshire Street; with the drink stall showing the wonderful liquid vibrant colours of pineapple, strawberry, raspberry and orange and sarsaparilla, which in summer were served cold and icy and would have the mouth watering! In winter, hot blackcurrant was the number one drink, not forgetting the roasted chestnuts and baked potatoes.

The mobile van could always be found, cooking apple fritters heavily coated with sugar, and other stalls selling second-hand false teeth and spectacles, second-hand shoes and just about every commodity in existence, both old and new, that one could imagine.

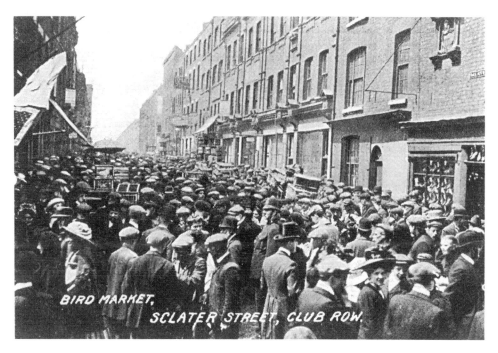

The Bird Market, 'Club Row', *c.* 1912. It remained unchanged throughout the 1930s and 1940s.

The Jewish delicatessens did a good trade outside in the street with their barrels of pickled herring, and inside, chopped liver, chopped herring, schmultz herring, smoked salmon, Vienna's (sausages), hot latkas and rye bread were readily available.

We used to sing a song that immediately brought Petticoat Lane and Brick Lane to mind:

I went down the Lane to buy a penny whistle,
A copper came along and took my penny whistle,
I asked him for it back, he said he hadn't got it,
Aye, aye, copper knob you've got it in your pocket!

Everyone dressed up in their Sunday best, men, women, and children alike. Men took the trouble to wear a collar and tie, a bowler hat, or a derby. A few donned an Anthony Eden (hat) and in summer these hats would be replaced with a boater or a panama.

Men would place a pocket watch in their vest pocket, an Albert strung across either side of the waistcoat, giving an air of stature and authority. They just loved to stick their thumbs into the lower arms of their waistcoats when being addressed, displaying that watch chain, with the stomach pushed out to its full extent. Why – it was almost like being the Mayor of Bethnal Green! Invariably as you walked down the street there was a piano playing in the front rooms. Several households possessed a piano, each house you passed playing a different tune, and the music emanating would merge into one melodious casserole. The smell of the Sunday roast cooking stimulated the appetite and aroused the taste buds. The front room windows facing out on to the street had their lace curtains parted to display a plant of some description; the aspidistra seemed the most popular, on a polished wooden stand or an upright gramophone cabinet.

Now and then as you passed a window, a curtain would slowly be pulled back. A face could just be seen, the best part concealed behind the curtain, interested only to see who was passing.

Quite a few of the families had dogs of well-known breeds; we were situated quite close to the Dog Market just off Bethnal Green Road. Airedales, Chows, Fox Terriers, Red Setters and Cocker Spaniels seemed to be the favorites, with a mixture of mongrels. It was quite commonplace, if the dog was black, to call him Nigger. It wasn't considered derogatory to use that word then, it was an accepted name without any racial overtones – it would not have entered anyone's head to question it. I shudder to think of how people would react if they were to use that name today, bearing in mind that in those days a black person was a rarity.

One of the few coloured people we ever observed was an Indian who would come down the street once a year selling 'Indian Toffee'. He tinkled a little bell to draw your attention, made a small cone from newspaper and placed the Indian Toffee inside the cone; it was a tinier version of candy floss. The other one was known throughout Britain as 'Prince Monolulu'. He was a racing tipster who you would find in Petticoat Lane practically every Sunday, and was always very easy to spot in a crowd. He was quite tall, wore brightly coloured clothes, and a head dress of highly coloured plumes. His favorite slogan was 'I gotta horse'. A prince he was not. His real name was Peter Carl MacKay. He claimed he was a Chief of the Falasha Tribe of Abyssinia. But he was born in St Croix, now part of the US Virgin Islands. He was regularly featured in a radio programme at the time called *In Town Tonight*.

Racial discrimination then, with the exception of some of the Jewish population, was never an issue. The anti-Jewish feeling was mainly stirred up by Sir Oswald Moseley and his Blackshirts, who preached their anti-Semitic doctrine around the East End. Little did I know that several years later when my curiosity took over, I would find myself drinking in his company!

Pubs were invariably full on Saturdays and Sundays; they were the poor man's opium, the working man's only form of temporary release from the drudgery of work, and away from the responsibilities of wife and kids for a brief period in their humdrum lives. To get drunk was a way of life; it wasn't anything unusual to see a drunk at the weekends. The pubs had a saloon bar, a public bar and a small off-licence bar for outside orders. Beer was served 'loose' for people bringing their own jugs.

The public bar was a man's domain, quite spartan, sawdust thrown on the floor, perhaps a dartboard, but you rarely saw women there. The saloon bar was better furnished with reasonably comfortable tables and chairs and always a piano. Most women would accompany their husbands on a Saturday night to the pub's saloon bar; it was the one occasion when they could get themselves 'dolled up'. Invariably a pianist was hired for the weekend, popular songs were played and usually a sing-song entailed. At the weekend you would see children outside the pubs waiting for their parents. They were usually given an Arrowroot biscuit to keep them quiet; this was a very large sweet biscuit that pubs sold in huge glass jars at a penny a time.

An accordionist would visit the pubs around the locality; he would stand outside and play a popular medley of songs, then go into the bars with a hat for a collection. Quite near to us in Old Bethnal Green Road was Lou. He was known to all of us; I can see him now, trilby hat, thin pencil moustache, cigarette dangling out of the corner of his mouth, a club foot that made him limp quite badly, the heavy accordion strapped to his back on his way to the next pub. The Salvation Army would come into the pubs on a Saturday evening selling their War Cry; hardly anyone would refuse them. Many of the pubs would have clubs, members paying in every week to provide a good dinner and Christmas presents come the highlight of the year. It was not unknown for a Christmas club's treasurer to suddenly disappear shortly before the festivities, leaving the poor subscribers 'high and dry'!

One day, bandy little Ginger Jago, the youngest of the very poor Jago family from Nelson Gardens, took a jug to the Oxford Arms to be filled up with beer. Albert Poole, the publican, went to fill up the jug and found a bed bug at the bottom of the jug. Remarking to the young boy that there was a bug in the bottom, young Ginger quickly responded, 'That's nuffink, we've got fahsands of 'em at 'ome'!

The whole Jago family was bandy. Mr Jago was a bookies' runner; you would see him standing on the corner of Nelson Gardens and St Peter's Avenue outside the Oxford Arms, on the lookout for the police and for the punters who would come along and place paper betting slips into his hands – the transaction being made as discreetly as possible. Should a policeman be spotted, Mr Jago would beat a hasty retreat down Nelson Gardens to his home at the very bottom of the cul-de-sac, out of sight.

On some Saturday nights Grandfather might be in a benevolent mood and take my Grandmother out to a public house, usually the Oxford Arms. It was the only time she had occasion to dress up, which was usually all in black. She would overuse the powder puff and wear every piece of jewellery that she possessed. We dubbed her 'Nancy Glitters'!

If ever you entered a pub around midday during the week you would find a few women sitting at a table sipping a glass of ale, wearing flat caps like the men, shelling peas for dinner, the pods of the shelled peas falling into their aprons that were collected up after the apron was full. It was a great place for a 'jaw', the term they used for a good chat.

Nelson Gardens formed a 'U' shape from St Peter's Avenue and back again. We had several school friends living there who also attended St Peter's School. Among them were the brothers George and Teddy Evans. Teddy talked me into joining the church choir and Johnny Renshaw, who when Sinatra became popular went completely overboard, and never stopped imitating him!

A girl who I liked very much was Iris Renfrew. I gave her my signet ring and Mother went berserk when she heard that I had given it away and promptly went round to the girl's Mother and reclaimed it. It was a romance that finished before it began, and although she was an attractive girl at the time, dear Iris became quite plain and lanky later in life, married and went to live in Norah Square. The strange thing was that having

Gran in her 'Nancy Glitters' attire.

grown up together, whenever we passed each other in our adult life, words of recognition were never exchanged!

On Monday mornings it was commonplace to see a queue forming outside Walter's the Pawnbrokers in Hackney Road. His full name was Leonard Moules, and Grandmother always referred to him as Walter Leonard, but we knew him as Walter. I can see him now standing behind the counter with his twirled waxed moustache taking in the bundles of clothing and other items from the queue that regularly formed there at the beginning of every week. Grandmother would say to us, 'go in the front door, not at the side door in the alley'. It was considered that only the real hard-up cases went in the side door. The 'old man's' suit or watch and chain went in regularly on Monday morning, coming out by Friday in time for him to go out at the weekend.

But tragedy was to come for Walter. On 30 April 1942 at 10.23 p.m., P.C. Clement April, in the company of other police officers, went to the premises of a pawnbrokers shop at 299 Hackney Road, having heard a dog barking in the basement, and found a door partly open. He had trouble in opening the door, and when he flashed his light he found a body behind the door. The body was identified as that of Leonard Moules (Walter), aged seventy-one years. At the Coroners' inquest, Detective Inspector George Keen was engaged in making enquiries into the death of the deceased. It was mentioned that £40 and a quantity of rings had been removed from the safe. On 9 May, two young men, Samuel Dashwood, aged twenty-two years, and George Silverosa, aged twenty-three years, were charged with the willful murder.

The evidence of a fingerprint expert had discovered somebody's palm print on the safe in the shop. Subsequently he received the palm prints of Silverosa from Brixton Prison and it was of his opinion that that it was made by the left hand of Silverosa. Dashwood had been discharged from the Army the previous August as a result of his mental condition. The accused were committed for trial at the Old Bailey.

Dashwood dismissed his counsel, resenting the fact that they considered him abnormal. Their petitions for reprieve were dismissed and they were sentenced to death and executed at Pentonville Prison on 10 September 1942. Later on, the bombing devastated the area surrounding the pawnshop, but it was one of the few buildings that survived.

In our young adventurous days, we used to climb into the pawnshop where poor Walter had been murdered. It was silent, dark and eerie. We climbed the stairs to the top of the building and all we could hear was the creaking of the pulley ropes of the service lift that ran from the ground floor to the top floor. The noise of those ropes creaking began to scare us. Our thoughts were focused on the murder that had been committed in the building. We fled down those stairs 'hell-bent for leather' and out of those premises, never to return!

Dying, and funerals if you could afford them, were very stately affairs and considered an event. The house of the deceased would have it's front room shutters closed – several others down the street would have their blinds half-lowered as a mark of respect. The undertakers, normally English's from Bethnal Green Road, came with their horses and carriages. The horses were black and harnessed in black leather, with silver embellishments and purple feathered plumes on their heads. The carriages were also black, polished to such a high degree that you could see your reflection in them; the undertakers wore black top hats. The direct relatives were always attired entirely in black, the women wearing veils, while other mourners wore a black armband or a black fabric diamond sewn on to their sleeve. Family mourners would remain in black for at least three months. Neighbours gathered outside the house on either side until the coffin came out, and remained until the coffin was placed in the hearse and the entourage moved off. Neighbors were left to talk amongst themselves and pass their comments to say 'what a lovely chap', 'what a lovely person she was' or 'what a lovely turnout they gave them'. If ever you were walking along and a funeral procession happened to pass, it was customary to stand still, raise your hat if you were wearing one, or if you didn't, touch your coat collar, and remain still until the procession had passed as a sign of respect for the departed. I really never understood why we touched our collars. Anyone who could not afford the full services of an undertaker would call on my Grandmother and ask her to lay the body out. She would wash them, comb their hair and make the corpse more presentable. If it was very hot weather, she would cut an onion and place it under the bed to hide the body odours of the corpse. She would return to our house and tell us how nice he or she looked, saying what a lovely hair parting she gave them. My sister would cringe in horror at being told about the dead. My Grandmother would tell us that if you didn't fear them in life, you would most certainly not fear them in death.

Many families had children of an age group similar to my sister and I, so we grew up together, played together, went to school together and remained together until we became that much older when, through diverse circumstances, we went our separate ways. There were the Arrowsmiths, the Andrews, the Kendalls, the Baldwins, the Gardeners, the Wards, the Mills, the Radfords, the Dearings, the Herberts, the Hudsons, the Beauvoirs, the Smiths, the Heywoods, the Kilburns, and so many other names. For some unknown reason the women would address each other by their surnames. Sometimes passing by their doorways, you would find a child sitting on the doorstep eating an enormous size piece of bread with 'Daddie's Sauce' or granulated sugar, or perhaps jam, spread over it. If it were a Monday it was usually a piece of Yorkshire pudding left over from Sunday's dinner, dipped in condensed milk.

The Dearings were one of the wealthier families in our street, often referred to as 'Big Pots'. Anyone with wealth was regarded as 'Big Pots'. They had a nicer furnished home, the children were better dressed. They had two red Chow dogs with purple tongues, which were forever in and out of their mouths, dripping wet saliva. We firmly believed that if you were bitten by one of the Chows with their purple tongues, they would poison you. So in our ignorance we kept clear of those dogs if we could! Their youngest boy, Ernie, and his older sister, Betty, would at times invite us to play in a small building at the back of their home that stank of the dog's droppings. It had a small stage where we would hold a concert of sorts but would never have given us entry into The Royal Academy of Dramatic Art!

On Sunday mornings it was commonplace to see pony and traps out, as it was a Sunday pastime for those who could afford it. You would be walking along, and suddenly that familiar sound would get nearer and nearer, the clip, clip, clopping at a very fast pace until they were alongside you. The ponies were beautifully groomed, the driver dressed up in his Sunday best with his whip in hand, with the trap gleaming; they were a showpiece, a lot of effort went into preparing pony and trap for their Sunday morning jaunt – you just could not help but admire them!

On Sunday afternoons we made a point of being outside the Dearings' house, as Mr Dearing would arrive home by taxi. A taxi down St Peter's Avenue was a rarity, with the exception of Mr Dearing's Sunday homecomings. He would alight from the vehicle, cigar in his mouth. The smell of a cigar would be associated with wealth, and I loved that smell. If you were lucky enough to be close to him, he would give you a sixpence; we would then buy sweets and share them with the other boys. To be given a whole sixpence was, for us, to be in seventh heaven.

The Hudsons and the Beauvoirs moved into the street shortly before the outbreak of war. They occupied the larger type houses with four or five steps leading up to their entrance doors. In summertime those families would sit out on the steps watching the world go by, something the other residents would never dream of doing. They were a rough and ready lot by comparison, lacking perhaps in social graces, very blunt, calling a spade a spade. On first impressions one would be put off by their appearance, yet they had hearts of gold, and once you got to know them, they would do anything for you. Despite their coarse nature, they were good people. One day, the insurance man called on Mrs Hudson to collect. It was apparent that she was in no position to pay him. Before the poor man had time to get off his bicycle she said 'You can fuck off for a start'! Mrs Hudson's diplomacy was non-existent, she knew no other way to express herself! When there was no money around to feed your family properly, the rudeness and profanities acted as a defence mechanism to ward people off.

The Hudsons were extremely hard-up, with a family of eleven. Their youngest daughter Renee was doing handstands one day with some other girls; they used to do them up against a brick wall. To the dismay of the girls, they saw that poor Renee wasn't wearing any knickers! My Aunt May, on hearing about this, promptly went out and bought the girl a couple of pairs. Renee turned out to be an attractive, eloquent lady; sadly she died of cancer at the age of twenty-seven.

Approaching September, the exodus of thousands of East End families would begin, making for the Kentish hop fields. Some of the families in our street, who were no exception, would travel with their babies in arms. The hop picking season lasted three weeks. 'Hopping', referred to as *'opping,* meant that lorries were hired to collect their essential family possessions, piled high with their mattresses, pots and pans and all the other necessities required for the season. It was their form of a holiday, albeit a working one, to get away from the rent collector, insurance man and any other person who might make payment demands on them, to be far away from the East End, far away from the everyday struggle for survival. Many of these families would write to the same farmer every year so that they could return to familiar surroundings. The quarters they stayed in were quite ramshackle, austere and basic, but come the end of the day when work was done, they would enjoy a sing-song and booze-up, joining other families whom they had befriended during the hopping season. They would return to the East End looking rosy-cheeked and healthier from Kent's fresh air. It was not too long before the pallor of the East End returned.

If you wanted one of your playmates to come out and play, you would go to their front door, 'holler' through the keyhole shouting 'Door, door, coming out, coming out'. If they were finishing their meal you would be asked to come in and sit in the passage until they were ready. Many times if it was raining, we would sit in the passage of one of the homes with a pack of cards, playing snap until it had stopped. I was never allowed to have boys in our home who played cards, they were considered bad luck.

There were six of us boys who were always together. I would not describe ourselves as a gang, we never thought of it as such. We were all born in the same year, went around together, left school together, and stayed together right up until our teenage years when our tastes and interests began to diversify. Horace Andrews, 'Orrie always appointed himself as the organizer, even writing and producing school plays that we participated in. When I think of the names of those boys now, I wonder what became of them; Jimmy Arrowsmith, his younger brother Peter, Ernie Gardener, Johnny Kendall, Horace Andrews and Peter Ward. I always remember young Peter Arrowsmith accompanying us to the cinema. If anything of a scary nature was shown on the screen, he would lower his head behind the seat in front of him so he couldn't see! We would have to tell him what was going on, amplifying the frightening scenes to make him even more scared. I guess we were just plain shockers!

Further up the street lived Gladys Sampson. She was a tall, gangly girl who always looked like she had just crawled out of bed, and had a Terry Thomas gap in her front teeth, while her hair was hardly ever groomed. Gladys in her younger years was 'boy hungry' and when she became older, 'man hungry'. At school, she sent 'Orrie Andrews a three penny piece to go out with him. I never discovered whether 'Orrie returned that three penny piece, or kept it. One thing for sure, he most certainly never went out with her! Like many girls in the East End, going 'Up West' at the tail-end of the war in pursuit of Yanks was an attractive venture. Gladys was no exception. At weekends, she would paint her face heavily with make up, lips thick with lipstick. She would board a bus in Hackney Road and head for the West End of London. The American GI's had far more money to spend on the girls than us. They would buy them gifts such as silk stockings that they hadn't seen for years.

Street games were played in a regular seasonal pattern. It often puzzled me how one game that lasted for a few weeks would suddenly be succeeded by another without anyone organising the change, they just happened to follow on, one after the other. There would be the whip and top, marbles or 'glarnies' which we carried in little cloth bags, those beautiful pieces of glass coming in every colour of the rainbow, some with coloured streaks running through, and we would roll them along the gutter in the road. The larger ones, 'glarnies', were used as a prize; that is, if you could hit it, it was yours. Those missing the target would be retained by the owner.

We also played yo-yo's and hoop-la. If you didn't have a wooden hoop, a bicycle wheel with the spokes removed, with just the metal rim, served as your hoop. Hop-scotch was chalked out in the road, as were tin can copper, knocking down ginger, roller skating, ball games, cricket, with the wickets chalked up on a brick wall.

When skipping we would sing:

> Rosy apple, lemonade, tart
> Tell me the name of your sweetheart.

You would then proceed through the letters of the alphabet, and if you caught the rope on a given initial, that would be the letter your sweethearts name began with.

The other skipping song was:

> Salt, mustard, vinegar, pepper.

If you were bouncing a ball the song was:

> One, two, three a lairy
> My balls gone down the airy
> Don't forget to give it to Mary
> One, two, three a lairy.

The 'airy' referred to the exterior basement area of the larger houses in our street, and was an opening beneath pavement level covered over by an iron grill; adjoining the airy was the coal chute. There were heavy circular iron patterned plates set into the pavement, to be raised by the coalman when delivering his coal by horse and cart. He wore a leather type hat, the back of which reached almost halfway down his spine, to protect him from the coal dust.

Aunt May, who lived at No. 2, had her coal delivered by the coalman who lifted the iron plate directly into the basement area. Our coal would be carried through the house and the sacks emptied into the coal cupboard under the stairs. Each time the coalman from Lebon's of Dalston would visit, he would receive a 'coating' (telling off) from our Grandmother She was always complaining about the size of the pieces of coal, and that she was only getting sacks of coal dust. On most occasions the lumps of coal were too large to be placed on the fire – you would invariably have to smash them with the poker to fit into the fire grate. I think those poor coalmen dreaded delivering to our house!

Boys or their fathers made scooters, the front board having coloured-metal bottle caps attached, displaying your lucky number or the number of your house; some scooters would even have side carts. We would scooter to Victoria Park and the Hackney Marshes, a considerable distance from Bethnal Green, stopping off sometimes at my nan's home in Clapton. She would give my friends and I tea in the garden. I loved her poppy seed crusty bread, the butter spread on the bread like a ploughed field in miniature, made by the marks from the blade of her serrated bread knife. Hand carts were made from an old pram chassis. We would make our own swings from the plaited straw rope that bananas were tied in, and discarded by greengrocer stallholders in Bethnal Green Road. The rope was tied to both sides of the crossbar of a street lamp, forming a loop that you could sit on or whirl yourself around by using your feet. Our favourite lamppost was outside Mrs Smith's house on the corner of Nelson Gardens. She would come out and tell us

Aunt May with Uncle Alf and our Grandparents at No. 74.

to 'sling your bleeding hook' – her polite way of telling us to go! I guess we must have been a source of annoyance in our over exuberance at play. We would stand at the top of Hackney Road by the tram stop asking the alighting passenger for their cigarette cards. At the time, every cigarette manufacturer would have a series of picture cards inserted in the packets. Some of these cards were quite beautiful, ranging from warships, military regiments, famous film stars, and flowers etc; little did we know that many years later they would become quite valuable. We would stick the cards into albums or use them in the school playground to flick down a card held upright, usually a rarer one that you did not have from a set you might be collecting. We would also collect the silver paper from any empty cigarette packet, wrap the paper around our index finger and form the silver foil into the shape of an egg cup. We would wet the base of the cup with our spittle and throw them up to the ceiling; sometimes they stuck, other times they did not! It did however give us a sense of achievement to see your little silver cup on the ceiling!

We would also collect bus tickets, and each denomination would be of a different colour. Bus conductors wore a peaked cap and uniform, a leather bag at their side for change, a small handheld wooden rack that would hold the bus tickets which ranged from white, blue, red, pink and green. The conductors would come down the aisle of the bus shouting 'Fares please!'. Many were natural born comedians and put people in a cheerful mood on their way to work, with others a little more serious. Bus inspectors hopped on and off the busses regularly checking for anyone trying to dodge a fare.

On some Sundays we boys would take a return journey by tram to the Kingsway Subway in Holborn. The shake, the rattle and the roll of those trams, especially if you happened to be sitting at the top, added to our delight; the highlight of the day was entering the subway in semi-darkness. To us, it was a thrilling day out.

Those of us who had roller skates would skate down Blythe Street, known to us as 'Jews Alley', as practically all the residents there were Jewish, using the houses not only for living in, but also for garment manufacturing. We liked skating there as the street had a smooth asphalt surface that made it a pleasure. On many an occasion some of the Jewish residents would ask us to light their fires, or turn their lights off on a Friday evening, their Sabbath or 'Shobbas' as it was known to them.

Our purchased weapons were either a catapult or a peashooter. The catapults were used on targets like tin cans or old deserted factory windows. Peashooters were used among ourselves, our missiles were brown lentils bought from Gunn's the Chandlers and Corn Merchants in Bethnal Green Road. We never did wanton damage or vandalized anyone's property. Law and order was held in high esteem, our misdemeanours and antics were minimal, and we also had a great respect for our elders, and never thought otherwise.

Crime in our street was non-existent. Some people would have their house key tied onto string that made it accessible by putting your hand through the letter box, pulling the string to reach for the key to let yourself in. Burglary of houses was unknown. There was nothing in the homes worth taking!

Muggings and rapes were also unheard of. The East End, to walk around at night, was secure, and never at any time did you feel threatened or unsafe. The East End villains would target Mayfair, St John's Wood, Kensington, all the wealthier boroughs to carry out their burglaries. If they happened to get caught, they accepted it with good grace saying 'Fair cop guvnor'. The only thing criminals really feared was 'the cat' (cat-o'-nine-tails) and the younger ones 'the birch'. Sentences and punishments were so much harsher then.

In the colder months we would play games in each other's homes. Black man's dark scenery was a game where we hid under a pile of coats and had to guess who was beneath it. There were doctors and nurses, mothers and fathers, when we would explore each other's anatomy, usually the nether regions which held more interest than other parts of the body! The girls were just as inquisitive as the boys. It was a natural innocent curiosity which made a boy want to see what the girl's private parts looked like and the girls wanted to see what the boy's willy looked like. The very word 'sex', or any thought of such, was never heard or thought of. We never even knew where babies came from!

We used to play our cricket and tin can copper in Nelson Gardens alongside St Peter's Church, the bottom half being a cul-de-sac. We called this area Le Bealing; funny name, we never knew where it came from, but I suspect that it was the name of a previous cabinet maker at one time. The existing cabinet maker's factory would have the smell of menthylated spirits and polishes that hit you if the factory doors happened to be open. In the morning and afternoon breaks, a tea boy would emerge, usually an apprentice, with several tea cans hooked up on a broomstick by their wire handles, dirtied and stained with polish from the constant handling to get filled up from Harry Orsi's Café in Bempton Street facing the church. He would return later with the steam rising from the cans of piping hot tea, the broomstick perched firmly on his shoulder, a package of cheese and ham rolls wrapped under his arm. In the afternoons the package would be cakes. Cabinet makers, French polishers and upholsterers were the main forms of industry around Bethnal Green.

Adjoining the cabinet makers was an area sectioned off by a brick wall with broken glass at the top to prevent anyone climbing over. We really believed that a witch lived behind that wall! Occasionally, when we were playing, we would hear an old woman's voice shouting at us to 'clear off', and we ran to escape her in fear of her casting of a spell on us.

This same area was reserved for Bonfire Night. There was a large circular inspection plate in the middle of the road which I think must have been an entrance to a sewer. It served as a base for our bonfires. We made our 'Guys' from any old clothing stuffed out with newspaper, a papier mâché mask placed across the head with an old hat perched on top. The Guy would be put in a pram and wheeled around the streets, asking for a penny for the Guy. Later in the day the Guy would be placed in Hackney Road by the tram stop, so that we could stop returning workers alighting from the trams and persuade them to part with a penny! The pennies we collected would buy our fireworks. The guy would always be placed on top of the bonfire for burning.

There was a fellow we all called Tucker, and we never knew where he lived, only that he was related to a couple of families in the street. Tucker was always dressed in a black suit, with a black flat cap we called a 'cheese cutter' tilted to one side of his ginger head, his complexion was always as white as a sheet, while his lips had a slight tinge of blue; I suspect he must have had a rheumatic heart and that he was somewhat retarded. Tucker would nominate himself to be in charge of the bonfire; he seemed to be able to acquire more wood than anyone else for the fire. One bonfire night Tucker came with a box full of Beecham's Pills, I think he must have pinched them and he handed them out to all of us kids. We thought they were sweets and swallowed several of those little pills. Lo and behold, we were in and out of the toilet a few hours later, and some never quite made it in time! Tucker was out of favour with our mothers for many months. I, in my innocence, did something very similar not long afterwards when I bought a packet of ex-lax thinking it was chocolate, and gave our little team of boys each a piece before we went off to the cinema. It was not too long after the performance began that there was a mad dash to the toilet – almost in unison! There was another character around the same time as Tucker known as Nugget; we didn't know his real name. His mouth was permanently open which exposed the only tooth he had in his head, heavily stained from smoking. It resembled a fang if anything, and like Tucker he was a little retarded. His appearance was off-putting and a little frightening to some of us, although he meant well and was always trying to be friendly and give us things, things that we believed he had removed from an unsuspecting proprietor of the local shops. We were just too young to understand that he was simply just trying to be kind and that he was lonely.

Bonfires were piled quite high with old furniture and anything inflammable that we could lay our hands on. We would place potatoes onto the fire until they were blackened and charred, retrieving them with a stick. We would dance around the fire like Red Indians with flaming pieces of wood. On one occasion my ear got burnt quite badly – my Grandmother took me to school the following morning and remonstrated with one of the teachers. What on earth this had to do with the school, I could never quite fathom, but that was my Grandmother!

Comics were regularly exchanged, from the *Film Fun* to the *Dandy* and *Beano*. There were cartoon characters like 'Desperate Dan' with a gargantuan appetite, usually finishing up with a 'cow pie' with horns sticking out of the pastry. Dear Keyhole Kate was always peeking into keyholes, never minding her own business. The *Film Fun* had comic strips with Laurel and Hardy. I used to imitate Laurel crying at the kitchen door. Arthur Askey and other stars of the day would also be depicted in cartoon form. As we became older, the more juvenile comics were discarded and we would read *The Hotspur, The Wizard* or *The Champion* with short stories of Sexton Blake, Tailspin Tommie and many others of characters long forgotten. Stories of rockets to the moon and outer space were beyond our comprehension, and to believe that by 1969 a landing on the moon would become a reality was unimaginable!

The cinema was a great escape from the poverty around us. To see Fred Astaire and Ginger Rogers, Busby Berkeley's kaleidoscopic dance routines, the sophistication, the glamour, the debonair men in white tie and tails, Nelson Eddy and Jeanette McDonald in *Rose Marie, New Moon, Rosalie, Girl of the Golden West* and many other films took you a million miles away from the East End as you sat there transfixed by the silver screen. We loved Eddie Cantor in *Roman Scandals*, the Marx Brothers, Shirley Temple, Our Gang, Freddie Bartholomew and a little boy singer called Bobby Breen who sang '*There's a rainbow on the river*'. On one occasion I befriended a boy in Dalston who showed me how to bunk in. I accompanied him feeling very nervous by what I had done as we found seats and sat there on needles and pins throughout the whole performance of *The Firefly* with Allan Jones and Jeanette McDonald. Allan Jones sang 'Donkey Serenade'. How I loved his voice and that song!

We had several cinemas around us that we frequented. The Odeon and the Grand Central in Hackney Road, the Standard in Goldsmiths Row, the Excelsior in Mansford Street and Smarts in Bethnal Green Road, which used to have wooden benches until it changed its name and became the Rex, The Foresters and the Museum in Cambridge Heath Road, The Regal, the Empress and Hackney Pavilion in Mare Street. It was not uncommon to have a film break down, and if ever this happened the audience would whistle, yell and shout at the projection box; the longer it took to repair the film, the louder the noise became, until the film resumed playing. Cinema attendants were dressed either in maroon, blue or green livery with gold aiguillettes worn from the shoulder and peaked caps with the name of the cinema embroidered with a descript motif on the front of the cap. They would line up the patrons in queues according to the price you were paying. A chromium stand would display 'Standing Room only in the one and nines' (1/9*d*). They would yell 'Full up in the nine pennies (9*d*), no more seats', carrying their torches like a Field Marshal's baton. There were times when one of us would get a bash over the head from a torch for 'bunking' into the cinema. At the Grand Central there was an iron bar missing from the gent's small toilet window that we were able to crawl through. The other method we used was to get wire from the orange crates from the greengrocer stalls in Bethnal Green Road; a hook was made with the wire and passed through the fire screen doors; the hook registered onto the crash bars, pulled the bar down and released the door. What an ingenious lot we were when money was hard to come by!

The Odeon Cinema in Hackney Road was the last cinema to be built in our locality; it was the most luxurious cinema around, with the plumpest upholstered seats ever with padded arms, so beautiful and comfortable to sit on, and thick carpeted aisles that felt like walking on air! It was our very first taste of anything luxurious. The other cinemas by comparison were 'bug 'oles'. The earliest films I recall seeing there were *The Count of Monte Cristo* with Robert Donat and *The Adventures of Marco Polo* starring Gary Cooper. The Odeon became my favorite; it was a little bit of heaven just to sit there. The Regal was next in line for a better class cinema. At intermissions an illuminated electric organ would rise up from the ground before the screen, colours flashing from the organ and changing as the music was being played. At times songs were displayed on the screen and the audience would join in singing.

Outside the Grand Central in St Peter's Avenue, a vendor was based at the curbside selling Percy Dalton's Famous Roasted Peanuts from a wheelbarrow. If you went in the cinema on the second or third performance, you walked almost knee-deep in peanut shells, empty ice cream tubs, cigarette packets, with sweet and chocolate wrappings around your feet, the air thick with cigarette smoke, so thick that an attendant would come around with a spray gun and spray over the audience a cheap perfumed vapour.

The performances then were greater value for money, giving far better entertainment than today for an evening out. You had the 'A' Feature film, the 'B' Feature film, a comedy 'short' of either Three Stooges, Charlie Chase, Andy Clyde or other comedy 'shorts'. The Movietone News or Gaumont News came next – the narrators of the newsreels with their clipped, cut-glass accents, and then the trailers of forthcoming attractions. The actors and actresses were shown before the commencement of the film, giving the names of the roles that they were playing; even the secondary players equally known to us were displayed in this fashion. Quite apart from the stars, you knew every supporting player in the film. Zazu Pitts, Nancy Kelly, Guy Kibbee, Eric Blore, Edward Everett Horton, Hugh Herbert, James Gleason, Frank McHugh, the names went on and on, great character actors. At the end of every performance the national anthem was played, and people would rise up from their seats and stand to attention for the duration.

Our Grandmother would sometimes take us to an afternoon performance, either to the Hackney Central, the Excelsior or the Rex. The Rex was formerly known as Smart's, where one would sit down on wooden benches. She would take a shopping bag that contained an alarm clock, a bottle of cocoa and some biscuits. The alarm clock would be set in case she dropped off to sleep. This occurred on several occasions when we were sitting with her. The rest of the audience never appreciated the clock's alarm bells sounding off in the middle of a film!

On Saturdays, having made some pocket money, we would go to the Standard in Goldsmith Row. We called it the 'Two Penny Rush', pronounced *tuppeny rush*. The Standard was very much 'a bug 'ole' as well, although as youngsters, we didn't really care. The seats were wafer thin, upholstered in rexine (imitation leather) with brass studs, so if you sat long enough your behind began to ache, shifting the cheeks one side to the other. To enter the auditorium was like bedlam; between 200 and 300 kids yelling and shouting at each other before the performance commenced! Our favourites were the serials of Flash Gordon battling against Emperor Ming, *The Adventures of Rin Tin Tin* the wonder dog, and of course, the cowboy films. Cowboys, like Tom Mix, Ken Maynard, Tim Tyler, Buck Jones, and Hopalong Cassidy. Comedies would also be shown like the Three Stooges, Andy Clyde, and Wheeler & Wolseley. We would vacate the cinema feeling like cowboys, pretending we had horses, holding out our arms as though we were holding reins and instead of walking, we would trot, making horse noises! At other times we would emulate some of the antics of the Three Stooges. Whoever had an impact on us at the time, we would invariably copy. Opposite the Standard was a fishmonger, selling wet fish and ready-cooked cold fish. If we had a penny or two to spare, we would buy a piece of cold fried fish and devour it in minutes.

Watching those cowboy films did have some influence on us; we regularly played cowboys and Indians. We had toy cap guns that were quite heavy, made from a cast metal. In those films you would often see a cowboy hitting another over the head with the butt of the gun. One day, I re-enacted this scene on a boy I was playing with, landing the butt of my gun on his head which immediately streamed with blood. He ran home. His elder brother came out and chased me through the streets, but never caught me and fortunately for me the matter did die down. That boy, Eddy Woollard, became an Amateur Heavyweight Boxing Champion.

The postmen in those days wore a hat more like a helmet, somewhat Germanic in style. Our regular postman had a large carbuncle on the back of his neck which made you feel as though you wanted to stick a pin in it, and make it disappear. Postal deliveries were prompt and efficient, and occasionally a telegram boy would appear down the street on his bicycle, wearing a pill-box hat held by a chin strap, a belt strapped diagonally across his upper torso holding a shiny patent rectangular pouch where the telegrams were kept. An official armband was worn on his sleeve displaying the Royal Mail crown. Usually they would be cycling to their next telegram delivery, whistling away, full of the joys of spring.

In the evenings the lamplighter would appear on a bicycle, his long pole perched over his shoulder. He would hook up the metal arm of the lamppost, gently raising it until the gas mantle was at full glow. Come daylight, he would repeat his rounds to turn the gas lights almost off. The cat's meat man would also deliver by bicycle, a large basket affixed to the front beneath the handlebars, piled high with sliced horsemeat, newspaper wrapped, and if you were not at home, he would leave the cat's meat under your knocker, or wedged in your letter box. Our cat's meat man was the brother of my Grandfather's best friend. He had rather a vacuous looking face, gold-rimmed glasses with tiny lenses, and an 'old bill' moustache. My aunts dubbed him Clark Gable and he was known as this by all the family, never as the cat's meat man.

Running behind horses and carts was a favorite pastime, the preference of these being Charrington's the brewers' dray horses and carts, towing a cart loaded with beer barrels at a very slow pace. We used to perch ourselves underneath the cart on the ladders, used for rolling the barrels down into the cellars of a pub. These ladders were secured by chains, and the motion of swinging side to side and the plodding of the horses made it a lovely illicit little ride.

In the summer time we would watch Carlo Gatti's, the ice makers at the foot of the canal bridge in Queensbridge Road, sending huge blocks of ice cascading down the chutes from the factory onto the carts. Carlo Gatti's horse and cart drivers were big, dark-skinned, muscular Italian men, mostly wearing a Garibaldi moustache, who tossed the ice blocks around with their huge ice tongs as if they were cubes of sugar. They hoisted them up on to their shoulders protected only by sacking to prevent water from the ice dripping on to them, and stacked the blocks until the carts were fully laden. Carlo Gatti's carts were unmistakable, painted in bright canary yellow and black. We loved to hitch a ride in the summer time and purloin some of the ice that had broken away from the large ice blocks that were being delivered to cafés and restaurants. If we managed to filch a piece, we would suck on it until it was small enough to place in the mouth.

Occasionally, if you were seen clambering on to the back of their cart trying to remove some ice, the driver would think nothing of raising his whip and lashing out at you. If you were seen running behind a horse and cart, someone always seemed to be there to shout out 'Look behind you 'guvnor – never pronounced governor. Fortunately throughout my days of running after horse and carts, I never received a whip lash or any other form of injury! Motorization had not reached its peak, and the horse and cart was still very much in vogue.

The horses' droppings left lying in the road were never there for long before a bucket and shovel would emerge from one of the houses, whereupon it was scooped up for garden manure. My Grandfather made a point of being alert whenever a horse appeared on the street to be ready to shovel up the horse's poop; if you heard a clip clop, you would be out of the house immediately! Some people would go around the streets gathering up the horse manure and selling it.

Our Grandfather's garden was his pride and joy. Many others down the street preferred keeping chickens outside instead of a garden to provide them with fresh eggs, and from time to time a chicken dinner; the poor chicken would be dispatched when her laying days were over. Some even kept rabbits for the same purpose, not only as pets but as a source of food. Mrs Baldwin next door kept chickens; she had no garden but managed to grow a few large sunflowers looking over the wall into our garden. To me those flowers always looked hideous; they were ugly and really not attractive at all. The rest of her space was just a dismal area of black soil where her chickens would be clucking away and pecking into it. Mrs Baldwin always looked very stern. She was a large women always dressed in black, her hair plastered back into a bun with a centre parting, a woman of very Germanic appearance who found great difficulty in raising a smile – in fact I cannot ever recall seeing her smile at all. Grandmother and Mrs Baldwin were never exactly neighbourly.

Mrs Hudson kept her chickens in the 'airey' (small outdoor space adjoining the house at basement level), a most unusual place to keep chickens! In the hot weather Mrs Hudson could be seen through her iron grating, chickens running around her, fag in her mouth, feet in a bowl of water, peeling potatoes and placing the potatoes in another bowl beside her.

Summers seemed hotter then. We boys would sit by the roadside well away from the drains where pink disinfectant powder had been placed by dustmen who came along in their horse and carts. It was believed that if we played near the drains you would catch scarlet fever. We dug up the melting tar from the tar blocks that made up the road, a weird pastime that fascinated us! Sitting there plunging a matchstick into the tar and lifting it from its blocks, removing it and shaping the tar into little balls. My Mother had just bought me a pair of white flannel trousers – I could not think of a better time to wear them. I came home with my trousers covered in tar and she went absolutely ballistic! As a summer drink, Grandmother would give us R. White's Cream Soda with milk; I guess it must have been a poor man's milkshake, although in those days we had never heard of them. If we were lucky we would have a vanilla ice cream placed in a glass of cream soda. This, to us, was a summer drink above all other summer drinks. Ginger beer came in two-tone stone bottles; these were used as hot water bottles in the winter.

There was a small road linking St Peter's Avenue to Warner Place named Bempton Street. It had a café there whose proprietor was Harry Orsi; we pronounced it ''Arry Orseye'. Harry was Italian and had once been a chef at one of London's leading hotels. His café had been a motor repair shop that was converted into an eating establishment. He was overweight and limped quite badly. He had a permanent ulcerated leg problem, the leg swathed in bandages, which at times worked loose and trailed around his feet, of which he seemed completely unaware. I suspect that he must have been diabetic, but in those days people didn't know about such maladies. At the weekends he would make the most fantastic ice cream ever and sell it from the front room window of his home in Nelson Gardens.

His café, like many others in London, had a large chromium tea urn on the main counter, and the lower counter displayed large plates of cakes, cheese rolls, ham rolls, Doubleday's meat pies and many other edibles on show to tempt the palate. He served a hot meal at lunchtime which attracted many lorry drivers who could park unseen from the main road. One particular cake he served was what we at that time called a 'cheesecake', although it never had the taste of or resembled a cheesecake in the slightest; a round pastry tartlet with a plain sweet filling, icing over the top with shredded coconut embedded into the icing. That man also cooked the best egg and chips in London! It was to be the bane of my Mother's life, since I often ordered his egg and chips, telling dear Harry that my Mother would pay – she did, of course, always settle up with him; she seldom scolded me for my audacity. I do reiterate even to this day they were, without question, the best egg and chips I ever tasted! His chips were thick cut and unsurpassed in flavour! A bottle of Tizer (red-coloured fizzy drink) to accompany the meal was, to me, like nectar of the gods.

As a source of earning a copper or two, we would run errands for some of the neighbours; we would canvas by knocking at doors crying 'any errands, any errands?' Invariably it would be a 'no' but sometimes you would strike lucky and have an errand to run. This gave us money to buy sweets from Belsham's on the corner of Warner Place and Bempton Street. Old Mr Belsham reminded me of the 'Old Bill' character from the First World War. He had a greying walrus moustache, was rather corpulent, and always wore a heavy black cardigan and a flat cap that he never removed! Depending on how much money we earned, we would buy a sherbet dip: yellow lemonade crystals that we sometimes watered down to make lemonade, but mostly we wet our fingers and dipped them straight in to the crystals to suck on. There were acid or pear drops, bull's eyes, jelly babies, liquorices sticks we called 'Spanish' and every other confection that might take your fancy. He would blow into a small white paper bag to make an opening to pour the sweets into from his weighing scoop. If we could not afford the sweets we would buy loose mustard pickle, served up from a large stone jar, and placed in newspaper or desiccated coconut.

In Old Bethnal Green Road in a small terraced house we knew as 'Silk's where we would buy homemade toffee apples. Their front room window was used as a shop window, and apart from toffee apples and bundles of firewood, I don't think they sold anything else; it was just another source of income.

Warner Place was situated just west of St Peter's Avenue; it had two public houses, the Baker's Arms and another called 'Moaners', which we never knew by its true name. It was given its name by a one-time publican that was always moaning, and the name stuck! Towards Hackney Road there was a cabinet maker by the name of Spiers. One of his children, Morris, was a playmate of ours. Morris had jet-black wavy hair, a cast in his right eye, and the most unusual laugh; it would have pauses in between the bursts

Old Bethnal Green, changed vastly from its old terraced cottages.

'Pub outing' outside the Bakers Arms, Warner Place, *c.* 1905.

of laughter. His laughter was the oddest I had ever encountered, very low in tone and almost sung! We would play in the yard at the back of his Father's small factory on piles of wood shavings, but unfortunately there was dog's doo-doo amongst the wood shavings which coated my hands on more than one occasion, so I decided not to play there with him anymore.

On an errand one day for a neighbour for a loaf of bread, I went to Wasm's the Bakers in Hackney Road. Arriving at the main thoroughfare, the road was cordoned off; trams were not running, and traffic was at a complete standstill. A very large horse stood in the middle of the main road, with blood pouring from its numerous wounds. The poor thing had bolted and gone straight through the shopfront window of the bakers I was about to visit. I stood there looking at that sorrowful animal; the scene upset me and remained with me for several days. Inquisitive crowds had gathered, watching that poor beast bleed to death. Eventually a couple of men came and led him away into Ion Square and shot him. When the entire furore was over and things were back to normal, I went into the bakers for the loaf; blood was still on the front window display which assistants were scrubbing in an attempt to remove it. From behind the counter an assistant weighed the crusty bloomer loaf, and also give me a square piece of mince. Normally this would have been devoured before I arrived at the recipient's address, but on this particular occasion it was the only time that I had lost my appetite.

At other times to earn money we would scout for wood suitable for firewood. When we had gathered up enough, we would chop it into convenient sized sticks, bundle it up, tie it with string and sell it. We never had any problem selling firewood, transporting it around the streets in an old pram shouting 'firewood'. The local shops couldn't compete with us, we were that much cheaper.

2

OUR PARENTS

They met at Miss Youen's Dance Classes at No. 18 St Thomas's Square in Hackney. Everyone knew it as Mother Youen's, and you got three dance lessons for 2s 6d. Father played clarinet and violin there and helped out with the dancing lessons, as he was very good on the dance floor. It was an age of sophistication and refinement. Father, I believe, modelled himself on a smartly dressed screen actor by the name of Adolphe Menjou, who wore a different suit in practically every scene he played. His work over the years was mainly in hotels, with an occasional stint as a temporary librarian. He was extremely knowledgeable of all the good restaurants and hotels in the West End of London, taking a great interest in food and was indeed, like my Mother, a wonderful cook and a great lover of classical music.

Our parents were married on 6 December 1927 at the Registry Office in Hackney; they resided at the time at No. 33 Balls Pond Road, Hackney. Mother was named Elizabeth Georgina and Father just plain Henry. The family called my Mother 'Niddy'- how she came by that name I will never know. Families seem to give nicknames to their offspring only familiar to themselves. Three children were to follow; Henri was born in 1928, and he died eighteen months later of meningitis. Sister Dawn entered the world in 1929 and I followed the following year.

Looking back on our Mother and Father's relationship, it was not too difficult to understand that they were really not meant for each other. It was hardly a match made in heaven, though it is easy to see how they were attracted to each other. Mother, in her younger days, was a very striking woman, the most attractive of all her siblings. Father was tall, slim, sophisticated, well-read and well-spoken; they married when Father was twenty-two and Mother was twenty-one. Regretfully, neither of them was cut out for parenthood, nor for that matter, wanted the responsibility of having children. They were poles apart both in their outlook and interests and came from two different worlds.

At some stage during Mother's first pregnancy, they moved into our Grandparents' home in St Peter's Street. With Father living in such a cramped and unfriendly environment, he found that conditions, and the relationship with his in-laws, were too much for him to bear and he could take it no longer. One day he just upped and left. It was about this time

Father looking his elegant self.

he met a girl with whom he fell in love, and continued to love throughout his life, and even though she eventually married someone else she remained in his thoughts, and he carried a photograph of her in his wallet until the day he died.

When my Mother heard about his relationship she gave him a verbal onslaught that lasted years; she sought him out at practically every place he worked, not caring in the slightest how she embarrassed him. She loved him, so could not take the rejection kindly. It was to last a lifetime. On the day he left No. 74, a very vivid day in my memory, she ran after him all the way up the street calling him names. I ran behind them crying my eyes out. It was one of the saddest days in my young life.

Growing up without our Father left a great abyss in our lives. Children can be quite cruel and very often we were taunted for having no 'ole man'. For a man to leave the home was considered something alien to the East Ender. It took a long time to reconcile ourselves that our Father was no longer with us. We no longer had his love, his affection, or his guidance.

Mother worked in the West End and the City as a waitress. Sometimes she would come home very late from a wedding or a banquet, bringing with her some of the left over tit-bits from the various functions she attended. This was considered an enormous treat; to have fancy food that we had never seen or tasted before. It was readily and

Mother, aged eighteen.

easily devoured. She gradually acquired additional pieces for the home which included a gramophone. We didn't have much of a selection of records at that time; consequently you would play the same record over and over. My earliest recollections were playing a song called 'Steamboat Bill', and the whistle of the steamboat would sound off several times during the course of the song – I just loved to hear it. Another was 'It looks like rain in Cherry Blossom Lane'. We had another record that used to be played that would depress both my sister and I called 'On we go through the snow'. It depicted prisoners being marched through the snow, eating carrots as they went singing 'On we go through the snow' (we only knew it as a song of this title). It was as though a black cloud had passed over you and left you in a state of despair. Even to this day, if ever we refer to that song, it has the same effect upon my sister and me as when we were children. Mother could play the ukulele and Father often played violin in a professional band. Mother could strum out a tune and sing 'Dinner for one please, James'. Sometimes if he had the money, he would bring us home delicacies such as Jewish Vienna's (sausages), Halva and stem ginger in lovely oriental stone jars.

Father had a peculiar sense of humor. One winter, my sister and I were quite hungry. He raised our small box-room window, collected some snow, and made some snowballs gathered from the window ledge, placed them in a frying pan, and lit the gas stove.

My sister and I stood by in total silence and watched the snowballs turn to water! He thought it was funny, but on reflection I think he was trying to humour us and take our minds off the hunger – there could not have been any money in the house for food.

He befriended a Jewish family, the Silvers, who lived at The Oval leading off Hackney Road. The Silvers were from Russia. Old Mr Silver, who spoke little English, would play Russian and Jewish folk songs on his concertina whenever we visited. We would be offered cake and lemon tea, and sometimes they would entertain us by hanging up a white bed sheet and perform behind it by candlelight, creating silhouettes, although I was too young to understand what they were supposed to be playing. They would have an intermission and drinks. The whole family were quite mad and their antics reminded me of the Marx Brothers. Tony Silver remained a friend of Father's for several years until he became mentally ill and was committed to an asylum. Father visited him once or twice; poor Tony did not recognize his friend and thought my Father was Raymond Navarro, a silent screen film star! One of Tony's other brothers took up the piano at the age of fifty-eight years, and became an accomplished player of classical music.

When Father was living with us, he would take us to see our paternal Grandparents. We called our Grandmother Nanna Sue. They, with our three spinster aunts, lived in Clapton. Clapton was then a lovely district; it was considered quite posh by Bethnal Green standards. I loved going there! They lived in Ashenden Road, where each house had a bay window and a walled or iron railed front garden. In summer, residents would leave their front doors wide open to allow cool fresh air to enter, covered only by a canvas door awning. When he took my sister and I, it was never by tram or bus, we walked the whole way. Whether or not he could afford the fare we never knew, but walk we did. Their house was a pleasure to visit, with the smell of lavender and furniture polish everywhere, a far cry from our home in Bethnal Green. They would allow me upstairs to play in a room that housed all their stock reserved for selling on their stall in Chatsworth Road. I always made a beeline for a large box that contained buckles and buttons in various colours, shapes and sizes that kept me amused for hours on end.

Mother was a complex character. She would make an effort to appear sophisticated and put on the 'accent' if she thought it was required. Strangely enough, all of her sisters – with the exception of Marie – did the same thing! Her accent could change from a gentle 'Gor blimey' to Mayfair at the drop of a hat! She took great pains with her appearance and was always smartly dressed whenever she went out. One great asset to her character was that she was a hard worker. This was a family trait, and no one in our Grandparents' household was allowed to be idle.

One Sunday morning, shopping in Brick Lane, she met a neighbour and they started chatting. During the course of the conversation, the subject of bad language was brought up. Mother was telling the neighbour how much she detested its use just as a dog leapt up at her. She immediately shouted 'Get down you bastard!'. Nothing could more aptly summarise or be more descriptive of our Mother than that incident!

Our paternal Grandparents were kind, gentle, conservative people and our three spinster aunts, Lil, Joan and Enid were very well-read. All the family were great readers and even at our young age, they would introduce us to books to read, as indeed our

Nanna Sue with Grandfather, 'Little Harry', in their garden in Clapton.

Father did. Enid, the youngest, was the fun one – a little bohemian, extremely artistic, a great mimic, and she made the most beautiful dolls.

It was interesting to hear that later on our aunts embarked on a family search and discovered that we were Huguenots – long before genealogy became popular. My great-Grandfather was a naturalist and before him they were all gentlemen, going back to 1645. Our Father was to end his days at the Huguenots Apartments and French Hospital in Rochester, Kent.

Huguenots can be traced from 1689 when they settled in the East End of London around Spital Square. They made an enormous contribution to the economy from their expertise as silk weavers, watchmakers, silversmiths and financiers. By 1700 there were nine French churches in the East End. The first was built in Threadneedle Street and the other at the Savoy. One of the churches in Brick Lane became a synagogue when the Jewish people lived in the area; it has now become a mosque. The very fine architecture of the houses built by the Huguenots still stand in and around Spitalfields. They arouse a great deal of interest amongst visitors to the area.

One day Nan took us to Chalkwell on the Essex coast. It was the very first time we had ever seen the sea or the seaside. Having never seen it before, we were both captivated and enthralled; it was like being transported to a magic land! The sun was shining, the skies were blue and we saw a beautiful expanse of sea! Nan bought us buckets and spades, we built sandcastles, paddled in the sea and chewed and sucked on a stick of rock. We ate sandwiches she had brought from home, while she sat back in a deckchair reading,

Our paternal Grandparents with Aunt Joan.

Aunt Lil, Father's
eldest sister.

Father's youngest sister
'Enid', my favourite aunt.

Chatsworth Road, Clapton. Our Grandfather had a hosiery stall there.

occasionally dropping the book into her lap and looking out to sea. She was so quiet and reserved, unlike our maternal Grandmother in Bethnal Green. That day was so wonderful, we never wanted it to end, and we never wanted to return home.

We called our paternal Grandfather 'Little Harry'; our Father was 'Big Harry'. Little Harry had a hosiery stall in Chatsworth Road which my Father sometimes looked after. Next to the Castle Cinema in Chatsworth Road was a café – well, it was really what we termed 'Dining Rooms'; each table was sectioned off by a wooden partition. When Father wasn't working the stall, he would have his break there, playing dominoes with some of his associates. He won at dominoes so many times his friends dubbed him 'Harry the fox'. He would buy me a college pudding and custard. I loved those puddings! It was always something to look forward to when going to visit him in Chatsworth Road.

In 1938, Mother opened a café in the Haggerston area, in a small lock-up shop in Scriven Street that ran from Queensbridge Road into Haggerston Road. I must have been her most frequent visitor! She was an excellent cook and it was not long before she established a regular clientele. I would help out either washing up or sometimes running errands when I was not at school. She had a helper from time to time, an elderly lady we called Emma, who was able to tell fortunes from tea leaves left in a tea cup. One rainy afternoon when the café was quite full, I was sitting with Emma and my Mother asked her to tell my fortune. Gazing into the tea cup I had drained, she proceeded to tell me that I would see more countries than anyone sitting there. In time, Mother decided to move to much larger premises in Haggerston Road. It had accommodation above the shop with much better facilities.

Ashamedly, one day I removed a two shilling piece from her till, and placed it in the cigarette machine for a packet of 'Craven A' cigarettes. Together with my play friends we went down an alley and smoked some of them. I became quite giddy, began to vomit and felt dreadful! I knew that I had been punished for removing that two shilling piece!

By this time, she had extended her working hours by opening up on Sundays, selling seafood outside the premises. The seafood came up by train, fresh from Leigh-on-Sea to Fenchurch Street Station. Mother may have been lacking in many things, but she was never work-shy.

By then, I was spending more time in Haggerston than in Bethnal Green. One day, I ventured into Ridley Road Market in Dalston. Ridley Road then was predominantly a Jewish Market. Jack Solomons, the fight promoter, had a fishmongers there. Barrels of pickled herring were at practically every shop and stall you passed. The Boobas and Yentas (grandmothers and talkative women) there would be haggling over the price of fish and kosher chickens, giving the chickens an inspection more thoroughly than guardsmen on parade would ever hope to receive! Yiddish was spoken more than our own tongue. This was Ridley Road. It was not uncommon for some of the local boys to pinch florins and half crowns from the open wooden tills on the stalls; one immediately recognized what a boy was up to when you saw him racing through the crowds, away from a stallholder that he had just taken money from.

In the market I once saw a huge crowd of people dressed in black shirts, with armbands bearing two streaks of lightning, which I later learnt was the party emblem. Shortly there was a huge roar from the crowd and arms were raised in a 'Seig Heil' Nazi-style salute. It was then that I saw Sir Oswald Moseley. He was standing high in an open car, returning the hordes' salute. His followers were going wild at seeing him, the frenzy and adulation gradually dying down when the car came to a halt and he prepared to speak. The whole scene was as daunting as it was awesome. I stood watching this man, not really understanding what he had to say, but carried away by the whole spectacle. I was not around that long to see if any fights and scuffles took place. It was well-known that these meetings, which were so well publicized by the newspapers, sparked off battles between the Blackshirts, and the Communist Party and Jewish organisations. On Saturday evenings after all the stalls had been cleared away, we would go to Kingsland Road to 'The Waste' and sort over the debris from the stalls. When I think of what was thrown away, I realise now it would have made an antique buyer very happy! If one could only have had the foresight then.

Prior to the outbreak of war, Father took us to Lyons Corner House, Coventry Street, in the West End of London. To go 'Up West' was always an exciting adventure. Lyons, or Joe Lyons as they were known, had a string of tea shops throughout London, which were easily recognizable by their white painted shop fronts and gold lettering. Their standards for quality, cleanliness, and affordability were about the best you could get.

We entered the restaurant, found a table, sat down and Father proceeded to order a selection of pastries and tea. They were brought to us by one of the waitresses who were

The author, aged four, in a sailor suit made by Harris's the tailor, Brick Lane. (Photo taken by Freeds Studio, Hackney Road, 24 March 1935)

known then as 'nippies'. They all wore the Lyons uniform of black dress, short white apron and white cap. The waitress placed the tea on the table and the pastries were nicely arranged on a two tier cake stand. Father began to talk to us in earnest, saying, 'You see those pastries, take a good hard look at them before you eat them, because you are not going to see anything like these for a long, long time'. Talking to us so seriously had a profound effect on us. It turned out that he was absolutely correct; we did not see them again until a long time after the war was over. We never forgot his words.

Father came to see us occasionally and gave us treats, taking us to the cinema in Dalston Lane, buying a box of Black Magic chocolates to devour in the course of the performance – he was a chocoholic! We saw Gracie Fields in *Shipyard Sally* – that wonderful soprano voice, as she sang 'Wish me luck as you wave me goodbye'. 'Our Gracie' was loved by the nation, as indeed was another artist at that time, George Formby.

Father would also take us to wonderful places of culture, such as the British Museum, the Science Museum, and the Natural History Museum. Pointing out and explaining things, he gave us a history of the exhibits that we revelled in. And he introduced us to books, arousing our interests in those he recommended that we read. These visits were to cement my lifelong interest in history and the arts.

Unlike our Grandparents in Bethnal Green, our other Grandparents in Clapton had an Anderson Shelter installed in their very long garden. Father had taken me to visit them. While he was in the house, I was left outside playing in the garden. I found a pot of bright blue paint and a brush and decided to paint the front of the shelter; on completion I thought it looked quite nice. When Father and Little Harry came into the garden, Little Harry normally a quiet and reserved man, went absolutely ballistic. An argument ensued between Father and son over my 'artwork'. I couldn't quite make out what all the fuss was about. I really thought that I had done a splendid job. Little Harry obviously thought otherwise!

3

LIFE AT No. 74 ST PETER'S AVENUE

Our address was No. 74 St Peter's Avenue – the house I grew up in. The very mention of the number catapults me back to Bethnal Green, whenever I see or hear it.

At the time of my childhood it housed fourteen of us! Grandfather, Grandmother, my Mother and Father, my sister and I, our uncles Will and Joe, plus their friend Alf Schofield, our aunts May, Lilly, Marie, Eileen and Winnie, and another aunt, called Ethel, whom the family called Noona. How she came by that name was never known to us. Noona left No.

74 when she married a man named George Marshall and went to live in Walthamstow. Marriage for many became a form of escape. It was claimed that our Grandmother had fourteen children in all: two sets of twins and two others who died. Fatalities in childbirth in her day were very high. There would have been five in our immediate family but for the loss of our brother Henri (he died eighteen months before I came into the world).

Records state that I was born in the Bethnal Green Infirmary, 214a Cambridge Heath Road. I never liked the sound of the word 'infirmary'; it has connotations of poverty and debtors prisons. The Bethnal Green Guardians purchased the Cambridge

Grandfather with our Mother in his arms, c. 1906.

Uncle Alf Schofield, drinking chum of 'Old Charlie', the Kray twins' Father. Their local was the Marquis of Cornwallis at the corner of Bethnal Green Road and Vallance Road, home of the Krays.

Heath Road site in order to erect a new infirmary. The site had previously been Bishop Hall Farm but was leased in 1811 by William Sotheby to 'The London Society for promoting Christianity amongst the Jews'. It became known as 'Palestine Place' and schools and houses followed.

The site was purchased by the Guardians in 1895 and the new infirmary built to accommodate 670 patients. The total cost of the land and buildings was £212,895. Many of its furnishings were made by inmates of the Waterloo Road Workhouse in Well Street, Hackney[1]. The Hospital was opened 5 March 1900, and included a Nurses Training School within the administration block. During the wars, the Infirmary was utilised as a military hospital. The hospital closed in 1990, and its staff and patients transferred to the new Bancroft Unit at the Royal London Hospital.

At home all our aunts, with the exception of Aunt Marie, married and gradually departed to live elsewhere with their spouses. Marie joined the Salvation Army in a permanent capacity and moved to various places around the south of England, eventually becoming a Brigadier. On the day my Grandfather learned that she had enrolled in 'The Sally Ann', he went absolutely spare. I had never seen him so enraged. He was brought up a Catholic, and although we never knew him to attend church, he was very rigid in his beliefs. He regarded the Salvation Army as a lot of 'Bible punchers'.

An uneducated man, but as honest as the day was long, his favourite quote was 'Tell the truth and shame the Devil'. His parents had hailed from County Cork during the Potato Famine in Ireland. He possessed a jaundiced mind on matters he never really understood. A Labour Party man through and through, he could never explain why he was a socialist, he just fell in line with the majority. If ever you mentioned conservatism, his feelings and that of many like him were 'what have I got to conserve?'. The general consensus was that the Tory Party was restricted solely to the wealthy. His views on homosexuality were just as bad. In his day, a homosexual was referred to as a 'nancy boy'. 'Put 'em up against a wall and shoot the bleeding lot of 'em' was his philosophy. Homophobia was then an unknown word; he was an East End product of his era.

He once told me that my maternal great-Grandfather, was a master japanner and grainer who, before the First World War, would specialize in painting public houses.

Aunt Marie the Salvationist, who rose to become a Brigadier.

All the masonry and stonework would be japanned and grained to look like wood, either a light oak grain or a mahogany grain, whichever the publican preferred. Work like this would take him approximately three months to complete; it would be painstaking, fine and intricate work. He would be paid in gold sovereigns, then proceed to go on a binge for several weeks, alienating himself from his family! He would go to Smithfield Market to buy a whole belly of pork, bring it home and roast it on a spit over a fire in the basement of the beautiful Georgian house in which they lived, smothering the belly of pork in mustard without removing his bowler hat and eating it alone, away from the family. At the end of his boozy period he would return to work to commence painting another public house.

My earliest recollection at No. 74 was of being in one small back room sleeping on the floor with my Mother, Father and sister. A small gas stove stood in the corner and a small food cupboard sat opposite. The picture becomes a little blurred as to how long we actually lived like that, but when my uncles married off and Alf Schofield married our Aunt May, we finally had a bedroom with our very own beds. Looking back, I still feel a sense of amazement how we ever managed, but manage we did. There was no water facility upstairs. It was carried up both to drink and wash with in an enamelled bowl. Lighting was by gas. Around the wooden disc that gave rigidity to the gas pipe holding the mantle, we would see bed bugs crawling about; small reddish brownish insects about a quarter of an inch long, with oval flattened bodies. They were resilient little buggers that we would squash with our thumbs and once squashed they gave off a sweet odour that I can almost smell to this day. We never knew a household without bugs. The pesticide appliance used then was a hand-compression gun that contained a small round tank of 'Flit'. Flit was a brand name disinfectant that was sprayed on to the affected areas. Trying to eradicate the bugs was a thankless task as they could spread from building to building, room to room, hiding in every crevice; they were the Romanies of the insect world which had little to do with the level of cleanliness.

The hall on the ground floor was never called a hall, it was always referred to as the passage. On either side of the passage before you reached the front room door, hung two pictures framed in light walnut depicting battle scenes from 'The Charge of the Light Brigade'. I would look at these pictures for lengthy periods. They were so animated and colorful, and the uniforms, the swords, lances and sabres would intrigue me. Further down the passage was a horse stand of bamboo and cane, and a mirror in the centre with a cane box beneath it. On the lid of the cane box stood a red china elephant. It had a castle-like structure on its back that would have been used for a tiger shoot had it been life size. That elephant became so embedded in my brain, I found that I started sketching it at every given opportunity. I drew it at school, painted it at school; in fact I became quite adept at drawing and painting elephants. This was a start of a lifelong love affair with drawing, painting and art.

District Nurses were a common sight in the East End, cycling along in their unmistakable navy blue uniforms and navy blue hats. Somehow or other, I contracted worms. The District Nurse called to attend to my malady, coming up the stairs to the bedroom with her bag of medicinal tricks. She pulled out of her bag an enema tube and a bag. She showed me what looked like wood chippings, which I think were Quasha chips. She placed them into a receptacle of boiling water and left them to take effect. Satisfied that the mixture was right, she then proceeded to siphon the liquid up into the rubber enema tube and proceeded to pump it up into my backside. I could feel the warm liquid swishing away inside me. Sitting me rapidly over a bed pan she removed the enema tube, and the liquid gushed out, along with hundreds of little worms wriggling about! It must have been an early method of colonic irrigation. She came for one or two more visits, after which I was free of worms. The District Nurse provided an invaluable service to the East End.

While Mother went out to work, we were left in the care of our Grandmother. Gran as we called her was about the hardest working woman I have ever known. She was no taller than five foot, if that. She had a job in the Strand at Shell-Mex, charring (cleaning the office). She would set off around six o'clock each weekday morning, and some days bring home brown bread rolls and cigarette ends, the largest cigarette ends she could find. Most of the brown rolls were for the widow Mrs Andrew opposite, as she had been left with four children to bring up. There was Teddy, Alfie, Hetty and Horace. Alfie permanently suffered from a red soreness around his eyes, Grandfather always referred to him as the boy with the 'salt beef eyes'. They were so they poor that they couldn't even afford a gas mantle; the bare flame would be the only form of lighting. I used to take the cigarette ends to 'Old Moore', as my Grandmother called him, who lived in Pollards Row, a continuation of our street. He would sit on the steps of his house, break the cigarette ends open, mix up the tobacco and roll them into cigarettes. To all intents and purpose he should have died years before, but he lived well into his nineties. Inhaling all that smoke and bacteria from those dog ends over the years, he defied medical science!

Home from her 'charring' in The Strand, Gran would commence box-making for a company in Hackney Road, The Stanley Box Company. Glue, and the smell of glue on the gas stove, was forever under our nostrils from morning to night. My sister and I would assist her in box-making, cutting the corners out of the cardboard which would cause blisters between our thumbs and index fingers. She would then glue the glossy coloured paper to the boxes. She hated making pen boxes that were small and fiddly. On completion of two gross or more, the boxes were tied up, and we would place them in a

Grandfather and
Grandmother with cousin
Brenda in Oxford Street,
London.

pushcart and take them to the box company to be paid. Payment was paltry, something like a penny farthing for a dozen boxes. Prior to our being paid, the boxes were checked and we were then given a new batch to take home. If what they had given you were awkward or fiddly to assemble, Gran would bemoan you as if you were personally responsible! When she was cooking, you would have the combined smells of glue and food. She also ran a loan club for Phillip's and Scoons in Bethnal Green Road. She washed all the towels used by the teachers at our school. She never had a holiday in her life, apart from days out at Southend, which were very seldom. If she managed a trip there she would be on 'needles and pins' to get back home. In the winter I would see her out in the yard doing the washing, scrubbing away on a washboard submerged in a galvanized bath, her arms red raw from the detergent. The larger clothing items would go to the bag wash. To come home from school and see laundry drying on the fireguard in front of the fire with steam rising up from the wet clothing would set me into a depressed mood. I hated Mondays, and the bad mood it placed me in never lifted until all the washing was put away.

Our Grandmother was an atrocious cook. Perhaps it was the size of her family that never allowed her the time to undertake any really good cooking, or perhaps she was just not interested. I think it was the latter. Sunday lunch, we never called it lunch, it was always dinner, was about her best effort. Normally it would be a joint of beef, pork, lamb or salt beef. Her roasted potatoes were virtually fat free, more like a baked potato, always accompanied by a dish of sliced beetroot and one of freshly grated horseradish, marinated in vinegar. The portions of meat were very sparse. Come Monday, you would have the leftover food from the day before, and if the meat could not stretch to reasonable portions, she would supplement your meal with a chipolata or a sausage. Your meal would be covered by a saucepan lid, chop covers were unheard of, and when you raised it you would find your chipolata embedded in a pile of potato. Fortunately, we always had a bottle of Daddie's Sauce on the table, and the flavour of the sauce was better tasting that the meal itself. At times I used to let my mind take over and really think that I was eating something quite delicious; mind over matter can be a wonderful thing. There would be a stew that the whole family would enhance with Daddie's Sauce, pouring it into the pudding basins and disguising the taste. When you came home the basins would be in the gas oven keeping warm. There must have been nine or ten meals with a crust forming on top of those stews! She would ask you to take one from the oven, and as you commenced eating, you would be told that you had taken the wrong one. I could never understand why, they were all the same size basins!

The remainder of the week it was pies and mash, fish and chips, sausages and mash, or liver and bacon. Gran would make a thick liver sauce from the flour that she coated the liver in for frying and stews. Sometimes we were given soused mackerel that I absolutely loathed and dreaded whenever it was placed on the table. Fridays would be fish and chip days, never cooked at home, and always bought from Little Annie's in Gossett Street. Annie was so short her head hardly came above the marbled top counter that held jars of wallies (pickled cucumbers), pickled onions and pickled red cabbage! Fish was about a penny or 2*d* then, and would nearly always be skate, rock salmon or cod. When we were not getting fish and chips for the family, we would buy a halfpenny worth of cracklings, the batter that dropped off the coated fish. We would put plenty of vinegar on the cracklings and suck the vinegar that passed through the small nuggets of batter at the bottom of the cone-shaped greaseproof paper and newspaper.

I was never given any fish in those days, it would be fried egg, sausage or a couple of rashers of bacon with the fish shop chips. All the perishable food was kept in a cabinet outside in the yard, known to us as a safe. A cabinet with a narrow wooden frame, a lower drawer, and metal mesh panels on three sides of the cabinet, the top covered in an off cut of linoleum to keep it waterproof. The only refrigerators we ever saw were at the cinema. Sometimes in summer, the bacon could be a little high, sausages sour, which we would term as being 'on the bugle', and the cheese a trifle pongy. If there was butter it was always a little rank. Everything was eaten regardless, we were a hungry lot! During the weekdays we never knew breakfast as such, usually a slice of bread was about all you got with a thin layer of margarine we called 'marge'. Butter was an almost unknown commodity, if we had butter which was very rare, it was known in our home as 'best butter'. Looking back I often wonder how we survived and how we never developed any sinister disease from the condition of the food we ate.

Birthdays and birthday parties were never celebrated, in fact, it never crossed our minds. We never saw a birthday cake, nor received a birthday card or present. We just never knew that a birthday was celebrated. Invitations to birthday parties by other boys and girls in the street were non-existent, like ourselves; they never knew they took place either. It was a case of what you never had, you never missed. Our cousin Sheila complained to her Mother, Aunt May, that she never had a birthday cake, and Aunt May promptly made her a marmalade tart and stuck lighted matches around the edges of the pastry, that is if you could call it pastry.

Cousins Sheila and Brenda in Grandmother's arms.

On Saturday mornings we would get a piece of cheddar cheese that had been on a shelf in the safe too long and hardened, and melt it in the coal-fire oven in the kitchen, creating the poor man's fondue. At times if my Grandfather had not eaten his supper, such as a sheep's head, it was passed over for me to eat the following morning for Saturday's breakfast. I would pick away at the meat on its head, even eating the sheep's eye, the teeth still in its jaws! I look back now and the whole episode revolts me. In those days we ate just about anything put before us. On Sunday we might be lucky and have a boiled chicken or duck egg. Our tea would be winkles, sometimes shrimps, with bread and butter, and sticks of celery. In winter we would have crumpets toasted in front of the fire as an added bonus. I was usually given the toasting fork and would sit in front of the fire and do the toasting. When we had winkles our Aunt Lilly would remove the little caps protecting them in their shells with a pin, sticking them on her face as though she had measles!

She was about the most humorous of the aunts, a tom boy if ever there was one! I remember walking alongside her as she slowly peddled her cycle through Warner Place, when a youth passed us, uttering an unpleasant comment to her. Without any hesitation she got off her bicycle and promptly smacked him about the face! He was as astounded as I was, not bothering to defend himself, and he walked away saying absolutely nothing. She got back on her bicycle and continued cycling up Warner Place!

Aunt Lilly's pen-friend boyfriend, came home from India, pulling out his 'topi' helmet from his kitbag and dropping it on my head. The thought of being with someone who had just come from India excited me. I wanted to hear about the country, its people and his experiences there in the army. We never really got around to hearing much. He was from Liverpool, drank too much and sang Irish songs that delighted my Grandfather, who thought that he was the cat's whiskers. He and Aunt Lilly married and moved to his native Liverpool. He turned out to be an absolute swine and a wife beater; they divorced after having two children. For reasons unknown she moved to Scotland and married a Polish ex-army officer and had a further three children.

I remember one Sunday afternoon in the winter time, my Grandmother gave me a saucer of tinned salmon for my tea. It had been standing on the window ledge in the yard. Placing the salmon before me I noted that it was frozen in ice. I was so hungry that as each piece thawed out I ate the iced, watery salmon devoid of any flavor, smothering it with vinegar and pepper to enhance the taste. On another occasion Winnie, the more refined member of the family, came home; it must have been a Friday. Gran served her up egg and bacon with two dumplings left over from the previous day's stew. Poor Winnie just did not appreciate our Gran's *haute cuisine*. We had a 'waste not want not' policy in our household. Our Grandmother was decidedly not *Cordon Bleu* material.

Sometimes we would arrive home to see Gran sitting cross-legged looking glum, her feet tapping away with the rapidity of a machine gun. We immediately knew that something had occurred that had set her off in this ugly mood. Usually it was one or two of the family who had emptied their meal in the dustbin. We then got the full blast of her displeasure, with her saying 'Fine bleeding crew I've got. Go and have a look at my dirt pail'. We never did of course. We ate our meal no matter how awful it was in order not to offend her any further. She had one or two sayings that for years I could never interpret. If anything was very dark she would say it was as 'black as Noogits Knocker'; eventually I discovered that it referred to the knocker on the door of Newgate Prison. This had probably come from the debtors prison and using Cockney jargon, it had become distorted over the years. The second saying she used if she was amazed at something was 'Gor blimey, blind ole kill cooper'. To this day, I have not quite worked out what this meant, the nearest interpretation I can find is 'We'll' or 'I'll' 'kill or blind a cooper', a cooper being a barrel-maker. Whenever she made these odd remarks I regret that I never asked her what they meant. If any family member should come down in the morning in a non too polite or grumpy mood her quote was 'They've woke up with their arse in their hands this morning'. On occasions she would ask me to go to Ellis's, the cooked meat shop in Bethnal Green Road, getting the usual purchase of brawn and luncheon meat. If my Grandfather was in earshot she would say in a louder voice 'and a quarter of pound of pressed beef for your Grandfather' – then whisper to me 'make it two ounces'. If Grandfather happened to be at home and there was a knock on the door from a neighbour, Grandmother would answer and stand in the doorway having a lengthy chat. This used to make my Grandfather irate; he would yell down the hall in a very guttural growling voice 'come in 'ere out of it, nothing but cackle, cackle bleeding cackle'. Grandmother of course would completely ignore the growling which made him even more irate. Such was a peaceful day at No. 74!

Gran's tea making was about the worst tea one could ever taste; you stood about as much chance of having a freshly made cup of tea as winning a lottery! It was simply indescribable, stewed beyond any resemblance of tea. She would leave the teapot over the gas ring to keep it hot and leave it there for hours. By the time it was poured into a cup, the colour of the tea was grey, mixed with a couple of ounces of tea leaves that accompanied the liquid for good measure! I can never recall a tea strainer ever being used.

Grandmother would take me shopping with her to Bethnal Green Road, which was a place of hustle and bustle from Mondays to Saturdays, stretching from just beyond Vallance Road almost to the Salmon and Ball. A long ribbon of canvas topped the stalls and the stallholders yelled and shouted to attract your attention. Greengrocers, grocers, fishmongers, confectioner's, the cat's meat man, tinkers, drapers and hosiers all had stalls. The stalls all faced looking into the shops. Halfway through the shopping we would stop off and she would take me into Kelly's, the pie and mash shop. Kelly's also had another shop just further up the road, but we favoured the Kelly's opposite the Rex Cinema. Kelly's interior was similar to practically every other pie and mash shop in the East End, with white tiled walls, marble-topped tables, condiments of salt, pepper and vinegar, and sawdust on the floor. Trays of pies would come out from the kitchen, with a huge vat of green parsley liquid that we called liquor. It never resembled parsley sauce in any shape or form; it was more floury and less creamy, more like parsley, flour and water. A huge bowl of coarse mashed potato would be placed behind the counter. If they were very busy and some of the tables had not been cleared you would have to sit with your food amongst other peoples plates and liquor spillages which formed into little puddles on the table tops. Even as a child, I hated this. My Grandmother used to order herself a bowl of stewed eels, and a bowl of mashed potato and liquor for me.

Kelly's Pie & Mash Shop, Bethnal Green Road, purveyors of the locals 'soul food'.

Pie and mash in those days cost about 2*d*, a bowl of mash and liquor was half a penny. Vinegar and pepper were applied and it was eaten with relish, though I thought that Gran might have been a little more generous and ordered me a pie. She would say to me, 'Don't tell anyone when we get home'.

A traditional London working class food, pie and mash shops have been in London since the eighteenth century. A pie from a pie and mash shop is quite different from any other pie; it has a flaky-like pastry top, completely devoid of butter or fats, a mince beef filling with the base having the texture and consistency of a steamed pudding. They would be served with liquor and mash, always flavoured with chilli in the vinegar, and salt and pepper. In my adult life I did take one or two people along to the East End to savor our delicacy, but not being raised on 'our soul food' they found it not quite to their taste! The customers nowadays in these establishments are very mixed in terms of social class, which is far removed from the 'working class only' customer image. Sadly a lot of these shops are disappearing now from the East End, a great shame for I feel that this is part of our heritage.

Opposite Webster's fish & chip shop there was a stall which would be used for weighing and cutting up wet fish, or taking live eels from a tray and chopping them up into edible sized pieces. If ever I saw them doing this in winter when it was really cold, seeing their hands almost blue with cold, I would feel even colder, and it would make me long for warmth and comfort. The adjacent stall on the corner of Mape Street was the cat's meat man, with 'Clark Gable', slicing away at huge slabs of horse meat and wrapping half pound's of the smelly stuff in newspaper.

I had a favorite stall in Bethnal Green Road, it was close to the Marquis of Cornwallis pub, and was a confectioner's stall making boiled sweets before your very eyes. I used to stand watching this man making sweets, absolutely mesmerized by the dexterity of his work. He would roll the confectionery into one long sausage and place it around two hooks about three feet away from each other, and commence twisting and turning at an incredible speed, finally snipping the confection into mouth sized portions. The pineapple twist, the bull's eyes, cough drops, pear drops and the sweet smells as he was making them would make the mouth water. In the dark winter afternoons and evenings, the stallholders would have their gas lamps ablaze, the lamps giving off a hissing sound. To see a long row of stalls lit up at night gave it a fairyland atmosphere. When it was really cold most of the stallholders would have a brazier burning to keep their hands and bodies warm; standing on a wooden pallet or wooden boards for hours and hours behind a stall was a feat of endurance. You would see them stamping their feet and quickly moving their arms around their shoulders to keep the circulation going. The cries from these people and their bantering, shouting out 'Ripe bananas!' or suchlike, usually followed by a witty remark or rhyme, made the whole market a wonderful place to be.

At the end of the stallholder's day, everything was packed up and moved away and there remained the debris of orange crates, cardboard, paper, discarded bad and bruised fruit, and vegetables stretching far down the road. Before the council came around to clear this away, children would be sorting through the rubbish, salvaging any fruit or vegetables worth retrieving for the table. Damaged fruit would be referred to as 'spunky'! With a spunky apple or orange, you cut away the bruised or damaged part of the fruit to make it edible.

On the corner of Mape Street stood Hailes, a German butchers. There were several German butchers around the East End at the time. He sold just about the best saveloys, pease pudding and faggots you ever tasted. His succulent saveloys were plump and juicy, his faggots were herby and meaty, served with wonderful gravy, and his pease pudding had a soft, creamy texture. This man had a large heated copper container outside his shop, and people would queue on Saturday nights, bringing their jugs with them to be filled with his faggots and gravy. Pease pudding and saveloys were wrapped in paper. To this day, I have never tasted anything that resembles his wonderful food. Whether it be Selfridges or Harrods, they could never have competed with that butcher's produce! We would go to Stoltz the Bakers for our bread and rolls. In those days they weighed the loaves of bread, and if the bread was underweight they would supplement the difference by giving you a portion of mince. This had a thin layer of sugared pastry on top, a bread pudding-like filling with another thin layer of pastry underneath. We never objected to running errands for a loaf of bread as there was always a piece of mince handed over that was eagerly devoured before the bread reached its recipient. Our meat was obtained from Tommy Halesworth, who always had a beautiful array of all types of cuts of meat in his windows. The road had two cooked meat shops that sold tripe, pig's trotters, brawn, often with the pigs bristles still sticking out from the meat and aspic jelly, pressed beef, luncheon meat, sweetbreads, brains; in fact every piece of offal that came from an animal. They were very popular with the locals because they were much cheaper than the regular butchers. Our grocers was the Maypole, an off-shoot of Lever Brothers who also owned the Home and Colonial, another similar grocers seen in the East End. Tins of Goats Brand condensed milk, margarine and cheese were bought here. Billy Adair had a seafood stall quite close to Kelly's pie and mash shop, and boys being boys we used to sing out 'Billy Adair, Billy Adair, all balls and no hair'. Billy was of course bald, a heavy set man and a former wrestler, and the boys took advantage knowing full well that Billy couldn't leave his stall to chase after us! Our shopping expedition usually finished up with Grandma buying me a packet of wine gums for my good behavior!

Come Fridays, it would be bath night in the scullery. The scullery had bare brick walls whitewashed over, a stone floor, a bare roof-tile ceiling with a small glass skylight shaped the same as the tiles, a ramshackle shelf holding pots and pans, a copper in one corner, a stone sink in another, and a gas stove. The scullery door led into the yard, its walls whitewashed to reflect light into the kitchen. A galvanized tin 'bungalow' bath, when not in use, stood out in the yard, upside down on top of the mangle. Our bath water would be heated in the copper, and as the water in the bath got colder, a saucepan of hot water would be added. We took it in turns to bathe in the same water according to seniority; I, being the youngest, was always last. Grandma would put soda in the bath and use soft brown soap that she brought home from Shell Mex used for scrubbing. The towels for drying were not real towels at all; they were old laundry bags that had seen better days and were never water absorbent; the cloth just slid over your body leaving your skin covered in fibres. Your face would be reddened by the soda. By the time it was my turn to bathe, the water would be tepid and a film of scum had formed on the surface. My Grandmother was never gentle when washing you, the face flannel was literally smacked into your face, the soft brown soap rubbed into your hair then rinsed off by having a saucepan of cold water thrown over your head!

If ever Grandfather took a bath, my Grandmother would open the yard door so that the cold air would blow in directly on to his back, standing back unseen in the frame of the kitchen doorway laughing her head off! The comments from my Grandfather were never exactly polite ones! A normal wash was never referred to as a wash; it was always a 'rinse' or a 'sluice'.

There was never any instruction given on personal hygiene at home; it was something you learned along the way and observed from others whom you mixed with. It was a long road to go down before you became completely knowledgeable and understood bodily cleanliness as it should be. I think my Grandmother just never had the time to explain or show us how or what you should be doing.

The scullery had a small inner window ledge where ointments, toothbrushes and toothpaste were kept. One evening when my Grandfather was preparing to go out; he picked up a tin that he thought was Brilliantine, and mistakenly applied the ointment, Wintergreen, to his hair. Wintergreen ointment was used for general cold symptoms, it has a strong medicated aroma. He could not quite make out why his hair did not have the smell of flowers from the Brilliantine. We kept quiet when he went to his local in Bethnal Green Road smelling like a chemical factory! We never heard if his drinking partners had made any comments! On another occasion I was so hungry, I ate part of Winnie's cake of toothpaste! 'Gibbs' was the brand name; the toothpaste came in little pink cakes inside a tin, and the peppermint smell appealed to me so much that I simply could not resist nibbling away!

There was very little room in the place we called the kitchen; I don't know why it was ever called a kitchen as it held no kitchen cabinets or appliances. There was never anywhere comfortable to sit, the room had hard wooden upright chairs and each door would be piled high with jackets and coats. It was a wonder that the weight of the clothing on the doors never pulled them off their hinges!

From the hall, or passage as it was known, you stepped down into the kitchen. It had a fixed dresser and a handmade side-dresser built, I think by my Grandfather at some stage. If you happened to sit by that dresser you had to sit bent over or hit your head. The only one who could sit there unaffected was our Grandmother, who was just not tall enough to be inconvenienced. There was a small cupboard built into a recess by the door of the coal cupboard running under the stairs. We had no 'easy' chairs, just plain wooden ones; there was no comfort at all. The room had one window facing out onto the yard, the daylight curtailed by a brick wall belonging to the adjacent property.

A single gas light stood out from a bracket. Grandfather used to sit quite close to the gas light, and from time to time the gas mantle, made of very fine gauze, would start to disintegrate from the constant burning of the flame and release its snow-like particles on to our Grandfather's head! We found this very comical while he sat there with his newspaper cussing and blinding. The fireplace had a small black oven range and fire grate. About the only thing that oven was ever used for was to melt cheese for our breakfast, bake an apple, or a rice pudding. There was an entrance door into the yard that was never opened.

We always had a caged canary or a budgerigar perched above the wireless, and every bird we ever had was called 'Joey'. There was also a very odd contraption that formed a shelf to hold the wireless. It must have been made by Grandfather from two brass chains which ran down from the ceiling to support it. It looked most odd but no one dared to pass comment.

The wireless was our main source of entertainment; we would sit around in the evenings listening to *Monday Night at Eight O' Clock*, or *Band Wagon* with Arthur Askey. There used to be a favorite of mine with a chap called Sid Walker from the *Monday Night* programme; he was a rag and bone man who used to open with ''Evening chums', then commence singing, ending with:

> Day after day
> I'm on my way
> Any rags, bottles or bones

Each week he would tell a different story, always of interest. We had 'The Ovaltineys' with their own Ovaltine programme and song which we all knew. We became members and proudly wore the bronze-coloured Ovaltine badge. It could be most infuriating trying to find the stations at times, twiddling and turning the knobs to locate them. The wireless was powered by accumulator batteries, and when they were running low, we used to take them to a shop in Hackney Road for recharging. It was known as the Oil Shop, and sold paraffin and various other oils for domestic use and hardware. I disliked going there as it was always so dark and dingy and had the smell of oils about the place. During the weeknight evenings, with one or two of the aunts, we used to do crosswords or sing the songs from the sixpenny song sheets.

If some of the aunts were going out they would put their hair in curlers for a few hours, then heat curling tongs, either in the fire or over the gas ring. The iron would also be heated over the gas to iron their dresses, with the kettle steaming away to freshen up their hats. It was difficult not to be in any one's way in such a small space when all this activity was going on!

At bedtimes the aunts and uncles would retire. They did not possess nightwear of any description. The uncles slept in their underwear and the aunts in their slips. In winter in their unheated bedrooms it could be bitterly cold. It was not unusual to see my uncles sleeping with their socks on, and the aunts with scarves around them, going up the stairs to bed in their coats carrying candles! The gas lighting was never used in any of the bedrooms. We as children were not as badly off; we both wore Mickey Mouse pyjamas that opened at the rear which we called 'trap doors'. During the early years I had a period of bed-wetting. However much I tried to prevent it and save myself from being scolded by either Mother or Grandmother, it didn't stop until I was about six or seven years of age. Much later in life I discovered that it was a medical condition known as 'primary enuresis'; night time bladder control. Both Mother and Grandmother were completely ignorant of this condition, and never ever dreamt of trying to find out its causes.

At weekends all the aunts would have a certain task in household cleaning. The whole of the dresser was stripped of crockery and washed; everywhere was scrubbed, swept and dusted. In Grandfather's garden the multi-coloured marbled crazy-paving was washed. Even the windows were cleaned, and the yard scrubbed with a birch broom. Our house, although lacking in many things, did not lack cleanliness.

Our insurance man was a Mr Hicks, representing the Liverpool Victoria Insurance Company. He was an ex-Army Officer and a tall, well-spoken gentleman. He would be invited into our home to make his payment entries into the insurance books on our dinner table. His bicycle would be perched at the curbside, and after removing his bicycle clips, he would come in. He was one of the very few outsiders who were ever invited in. The younger aunts rather fancied him I think; their voices, although never a 'Gor Blimey' accent, would suddenly become terribly affected whenever he paid us a visit! They even addressed my Father, their brother-in-law, in the same manner. It was a natural instinct for them to behave like this whenever they were confronted by people who spoke better than they.

At Christmas, a pudding was made in a white enameled bread bin. Mixed fruit, dark sugar, flour and stout would be poured into the bin, and a silver 'Joey', a tiny silver three penny piece, was dropped into the mixture for good luck. We all had a stir with a large wooden spoon and after a really good mix, it would be shaped into large balls, wrapped in muslin and boiled for a few hours. We would make paper chains from coloured strips of glossy paper, paste them together into a chain and fix them across the kitchen with balloons and a few manufactured decorations, although there were not very many of that kind. It was the one time of the year when we had chicken, which was a delicacy to us, and I looked forward to Christmas for the sake of the chicken alone!

Our front room or 'parlour', as it was called, was the inner sanctum. Its door was always locked, and it was never used except at Christmas time, or if there was a family wedding. A party would be a gathering of my Grandmother's sisters, their husbands, cousins and some of Grandfather's friends. A primitive type of bar would be set up on the stairs, with a small wooden barrel of beer, crates of beer and lemonade, and a few bottles of spirits. The piano was about the best piece of furniture in the room, a richly colored walnut cabinet with two decorative brass candlesticks situated on the front panel, the piano keys yellowed with age. There were few pianists in the whole family and not very good players at that, and they managed with difficulty to accompany anyone rendering a song. Each year practically everyone partook in a song, or a monologue!

One Christmas whilst all the elders were in the parlour drinking and singing and singing and drinking, I sat on the stairs by the bar. I drank a glass of port, or perhaps a couple, finishing up falling down the stairs. My sister was the scapegoat, and got a good hiding for allowing me to get into that state. Another time I locked the parlour door when the party was at its height. No one but no one could get out, as the lock had jammed due to its infrequent use, resulting in everyone having to climb out of the front window into the street and re-enter the house again through the front door. I thought the whole thing funny; the party guests however did not.

There would be the same songs and the same monologues year after year. Uncle Tom would whistle one of Albert Whelan's popular songs, 'I want to play in a big review'. Aunt Jane who had a dreadful, nasal voice would sing 'Franklyn D Roosevelt Jones' 'I've been told there's a new arrival in the Jones's family, yesireee, yesireee, yesiree-ee-ee'. Grandfather would sing 'The Rose of Tralee' or 'The Mountains of Morn' and cry. He loved Irish songs, though why he should cry I never knew; he had never seen the skies of Ireland. His friend, Ted Ferry, would sing 'I had a Wheelbarrow that went round and round'. My Aunt May regarded him as a dirty old bugger; he was always trying to grope her. Grandmother would sing 'Just a song at twilight' If anyone happened to speak while someone was singing there would be a cry, usually from my Grandfather shouting 'Order please, order', just as they did in the music halls.

There would be an intermission from the piano playing and singing; ham, corned beef and cheese sandwiches, sweet pickles and pickled onions would be passed around, hardly fine cut and more like doorsteps, but the bread was fresh so there was never any complaint. Grandfather would normally finish up drunk and had to be put to bed. We could hear his ranting and raving as he lay on his bed. The party guests would ignore it all and carry on partying.

One year when we were very young my sister and I were invited to participate in a party piece we had learned at school. She was the patient, I was the doctor. When I was supposed to say 'Let me feel your pulse', I inadvertently said 'Let me feel your parts'.

The whole room burst into laughter and I ran out of the room in tears for having been laughed at. I really didn't know what I had said that could have been so funny.

Uncle Harry would sing old East End songs that I guess were almost Dickensian. I often wonder how many of the true old East Enders are still around that remember any of these old songs that could, and should, have been placed on record for all time:

> Bash me again Bill, Bash me again,
> You caused me no heartache, you caused me no pain,
> You called me a flirt and a flirt I'll remain,
> You bashed me last night Bill, so bash me again,
> He comes down our alley he knocks me about,
> When ever he does so you'll hear them all shout,
> But still I love him I can't deny it,
> I'll go with him wherever he goes,

Everyone would join in on:

> Come round any old time, make yourself at home
> Put your feet on the mantle shelf,
> Open the cupboard and help yourself
> The meats in the oven, the breads on the shelf
> If he doesn't eat it, I'll eat myself
> We don't care if your friends have left you all alone
> Rich or poor, knock at the door and make yourselves at home.

When *Me and My Girl*, the musical with Lupino Lane, was showing in the West End of London, one of the songs from the show 'Doing the Lambeth Walk' became an instant hit. It was sung everywhere, not forgetting the East End parties who brought it into their parlour repertoire. 'Doing the Lambeth Walk, Oi' was invariably included into a sing-along. Other songs that resulted in a 'knees up' would be 'Knees up Mother Brown' or 'How they going to keep them down on the farm / After they've seen Paree'.

Come the weekends, my Grandfather would go out. Hardly a weekend ever went by without him coming home drunk. It was a way of life with him, as indeed it was with many other men. We accepted this and grew up with this around us; it was the norm. At times he would fall down in the hall and had to be helped to bed. Sometimes there would be terrible arguments between my Grandmother and him when he came home in that state. There were times you dreaded him coming home knowing what was in store. He could be quite violent and at one time broke my Grandmother's arm. We could hear the screams, my Mother and sister ran down the stairs to her aid. Weekends could be very unpleasant. Why women stuck with men who made their lives so miserable is hard to comprehend, but leaving the home was out of the question. The song 'Bash me again Bill, bash me again' just about sums up the East End women's philosophy of those days; they did not run away.

They had a saying, 'You've made your bed, now lie on it'. Grandmother could be rather canny. Whenever Grandfather was going out, she would turn the clock back one hour to reduce his drinking time. She referred to his drinking as his 'suction'; he never checked his pocket watch, just observing the time by the clock on the mantelshelf.

Grandfather had once been a Hansom cab driver, and we used to have a photo of him wearing his livery – he was then a smart, good-looking man. He then became a dock worker for the next forty-five years. If ever you asked him for a direction, he would give you a route by naming pubs and who the brewer was to verify you had the right pub. It would become something like, 'Go down the hill, you'll see the Queen's Head, it's a Truman's House. Do a right at the top and you'll come to The Good Hope, that will be a Taylor Walkers House…' and so it went like that, rarely by names of the roads. My Father would have defined it as 'the fine art of tavernry'. My Grandfather would clean his boots and shave the night before, and repair his boots if they so required from an iron boot hob

Grandfather seated with Uncle Joe, Grandmother's brother, in uniform.

we kept under the dresser. Apart from a dock accident, I never knew him to have a day off work. He was working in the docks when they had to fight for work to unload a ton of sugar at sixpence a ton. He crushed his thumb on one occasion and was unable to work, so I had to go with his book down to St Katherine's Dock for him to be 'bomped on' to claim his sick money. Work clothes, protective clothing overalls and the suchlike were not around in those days. They went to work in old clothing. In the winter overcoats would be worn, and he would come home at times with his coat soaking wet, weighing a ton from the rainwater it had gathered. The garment was placed over the fireguard in front of the fire to dry. The steam that rose from the coat smelt of the stale cigarette smoke from pubs and buses that had impregnated the cloth. Other than an interest in a newspaper, I never saw him read a book throughout his life. There was no quality of life, just work and the pub at weekends. Like my Grandmother they never had a holiday between them.

Grandfather was known to us when we were very young as 'Paba'. 'Paba' belonged to a Working Men's Club in Pollards Row. It was his regular haunt. My Grandmother called it 'The 'Ole' as the 'Men only' bar was down in the basement. It was often my duty to go and get him out of 'The 'Ole' to come home for his Sunday dinner. I would climb the stairs to the entrance hall to be met by two of the club's officials who would shout down into the depths 'Bill Cunningham down there?', which of course he always was. I would be given permission to go down to the bar. Behind it in a large glass cabinet was a display of gleaming silver sports cups and trophies from both past and present events. 'What does she bleeding well want now?' would be his remark, nearly always the same. He would proceed to buy me a large glass of cola, quite different to the American version of today, and sit me on one of the raised benches to watch men playing billiards while he finished his drink with his friends. The coloured billiard balls would hold me spellbound; the colours were so vibrant on the green baize under the low hooded lights. When he had finished drinking we would walk the short distance home together. He would sit down to his dinner alone in silence, and then go to his bedroom for his afternoon siesta. After his afternoon sleep he would have his tea then prepare to go out for the evening again.

We were sent to the Jewish grocers for his Sunday tea, either to Mickey Nemko's in Pollards Row or one other in Old Bethnal Green Road and the corner of Jew's Alley. Mickey Nemko's shop was completely disorganized; you entered into semi darkness and tins, cartons, bottles and jars were all over the place. He hardly had enough room to work from behind the counter with the stacked boxes around him. Mickey's knowledge of hygiene was very limited; you would see him put his hand in a barrel of pickled herrings, never washing or wiping them before serving you with the next order. Most off-putting to see was the sticky fly paper hanging from the ceiling with a host of houseflies and bluebottles stuck to it. He had a good clientele and people bought from him unconcerned about his lack of hygiene and his habits. Normally we would have to get Grandfather a Dutch herring or a brown herring. The brown herring was placed in a small earthenware bowl and immersed in hot water from the kettle; it smelled and tasted revolting. How he ate it I shall never know.

The club had an ever-present odour of stale beer that hung permanently in the air. On some Saturday nights, they would have 'turns' or acts in the club's mini music hall

The Working Men's Club, Pollards Row. Grandmother referred to it as the 'Ole.

style theatre. The seats in the hall were thin, covered in red rexine, studded with round brass headed upholstery tacks. Behind each seat in every row was a shelf running along its full length with a metal guard where you could place your drink while you applauded, without fear of the glass falling down. Each turn would display a large placard giving you the name of the act! They were run very much in music hall style. Men would bring their womenfolk and children, if they were old enough, to see the show. We looked forward to going there on these particular nights.

The club arranged a pantomime each year for its members children. For us, it was one of the highlights of the year to see *Aladdin* or perhaps *Puss in Boots*. We were given a bag of fruit and chocolate or sweets and a three penny piece; it was wonderful. The colours, the music, and the singing captivated us.

In the summer they arranged a coach outing for all the children. We loved these outings to Loughton or Theydon Bois, they were only parts of suburban London, but we used to think they were miles and miles away. The days were always sunny and hot, I can never recall having rain on any of the days. The coaches would be lined up outside the club, the children's excitement building up! The coaches or 'charabancs' as they were then known, would be the Grey Green Coaches of Albert Ewers. We would be given an apple, an orange and a three penny piece as we stepped on to the coach. There would be a sing-song all the way and much merriment between us! The appointed area had a small fairground with a helter-skelter, a large wooden tower with a chute descending around it for sliding down its length on a coconut mat. Under a large marquee, tables were laden with sandwiches, blancmange, fruit jellies and cakes. A photographer would be present at these events to take your picture; little tinny efforts that would gradually fade after a time. Many of us would get stung by wasps that always seemed to accompany us to these outings. The St John's Ambulance was always on hand to attend to us. I once needed treatment for a large splinter I got from sliding down the helter-skelter, and a wasp sting on the backside!

When tea was announced, there would be a mad scramble for the marquee to get a seat. Wasps were everywhere: over the jams, over the cakes, over the sandwiches. Through the whole of the tea we would be half eating and half driving away the wasps. There would, of course, be more work for the St John's Ambulance people attending to stings. But it was a glorious day out and we could hardly wait for the next year's outing to come around!

Newspapers at home were the *Daily Sketch*, *News Chronicle*, *Reynolds News* and the London evening papers *The Star* and *Evening News*, and others brought in by the rest of the family. On Sundays, Grandmother would hide the *News of the World* in her bedroom lest we saw anything she might disapprove of. Normally we would get around to reading it, and there was never really anything in the articles that would destroy our morals or put us on the wrong road! We were street-wise at a very early age. If there happened to be something of a sexual nature she would say 'That's lust my child'. The subject of sex was never discussed, it was a topic that was shoved under the carpet. Also never mentioned was any girl who had had a child out of wedlock, as she would be considered a social outcast. It was a dreadful stigma, and divorced people were also looked on very much the same. They were two taboos that the East Ender viewed as something dreadful.

Some afternoons, quite by chance, we might come home early, and we would catch my Grandmother lying down on the floor in front of the fire, having made a comfortable bed for herself under a couple of coats, reading one of the cheap romance magazines, *The Red Letter*. She hated being caught in this situation. She would tell you that she had 'just lain down' and 'hadn't stopped all morning' – not that anyone resented her resting whatsoever.

Every week I would have to take the bag wash. In the winter she would wrap a scarf around my head secured by a safety-pin under the chin and send me with a hired wheelbarrow or pushcart to the Gas, Light & Coke Company in Whiston Road. Through the gates of the gas works you purchased tickets from a small office requesting the number of bags of coke you wanted, and then took them to where a workman who stood shoveling coke into the bags. He took your tickets and filled the sacks. I would take the sacks of coke first to my Aunt Jane, who resided in Hackney Road in a Georgian house that I loved and which was initially the home of my great-Grandparents. It then housed my Aunt Jane and her family. It had such a long front garden, a basement and rooms on three floors. Her daughter converted the large ground floor rooms into a hairdresser's salon. Aunt Jane would give me a copper or two, and I would then take the remaining bags to my Aunt Becky in Norah Square. As Aunt Jane was nasal in her speech, Aunt Becky had a slight impairment in hers. She was also a little more generous in parting with her coppers, so I always gave her preferential treatment. Grandmother never had coke in the house; she always had coal delivered by Thomas Lebon's. The delivery was by horse and cart; coalmen carried the sacks of coal into the house on their backs, wearing a leather-type helmet with a leather covering running down to the small of their backs. The coalmen nearly always got a hard time from my Grandmother who would berate them for the previous delivery of being nearly all coal dust and small lumps! I think they must have dreaded coming to our house, as indeed did any builder. They would have the same treatment. The money collected from my aunts was my cinema money, plus a few little extras.

With so many of us living at No. 74, it was a wonder there was no queuing for the toilet, situated outside the house! What a cruddy place our toilet was! Distempered plastered walls flaking away from the dampness, an iron cistern with a pull chain and a scrubbed wooden pine seat that went from wall to wall – it could never be raised. There was no such thing as toilet paper; old newspapers would be placed at the side of the seat for you to tear off. Some of our neighbors went to the trouble of cutting their newspapers into convenient squares and placing them on a nail, but not us; I suppose there was too much cutting involved. At Christmas time a supreme effort might be made to place a toilet roll there for guests' use. More time was spent in there reading newspaper articles. Uncle Alf would request comics to give his backside a laugh! At weekends, it was in regular use from our Grandfather's imbibing. The smell from his drinking had a defined odor that became so familiar to us come Sundays. We hated it but had to put up with it until that brewery stench had disappeared. Even today if we search deeply enough in our minds, we can conjure up that awful, unforgettable smell.

Our garden, if one could call it that, was a small patch of earth and was the one thing that my Grandfather would take an avid interest in. A small picket fence, painted green, divided the yard from the garden, and the earth had been paved over by small wedge like shapes of various coloured marbles. There were three flowerbeds; a rectangular one either side of the garden, and a centre circular bed, bordered by triangular pieces of white marble. It had a green painted trellis arch stretching from side to side, and a small wooden windmill with a little man at the side who would turn the windmill handle when the wind blew. Alexander roses grew in abundance on the trellis, and wall flowers, lilies, peonies, marigolds and a host of other types of flowers flourished. I would play out in the garden amusing myself catching caterpillars, spiders and flies, and doing horrible little things; pulling the wings off flies, and the legs off spiders, dissecting the caterpillars and placing them in an old 'Mortlake' wax milk carton half filled with water, watching the results of their torture and final demise! The garden was overshadowed by a wood yard called Cripps, named after its owner. Our cats spent most of their time there and would only emerge when they were called for food. Cat's meat was the bill of fare for them on most days, plus any other scraps that were left over from the table. One cat was named George, an unusual name for a cat, the other Blackie on account of his black fur. George was my favourite. He was quite old with grey fur and black tiger-like stripes. Because Blackie was not my favorite, I gave George lots of stroking and affection. For reasons unknown, my Grandmother didn't really like him and was not particularly nice to him. If they did their business in the yard, she would put pepper down and rub their noses in it. Dear old George, I found him dead one day in the wood yard.

You could never be ill in our house, it was not allowed. No matter how ill you felt, you just had to carry on until it came to bed time. A doctor was never called; most of our ailments were treated at home with old wives remedies and ointments such as Wintergreen, Germolene, Thermogene, Bella Donna plasters, Linctus, Fry's Balsam, White Horse Oils, Camphor Oil, and Union Jack Chilblain Ointment that came in tiny little tubs. One day Winnie was in bed with, I think, tonsillitis. She was sitting up with a slice of burnt toast soaked in vinegar on her neck tied with a scarf, one of my Grandmother's old wives' remedies. How effective it was we shall never know, although Winnie did get better. Being the more refined member of the family she looked completely out of place. For Grandmother's personal medicines she would send us to The Old Maids, a chemist in Bethnal Green Road. It is still there today, under that name, though I doubt very much if it belongs to the same family. You would collect the medicine and tell the dispenser that the last lot was not as good as the previous one; little did our Grandmother know that they were just changing the colour of the same thing! She would tell them that she felt much better when the blue medicine was given instead of the red! Winters brought on chilblains, chapped hands and legs, coughs and colds; it was a common sight to see women with red, mottled legs from sitting in front of the fire too long. Fry's Balsam was often used for our colds. We had to sit under a towel with our heads over a pudding basin breathing in the fumes of the balsam. If you had a chest cold you would be rubbed with camphor oil or white horse oils. There was never any form of heating in the bedrooms, they were freezing. Nor was there any gas light, we went to bed with a candle. Chamber pots were placed under the beds; we called them a 'po' or a thunder jug. Sanisal disinfectant was always placed in the bottom of the chamber pots. I remember one night, Grandmother had been overg-enerous with the disinfectant, so when I got up in the middle of the night for a pee, I found my testicles had accidentally dipped into the Sanisal! I was unable to sleep for most of the night, with my testicles on fire!

Grandmother's maiden name was Biggs. She had five sisters and one brother, Joe, who died prematurely from being gassed in the First World War. Aunt Jane remained in the lovely family home in Hackney Road, and Rebecca, whom we called Aunt Becky, lived in Norah Square, Bethnal Green. Aunt Sarah lived in Clapton, and aunties Francis and May lived in Barking. We liked visiting our aunts in Barking. The married surname of Aunt Francis was Fitzgereld; it sounded so aristocratic. I used to think that if ever I were to change my name, Fitzgerald it would be. They lived in nice suburban-type homes and at that time Barking was considered to be a very attractive area. In their early days, when they all lived together in the family home in Hackney Road, the sisters were feather curlers. The curling of feathers was quite an art. Feathers were always used on the fashionable hats of the day.

Grandfather had two brothers, Harry and Arthur, and one sister, Charlotte. Harry died prematurely, Arthur was a docker like Grandfather and Aunt Charlotte's husband deserted her and went to Canada. Aunt Charlotte worked as a cook for Allen & Hanbury's close by. We would visit the aunts as a matter of duty and respect from time to time. Aunt Charlotte lived in Finnis Street in Bethnal Green. Her home was like walking into a piece of Victorian history; glass cases of birds, animals and artificial flowers everywhere, heavy drapes and gloomy. Whenever you called on her you could guarantee she was always cooking something, and you had to sit down and eat. She had a strange habit

The Old Maids, modernised beyond recognition. It was our Grandmother's lifeline of providing her with red medicine one week, and blue the next. She maintained the 'red' made her feel better!

when talking to you of picking at your neck. A very weird sense of affection! When you left you were guaranteed to have a pink neck!

Behind Shoreditch Church, famously included in the nursery rhyme 'Oranges & Lemons', stood the Mildmay Mission Hospital. We went there for all our dental treatments, the main reason being that you were never charged. Sometimes you perhaps put a few coppers in their collection box instead. They made it a point of encouraging you to say prayers prior to having any work done on your teeth. I recall, despite having a raging toothache, having to partake in prayer and feeling pretty sure that the way I felt, the Lord was not receiving my prayers loud and clear! After prayers, you were led into the dentistry section. Gas was the method used to anaesthetize you. A rubber mask was placed over your nose and mouth and within a short space of time you awoke to find the tooth extraction over and you were being led out, semi-conscious, by the dentist's assistant into a room and put to sit at a large table. Gradually you began to focus and would see five or six other people, sitting around that same table, small, white, blue-rimmed enameled bowls in front of them spitting out the gunk from their mouths following their tooth extractions.

At a very young age I was in the Children's Hospital, later changed to The Queen Elizabeth's Hospital for Children in Hackney Road. It was virtually opposite our street. I was only there for a short period, as there was something wrong with my knees and I was unable to walk. The smell of that hospital always scared me. It represented pain, or pain

The wedding of our Great-Aunt Francis, Grandmother's sister, to Uncle Dan Fitzgerald, *c.* 1912.

The wedding of Great-Aunt May, Grandmother's sister, to Uncle Harry Bryant. At the bottom row far right are my grandparents with their children, our Uncle Joe and Aunt 'Noona' seated on the ground.

Great Grandmother Biggs, also seen at wedding of Aunt May's, at the back row centre. She could neither read nor write.

inflicted by a nurse or doctor. My stay was rather pleasant in fact from what I remember; crisp, clean white bedsheets, a comfortable cot, bread with butter, and for the first time in my life I tasted Marmite. It took me ages to find out what they had given me, the taste was something I never forgot. If it was a sunny day the nurses would wheel you out onto the balcony looking down into Hackney Road. Family and friends were able to wave to you. Literally all the boys and girls in Bethnal Green went there at some stage or another. An expression used at home if you were seriously ill was that 'you were on the gate'. I never quite worked this one out, at least not for a long time. Grandmother loved to say to people, if someone she knew was seriously ill, they're 'on the gate'. Actually it meant that the patient was in intensive care, but at that time, the term 'intensive care' was never used or

The Queen Elizabeth Hospital for Children, Hackney Road, known to us as the Child's Hospital.

even heard of. She was always concerned that if ever my Grandfather got knocked down in the street, he hadn't changed his underwear. She feared the embarrassment, as indeed did many women in the East End. The very thought of your husband being knocked down and not having changed his underwear for over a week just didn't bear thinking about!

Come the early part of winter, London would start to have fogs. The fog would begin white and damp in the early morning and by evening would develop into a 'pea-souper' – a dense yellow fog, you could taste its sulphuric tang and it was thick enough to cut with a knife. Visibility became so bad that you could hardly see your hands in front of your face. Coal burning from industry and people's home fires were the contributing factors. Many elderly people died during these times, the pungent, polluted air choking them. It was not until twenty years later that Parliament enacted the Clean Air Act, after 4,000 Londoners had died, spurring the government into action.

One sight gone forever, but the recollection of which brings back happy memories, was to see the night watchmen in their huts at a road works or a building site. Red lanterns were placed around the work area as cautionary signs. You would often see a brazier burning with the night watchman cooking his meal over the fire, sausages sizzling away in the frying pan. Now and again you might be lucky and be given a sausage. On most occasions they would be happy for your company to relieve them from the loneliness of the night. Most of the streets comprised of tar block surfaces, and if the night watchmen were not that vigilant, tar blocks would rapidly disappear from the site for the fire at home. They burnt beautifully but spat the tar out all over the place.

4

SCHOOL, CHURCH AND CHOIR

ractically all the boys and girls in the street attended St Peter's school, a Church of England school affiliated to the church. It was a well run, disciplined school with good teachers. Our flag, King, and country were held in great esteem. We started at the age of three and remained there until we were twelve years of age. My earliest recollections were being in the primary class; it had a large dapple-grey rocking horse that I loved riding on; the memory of that horse has never left me. It was some sixty years later that, with my sister and cousin, I paid a visit to our old school which was still standing, and now an

St Peter's School, showing the doorway where Mr Loft the caretaker would stand ringing his bell, beckoning us to school.

St Peter's School, now an organ-maker's premises. The playground's only vehicle then would be Mr Thomas's car.

organ-makers' establishment. A lady came out while we reminisced in the playground, enquiring what we were doing there. We informed her that many years ago it was our school. She was very gracious in showing us around all the classrooms that we had once sat in. We came to the primary classroom, and I happened to remark that this was where a rocking horse I loved as a child was situated. I described it in detail and to my surprise and joy, she told me that her sister now owned it! It felt good to know that the dapple-grey had survived the ravages of time. We felt that our school was extra special to us.

The caretaker, Mr Loft, known as 'Lofty' was a heavily moustached, large, kindly man who wore a brown felt trilby whenever he entered the playground. He would ring his large brass hand-bell calling us to school, sometimes allowing us to ring it. We would then line up in our respective classes and enter the school. Our teacher would call out our names from the register, marking down those present and absent. Absenteeism was almost unheard of; the prospect of the school board man coming to your house was feared. Our Headmaster, Mr Thomas, used to park his car in the playground next to the house of Mr Raymond, the choirmaster. We boys loved his car; it was like an American gangster's, similar to those we used to see in the *Crime Does Not Pay* series. It had a soft-top, yellow coloured 'plastic' windows, although plastic wasn't around then, I guess it must have been celluloid or some other substance manufactured at the time. We would jump onto the foot boards, moving his chromium headlamps like searchlights, playing 'cops and robbers' crying out 'Calling all cars, calling all cars'. I don't think Mr Thomas ever came out and remonstrated with us, he was a very kindly headmaster. In fact,

I cannot recall any of the teachers at St Peter's being unpleasant; they were firm but they were fair.

We were frequently visited by a nurse who would comb through our hair for nits; we called her 'Nitty Nora', though I do not recall any resentment felt when her visits came around. She would stand there in her dark blue uniform and white cap, dipping the silver metal comb into a small blue-rimmed enamel bowl filled with disinfected water and comb through our hair.

A short prayer was said every morning before the commencement of class and our lessons. Normally we had one subject in the morning, changing to another in the afternoon. Once or twice a week we would have school drill which involved exercising in the playground outside. We wore coloured bands worn diagonally across the upper part of our bodies and formed into groups. I always tried to select my favorite coloured band, alternating from red to blue to green depending upon my colour preference at the time. The exercises were shoulder, arm, leg and body movements; time permitting we would have the game of O'Grady. You followed to the order of 'O'Grady says'. If you made the movement, and O'Grady never said it, you were out.

In the junior classroom you made a point, if you could help it, of never sitting with Edna Hoskins. She was always peeing herself and stank constantly of urine. If the teacher so ordered you to sit next to her, you suffered in silence. This also applied to Horace Andrews, who we called 'Orrie; as a small boy he used to wear brown velvet trousers with two pearl buttons either side. He always stank; he was constantly messing himself, and during summer time if ever you had the misfortune to sit next to either of them, it became an endurance test; you did your very best to try and keep your mouth shut tight to prevent breathing in the fetid odors.

Our swimming classes took place at Haggerston Baths, a good fifteen minutes walk from the school. We would take swimming costumes, which we called 'cossies'. These were usually a two-tone affair made of cotton. The colours always seemed to be an orange top and black lower half which we purchased from Dunne's the Drapers in Hackney Road, for about three and a halfpence. The 'cossies' were rolled up into the towel and placed under your arm. We were formed up in pairs and marched from the school to the baths. At that time we had a rebel in the school, who was never out of trouble of some sort, named Frankie Walker. At the baths, in order to enter the main bathing pool one had to walk through a small shallow pool known as a slipper bath. Frankie, for reasons known only to himself, refused to use the slipper bath which angered our teacher, Mr Desborough, to such an extent that he slapped him all around the slipper bath. During the whole of that scuffle and those whackings, I never saw Frankie shed a tear – he was a tough little sod.

One of the highlights of the year was Empire Day. We would proudly display our Union Jacks and march around the playground to music and songs. The large map in the school indicated every country marked in red belonging to the Empire. The red made up practically two thirds of the world and we were very proud. Everything was red, white and blue. The green lawn behind the church would be opened up for this special day to extend the activities, egg and spoon races, sack races, relay races, drinks and cakes on large wooden trestle tables to be consumed by an ever-hungry horde of school kids. If ever you asked one of them at school what they had for dinner, they would reply, 'meat, 'taters and greens' regardless of what meat it was or what type of vegetables they had eaten, it was always the same reply. Every school kid's favourite dessert was jelly and custard; if you ever asked what they had for 'afters', we never ever used the word dessert or sweet, it was not in our curriculum, if it had happened to be jelly and custard, they would rub their tummies in a circular motion of sheer delight. On Monday mornings you handed in your milk money for the week; the milk was delivered in silver-topped half pint bottles, together with a straw, and was drunk in the morning. From the silver tops and the straws we would fashion small spears and throw them at each other when teacher wasn't looking. Come the winter we would place our milk bottles close to the large combustion stove, so by the time we had our break the milk would be nice and hot.

It was King George V and Queen Mary's Silver Jubilee in 1935, and every schoolchild received a china mug with the pictures of both King and Queen in an oval framework surrounded by draped flags of the Union Jack and Royal Standard. In 1936 the King died. I recall standing with my Grandmother listening to the funeral commentary over the wireless, and even at a young age I was quite moved. In 1937 George VI became King and we were all handed a coronation beaker with the pictures of King George and Queen Elizabeth with the initials 'L.C.C.' (London County Council) emblazoned beneath. This was followed by a street party, with the street decorated with flags and buntings, a sea of red, white and blue. Trestle tables were erected and joined into one huge table where we all sat. Piles of sandwiches of fish paste or cheese, jam, cakes, buns and jellies were placed on the tables together with lemonade and tea. On sitting down, the food was rapidly demolished. It was the most wonderful thing ever. East Enders were a very patriotic people.

Invariably, boys being boys, we would fall down in the playground and graze our knees. Every other boy seemed to have a scab of sorts on their kneecaps. Their jersey sleeves and jacket sleeves at the cuff were often shiny from the mucus being wiped from their noses. Parents could not afford handkerchiefs and tissues were not around then, so the poor boys used the only method they knew to wipe their noses, there was just no alternative.

Trousers were held up by snake belts which were two-tone and elasticized, boots were bought from Wickams in the Mile End Road or Gammages in Holborn. I never got to wear boots until called up for National Service. I just wanted to be like the other boys, but my Mother made me feel very much out of it by making me wear patented Cromwellian shoes with silver buckles that left me open to unkind remarks and ridicule from the other boys. In the summer we liked wearing plimsolls, light on the foot and as we firmly believed, you could run faster in them. Many was the time where I had to sneak by my Grandmother so that she could not see me wearing them. I was not allowed to wear them in the street.

Another fallacy was that if you peed on a lorry's tires, it would go faster. At every opportunity when we saw a lorry parked part hidden from public view, we thought that we were doing the lorry driver a great service by having a pee on his tires!

Emptying out a boy's trouser pockets was like emptying his treasure trove: a catapult, a Jew's harp or a mouth organ; if you didn't have a musical instrument of sorts, a comb and tissue paper would suffice; as well as marbles, string, penknife, and a lucky charm.

It's funny how certain things stand out in your memory. I recall being in class when we had to read out essays we had written. One boy named Lenny Davis, a tall, thick-set, blond haired boy from Warner Place, was asked to read out his essay. He commenced reading, 'My dad is a dustman and goes to the beer pub'. I pondered and thought why did he make the comment about his Father in public? Why should he let it be known that his Father drank? Why the words 'beer pub,' and not public house? 'Beer pub' was the term often used instead of pub or public house, but to write it down as such did not seem quite right. This was my first experience of becoming critical, though I never recognized it as such at the time.

My sister became infected with scabies, a horrible disease that left you itching and scratching, day and night, gradually developing into sores all over her body which eventually turned to scabs. She believed it was caught from swinging on the toilet doors at school. Scabies is a highly contagious disease that quickly spread both to me and my aunts, May and Winnie. The family had great faith in St Bartholomew's Hospital (Bart's) in Smithfield. We visited there for both examination and prognosis. Aunt May must have given permission, not really fully understanding what we were about to experience, as we were paraded before a whole class of medical students. The next thing we knew, we were all undressed and led into a lecture hall, totally starkers on a platform, staring out at forty to fifty students, while the lecturing doctor pointed with his stick at the sores on our bodies! I felt very uncomfortable and embarrassed not only for myself but for my sister and aunts at being exposed like this. It seemed an eternity standing there while a banter of questions and answers bounced between the doctor and his students. It was a great relief to us when the ordeal was over and we were allowed to dress and go home. Our ensuing treatment was to have sulphur baths at a clinic in Russia Lane, behind the Bethnal Green Town Hall. Russia Lane at that time had a notorious reputation for thieves, cut-throats and squalor. The squalor was most decidedly there, the reputation of having thieves and cut-throats was unfounded. The name Russia Lane and the square at the side of the Town Hall, Patriot Square, were the names given, no doubt, by some very Leftist councillor who had been brought up on a diet of Communism, revolutions, Marxism and Lenin. The name, so close to the leafy Victoria Park Square and the library, never quite befitted the surrounding area. Names of a more serene nature, rather than revolutionary ones, would have been more apt.

The school organised a Country Holiday Fund. For a small sum, underprivileged children could take a holiday in the country. I started to save my pennies, religiously putting them away each week into a china basin in a cupboard in the kitchen. Shortly before I was about to go away, my money went missing. We never knew who had taken the cash. I was absolutely distraught. The family somehow got together and saw that my holiday did not go amiss. I went to Harwich from Liverpool Street Station with 'Orrie Andrews, we stayed with a fisherman and his family. He would take us out in his rowing boat to fish. 'Orrie and I went out one day and got stuck in the mud. Fortunately before the tide came in we were rescued and never went near the mud flats for the rest of the holiday. I loved the smell of the sea, the smell of the seaweed washed ashore in black and dark green heaps lying across the pebbles, and we loved to pop the little pods of the seaweed, looking for small crabs and picking up interesting sea shells to take back home to London as a memento.

On school holidays our Grandmother would say, 'I put my hands together the day you go back'. She dreaded them as it would entail our being at home for a certain length of time, which would upset her routine. We boys would form into our little team and go to the parks. Victoria Park was the grandest and our favorite park, we called it 'the Vick'. Leaving our street we would trek along Hackney Road to Cambridge Heath, crossing the road into Bishop's Way, then on to the park. We would invariably make up bottles of lemonade from the yellow lemonade crystals that dissolved in tap water, shaking the bottle to give it a fizz. Stopping off in Bishop's Way, we would buy a bag of broken biscuits. I would always try to pick the ones with the pink icing on the back, or ask for any stale cakes as these were always cheaper. Victoria Park had a magnificent wrought iron gate you passed through, with a stone statue of a dog, which we understood had saved someone's life from drowning, as you crossed over the Regent Canal Bridge.

The park had a large boating lake and an island in the middle with a Chinese pagoda that you could reach by bridge. You could hire a boat to row, hire a skiff if you were a good oarsman, or take the larger motorized boat that would give you a tour around the lake. We would sit by the lake, drinking our jaundiced-looking fizz, eating the biscuits or stale cakes and feeding the crumbs to the ducks and swans that would come to you if they saw you were eating. We would remove our shoes and socks and paddle in the lake for a spell. The park, so prolific in trees and greenery, was a happy escape away from the streets. It was wonderful just to walk across open fields where all sorts of activities took place. It boasted a Lido where we would occasionally go and swim and sunbathe. We considered going to the park an exciting adventure. Other days would be divided by going to London Fields which had a large pond. We didn't like going into that water, it was said that bloodsuckers lingered there.

One day I fell into the pond and returned home soaking wet. My sister got a walloping for allowing me to fall in! Our other park ventures nearer home were Ion Square and Piggy's Island. These parks were just tiny open spaces with swings, seesaws and a round-about. It was not unusual to fall off of these leisure contraptions and go home with a bump on your head or a grazed knee.

At about the age of eight I joined the St Peter's Church Choir. Choir practice was twice a week, our choirmaster and organist was Mr Raymond. He was quite a martinet and would stand no nonsense. On two occasions I was dismissed from the choir. I cannot recall the actual reasons but suspect it was for larking around during practice or some other misdemeanour. On the second time of being thrown out I cried all the way home. One of my aunts, Aunt Winnie, took me back and pleaded with Mr Raymond to reinstate me. He succumbed and I was back in the choir. On Sundays we would change into our cassock and surplice, with fresh scrubbed faces and hair parted looking like little cherubs when, in fact, we were quite the opposite. In procession we would enter the church,

London Fields.

ascending the three stairs to the altar, pair off to be seated in the pews directly opposite the church organ. Mr Raymond had a small mirror facing him, and as he played he would look into the mirror to see if we got up to any antics during the service. Our delight was if there happened to be a choral wedding as we would be paid a shilling. Out of this we would have to pay for our own white high stiff collar and small black bow purchased from Dunne's the drapers. The cost of collar and bow was a penny and three farthings. When we were handed that shilling after a wedding service we felt like millionaires. We could then afford to buy a bar of Double Six chocolate from 'Arry Orseye's. This was a chocolate bar with twelve sections of differently filled chocolates, ranging from strawberry, coffee, caramel and other flavors, or perhaps one of his freshly made ham or cheese rolls, or even a Doubleday's steak and kidney pie. That shilling meant the world to us!

At Christmas time we choirboys, accompanied by Mr Raymond, would go around the streets clothed in our cassocks and surplices singing carols and making a collection. Money from the upper floors of houses would be thrown out into the street, and it would be our task to run around picking up the coins. We thought nothing of retaining a few coppers for ourselves and giving the rest to the church; even at that age we had learnt to charge a commission! At the end of the singing we would be invited to his house in the school playground for hot blackcurrant cordial and mince pies. It was his way of thanking us for our efforts.

When I was about twelve years of age the vicar at St Peter's church informed me that he could find no records of my baptism. I was always given to understand by my Mother

St Peter's Church,
Bethnal Green,
the only building
remaining in what
was once St Peter's
Avenue.

that I was christened there. Our vicar decided to take matters in hand and promptly baptised me at the church font with 'Orrie Andrews as my godfather. Much later in life, it proved to be very hard to understand that 'Orrie, a boy we had grown up with, turned out to be different; not interested in girls like the rest of us. There were signs, even at an early age, that his interests were not quite the same as ours, but we were too young to recognise it.

The church had a hall in Warner Place, St Peter's Hall, which is still standing. We enrolled in the Cubs. It was a junior version of the Boy Scouts. We 'dib, dib, dobbed' and our Cub Leader was called Akela. It was another world. We wore green pimple caps with yellow cord, our scarves were plaited blue and yellow held by a leather toggle. We felt very proud of our outfits. Most of the 'pack' had names of the animals from Rudyard Kipling's *Jungle Book*. I loved the activities and hearing about the animals from his stories. It was a great institution that taught us many values .The girls enrolled in the Brownies, the junior body of the Girl Guides. There would be functions and concerts from time to time in the hall when both Cubs and Brownies would share the evening.

Each week I would pay a visit to the library. The books and the selection of subjects opened up a whole new world for me, I would spend hour upon hour there quenching my thirst for knowledge and broadening my horizons. It introduced me to Rudyard Kipling and Jack London's *Call of the Wild*, never realizing that later in life I would be standing in the very places that Jack London wrote about. To buy a book or to be able to afford one was out of the question. Thank God for those libraries. I became a member and recall going into one of the smaller sections which contained an electric fire. I had never seen one in my life before and became terribly curious as to how it worked. Poking my fingers up behind the elements I was thrown by the electric shock to the other side of the room. Might I say from that moment on I never tampered with electric fires again.

St Peter's Hall, Warner Place has remained unchanged.

The walk to the library, along Bethnal Green Road via the Salmon and Ball public house, housed a secret that I never knew for many years. Outside the Salmon and Ball public house two men were hanged for participating in the Spitalfields Riots of 1769. One was John Doyle (an Irish weaver), the other John Valline (of Huguenot descent). The riots were actually centred to the east, and were put down with considerable force [2].

The Bethnal Green library building is close to the original village green, now Victoria Park Square. The building erected by the green was Blithe Hall, recorded in an eighth-century document. Taking the toll over the years of different accents and bad handwriting, by the fourteenth century it had become known as 'Bleten Hall Green'. Another hundred years on, Samuel Pepys recorded his journey to 'Bednall Green'. Behind the library, a large mansion was built called 'Bednall House', by a rich merchant named John Kirby, which eventually became known as 'Kirby's Castle' by the villagers.

In 1727 the mansion was turned into a private asylum for what were then classed as mental patients or 'lunatics'. The original building stood until 1843 when it was demolished. A new asylum was opened in its place and existed until 1920, before being closed to make way for a housing estate. Its inmates were transferred to Salisbury.

My Grandmother used to tell us that when she was little, she used to see the inmates in the grounds, making faces behind the wire fencing at whoever looked in. It was known to all of us, and is still called, 'Barmy Park'.

5

THE EARLY WAR YEARS

*O*n 3 September 1939, war was declared. It was a glorious Sunday morning, just like a mid-summer's day, the sun was shining and the azure sky cloudless. Halfway through the morning, the warning siren sounded, I think, for the very first time. It was the first of hundreds of times we were to hear it over the next five years. Mr Irons, the proprietor of a newsagents and tobacconist shop at the corner of Gosset Street and Kite Place, came running up the street with great difficulty; he was grossly overweight, wearing a tin hat and gas cape, with a wooden rattle in his hand. The rattle was to be used to alert people if we had a gas attack. Mr Irons was in the ARP and looked extremely worried, as if the Germans had already landed.

Grandmother, on seeing Mr Irons running up the street, dressed as if he was about to go 'over the top' from the trenches, started to have a panic attack and screamed almost to the point of being uncontrollable. I took her back into the house, sat her down on the stairs, and calmed her back to her normal neurotic self!

People began to be issued with gas masks; these were skin-tight against your face so that when breathing out they would quiver and make sounds like a flatus (fart).

Babies' masks were like a space capsule called the 'Mickey Mouse.' With their bare legs protruding, many babies were frightened at being placed in these capsules and would scream their heads off. Gas masks were carried in small cardboard boxes that we tied with string and wore over our shoulders; we carried them everywhere. Homes were provided with either Anderson shelters or Morrison shelters. Grandfather would have none of it; he was not going to have his garden dug up for an Anderson shelter! So we became one of the few in the street who did not have one.

Barrage balloons started to go up all over London. They reminded me of huge silver elephants without trunks. The Committee of Imperial Defence authorized an initial barrage of 450 balloons for the city's protection. During the Blitz, 102 aircraft struck cables, resulting in sixty-six crashing or being forced to land. The best example of these 'balloons in combat' occurred during the V-1 offensive against London in 1944. They proved an integral part of the air defence system and in this case formed the third and final line of defence against this low-flying weapon. Approximately 1,750 balloons were amassed from all over Great Britain forming the largest balloon curtain in history. Although guns and fighters destroyed most of the V-1 bombs (1,878 and 1,846 respectively), balloons were credited with 231 'kills'. That was the last 'hurrah' for British balloons when the war came to a close in 1945 [3].

The blackout began two days before the war commenced. Blackout rules were enforced and everyone had to cover up their windows at night with black material. Street lamps were turned off, so people walked the streets in total darkness. Some had nasty accidents, walking into walls, falling down unlit staircases and walking into the canals and ponds. There were several fatalities, particularly through road accidents. It took quite a while for people to become accustomed to the darkness. In the homes, families were putting up blackout blinds and curtains. They got used to turning off the lights before opening a window or door. To expose your home with any light showing, you would hear a cry from an ARP Warden shouting 'Put that bloody light out!' Practically everyone carried a torch; they bought 'No.8 Ever-Ready batteries' regularly to keep the torches powered. Strips of brown paper were stuck on windows in a diamond pattern to prevent shattering from bomb blasts. The blackout was intended to make it difficult for German bombers to find their targets. Each week in the *Hackney Gazette* people were being summoned to the courts and fined for not keeping their premises in total darkness.

The Ministry of Food instituted a rationing system. Who would have believed that it would remain for fourteen years until it finally ended in 1954? We would register with our local shops and were provided with ration books.

On 8 January 1940 bacon, butter and sugar were rationed. This was followed by meat, tea, jam, biscuits, breakfast cereals, cheese, milk, eggs and canned fruit. One of the few foods not rationed were fish and chips. The scarcities created by such strict rationing led to the black market. There was hardly a thing that was not rationed. People were deceived into buying horse meat, thinking it was beef. As the war progressed, clothing was rationed on a points system, as was petrol. It became a black marketeer's paradise. If you had money, you could buy anything. This was the birth of 'the spiv'.

The average standard of rations was:

> 1lb 3 ozs meat
> 4 ozs of bacon or ham
> 3 pints of milk or 1 packet of milk powder per month
> 2 ozs of butter
> 2 ozs of margarine
> 2 ozs of fat or lard
> 2 ozs of loose tea
> 1 egg per week or 1 packet of egg powder per month
> (1 packet making the equivalent of twelve eggs)
> 2 ozs of jam
> 3 ozs of sugar
> 1 ozs of cheese
> 3 ozs of sweets
> 2 lb of onions (onions were rationed between 1942–1944)
> These amounts were per week, unless stated

In the second week of the war, Aunt Eileen married her cousin Harry; both were Catholic and had to obtain special permission from the church to marry. Winnie, with a work colleague and my sister were bridesmaids, and I was selected as page boy. No suitable shoes could be found for me, so urgent improvisation was required which resulted in my sister having to give up a pair of her shoes, which were then painted in a metallic bronze to match my page boy outfit! The wedding arrangements were brought to a halt as I refused to budge until I had a buttonhole flower like everyone else! My Mother was shouting and becoming quite hysterical. I tore the bronze coloured satin shirt I was wearing in anger! I was screamed at, shouted at, until finally a buttonhole carnation was found. I relented and the wedding proceeded without a hitch!

A few months went by in the 'phoney war' period when the evacuation of children was implemented. Schools began to close down, and no longer did you see children playing, the streets were empty. Most of our playmates and school friends had departed for Somerset, Norfolk and other counties. St Peter's' school teachers and its children had gone. I never knew the reason why we were not included. Since there were no children I knew left around the neighborhood, I started to befriend other boys and girls in the area where my Mother had the café, who had not yet been affected by the evacuation.

We were invited to cousin Stanley's twenty-first birthday party above a public house in Brady Street. I can still see Stanley, with his black wavy hair and beautiful smile; he was a

The wedding of Aunt Eileen, my Mother's sister, and cousin Harry at St Anne's Catholic Church, Bethnal Green, September 1939. The author is the page boy, Aunt Winnie stands behind him and sister Dawn is the young bridesmaid far left.

handsome young man. He had joined the RAF as an air gunner but was shot down in a raid over Germany; he was placed on the missing list for a long time, and eventually given up as 'presumed dead'. Two other cousins were to follow him – Charlie and Sonny were killed in the D–Day landings.

My Mother had enrolled us into Ruby Bond's dancing school in Queensbridge Road; I was thrown out for having two left feet and returned to the streets! My sister Dawn became an accomplished singer and tap dancer and appeared in quite a few concerts. Clad in tartan, she would perform her song and dance routine of 'McDougall, McNabb and McKay'. I went to see her at the Excelsior Cinema. I was a little out of my depth at the time and didn't appreciate how good she really was, but her talent sadly was never pursued.

Things were beginning to happen in London. Official establishments were beginning to have sandbags placed around their entrances and at other weak areas, prone to blast. A group of us children participated in the war effort by filling up sandbags at Kingsland Road fire station. It was exciting and great fun but short lived. At that young age it was impossible to understand or comprehend what was about to take place.

Father was found to be unfit for military service and was directed to various jobs, some of which were quite unsavoury. Some of the jobs he was sent to were quite demeaning, and if he felt that the work was not for him he developed a ploy that prevented him from obtaining the position. He would be interviewed, mentioning to the interviewer that he felt it was his duty to tell them that he took things. The interviewer would say, 'Well, how do you mean, you take things?' Father would reply, 'I can't help it, I have this compulsion to take things'. He never did of course, but it worked every time and the interviewer would politely say, 'I don't think you will be suitable for this position' and Father was sent back to the Labour Exchange to re–register.

Having the foresight in what was to come, he found a small cottage in a village on the outskirts of Tring, in Hertfordshire, for 3s 6d per week and evacuated our Grandparents and three aunts. The village of Wiggington was hidden away up in the hills on the fringes of the Rothschild's estate. They remained there for the rest of their days. Both Nan and my Grandfather are buried in the village cemetery, and Father and my aunts are buried in Tring.

Over the years, I would go back there many times. Visiting my Nan's in the country was always a very welcome escape from Bethnal Green. Whenever one of my aunts invited me, I would jump at the chance. Aunt Enid was the favourite of my Father's sisters, she was full of fun and laughter. We would meet at Victoria and get the Green Line bus to Tring. She used to make the most delicious sandwiches for us to eat on the journey. I used to think it was miles away, which of course it was not. It was fantastic to be away from the drabness of the East End, if only for a few days. Amazingly, there were people in the village of Wiggington who had never been to London. Some still adhered to folklore, such as if a single girl wanted to find a man, she had to place a 'besom' (like a witches broom) outside the door!

I loved the bedroom I slept in at my Nan's cottage, old and countrified, with a sloping ceiling and a bookcase full of books. All the family read and the mobile library would call weekly at the village. Nan, even into her late eighties, would read on average six books a week and could relate all the characters in the books she read. Aunt Enid and I would get up very early and go into the fields mushroom picking and Nan would cook them with bacon. We also had fresh bread from the local bakery, everything tasted so wonderful! Nan would take me by local bus into either Chesham or Amersham. We would dine at a fish restaurant and her table manners were so ladylike, I loved her quiet reserved manner. Sometimes she would take me down the country lanes gathering cob nuts; she would hit the branches with her walking stick and I would do the picking up of the nuts. She was a magnificent cook, particularly her steak and kidney puddings. Grandfather would cut the cabbage and dig up the potatoes for cooking that day, no pesticides, just pure natural food that tasted out of this world.

The village had two pubs; although under age, I could sit with my aunts and have a glass of lemonade. Aunt Joan, who was an accomplished pianist, would play and Aunt Enid would mimic an East Ender singing in a 'Gor Blimey' accent. One evening I bought a raffle ticket and completely forgot about it – the pub promptly informed me that I had won a cockerel! Taking home the bird, still feathered, Nan had my Aunt Lil pluck the feathers out in the garden, where I assisted in part, until it was made ready for the oven. Those were idyllic days!

6

THE EVACUATION

e were eventually rounded up for evacuation. Neither our parents nor Grandparents were there to give us a hug or a kiss goodbye, or to wave us off. We were tagged, labelled and shipped off by train like refugees from Euston Station and informed we were going to Bicester. I had never heard the name before. In fact I don't think any other evacuee on that train had heard of it either. I carried a small suitcase of clothing, that broke open on the train, spilling all its contents and which was beyond repair. The journey on that steam train seemed to go on forever, I remember the clickety-click over the rails. Lowering the compartment window by its leather strap to relieve the monotony of just sitting there. I poked my head out, only to receive an unsuspecting hardened speck of soot from the engine flying into my eye. I spent the rest of the journey attempting to remove the offending particle.

Bicester was a small agricultural market town. The main street was Sheep Street, at its heart. It had a population of approximately 20,000-30,000.

I returned to Bicester on a few occasions long after my evacuation days. To my sadness, the town has been torn apart by a modern ugly supermarket and other buildings erected in such a small area so that it has lost its character. The cottage where we once lived, and its occupants, like the decimation of the town, are gone forever.

On arriving at Bicester, we were transported by bus from the railway station to a school where we were assembled, and the locals came to collect us. I was never sure whether it had been pre-decided who would have us, or whether they simply came along and selected us by how we looked. I will never know. My sister and I were separated; seemingly most of the people did not want a boy and a girl together, rather boy and boy, or girl and girl. I was paired up with a boy named Lenny Ebbs from around the corner to us in Bethnal Green. We were sent to a house on a council estate on the outskirts of town; we didn't like the house or its occupants and made a hasty departure back to the school. We arrived back to an empty assembly point; all the other children had been claimed. Eventually a woman, a Mrs Baughan, and her son Jim came along and took us a short distance from the school to their home. The address was No. 3 Ladysmith Terrace; a small row of flint-stone terraced cottages. When we entered their home it was apparent that they were as poor as we were. There was a small low-ceilinged living room, with a dining table in the middle of the room on which stood an oil lamp. Most noticeably, there was no wireless. Candlelight was the only other form of lighting in the house. The kitchen was half scullery, half kitchen. An open staircase led through to two open floor bedrooms. Husband, wife and daughters shared the first floor bedroom; we, with their youngest son, shared the room at the top of the house with a sloping ceiling. Lenny and I shared a bed. The toilet was in a shed way across at the back of the house where potatoes and vegetables from their allotment were also stored.

The Baughan family was an ordinary working class family. Mr Baughan worked with the GPO repairing outside telephone lines. The eldest son Joe was away in the Royal Navy, the eldest daughter Mary was in the WAAF's, and Jean was away in domestic service. Ray, the youngest daughter, was still at school, as was Jim, the youngest son; he was a similar age to us. They were a good-looking family, the daughters were all attractive girls, and as evacuees we got on extremely well with them all. I cannot recall having any disputes the whole time we lived there. After settling in and acclimatising ourselves to our surrounds, we reported for school. The school specialised in boxing and singing, and fortunately I was able to manage well in both subjects.

We were all assembled in a Methodist church hall and addressed by the head teacher regarding future arrangements for schooling. During his address I was rubbing my hand; I was called out in front of the whole assembly and caned six times over the palm of my hand for not paying attention! The school, along with its teachers and evacuees, had come from West Ham. After my caning I didn't hold this West Ham school in very high esteem! It was the first time that I had ever been caned. A suitable place was found to educate us, which I loved, on the outskirts of Bicester. Bignall Park was on the fringes of the village of Chesterton.

Bignall Park was a lovely grey stone manor set in the most beautiful grounds. It was the finest building I had ever entered. All the manor's contents had been removed to make way for classrooms, leaving the beautiful paneled walls and polished wooden flooring that had become stained with writing ink from careless and thoughtless evacuees like us. Each school day we were transported by bus from the town square to Bignall Park.

Singing and boxing were given precedence over other subjects, and I happened to be chosen for both. The music teacher would take me aside privately and sit at the piano, with me standing beside her, practising the scales for a school production of *Aladdin*. Come the time nearer to the concert I backed out through fear. I was terrified at the thought of having to perform in public. Fortunately, there were no repercussions for not participating.

One glorious summer's day, the class was out on the terrace for singing lessons. We were singing 'Do you ken John Peel'. Part-way through the song, a hunt came into view, riding across the fields at full gallop with their hounds, hunters in hunting pink, to the sound of the horn. Quite apart from being a splendid and exciting picture, I could not think of anything more apt for that particular moment! The gamekeeper was often seen walking through the grounds with his shotgun, stopping at trees that housed crow's nests. He would shoot right through the nests, sometimes blowing a crow completely out of its residence. Our main meal of the day was provided at one of the outer buildings which served as our dining room. Considering that rationing was in full force, with shortages of certain foodstuffs here and there, the school managed remarkably well. The food was adequate and not ghastly as school dinners often were.

Under the guttering of the building of where we ate, swallows nested. After lunch and before we had time to return to the classroom, I would sit and watch those lovely birds darting backwards and forwards, sweeping low and ascending high into the sky, diving, skimming the earth before soaring up again, and repeating the whole process over and over again. I could have sat there watching them forever.

We had a mobile shower unit visit the school regularly; it was set up like tents with canvas roofs and sides. We would line up, strip off, and ten to twelve of us would shower at one time. This was much better than having to bathe in a tin bath back at Ladysmith Terrace. The dentist would visit the school and literally everyone had a fear of his visits, as dentistry was nowhere near as sophisticated or technically advanced as now. In fact, it was quite primitive. To have a tooth filled or extracted was enough to put the fear of Christ into anyone.

Both Lenny and I became infected with scabies. For me it was the second time around. Mrs Baughan did not pursue professional treatment for us; she obtained the services of a woman who lived opposite us who made her own herbal ointments. We applied her ointment to our bodies and in two weeks the sores had disappeared. This was long before the general public knew anything about homeopathic medicine.

Boxing events were a regular feature on school sports days and fete days, which the town of Bicester would organise, our school being included. I did not particularly care for boxing, but you had to do it. Being left handed, always jabbing with my left gave me an advantage and I would gain more points than my opponent and usually finish up the victor.

The family's youngest son, Jim, would show us the ways of country life, taking us on numerous walks through the countryside, across fields and meadows, crossing and leaping over brooks and streams, into woods, fishing for minnows, collecting birds eggs, and teaching us the names of birds, flowers and trees. He showed us which springs were to drink from, the crystal clear ice cold water tasted like no other water that had ever passed our lips.

We watched the frogs' spawn in the ponds and their development into tadpoles, catching them and doing some horrible things to them that even now I feel ashamed of. Those poor creatures! We enjoyed eating elderberries, gathering blackberries, seeing the bluebells in the woods, primroses growing wild, listening to the songs of the birds and the buzz of the bees. It all merged into one beautiful harmonious picture. The countryside evolved into an everlasting love that I became eternally thankful for.

Walking down a lane one evening on our way home, as darkness was just descending, I was with a group of boys and we were talking rather loudly about Germans and parachutists. I mentioned the police station keeping rifles. From out of the blue, a wartime sergeant constable appeared, wheeling his bicycle, looking every inch like a taller version of Barry Fitzgerald, the Irish film actor, and giving me a shocking telling off, quoting the 'Careless talk costs lives' poster slogan. This was not to be my first run in with a policeman; I got a firm cuff behind the ear from a good old country copper for swearing on a Sunday, in the heart of town. I never forgot that cuff.

Since there was a shortage of hen's eggs, we would go looking for moorhens eggs. There was very little difference in taste. Rabbit and game were a regular feature on the menu at No. 3 Ladysmith Terrace. Mr Baughan had an allotment so we were fortunate enough to have plenty of fresh vegetables in the home. At that time I hated parsnips.

Mrs Baughan insisted on placing them on my plate and told me to eat them up. Craftily, when no one was looking, I would pretend to cough, grabbing a few at a time and shoving them into my trouser pocket This mushy matter would harden and leave a coating on the inside linings. I used to empty the white-yellow gunge down the toilet in the outhouse.

Returning home at night, tired from the day's excursions, we would sit in the small living room, with the oil lamp glowing and casting shadows across the room. Mrs Baughan would give us a cup of Oxo and a slice of bread before sending us up to bed.

The other evacuee and I had different interests with regards to friends. He found his friends and I found mine. I befriended a Johnny Venner from Punderson Gardens in Bethnal Green. If anyone knew Punderson Gardens you would wonder where on earth the gardens came into it. It was just a street of houses. Johnny lived at the most prestigious address in the whole of the town, Bicester House, occupied by the town's most illustrious couple, Major and Mrs Coker.

The Major was the epitome of a British Army Officer; tall, erect, moustached, with a clipped military accent. The locals would speak of his wife as 'Lady Coker'. Whether or not she was a titled lady we never knew. She was a very attractive woman, always very friendly to us and forever accompanied by her two dachshunds, Roma and Romeo. Bicester House was a manor; the manor's stone walls surrounded two-thirds of the estate, with a spinney and brook at the extreme end of the grounds. My friend, along with another evacuee, did not live in the manor; they were accommodated in an outhouse quite close by, somewhat austere in its furnishings, but quite comfortable. The Major kept two large wooden chests in the outhouse, his rank and name painted on them. As inquisitive boys, on one particular occasion we rummaged through them, delighted to find belts of machine gun bullets, swords and various other items of memorabilia from the First World War. We simply played with them, returned everything back into its place and forgot about them.

Bicester House became a regular feature in my comings and goings, and I gradually got to know the servants of the manor. One day they invited me into their kitchen for tea. One of the maids, Olive, was having a boiled egg. It was the very first time I had ever seen anyone slice the top off of a boiled egg with a knife, it intrigued me! I had so much to learn, both in table manners and etiquette. We did, at times, venture into the manor's living room; Johnny would remove a few cigarettes from the Major's silver cigarette box and smoke them, unseen, elsewhere on the estate. Occasionally we would attempt to crush the dried leaves from the trees, roll them in newspaper and smoke them, although not very successfully I might add! We were told to refrain from this as it would give you lumbago!

We played on the estate, running through the fields, down into the spinney, and climbing trees. In the walnut season, we scaled the trees for walnuts, removing the hard green skin; our fingers becoming yellow-stained as the nuts emitted their juices, releasing a smell like iodine. The Major and Lady Coker would hold fetes in the grounds; to us it was always an exciting event though we had hardly any money to spend on the stalls selling edibles.

Uniforms were beginning to appear around the town in numbers. Soldiers were being drilled on the asphalt road close to Major Coker's estate. We would watch them marching up and down to the orders of the Drill Sergeant, wearing forage caps and trying to keep them on their heads as they had not yet got used to wearing them. Older men started to join the Home Guard and formed units; convoys of army lorries, Bren gun-carriers and tanks were driven through the town quite frequently. The RAF were very much in evidence too, there were so many airfields around us.

At this time, with the amount of aircraft seen in the skies, I took a great interest in planes and became quite adept at plane-spotting. I could identify a Wellington, Blenheim, Beaufort, Avro Anson, Airspeed Oxford, Hurricane and Spitfires, as well as Gloster Gladiators from Weston-on-the-Green, towing gliders, and also German aircraft. Returning home one afternoon the clouds were very low, and I heard the drone of an aircraft. By the sound of its engines I knew that it was not one of ours. The whistle of a bomb was heard, then an explosion. The air raid siren sounded immediately. The bomb had detonated in the village of Launton, a mile and a quarter away from us. Fortunately, no damage was done. It was to be my very first taste of the war.

Lord Beaverbrook, as Minister of Production, was asking women to give up their pots and pans. We would play our part in helping the war effort by going around the town collecting scrap metal; aluminium appeared to be on the priority list for helping to make Spitfires. It was a bonus every time we were given an old aluminium saucepan, and we hoped that we had gathered enough to build a Spitfire. The railings of churches, parks, and people's front gardens were removed along with tramlines in London. There was a real spirit amongst the people all helping with the war effort.

Bicester on Sundays was not my favourite day; we were made to go to church two to three times. Our place of worship was the Methodist Hall in Sheep Street; the preacher, Sydney Hedges, knew us all by name. We would go there in the mornings and again to Sunday school in the afternoon, to a class run by Blind John. In the evenings we would go to the chapel opposite and, if we were lucky, they would show a film. The whole town closed down on Sundays, nowhere was open. If the day was fine it was bearable, but if it rained it was a miserable place to be in. In summer we used to have a marvellous Sunday school outing on the river from Oxford to Abingdon. It was one of those memorable days that was essentially English, and how you would always like it to be.

The cinema was the place to take you away from the harsh realities, into another world. Bicester was blessed with two. One was at the far end of town, the other formed part of the Crown Hotel in Sheep Street, Bicester's main thoroughfare. Outside the Crown there would be cabinets displaying picture-scenes of the current film being shown. I remember looking at some with Ray Milland, secretly hoping that when I grew older I would look like him.

In the evenings the town was very active with uniformed personnel. Pubs were always busy, though you never saw any drunkenness, firstly because the beer was watered down, and secondly spirits were hardly ever obtainable.

In the little enclave where we lived, the local milkman, Mr Tuffrey, gave me the job of helping him out on his milk round. This was on a council estate on the fringe of the town. He drove a pony and trap, almost at a racing pace, leaning straight back and holding on to the pony's reins. I would quickly collect the jugs from his customers and he in turn would fill them from the large metal churns. I would then return the milk to the customer post-haste. I loved helping him! I felt like a charioteer alongside him in that trap! His wife, very much a country woman, large in stature, enormous arms and as strong as a horse, kept pigs at the back of the town. Effortlessly, she could carry a sow in those huge arms of hers and throw a half-hundred weight sack of potatoes over her shoulder as if it were nothing!

Very often I would accompany her and watch her cleaning out the pig stys and feeding them. I have always retained a fascination for pigs; I could watch their behavior for hours on end. It was my first experience in seeing a pig being slaughtered, which at a young age I found barbaric. The poor animal was hit hard on its forehead with a mallet, stunning it and then a spike was driven into its brain. It was strung up and cut all the way down its belly, with its entrails dropping out. A bucket was placed underneath to collect the blood draining from its body. The slaughterer placed his arm into the bucket of blood, moving it in a rotating motion and black pudding was then made with it. Finally the pig was taken down, laid on the ground, and straw spread over its whole body before it was set alight, burning all its bristles off. It was then removed to the butchers. That scene never left me.

The town had a small open air swimming pool that we frequented at weekends. I think all of Bicester's boys and girls must have attended there on the same day. It was here, unaided, that I learned to swim. The sense of accomplishment gave a great boost to one's self esteem, something at that age which made you feel very proud.

We were destined to be immunized in a chapel close the town's main square. There were quite a few of us waiting to go in, sitting outside on a very low stone wall that was situated six foot above a stream. The wall's stone surface was extremely smooth and before I knew it, I slid backwards, dropping into the stream, cutting my forehead and drenching my clothes. Arriving home, I got a telling off for getting my clothes wet. It was the first and only time that Mrs. Baughan was ever cross with me – though I felt the reprimand was a little unjust.

In the fields close to the milk round an Italian prisoner of war camp was installed. They wore dark-brown dyed battle dress, with red patches sewn on. Some of the local girls became friendly with the prisoners – but how friendly I shall never know. My curiosity aroused such an interest that I started visiting the open camp. I sat with them around an open fire and spoke with them. I would ask them questions, and they would ask me questions. They showed me photographs of their families and girlfriends.

One very pro-Axis Italian prisoner had made a ring depicting the swastika of Germany, the column and the axe of Italy, and the rising sun of Japan, all filed and shaped from a piece of aluminium. Other prisoners made the most inventive things from aluminium, metal, perspex and coloured toothbrush handles. I was impressed with some of the rings they made from the metal, inserting multi-coloured fine lines on the face of the ring from toothbrush handles. They would offer me coffee and sometimes wanted to share their food. They were, in most part, a friendly lot, longing to return home when it was all over.

Throughout my time as an evacuee, I only saw my Father once. He brought me a Meccano set that I shared with the other boys in the house, making various models from the Meccano catalogue. My Mother paid me a visit only once. Things got so bad that the clothing I had was wearing out. No letters or parcels were ever sent to me that I can recall. Through the school, they arranged for me to be sent to a woman who took apart a lady's old two-piece costume that someone had donated, making it into a jacket and trousers for me. It looked most odd; it was too narrow at the waist and looked too feminine, but there was nothing else for me to wear. I felt embarrassed to wear it and hated it.

Lenny, the other evacuee, was taken back to London by his Mother. I had seen my sister only once; she was staying at the Fox Inn with a nice couple who moved away from the town, resulting in her being returned to London. After Lenny's departure I was left alone, until a few months later my Grandmother appeared out of the blue and took me back to London.

My sister, having already returned to London, had made arrangements to meet my Mother at her café in Haggerston. Dawn waited and waited for my Mother; she went and sat in a shelter. There were several of these brick shelters in the streets that could accommodate around forty people. Families were already sitting in the shelter in readiness for the next air raid that night. Fortunately, with their foresight, anticipating a raid taking place, they were all safe when the German bombers came over and dropped a land mine quite close to the church on the other side of the road. Mother never turned up, leaving my sister in that shelter alone. My sister and I did not see her until the war was over.

7

BACK TO LONDON

rriving back at No. 74, my Grandmother made a bed for me on the floor in the parlour, alongside the piano. There was no more sleeping room in the house, so I slept like this for several months. My aunts' husbands were in the forces, so they had returned to No. 74 with their children. Eventually, I had my own bedroom for the very first time. It was the same room where I used to sleep on the floor with my parents and sister. The fireplace had a small black iron oven range and fire grate. I used the oven as my safe. It became a hobby going around the streets the morning after an air raid, and collecting shrapnel and silver metallic-backed black strips of paper, dropped by German aircraft to confuse our radar system. As fast as I placed the shrapnel in my 'safe', Grandmother would remove them. She thought that they would explode!

Our Grandmother and Grandfather were left with the responsibility of raising us. Our parents, during their long absence, never provided anything for our support, financially or otherwise. We could have very easily been placed in a home.

The younger aunts felt resentment at having to help financially to clothe and feed us, and at every opportunity they would make this apparent. My sister was treated quite badly by them, and they used to taunt her, reminding her that we were charity children. If the aunts happened to be in conversation and my sister appeared, the talking would cease, and she was made to feel a social pariah. Nothing could be more hurtful at a young age, having no one to turn to, or a shoulder to cry on. It had an everlasting effect on her. Because I was a boy, and having so many women in the house, I was never treated in the same way, or if they ever did pass remarks like they had to my sister, they went right over my head. It's hard to understand how members of your own family could have been so cruel and insensitive.

Later in life, I have tried many times to analyse our family; summing it all up they were not a family as one would expect. They were never close-knit, each person seemed to go his or her separate way, devoid of love and harmony. I never saw any show of affection by our Grandparents to our aunts and uncles, not even a hug or a kiss. They just didn't know how to express love, or any form of tenderness. My sister and I, being the youngest, were just an extension of the family. We too never experienced any love. The sisters, our aunts, could be bitchy, envious and even jealous of each other. It was only much later in life when I was the only one left at home that a very close bond developed between my Grandmother and me.

From my period as an evacuee I had developed a slight country accent, so that when I teamed up with my old schoolmates again, I must have sounded to them like a country bumpkin. This left me open to some ridicule for a while. I enrolled at Teesdale Street School, as sadly St Peter's was never to reopen. Teesdale Street was a mixed school, with separate classrooms for boys and girls. It was at this school that we had two special teachers; the headmaster Mr McHarry who sang, and Mr King who played the piano. Classical music was introduced to us, with explanations of the pieces and composers by Mr King. It was never a boring experience and I have been forever thankful for it, in arousing our interest in music. The school had excellent teachers. Initially, I was in Mrs Jarvis's class. A lovely lady who always wore her hair in a bun, she was quite attractive. There was a period when sex education was introduced for the very first time into schools; by then we boys knew all the answers and there was very little that you could teach us! Out of devilment, I remember embarrassing Mrs Jarvis by asking her how the cockerel implanted its seed into the hen! The poor lady's face reddened and she had great difficulty in trying to give the answer! By the time she had finished fumbling and stuttering, it became as clear as mud! Even now, I feel sorry I ever asked the question! The school had a playground on the roof of the building, surrounded by high wire mesh fencing. Cricket and football were played along with general exercises and games. I recall St Paul's Cathedral being quite visible from here.

To get to school there was a shortcut through Hadrian's Estate. This was a council estate of grey-white brickwork, green painted doors, windows and balconies. The flats were fringed with back gardens, and a large enclosed garden was in the centre. We knew several families who resided there, with many of the boys and girls attending the same Teesdale Street School. Hadrian Estate had a caretaker, Mr Johnson; he was an absolute tyrant. If we were seen walking though his domain, he would chase us, shouting at us until we were off the estate. At times we would go to visit a friend, and if he saw you he would question you until he was satisfied that your visit was genuine. Mr Johnson was not very much liked by us, as he would scare many boys and girls who simply wanted to make a shortcut. One day passing through the estate, I happened to look down into a garden and saw something silver glinting; removing it from the soil, to my great delight I realised it was a half-crown piece; I had never possessed such a sum in all my life! I felt wonderful, I felt marvelous, and I felt rich. Making for the nearest shop en-route to the school, I stopped off at Mark Costa's. Marky, as he was known to us, was a small Jewish grocer and confectioner who reminded me of Groucho Marx, bespectacled with a moustache just like him! In harder times, we would fiddle this poor man with empty lemonade bottle deposits, returning a bottle, getting a penny back, and on the way out, removing two more empty bottles from the crates and taking them back the following day! On this particular day, with a half crown to spend, I bought bars of chocolate and sweets and shared them with some of my classmates.

There were many times when we went to school with holes in our shoes; we had to cut out cardboard and place it over them. If you had a 'downpour' the cardboard would get wet and soggy, and you would have to wait until you got home again to tear off a piece of cardboard from an old shoebox to re-plug the hole. When our clothing got beyond repair, or too small to wear, Grandmother would take us down to the 'Shallorams' in pursuit of something suitable. I remember looking with her for suitable shirts. We rummaged through piles of them on different stalls. She sorted one out for me that was pale blue with little silk star motifs and a frayed collar saying, 'There that'll do you nicely for school'. With great reluctance, I wore it to school, making attempts to hide the worn area as much as I possibly could by raising my jacket and looking as if my neck had disappeared!

Opposite our house, on the other side of the street, lived the Abrahams. After the blackout was lifted their house was illuminated all night by a lamp post situated immediately outside, it poured light into the front rooms of our house. The Abrahams were a most gentle and nicely spoken couple. We were never sure whether they were brother and sister, or husband and wife! We also never knew of the status of the young girl, Lilly, who lived with them. Rumour had it that she was an orphan, but she could have been their daughter for all we knew. They were very private people and we respected them as such. With the Abrahams, only brief pleasantries were ever exchanged, conversations never ever occurred.

The neighbouring Pattern's, who lived a few doors away from the Abrahams, were below average height. Mrs Pattern was the same height as Grandmother; they could easily have been mistaken for twins! Both of them loved the doorstep gossip and could always find the time to chat for hours about nothing. Very often we would hear 'I'll just pop across to see Pattern' – the Christian name was non-existent. Connie, the daughter and my sister's school friend, seemed the same height all the time I knew her; she never ever appeared to grow! You were lucky if ever you saw the Father, he would pass you in the street as if he never knew who you were. I'm not sure now if he was just plain shy, or he found it too much of an effort to acknowledge you.

There was a public telephone box on the outskirts of Hadrian's Estate, and a blue police box next to it in Hackney Road. The telephone had a button 'A' to press so you could register your call and speak. The other button 'B', was to return your coins if the call was not made. We used to stuff the opening slot with paper where the coins were returned. We would leave it there for a couple of days and then with a strong piece of wire remove the paper so that the coins would fall out.

Aunt Eileen and Uncle Harry had moved to Croydon, since his work was there, but Eileen came to Bethnal Green daily to work at the Lion Mills in Hackney Road. Grandmother also worked there as an office cleaner. Occasionally, I would go to help her do the dusting and other little chores. One morning, she gave me some A4 paper to take home. Placing this under my sweater, I was walking home along Hackney Road when the paper fell from my sweater blowing out onto the main road directly outside a police box. A constable very kindly went out into the road and picked up the papers up for me. Duly thanking the officer for his kindness, I gave a sigh of relief when I got home. Dear Grandmother was dismissed from her job at the Lion Mills for leaving puddles of water on the stairs. I think by this time, she was past her office cleaning days but she could not accept it. Eileen, at the finish of work from Monday to Friday, would collect Harry's dinner, which my Grandmother made, and take it home in a saucepan all the way back by train to Croydon.

In summertime after school, we would race to the bridge in the Broadway, climb though an opening in the metal railings, take off our clothes while we were still hot from running, and dive immediately into the Regent's Canal, known to us as 'The Cut'. The water was dark green, and you could not see a thing beneath, it was quite eerie. From time to time, you would see water rats scurrying along the bank on the opposite side; it was even said that there were dead donkeys in the canal, although I never saw any! Boys would be fishing from nets; a small bamboo cane with a white piece of gauze serving as the net, jam jars at their sides to place their catch in. Other boys would be dragging the canal with the rim of a bicycle wheel, and sacking stretched across the wheel, which improvised as a dragnet. Barge horses would be walking slowly along the towpath pulling canal barges, the tow rope running slack and dropping into the water, then tightening and coming up out of the canal, water dripping with green slimy matter that had been floating in it. If you were to fall in that canal today, you would be placed in quarantine for forty-eight hours.

We used to go swimming at the York Hall baths several times a week throughout the year. The York Hall baths, as with Bethnal Green in general, has a long association with boxing. Daniel Mendoza, champion of England from 1792 to 1795, lived in Bethnal Green. In my younger days our Bethnal Green boxing hero was Arthur Danahar. Boxing

The York Hall, noted for its boxing matches, swimming and public baths.

matches and dancing were held there. It is still used today for professional boxing matches. £2million has recently been spent in refurbishing York Hall, including a new gymnasium. We started to use The York Hall public baths frequently when we were older, rather than endure that awful tin bungalow bath back at No. 74!

At the kiosk in the York Hall you bought a ticket for a bath, towel and soap. The towel was hardly a bath towel size, and its texture was as rough as anything. The small cake of soap hardly lathered! The baths were in numbered cubicles, so if you got into the bath and found that the water was too cold, you would shout out 'more hot in number nine!' or whichever cubicle you were in. The attendant would then come along and release the water from an outside connection, which then came gushing into your bath at such a pace, that at times it became too hot. You would then have to yell back 'a little more cold!' Fortunately, most of the time you got the balance right! They had a small canteen/cafeteria where you could buy cups of Oxo, toast and other little snacks that were always welcome after a bath or a swim.

Sometimes we would go 'up the Roman' – the Roman Road market, where there used to be a shop by the name of Tolliday's. I knew of no other shop like it. It specialised in steamed suet puddings of every description. Our faces would be placed hard against their windows to see steak and kidney puddings, bacon roly-poly, treacle pudding, jam roll and spotted dick. Our mouths would drool at the sight of seeing all this wonderful food; alas, we never had the money to buy anything!

Each week we would attend woodwork classes at Daniel Street, and the girls would go to domestic science classes on those days. On one particular day in class, I walked past

The Broadway, London Fields, once a thriving market of stallholders.

a bench that a boy was working on. Suddenly, I saw a spurt of blood rising out of my sock like a fountain. He had knocked a brace and bit off the bench, and the bit had gone straight into the vein of my foot. The teacher applied some rapid first aid to the injury and, with the help of two boys, placed me on a wheelbarrow and wheeled me to the Mildmay Mission hospital! After treatment, I was wheeled home in grand style on the wheelbarrow, to the dismay of my Grandmother. She hated anyone being ill or injured, she lacked empathy in such matters.

Our lessons were interrupted from time to time by daylight air raids. Our shelter was on the first floor. It was a cloakroom that had been reinforced with an extra brick wall on all four sides. Mr Ridgeway, our teacher, would produce his newspaper – the *Daily Telegraph* – and have us read articles from the paper until the 'all clear' had sounded and were able to return to class.

Every Wednesday, my Grandmother would give me a note to take to school requesting permission for me to leave class early to get pies and mash for the family. The notes were never refused. Off I would go with an oilcloth-type shopping bag and a china jug for the liquor to Cooke's pie and mash shop in the Broadway, London Fields.

I used to carry about twelve to fourteen pies, with the potato mash and liquor. With regularity, the liquor would spill over my hands, the thick hot green liquid running over my thumb and the back of my hand. There was nowhere to stop and wipe that horrible mess off. I just kept going until I arrived home!

The Blitz was to last from 7 September 1940 until 15 May 1941. During the air raids we never went to the shelters. Some went to the underground stations at Bethnal Green and Liverpool Street, others to the brick shelters in the streets. Bethnal Green became the

Every Wednesday the author would go to Cooke's with a note to collect pies and a jug of liquor (coarse parsley sauce) for the whole family.

epicenter of the Blitz with bombings day after day. At the sound of the siren, a sound that made your stomach turn over, we would all go down to our Grandmother's bedroom and sit around the bed having cups of tea until the 'all clear' was sounded. Sometimes the raid was short-lived, at other times it would go on for hours. I think we found being together gave us comfort. We would listen to the bombs dropping, some getting quite close, and anti-aircraft guns would be firing away from Victoria Park, the ping of shrapnel hitting roofs and iron guttering. Some nights it became so very bad the house shook, other nights a little quieter. Many of the residents down the street were either in the ARP, Firewatchers, or AFS; many teenagers became ARP messengers on bicycles.

The Ministry of Home Security, in response to Herbert Morrison's appeal for more firebomb fighters, initiated a nationwide scheme for The Boy Scouts Association to act as fire spotters in their own district. The patrols consisted of eight boys with a patrol leader. Fire watch was compulsory for all civilians of both sexes between the ages of sixteen to sixty years of age. A part time service of the Civil Defence required forty-eight hours service per month. Not to turn up for a fire watch would result in a fine.

Our local rag, the *Hackney Gazette*, that most in the East End referred to as the ''Ackney Gazette', continued to report court findings and at times, even in the country's darkest hours, could be found to be amusing. A Mrs Minnie Winter, aged thirty-seven, of No. 34 Pollards Row was fined £5 for concealing a naval deserter for fifty-one weeks. 'I didn't know he was a deserter' she said, 'I met him in a pub'. The paper also requested its readers not to write and address letters to Adolf Hitler – 'The G.P.O (General Post Office) is not able to deliver them for the time being'.

Uncle Joe was in the AFS (Auxiliary Fire Service) based at Bishopsgate in the City of London. He invited me along to the station one day, showing me all the apparatus, the fire engines he drove, and best of all, I was allowed to sit down and eat with all the firemen! Firewatchers were armed with a stirrup pump and a bucket of sand, not very effective when practically the whole of the City of London and the East End were ablaze!

In mentioning Bishopsgate and the City of London, I feel that I should cite a former colleague, sadly no longer of this world. He was at that particular time a City of London policeman, based at Bishopsgate. Joe was a very tall man, as indeed most of the City of London policemen were. He was a loveable, charismatic rogue. His beat took him from Bishopsgate to Aldgate. The beat had seven pubs, and each night on duty, Joe would consume two pints of beer 'on the house'. If there happened to be a raid and some of the shops were hit and others damaged, Joe would arrange for a lorry to come along and remove the whole of the shop front, including the contents. If the shop fronts were chromium like the 'Fifty Shilling Tailors', so much the better, they brought a better price and were easier to get rid of.

One evening on his beat, he came across a row of garages that interested him – he found one garage locked. With no further ado, Joe gave the padlock a hard blow with his truncheon and gained access. It was like walking into Aladdin's Cave! The garage was stocked high with black market goods; chocolates, nylon stockings and a few hundred eggs. Joe very rapidly dispensed with the nylon stockings and chocolates, and then commenced marketing the eggs!

He knew of a Jewish club owner in Aldgate who was very eager to buy. The club owner, at his request, wanted to see the eggs. Joe took him round to the garage but the club owner almost had a fit as he discovered that it was his! Since the goods were black market he could say absolutely nothing. On another occasion, Joe was in one of the pubs on his beat having a crafty pint, and while downing it he could see out of the corner of his eye, his Inspector. Joe, quick as a flash, shoved his pint under his cape. His inspector walked over to him and said that he would like him to accompany him around a couple of blocks. Joe held that pint for the whole of the walk! On returning to the pub, the Inspector said to Joe, 'I do hope that you haven't spilt any of that beer'. Joe had the luck of the Irish!

At some stage when the air raids were at their height, we gave up going down into my Grandparent's bedroom. It was decided that we would all bed down in the kitchen at night. Our grandparents, aunts Eileen and May with their daughters, my sister Dawn and I all had our allotted sleeping places. Grandfather was at the end of the room with his feet under the dresser, Grandmother and I were under the table, divided by the table's spar, my feet hanging over the end one. Aunt May and Sheila slept beyond me under the wireless and birdcage. Aunts Eileen, Brenda and Dawn were in the opposite corner; Dawn's head perched against the coal cupboard. If Grandfather had gone out for the evening, he would return after we had all bedded down for the night, resulting in our having to get up to make room for him to find his sleeping position. Brenda, being the youngest, would pee over my sister in the night! Having no change of clothes, she would have to go to work the following day still wearing the soiled petticoat.

During one particular raid, we had an explosion so powerful in its force that it lifted me over the wooden spar of the table on to the top of my Grandmother! My sister slept on, she didn't even hear the noise. The Oxford Arms, Jones's Dairy, and several other houses were hit and completely demolished. The site made way for an auxiliary water tank for the Fire Service, as indeed were many bombed out sites. It later became an allotment for a time, to which the Queen paid a visit. It was later cleared for prefabricated houses to be erected.

During the cold weather, my aunts and cousins would sleep in their pixie hoods – a hat that was quite fashionable during the war. One of my aunts christened it the 'Pixie-Poxie Hood'. It got so cold that on some nights they would wear a balaclava and mittens! The cold draught would blow into the room from under the coal cupboard and the passageway.

As the war progressed, most foods were rationed, with the exception of offal. Restaurants were exempt from rationing which created resentment. The wealthy could eat out frequently and extravagantly, supplementing their food. Because of this resentment, certain rules were put into force. No meal would cost more that 5s, no meal could consist of more than three courses, and only one of meat or fish could be served at the same sitting.

The London County Council established the Londoner's Meal Service in September 1940 as an emergency system, feeding those who had been bombed out. This became known as 'The British Restaurant'. By mid-1942 the L.C.C. were operating 200 of these

HM Queen Elizabeth with Councillor Saunders, our neighbour, visiting allotments that were once the site of the Oxford Arms, Jones the Dairy and several adjoining houses, 17 June 1943. (Tower Hamlets Local History Library and Archives)

HM Queen Elizabeth visiting the allotments of St Peter's Avenue and Nelson Gardens. Note the old terraced houses behind the fencing of Old Bethnal Green. (Tower Hamlets Local History Library and Archives)

establishments. In Bethnal Green there was one restaurant in the Children's Museum in Cambridge Heath Road. A V-1 flying bomb came down opposite the museum in 1944, and there was hardly a window left after that explosion. The other British Restaurant was in Bethnal Green Road, quite close to Brick Lane. A three course meal only cost 9*d*. Standards varied. I ate in both of these and it was dire. The soup was watery, the main meal bland and tasteless, the dessert… well, on one occasion, I ordered jam tart and custard. The jam tart was a hardened, sweetened piece of dough served in a square, a razor thin line of jam running through the centre and the custard ladled on to the 'jam tart' had the consistency of water. In fact it tasted like water. These British Restaurants were not my favourite eating places! The tastier meals were found in the ordinary cafés. Corned beef and spam fritters were regularly on the menu, along with a lot of offal dishes. One of my favourites was stuffed sheep's hearts with roast potatoes, something you rarely see on menus now. There was, of course, a general saying that if you asked for something not necessarily out of the ordinary, you would invariably be told 'There's a war on you know'.

My Grandmother used to rant and rave about the stringent allowances, wanting to 'string up' Lord Woolton, the Minister of Food. 'A cess on him!' she would say, meaning that he should have a cesspit dropped on his head. Much later in 1946, a new Minister of Food was appointed, John Strachey, whom she also wanted to 'string up!' Among our rations, I remember having a tin of corned beef, dated 1917, some twenty-four years old. That tin was still edible, even after all that time! The cooked meat shops in Bethnal Green Road were a blessing, supplementing the meager food rations. Offal was not rationed, so we were able to extend the weekly bill of fare with tripe and onions, brawn, sheep's hearts, luncheon meat, pig's trotters, and many other forms of offal. The only item in these shops that was hardly ever available was liver. Things got so scarce that one week there was no meat available, only corned beef. It was the first time we were to see our Grandmother break down and cry. A vegetable dish was named after the Minister of Food, Lord Woolton – 'Woolton Pie'. Oddly enough people were much healthier then than now, and certainly there was no obesity.

Recipes from the Ministry of Food were advertised, and were the most uninspiring dishes one could ever imagine. Some were really awful. Characters were introduced, such as 'Dr Carrot' and 'Potato Pete' to encourage people to eat home-grown vegetables. 'Eat more carrots, you'll see in the dark better', we were told. It was rumoured that night-fighter pilots ate carrots to see in the dark.

A white loaf of bread was no longer available. We were introduced to the 'national loaf'; it was practically all grain. Supposedly a 'brown loaf', the colour was nearer to grey. There was no other selection of bread and the 'national loaf' stayed with us throughout the war.

Sausages were made in three grades, 'A', 'B' and 'C'. After 20 January 1941, sausage grades 'A' and 'B' were prohibited and only grade 'C' sausage was allowed. Grade 'C' permitted a meat content of less than 45 per cent but not under 30 per cent. The maximum prices per pound of grade 'C' were:

> Beef 7*d*, pork 11*d*, Kosher beef 10*d*
> Sausage meat: beef 6*d*, pork 10*d* Kosher beef 8*d*

Fruit such as bananas and oranges had completely disappeared; they were not to return until well after the war was over. Everyone was told to 'Dig for Victory' and to grow our own vegetables. We boys made ourselves a vegetable patch in the garden of a bombed out house, 'doing our bit'. Posters were everywhere. 'Is your journey really necessary?', 'Careless talk costs lives', 'Even the walls have ears', 'A slip of the lip may sink a ship', 'Dig for Victory', and 'Buy national savings bonds' were just a few of the slogans.

Every Wednesday and Friday the *Hackney Gazette* would publish the court cases of shops fined for overcharging on food. Owen Brothers of Bethnal Green Road were fined £50 and £5 guineas costs for selling three eggs at 4¾d each, the real retail price being 3¾d. The Home & Colonial was summoned for contravening the Jam Order (maximum price) for charging 1s8d on a 2lb jar of raspberry jam instead of 1s6d and for selling twenty-one 1lb jars of raspberry jam at 10½d instead of 9½d. The manager apologized to the court saying he misplaced the schedule as he was always at the butter and bacon end of the shop. All summonses were dismissed on payment of one guinea costs, it was an honest mistake! Albert Franks, butcher of No. 164 Ridley Road was summonsed for overcharging on two best neck imported lamb chops weighing 9ozs, at 8d, when the price should have been 6¾d. The case was dismissed with one guinea cost.

Grandmother started to use her culinary skills and made a cake. The nearest description would be, 'rock cake gateau' that we called 'her quick'. It weighed a ton! Grandfather was sent up to the docks at Greenock with his brother Arthur, with a parcel containing a whole 'bit of quick'. Uncle Alf in the army and Uncle Harry in the air force up in the Orkneys were each sent the cake on a regular basis, and I was to receive them much later while I was doing my National Service in Germany.

We would clamber over the bombed-out houses, rummaging through remaining rooms, removing, above all things, medicine bottles. We once found the metal insert of a copper and poured all the medicines into it and lit a fire, boiling the liquid up until it was bubbling. We waited for something magical to happen. As budding make-believe scientists we expected to develop some wonderful solution for mankind! Sadly nothing happened!

At odd weekends I would go and visit my Uncle Joe and Aunt Dolly in Clapton, by which time I had two young cousins, Jose and Valerie. I liked my Aunt Dolly a great deal. During one visit the air raid siren sounded and I had to spend quite a few hours in their Anderson shelter with my two young cousins until the raid was over. Uncle Joe and Aunt Dolly were to divorce; sadly we were never to see Aunt Dolly and our cousins again.

During these years the wireless used to play the songs sung by Vera Lynn and Ann Shelton, the music from the bands of Geraldo, Jack Payne, Harry Roy, Ambrose, and Victor Sylvester, the soft melodious voices of Flanagan and Allen, the monologues of the Weston Brothers and Cyril Fletcher. There were also broadcasts by comedians Rob Wilton, We Three: Enoch, Ramsbottom and Lovejoy, Tommy Handley's ITMA, and that wonderful routine of Rob Wilton's, 'The day war broke out', in his slow, dry, droll delivery.

It was at this stage that each Saturday I would get a No. 6 bus to Trafalgar Square to visit the National Art Gallery. All the old masters had been removed to safety in Wales; they had, instead, paintings of artists from the armed forces. Most of these were of war scenes, of well-known high-ranking officers, admirals and generals. Bomber Harris, General Montgomery, Air Marshall Tedder, and Admiral Cunningham were all there, along with paintings of land battles, sea battles, paintings of dog fights, of ships, destroyers, cruisers and battleships, Hurricanes and Spitfires. Every war scene that one could call to mind would be here. They were changed quite frequently and the National Gallery became my weekly Saturday venue. During the week, the National would hold gallery concerts, seating 1,500 people. American GI's were always hanging around Trafalgar Square hoping to pick up a girl. We used to approach them with 'Got any gum chum?', and in most cases they would pull out a packet of gum and hand you a strip. Being handed a strip of 'juicy fruit' gum, unlike our Wrigley's coated tablets of spearmint, was something quite different. Servicemen and women from all parts of the globe would come to Trafalgar Square sightseeing. I went to cross the road one day and a wartime constable took my hand to escort me across. I looked up and found that the man holding my hand was Wally Patch, the film actor. He was in so many British films playing character parts and I felt rather honoured that Mr Patch had held my hand.

I recall seeing airmen's faces burnt and scarred. Those very brave men were so badly burnt that they became known as the 'guinea pigs'. Eventually, some 600 'reconverted' men of sixteen different nationalities formed a group called The Guinea Pig Club. Sir Archibald McIndoe, then just plain Archibald McIndoe, the plastic surgeon, would send groups of fliers up to London with tickets to the theatre and night club reservations. As the Battle of Britain raged, some 4,500 airmen would be pulled out from the wreckage of their flaming aircraft. Many years later I was to meet Lady McIndoe, a lovely lady who at that time was involved in charitable work in the Caribbean.

Every other person then was in uniform and carrying gas masks. The American officers looked so smart in their olive green jackets and beige trousers, as did the Australian airmen in their navy blue uniform. I would look at the insignias, divisional signs, ranks and flashes on the shoulders of their different countries. There were Poles, Czechs, French, South African, and New Zealanders; so many nationalities passed by. One Saturday I arrived at Trafalgar Square during a Victory Bond drive. Standing on a rostrum addressing the crowd was Ivor Novello and the actress, Roma Beaumont. I could not take my eyes off them, they were the most glamorous people I had ever seen! Ivor Novello, had blue-black wavy hair, and was wearing a camel overcoat with a polka dot red silk scarf. Roma Beaumont looked absolutely stunning. After the drab war years, to see those beautiful glamorous people up on that rostrum was too wonderful for words! A young fellow approached me of a similar age with an autograph book and asked me if I had their signatures, which I had not. He then showed me their autographs. He invited me to accompany him to the Garrick Theatre in Charing Cross Road, where Michael Redgrave was appearing in 'Uncle Harry'. We waited at the stage door for a while and finally Michael Redgrave appeared. He gave me his autograph on a piece of paper, and signed the boy's autograph book. Some twenty years later, I was sitting in the buffet car travelling from Victoria Station to Bognor Regis, when who should be sitting next to me but Michael Redgrave! We got into conversation; he was on his way to Chichester where he was playing in 'Uncle Vanya'. I related the story of meeting him at the Garrick all those years ago. He asked me if I had seen the show, so I informed him that at that time I could hardly afford my return bus fare back to Bethnal Green, let alone go to the theatre which, of course, was absolutely true!

A newspaper agent in Hackney Road hired me for a paper round after I had first obtained permission from school. A medical was also requested, and it was found that I required dental treatment. The school, in the meantime would not allow me to work. Managing to get the dental work attended to, I had to be re-examined again and was found fit to work. Part of the news round involved delivering to a large council block in Pritchard's Road. There was a woman on the second floor; her flat was at the far end of the balcony. Each time I neared that flat, I used to wretch and gag my mouth, as the smell was appalling. I couldn't put her paper thorough the letter box quickly enough, hand across my mouth and pinching my nose at the same time. That lady got lightning newspaper delivery! Worse was yet to come on Sundays, when I had to collect the money and face her. Opening her door, she would keep me engaged in conversation, and it was unbearable. I had to keep a perfectly straight face, pretending that everything was quite normal, when all I wanted to do was to get away and breathe fresh air into my lungs! It was my worst delivery out of the whole newspaper round. I dreaded going there.

It was a relief to go to the cinema to forget the austerity of war, if possible, with its drabness and rationing. We were deluged with British and American propaganda films to boost our morale. Cinemas were showing *Night train to Munich*, *Hitler's Children*, or *Confessions of a Nazi Spy*. If someone appeared in a German uniform on the screen, the audience would hiss like a snake, not just one hiss but several. If, in a scene, a German did something cruel, such as hitting someone with a rifle butt, one or two of the older men in the audience would shout out, 'You dirty, rotten, German bastards'. It became quite commonplace when visiting the cinema to hear hissing, cursing, and swearing whenever Germans appeared on the screen. The audience became so carried away. With films like *Mrs Miniver* however, a wartime family story, you were guaranteed to watch without any noises or remarks.

On Wednesday 3 March 1943 Bethnal Green suffered its Tube shelter disaster; 173 people died from a terrifying crush, as panic spread through the crowds trying to enter the shelter. The underground station was one of the few deep level shelters in the East End. Situated in a densely populated urban area, it had, at times, held 7,000 people and contained 5,000 bunks. Approximately 500 people were already in the shelter when the air raid warning sounded [4]. It was 8.17 p.m. At 8.27 p.m., a terrifying roar was heard as an anti-aircraft battery fired a salvo of sixty rockets from Victoria Park.

This sound was unfamiliar, creating anxiety and panic as the crown surged forward, with only a twenty-five watt light bulb to guide them in the dark of the blackout. The station's steps were wet and treacherous as it had been raining. A woman, holding her child, fell near the bottom of the first staircase. A man tripped over her, starting the whole tragic event with each person tripping over another, creating a human domino effect. There were many rumours flying around at the time. Some said that it sounded like the noise of a train going over the railway bridge at the Salmon & Ball; others said it was Dickie Corbett, an ex-boxer and his gang who stationed themselves around the

Salmon & Ball. It was rumoured that Jewish people took all their jewellery down to the tube with them, and that the gang created the panic as a diversion to rob.

Despite the best efforts of rescuers, twenty-seven men, eighty-four women and sixty-two children died. Another sixty-two were taken to hospital. It had been alleged that the woman who originally fell had survived, but her daughter had not. Fearful that the news of such an unnecessary disaster would demoralise the people, the government ordered that both the location and the precise number of fatalities should be kept secret. There were boys and girls from our school who lost their lives on that dreadful day.

One of the boys in our class who died in that awful disaster lived in Mansford Street. He lived in the lower part, which housed tenement dwellings. One block, next to St Lawrence School, was Meadow Dwellings. That building depressed me each time I passed by. There were two flats on each floor; a toilet was shared between two families on an arched open landing, with an iron balcony facing into the street and cold stone steps leading all the way to the top. Between 1830 and 1898 there were many similar buildings erected in the East End to accommodate the poor; they were easily identifiable by their sombre and drab appearance. However, in those days the buildings must have seemed like palaces to the poor wretches who were transferred from hovels of poverty and squalor to clean and decent housing.

They must have seemed a godsend, the great benefactors such as George Peabody, the Guinness Trust, and Lord Rowton, who gave their names to the buildings they erected. The East End is indebted to Peabody, an American philanthropist who provided $2.5 million, an enormous sum at that time, for low cost housing for Londoners who had to be poor, of moral character and good members of society to qualify. Lord Rowton also founded and built the famed Rowton Houses with his own money. One was in Whitechapel, the other in King's Cross; a working man's hotel, providing a single bed in a cubicle, and a bath, for 6d per night. Most of these buildings have since been converted into private, luxurious abodes, and some demolished. To hear of anyone staying at Rowton House, you instinctively knew that they were literally 'on the bones of their backside!'

St Lawrence School had reopened as a play centre which we attended in the early evenings. Here you could participate in cricket, football, gymnastics and art classes. I spent very little time on gymnastics, but an excessive amount on art. In the summer we played cricket. It was nice to be away from home and find a place with those facilities. In those days, sportswear did not exist; we carried out our gymnastics in the same clothes which we wore on the streets.

It was at this age that I started noticing girls; one girl in the art class whom I became attracted to was Betty Wright. She was blonde, hazel-eyed and had a lovely lilt to her voice which I found appealing. I sent her a note asking her if she would 'go out with me'. She replied on paper, saying 'yes'. I was elated. This marked the beginning of discovering that I liked the opposite sex. The sole company of boys would begin to wear thin somewhat in its appeal! The romance with Betty was innocent. We would meet, going nowhere but the play centre, holding hands with an occasional peck. After some time our innocent little romance faded.

Quite close to St Lawrence School was another, the Mansford. This was a secondary school that closed at the beginning of the war like many others in Bethnal Green. During its heyday it had a fine reputation. Our Aunt Winnie attended it. It later reopened for evening classes and as a restaurant for high tea. The high tea was first rate; it was my introduction to pilchards in tomato sauce and spam; it was far nicer than anything I received at home. I would go there whenever I could afford to do so. I continue to eat both spam and tinned pilchards to this day.

On the odd Sunday I would go and visit Aunt Noona (Ethel) who had by then divorced her first husband and remarried a very quiet agreeable man, 'Uncle Sonny'. They resided in Clapton. Very craftily my main purpose of visiting Aunt Noona was that she was such a wonderful natural cook. Her Sunday roast dinners were unsurpassable, my sister and I were never sure where she acquired this talent, because she most certainly never gained it from our Grandmother. She would give me odd little jobs in the kitchen, like beating up the butter and sugar for her cake-making, a small price to pay for a wonderful meal. She was blessed in giving us two cousins, Mavis and Tony.

Like the other boys in the street, it suddenly became the craze for us to have bicycles. Not wishing to be left out, I badgered my Grandmother until she relented and we both went along to a second hand shop in Three Colts Lane that sold bicycles. I selected one that, with a new coat of paint, would be fine. Agreeing on a price of 30s, I walked home with her and the bicycle absolutely elated. It did not take long before I purchased a small tin of paint and decided to paint it in a Cambridge Blue. Grandfather, in his supervisory role, watched me paint the bicycle out in the yard and was constantly telling me that I was 'treacle-ing' it on. There's nothing quite like someone watching over you when trying to make a first class job. With the paintwork dried, I could not wait to get out on the street with the rest of the boys who would assemble outside the church and ride off to Victoria Park. The time taken from when we used to scooter there was next to nothing! The traffic around the junction of Hackney Road and Cambridge Heath Road, before entering Bishop's Way, could be a little scary, but the more you were on the road the more confident you became. The bicycle gave us a greater amount of freedom in that it enabled us to go further afield.

John Finch's Yard was in Mansford Street. I would sometimes go this way to school as a diversion from the regularity and monotony of the same old route. John Finch & Sons were carriers. They stabled some of the finest horses you would ever see in London, magnificent animals, beautifully groomed, which pulled only light goods vehicles. Their drivers always looked splendid in their livery. The horse-drawn vehicles and polished side lamps were always an impressive sight. Whenever they drove by, the sound was unmistakable; the fast rhythm of horse's hooves striking the road, and the rapid turning of the wheels. You felt compelled to look up and admire equally both man and horse. They would come out of the yard on to a cobble-stoned ramp, the horse's shoes creating sparks as they eased their way out into the street. Close by in Claredale Street, was the blacksmiths. John Finch's horses were taken here for shoeing along with horses from other companies. The blacksmith fascinated me; I would love to watch him working. The striking of red-hot metal, the metallic ringing, cling, clang as the metal was struck on the anvil, shaping, and forming it into horse shoes, then filing the horse's hooves, the hot metal shoe being placed on the horses hoof, sizzling and smoking into a miniature cloud. I adored the smell that arose when this was done! Finally, the blacksmith would hammer the nails into the hoof with such speed and dexterity it would leave me gazing in awe.

The war was now turning in our favour. I lay in my bed at night, listening to the sounds of our bombers flying overhead, on their way to Europe to discharge their loads. Each night the aircraft grew more numerous, until the sounds of the engines seemed endless, and it became impossible to sleep. Looking out of my bedroom window, there would be an armada above. It was a most wonderfully reassuring sight and sound, knowing that the chances of a German air raid reprisal would be remote.

8

THE TEENAGE YEARS

he school years at Teesdale Street passed. We were still at war, and having reached the age of fourteen, it was time to leave and go out into the world. When the day finally came to leave, I cried. I was at a point where I was just beginning to grasp maths and English, and had really become attached to the school. We were given the opportunity to state what we would like to do; I did not have one iota of a clue. Most of the boys in the class opted for engineering and raised their hands, so not to be left out, I stupidly raised mine.

I was selected for a job in electrical and telephone engineering with the firm of H.H. Electrics Ltd, in Clerkenwell (Little Italy). My Grandmother bought me a pair of brace and bib overalls, and a small attaché case which on my first day she packed with a stotty cake (a Tyneside flat loaf) given to her by a neighbour, Mrs Pattern, who lived opposite, and an apple!

The author in his late teens at No. 74.

Sister Dawn in her late teens.

Off I went out into the world. I was engaged at 15s a week, for a five and a half day week. My very first task was to push a builder's barrow with another boy, laden with heavy electrical equipment, from Clerkenwell to a factory being rewired in Holloway. We worked at this factory for a few months, experiencing a series of air raids from the V-1's (Doodlebugs). As soon as the air raid siren sounded, we would dash up to the factory roof which had an excellent view over London. We could see the flying bombs coming over quite clearly, the throb, throb, throb of their engines, with flames spurting out, suddenly coming to stop and gliding down to earth, creating death and destruction. They hardly ever came in our direction. We were able to catch first sight of them as they flew over London, the explosions and the plumes of smoke rising up dramatically. Each time, we debated where we thought they had come down. We were rarely accurate in our guesses as they could be very deceiving.

H.H. Electrics sent me on numerous jobs in and around London. One in particular I did not like was in Park Royal. I disliked the electrician I was working with constantly addressing me as 'Bill'. In today's terms he would have been referred to as a 'smart ass'. He loved to give the impression of being superior, which, of course, he was not, sending me to do tasks that really I should not have been doing. We were re-wiring a machine shed and he had me climb up into the rafters to a fuse board that was quite old, where some of the old porcelain fuses had cracked and the whole board was live. I fell off the rafters on to a lathe that was turning and gashed my wrist. He neither reported it nor bothered to take to me have it seen to. Each day when we finished work he would have me carry a heavy wooden tool box to Park Royal Station, which was a considerable distance from where we were working. I was very pleased when I never had to work with him again.

The same boy I had worked with in Clerkenwell was sent with me to an establishment in Clerkenwell Green, The Uniform Clothing Company. The basement of those premises to us boys was like an Aladdin's Cave. It contained uniforms, helmets, holsters, swords, and all kinds of wonderful things that would appeal to any youngster. At lunch break we would start playing around with some of the articles. One day, we donned fencing masks and started fencing with very lethal swords. I lunged with a thrust at the other boy's mask, thinking that the wire mesh would protect him. Regretfully the sword went straight through and cut him just under the eye. Fortunately the cut was very slight. It certainly stopped any further playing around with swords after that event!

The company sent us to some very interesting places at times. Not far from Clerkenwell Green was St John's Gate. During the war, I do not think it was open to the public, but as a boy it held me enthralled working there. St John's Gate has a rich history of the Knights Hospitaller. It was a monastic order, serving the sick and defending the faith, and was built in 1504. It was once the entry to the Knight's English Priory. The museum today has the most wonderful treasures that include arms and armour, silver, paintings and furniture from the Order's time on the island of Malta, a fifteenth-century Flemish altar piece, and decorative jugs from the monks' pharmacy. After the dissolution of the monasteries, Henry VIII used the sixteenth-century Priory precincts for storing army supplies, and under Elizabeth I, it housed the Revels Office, where thirty of Shakespeare's plays were registered. In the Gate's east tower, Hogarth's Father ran a coffee house, and Edward Cave's *Gentleman's Magazine* was published with a young Dr Johnson writing the articles. In Victorian times, the St John Ambulance was founded here, inspired by the medical traditions of the Knights. People passing this very impressive gate daily are unaware of the wonderful treasures that are held there!

When we were working in Victoria I was sent to the Sun Electric Company in Charing Cross Road to obtain some silk flex. On leaving the premises with the flex, I crossed the road and decided to spend a few minutes in an amusement arcade on a pinball machine. I placed the flex on a machine at the side of me, and became engrossed in the play. At the end of the game, I looked around and found that the flex had been stolen. I went into the decline of a fourteen year old and cried and cried! Eventually I plucked up enough courage to return to Victoria, face the music and explain the loss. With the stars shining down on me, the people I was working for were sympathetic and I was let off the hook!

On one of the jobs in the West End, we were working quite close to Wardour Street. Each day I would pass by 'Ley-Ons', one of the very few Chinese restaurants in London at that time. I could not pass without looking at the huge menu displayed in the window. All those lovely, exotic, oriental mouth-watering dishes that I was bursting to try and taste, but I could never afford to dine there. I said to myself 'One day I shall eat here'. And I did…

I began working with a Belgian electrician named Henri for long periods. He was a delightful man, and would take the trouble to explain everything in depth; not only electrical matters, but also worldly affairs, and especially romance, arousing my interests in so many subjects! London at this particular time had several continental butchers, which you do not see around today. They, of course, sold horse meat. We were still on rationing and meat was very scarce. Henri took me home one Saturday afternoon and introduced me to horsemeat. He cooked steaks for both of us, I thought they were delicious. I bought some from a continental butchers in Farringdon Road and took them home.

A Bethnal Green Memoir

My Grandmother was as pleased as anything; not knowing that it was horsemeat! I informed Grandfather of the truth, thinking that he would readily accept it. How wrong I was! He went absolutely ballistic at the very thought of eating it. Consequently, I never brought any home ever again. Henri was having a love affair with the company secretary. Our boss greatly disapproved of this relationship, and of Henri, and showed his disdain whenever they were together. Eventually they were married. Henri would certainly have been sacked were it not for the fact that the secretary was so important to the company.

Very often I had to remain at our office in Clerkenwell Road. Close by was St Peter's Catholic Church where Gigli had sung, and opposite was Leather Lane and Hatton Garden. Facing us was Lloyd's Tobacco Factory, so sweet-smelling pipe tobacco permeated the air all day long! Each morning I would leave home and catch the No. 555 Bloomsbury trolley bus to work. Sometimes, when I was a little short of money, I would walk. Close to where I worked was a 'dining rooms', then numerous around London. The interiors all looked alike; dark-stained seating, partitioned by wood-panelled sections, accommodating four to six at a squeeze, with marble-topped tables. The menus were very basic, but offered good wholesome food. In the mornings smoked haddock, kippers, bacon and bubble (bubble and squeak), porridge, toast, dripping toast, large tea and small tea was available. At lunchtimes there would be steak and kidney puddings, steak and kidney pie, liver and bacon, and sausages and mash. The vegetables were all boiled; potatoes, cabbage and peas. Nothing was ever fried; chips in these establishments were unheard of. Sweets, the word 'desserts' never in our vocabulary, were always suet pudding, treacle pudding, marmalade pudding and jam pudding, all served with custard. The proprietor, Ted Driscoll, forever-smiling Ted, employed me early in the mornings before I started work to toast the bread for him. I would sit in front of his coal fired range holding the bread in front of the fire with a toasting fork. For this I was given a large mug of tea and two slices of dripping toast. I was allowed to spread the dripping on my toast, which would have me going to the bottom of the dripping basin for the dark brown beef jelly, the tastiest part!

Catching the 555 trolley bus to work one morning with my sister, we were very near our destinations when the air raid warning sounded. She got off at her normal stop; I decided to alight from the bus before I reached Leather Lane. Getting off at Farringdon Road, I heard the familiar droning of a 'doodlebug'. Looking towards Smithfield Meat Market, directly in line with Farringdon Road, I could see a black V-1 that suddenly had cut its engine, and was gliding down towards me. Not knowing which way to turn, I stood in the doorway of a pub directly on the corner. It had huge plate glass windows which I never took any notice of at the time, as I was too focused on where the 'doodlebug' was going to land. It hit the concrete building opposite to where I was standing, taking off the two top floors. Plumes of smoke soared high up into the sky, debris flew everywhere, and people were coming off the buses cut and bleeding from the glass. The glass from the pub next to where I had been standing had blown in – not out. My sister had run up Clerkenwell Road looking for me and was crying. She felt sure that I had been hit. On seeing me safe and sound, she turned around and headed back to her workplace, and I, in turn, carried on to mine. Amazingly, being so young, I don't think you have any sense of fear. I used to stand out with a neighbouring friend during raids, when shrapnel was flying around, and recall the unmistakable 'ping' noise it made when metal hit metal. We would stand there looking up to the sky laughing! His Mother would be screaming and yelling at us to come inside!

One of the first V-1's to hit London came down in Grove Road, Bethnal Green on 13 June 1944, killing six people, injuring thirty and making 200 homeless. On the final day of the V-1 and V-2 campaign, Tuesday 27 March 1945, at 7.21 a.m., V-2 hit Hughes Mansions in Vallance Road, Bethnal Green, where 134 residents lost their lives in a single stroke. That rocket was the 1,114[th] of the assault. A total of 2,550 V-1 and V-2's reached London between 12/13 June 1944 and 29 March 1945.

As a relief from the office in Clerkenwell, I was sent to Brimsdown to assist with the installation of an automatic telephone system. Brimsdown had a large cableworks company, spread over a very large area. It was pleasant, light work that suited me far better than threading conduit pipes and bending them at angles like I had to do at the factory in Holloway. Hammering holes into concrete by hand wasn't really my scene at all. The works had a large canteen that I rather liked going to, since they served chips with just about everything, and with spam and corned beef. In fact it was one of the few places that served chips at all. One lunchtime I could hear live music. Entering the vast hall that housed the canteen, I saw Big Bill Campbell and his Rocky Mountain Rhythm, with Peggy Bailey and his female vocalists 'Sweetheart of the Golden West' on the stage. It was *Workers Playtime*. This went out three times a week as a lunchtime road show, from factories and shop floors up and down the country. You would hear the announcement 'Workers Playtime comes to you from somewhere in England'. I found the whole thing quite entertaining, being amused by Big Bill passing round the applejack and moose meat sandwiches, when there was nothing to pass around! There was, of course, the other radio programme of *Music While You Work* that kept the war worker singing and humming through their working hours.

Occasionally, I would have to go through one of the factories making copper wire; white-hot metal stretching yards and yards, with banging and clanging as it passed through the huge rollers, and sparks flying everywhere. From that moment on I knew instinctively that I cared not for factories and foundries, or anything of an industrial nature, though circumstances then meant I did not have the choice.

Returning from Brimsdown one day to Clerkenwell, we were diverted. A V-2 Rocket had hit Smithfield Market killing over a hundred people. Smithfield Market's rooftops were all encased in glass, it was literally everywhere. With the 'doodlebugs' you could hear them coming; with the V-2, there was never any time for sirens to be sounded, as they travelled faster than sound. The first experience of the V-2 was when I was walking home; it was close to midnight and I was just a few doors away, in total darkness, when suddenly a deafening noise shook the whole street from side to side and an enormous flash, almost like daylight, lit up the sky. A rocket had hit the other side of Bethnal Green Road, nearer Whitechapel. My first reaction was to fathom out what it could possibly be, since I had never heard an explosive noise like it before, and why was there no warning? Eventually information filtered through to enlighten us.

Mother in her 'missing years' in Coventry as a bus conductress.

We were shortly to be diverted again, travelling up from Brimsdown to Liverpool Street Station when a 'doodlebug' hit the railway line at Potters Bar. During these times you took everything in your stride and had to be philosophical, accepting whatever fate's hand was to deal you.

Still as young teenagers, come the weekends we would 'go up West'. My weekly wage of 15s would be approximately 75p in today's money. I would place my wage packet on the dinner table every Friday night, unopened, to present to my Grandmother. 10s was taken for my keep, the remaining 5s was my pocket money to include fares and anything else.

We would take a bus to Tottenham Court Road, buy a packet of five Player's Weights cigarettes for the cinema and go to the Dominion in the 1s 9d seats. Coming out of the cinema, we would have a milkshake in the Black and White Milk Bar in Charing Cross Road. To us at that time it was really 'living', though a dreadful drain on our pocket money to get through the rest of the week!

My sister had taken a position at the Bethnal Green Town Hall, and it was through her working there that she was able to trace our Mother to Coventry. Through practically the whole of the war we did not know of her whereabouts. Communication was re-established with her, and having no legitimate reasons or excuses for her absence, she returned to London for the day to see us. It was an odd feeling, seeing her again. I felt no anger at what she had done, I was just happy to see her. If anyone was a good actress, she was. The years of irresponsible motherhood were swept under the carpet, the subject of her behaviour never raised, never questioned. She came home to No. 74 like nothing had ever occurred; our grandparents behaved in the same manner. Not one word of reprimand for deserting her children was uttered. My own belief is that she must have given our Grandmother some money, and that made everything fine.

On 7 May 1945, Germany surrendered. VE Day was declared on 8 May 1945. With some of the boys in our street, we decided to 'go up West' If ever one experienced a city going completely wild, this was it! GI's were hanging out of windows at Rainbow Corner, people had clambered up lampposts, dancing, singing everywhere, smiling, laughing, crying and shouting. The crowds were 4ft deep. Piccadilly, Leicester Square, Coventry Street, Regent Street, Oxford Street, and Trafalgar Square were all just a huge conglomerated mass of people, rejoicing that the war was finally over! Huge crowds had gathered outside Buckingham Palace, many dressed in red, white and blue. The King, Queen and the Princesses came out on the balcony and waved to the crowd.

In Piccadilly Circus I began to feel quite sick and started to vomit. It took over an hour to get out of the crowds and get a bus home. I told my Grandmother that I didn't feel well and she immediately came to the conclusion that I had been drinking. The following day she realised that I was genuinely ill, and accompanied me to the doctor. Doctor Rockfeldt in Hackney Road diagnosed a grumbling appendix. The doctor informed me that I would probably have to have it removed the following year. How wrong his diagnosis was! I got peritonitis twenty-five years later! Grandmother saw to it that I did not go sick; there was never any sympathy in that area. I went to work, doubled-up in pain and came home from work still suffering. Her remedy was always to go to bed when you came home.

It took me a long time to realise that I was not really cut out for the job I was doing. At that young age, I still did not know what I really wanted to do. Having no one with whom I could rationally discuss where my talents lay and what I would be better at doing, I soldiered on. It didn't matter what you did in our Grandmother's eyes, so long as you worked. One day I suddenly decided to take a sabbatical and visit my Mother in Coventry.

Victory party in Norah Square, Bethnal Green.

I found her living with another man, whom, from day one, I did not like. I didn't like his looks, his manner or, anything else about him. I was deeply hurt that my Mother was living with him. Having been brought up in an environment where morals, ethics, and codes of conduct were high especially if you were married, unmarried couples who were living together were considered as something alien and shameful. I carried this sense of shame within me for a long, long time. Apart from my sister, who felt the same way about our Mother's choice, we never mentioned it to anyone. We were perhaps sitting in judgement, comparing him to our Father, but as far as we were concerned there was no contest. He didn't have our Father's intelligence, manners or breeding. Our Mother recognised our feelings but ignored them, and tried to engineer a way for us to accept him.

Arriving back from Coventry, I found a job in a distribution warehouse in Cambridge Heath Road It was a little more interesting than the electrical work. Most of the employees there had returned from the services, unmistakable by their 'demob' suits, raincoats and hats. It was hard for them to re-adapt to civilian life and work in a warehouse after being to far-flung places. For me, it was interesting to hear their stories of naval engagements, desert battles and the theatres of war they had been involved in. The managing director came to me one day, and told me he would like me to work in the office. He asked to see my Grandmother to discuss my prospects, so a meeting took place and I was promoted into the office. I was given lessons in typing and general office procedure; I learnt by heart the prices and tax on every item we sold. I used to take sandwiches that my Grandmother made, which were of doorstop magnitude! When it came to lunchtime I was too embarrassed to put them on top of the desk, so instead I would break a piece off in the desk drawer, and place the food piece by piece into my mouth. If I could afford it, I would buy a tongue sandwich from Lou Napolitano's on the corner; they made fabulous ones, the bread was so fresh, with real butter and the tongue melted in your mouth. Grandmother could never match it.

Later on, I was given the task of making out all the invoices for clients. This was to prove a grave mistake; I was left solely on my own to execute the invoices on a portable typewriter. What should have been a 'call over', a checking over of the items with another person, was never carried out. It was never even suggested. I don't think they realised that an accuracy check should have taken place. This resulted in errors being made and customers complaining. I was sent back to the warehouse.

Mother was later to return to London with her beau. It was hurtful to us that after she obtained a flat, there was never any mention of her providing a home for us. Her boyfriend took first place, while we carried on living with our Grandparents at No. 74. We could only describe it as selfish, insensitive behaviour.

Some of the boys down the street and I decided to join the ATC (Air Training Corps). There was No.416 Squadron in Bethnal Green Road where we duly enrolled. It was great fun, learning Morse code, tapping away on the Morse keyboard, sending each other rude messages! The greatest thing of all was flying. On several weekends we would go to Wethersfield in Essex. I was very small for my age, so the parachute pack practically covered me! We would fly in Avro Ansons or Airspeed Oxfords, both of them training craft. Some pilots were not too happy as they were unable to have weekend leave, having to stay behind at the airfield to take cadet brats into the air. Some pilots would try to frighten us by doing all kinds of manoeuvres, but the more dives and circles in the sky they made, the better I liked it! The cabins were not pressurized, and you could feel your head being pressed down, a most unusual sensation. We had to keep a log book of the flights and of the altitude climbed. We spent a week away in Felixstowe on Sunderland aircraft, draining out the floats and general aircraft maintenance. I was as happy as a sand-boy, being involved on those Sunderlands, and was very sad when that week came to an end. The ATC would occasionally hold a dance on a Saturday night, my first introduction to dancing, which I discovered I liked. Our hall was behind the Post Office in Bethnal Green Road. One thing that sticks out in my memory was the mirrored globe on the ceiling, turning when the lights were dimmed, and multi-coloured rays bouncing off that glittering ball to the tune of 'Goodnight Sweetheart' at the closing of the evenings dance. I think the tune of 'Goodnight Sweetheart' was the finale to nearly every dance.

On one occasion I popped into my Grandfather's 'new' local, the Shakespeare next to Bethnal Green Police Station. We had given the pub the name of the 'The Shake'. He was there with his cronies drinking, his favourite beverage 'mild and bitter' straight from the barrel. In those days flying was not a way of life as it is today, with the exception of RAF personnel, very few then had the opportunity to fly. For Grandfather and his friends, flying was something they had only read about. He would proudly have me tell his friends of my endeavors, the altitude I had flown at, about the aircraft I had flown in, and the aerodromes I had visited. His friends would nod and look up in awe. Grandfather would repeat some of the questions I had already been asked. 'How many thousand feet did you fly at?' he would say, he just liked to hear it! If you remained, it would invariably turn into a few songs being sung, mostly Irish. It was hard to convince my Grandfather that most of these Irish songs that brought tears to the eyes were written mainly in Tin Pan Alley, New York by some Jewish composers.

Being so close to 'the nick', the police used to drive black Wolseley cars to the back of the station into a yard. The yard also accommodated horses used by the mounted police. What fascinated me about these cars was the illuminated Wolseley sign on the radiator. You could spot a police car a mile off, by the light of the logo. There were stories about this particular police station, which once had a detective by the name of 'Nutty Sharpe'. He got the name 'Nutty' from the angle he wore his bowler hat. It was alleged that he arrested the whole of the 'Whizz Mob', a pickpocket organisation operating at a racecourse, put them all on a double-decker bus and drove the bus all the way back to the Bethnal Green station! In the winter evenings, just outside the police station, was 'Potato Jack's', his barrow containing glowing coals and large potatoes stuck on spikes, ready to serve to the customer. Jack would remove a potato from the spikes, and serve it to you doused in vinegar, peppered and salted, and placed in newspaper. Off you would go, warming your hands on the large pebble-shaped tuber, enjoying every mouthful as you walked down Bethnal Green Road!

Along with our aunts, we would continue to go to the local cinemas. At this time on the radio, Charlie Chester had a show called *Stand Easy*. There was a character called 'Whippet Quick'. My Aunt May with her daughter Sheila went to the Excelsior.

Grandfather's local The Shakespeare next door to 'B.G.'s nick'. The façade was once all green tiling.

During the performance they observed a man masturbating a few seats away from them. Aunt May dubbed him 'Whippet Quick' thereafter, and whenever any one of us went to the cinema, we would be asked if 'Whippet Quick' was there!

Aunt Winnie, the youngest of Grandmother's daughters, was more like a sister; she was eight years older than us. At night, when Winnie and my sister went upstairs to bed, I would hide in the darkness of the recess of my bedroom door. As they passed with a solitary candle, I would make noises to frighten them. It got to a stage where my sister was too frightened to go to bed! They would yell down to my Grandmother to get me to stop it. My Grandmother would shout up at me to behave, but could never refrain from laughing when doing so.

Winnie held a clerical position for a firm which owned a chain of butchers; it meant her staying at home less and less. Eventually, it came to light that she was romancing her boss, who was already married. A chauffer-driven Armstrong Siddeley would arrive outside our house to collect her, and on the odd occasion her boss would come in. Out of all the family, Winnie was the only one who married into wealth.

Returning from work one evening, I caught a No. 8 bus at the corner of Shoreditch High Street and Bethnal Green Road. There was no room at the bottom of the bus, so I ascended to the top. I was met by a thick curtain of cigarette smoke that you could cut with a knife. Looking around for a seat, I found my Grandfather sitting there. He was returning from the docks. I sat beside him, and everyone upstairs in that must have been smoking. A man sitting at the front of the bus was having a coughing spasm; it sounded awful, but my Grandfather, much to my horror shouted out 'Die, you bastard, die!'. I wanted to fold up and die with embarrassment!

There was a saying we used to quote in such circumstances:

> It ain't the cough that carries you off
> It's the coffin they carry you off in.

One of the few music halls still remaining is The Hackney Empire. It was another form of live entertainment that we cared for. The ''Ackney Empire' was built in 1901 and, thank God, it is still going strong. It was here that some of the old time greats trod the boards: Charlie Chaplin, Stan Laurel, and Marie Lloyd. We also saw Max Miller, Arthur Askey, Cavan O'Connor, Leo Fould, Maxie Bacon, Cyril Fletcher, Derek Roy, Phyllis Dixie and Jane of the *Daily Mirror*. I can also recall Peter Sellers when he was third on the bill. Later, Ted Heath and his band, accompanied by vocalists Lita Rosa and Dickie Valentine, appeared. We were mad about the' big band sound'.

On 8 June 1946 our ATC Squadron was invited to the victory parade. We assembled at St Paul's Cathedral with other ATC squadrons and marched from the cathedral through Admiralty Arch and down The Mall to the Victoria Memorial, immediately in front of Buckingham Palace. We sat on the lower steps of the memorial and watched the finest military parade from the four corners of the earth. The King and Queen, together with the Princess's Elizabeth and Margaret, drove past in an open landau, so close that you could almost reach out and touch them. They looked absolutely magnificent! Military bands, U.S. Marines and GI's, Arab legions, contingents from New Zealand, Australia, South Africa, India and the Commonwealth, regiment after regiment, then the British Army, tanks and armoured cars paraded before us. There was a Royal Air Force fly-past. Wartime celebrities such as Winston Churchill, Lord Mountbatten, Field Marshall's Alexander and Montgomery, General's Dwight Eisenhower, Mark Clarke, Charles de Gaulle and Emperor Haile Selassie all passed by, so near to where we were sitting. We had one of the finest views of the whole parade. It seemed endless, it went on and on. This must have been about the most magnificent display of all times. I doubt very much if we will ever see the like of it again.

Close to our ATC Headquarters in Bethnal Green Road, a bomb site had been turned into a fairground. There was a boxing marquee which used to be quite popular with the locals. You were invited to put on the gloves and go three rounds with one of the fairground's appointed pugilists for a fiver. Bethnal Green has been the birthplace of many well-known boxers; practically everyone had, at one time boxed, either at school or at one of the boxing clubs that existed in the East End. It was therefore no surprise that the fair had many takers willing to get into the ring.

We were quite enthusiastic at following the amateur boxers, and would see boxing matches at the York Hall, Hoxton Baths and Shoreditch Town Hall. We had the boxing clubs at the Oxford House in Mape Street, The Repton in Victoria Park Square and at Eton Manor. Several of the boys from these clubs became professional. Two of our favourites were Joe Lucy and Sammy McCarthy; they had style and craftsmanship, and you were guaranteed a good performance from both of those boys.

At about this time I joined the Mansford Youth Club, which was for the sixteen and seventeen year olds, although much older girls and boys attended. It was held in a converted two-storey garage; the ground floor had wooden parquet flooring, ideal for dancing, and a stage. Upstairs were billiard and table-tennis tables, and a small bar that served tea and biscuits. It was here that I learned to dance, and for the next six years dancing became a non-stop pursuit. This was the age of the big bands. Glenn Miller, Artie Shaw, Count Basie, Tommy Dorsey, and Lionel Hampton; and the age of great singers such as Frank Sinatra, Perry Como, Billy Eckstein, Ella Fitzgerald, Jo Stafford and a host of others.

It was here that I came into regular contact with Reggie and Ronnie Kray, who were also members. We never dreamed that in later years they would receive such notoriety. When they were about ten years of age they would come to St Peter's Avenue to visit their friend from Daniel Street School, Patsy Beauvoir, who lived opposite St Peter's Church. Patsy had the making, even then, of a tear-away, and grew up to become a genuine one. Patsy's Father, a short wizened man who looked much older than his years, was plagued by ill health, his weakened body bent over, a cigarette permanently dangling from his mouth, coughing his heart out, never realizing that his smoking was killing him. His Mother was tall and slim. She made a radical 'Eliza Doolittle' change from being a plain and drab female to an overnight glamour girl when the American GI's came over. At weekends, she would put her make up on, get herself 'dolled' up and 'go up West' in pursuit of pleasure. For her, and many others like her, living in the East End was a hum-drum existence, and it was not difficult to understand that they needed a stimulus of colour and excitement in their lives, to compensate for the grey drabness of their environment.

On one occasion when the twins came to see Patsy, my cousin Sheila was playing with the vicar's daughter in St Peter's Churchyard. Reggie and Ronnie came over from Patsy's house and tied cousin Sheila's long blonde plaits to a tree. They got up to boyish, mischievous pranks just like the rest of us. They lived in Vallance Road, the other side of Bethnal Green Road. We regularly saw them with their brother Charlie at Pelicci's café, which we all frequented. Uncle Alf used to drink with Charlie, their Father. in the Marquis of Cornwallis. Several years later when I was catching the No.8 bus in Bethnal Green Road, Reggie Kray was standing at the same bus stop, we both got on and sat together upstairs- Reggie paid the bus fares. Even at that time, I had no knowledge of their infamy. He was quietly spoken, just as I had always known him to be, and we chatted casually all the way to the West End. I got off at Tottenham Court Road and Reggie remained on the bus. I never saw either of the twins again. It later became known to me that they were accompanying George Raft, Judy Garland and many other celebrities whilst running 'The Firm'(The Krays organization). I was absolutely astounded when I read articles about them in the newspapers.

This was an age when we were 'jive' mad, the drape suit, 'guards-back' overcoats and Stetson hats were the height of fashion in the East End. I was not yet in the money league to afford the type of clothing I would have liked. I bought a blue serge suit from Billy Saunders in Wellington Row, but whilst giving it a good pressing from the iron heated on the gas stove for a dance that evening, I badly scorched the trouser turn up. With ingenuity, I cut a piece of cloth from behind the jacket lapel and glued it to the burnt part of the turn up! That night, I stood well back in the dance hall, in case anyone should spot my handywork, dancing only when the lights were dimmed!

We would dance at the Mansford two to three times a week; you would see the same following of people. Tubby Hutchinson would come into the club wearing a white riding belted raincoat and a grey Stetson that he never removed, even when he was 'jiving'. No one ever dared to tell Tubby how ridiculous he looked, jiving in them! Storky Walker, with his frizzy hair and horn-rimmed glasses, was a great jiver, dancing very erect with the most serious of expressions. You would hardly ever see Storky smile when he was on the floor! Tony Martin was also a terrific dancer, great with the girls too! Stocky in build, blue eyes and dark wavy hair, with a charming smile! Dumpsy Davis, whose brother Jimmy was a professional middleweight, would come up behind you if you were not watching, clench a fist and place it on your head, and with his other fist hit it like a hammer! I am apt to believe he got this from watching the 'Three Stooges' too often. It was not very pleasant if you were on the receiving end, but everyone accepted that nothing would ever change him! It was here at the Mansford that I learned to fox trot, quickstep, rumba and tango. The club introduced us to opera, and I saw my first major opera 'La Boheme', at Sadlers Wells, followed by several others at this theatre. These experiences broadened my horizons in music, firmly establishing me as a fan for life.

The club would also arrange weekends under canvas alongside the river close to Runnymede. We had some wonderful times there! Someone once brought a portable gramophone player, one of those old wind-up handle types; the record selection was very limited and the same ones were played over and over again which drove you to distraction! One I recall that virtually seared my brain was '*I met Sally Pringle when she was single, dat, dat, data, dat dow sir*'. Each time I heard that record played I felt like jumping in the river.

Wanting to look as smart as several of the other boys and feeling a little bit out of it, I wore my Grandmother down enough to persuade her to take a loan on my behalf, so that I could have a tailor made 'drape suit', When she asked me how much the suit was, and I told her £25, she absolutely went into orbit! However, she arranged a loan with Mrs Andrews across the street. Having got my way, I went to Levine's in Green Street, now Roman Road and ordered a mid-blue pinhead suit. The suit, when I put it on for the very first time, elevated me! I thought I looked the cat's whiskers and could now join the others with confidence.

'Barry's' was now my first opportunity to wear my new drape suit, as it was a dance hall above Burton's the Tailors in the Narrow Way, Hackney. It was run by Barry Langruish. Barry was softly spoken, tall, elegant, and refined with dyed-blond wavy hair. He had two sisters, Doris and Winnie, whose hair was as black as Barry's was blonde, and as Barry was handsome, they looked as though they were the unfortunate ones related to Cinderella! For the boys who attended Barry's, the trademark was to wear white socks. If you were walking down the street and you were seen wearing white socks, you would get a shout of 'Barry Boy'. Barry never had live music, only records. It was more like a club than a dance hall; here you got to know everyone. The girls would be sitting, the boys would be standing. To approach a girl to dance, you would just say 'Coming round?'. To say 'Would you like to dance?' was not in our vocabulary! In those days, I must have taken many girls home, but I must say they were never promiscuous. It was mainly a smooch, we called it a 'lumber'. At Barry's, two brothers from Bethnal Green used to attend, George and Lenny Walker. George was of medium height, with straight, lank blonde hair, while Lenny was short, dark-haired and like a tiger if upset. George would talk in a flat monotone voice; there were no highs, or lows, or heights in his conversation – it was devoid of expression! Whenever I said to George 'How are you?' he would reply 'How am I?…'umping those fucking 'taters up and down those cobbles, 'aint worth a carrot!'. George, of course, worked as a porter in Covent Garden, so he was telling me that 'Wheeling a heavy load of potatoes in a wheelbarrow over the cobbled streets of Covent Garden just wasn't worth it!'. George later became a taxi driver. At Barry's he always seemed to know which girl I had taken home. On one occasion, I took a girl back to her home in Walthamstow; the following day, dear George, always inquisitive, wanted to know how I got on. I was always non-committal in such matters. I simply replied 'Nothing'. George found this very hard to accept. 'Listen', he said, 'you don't go all the way to Walthamstow for nothing!' George never ever believed me; the truth was that apart from a smooch, nothing did happen! Lenny, his brother, was as small as he was, and as tough as they come. One evening at Barry's, he got involved in a dispute with some boys from Bermondsey who were twice his size. They went down into a little courtyard at the side of The Mermaid Pub for a 'straightener'. A 'straightener' was a term that was used to 'fight it out'. Lenny put the three Bermondsey boys down, left them lying in the courtyard and came back to the dance completely unperturbed!

In the 'Barry' dancing years, I befriended three boys from Goldsmith Row: Albert Styman whose Mother owned a pub, the Star of the East, Franie Evans, whose parents were proprietors of a dining rooms; and Terry Saunders, who was in the Merchant Navy. Albert was a beautifully sophisticated pianist who trained under Sidney Bright, Geraldo the bandleader's brother. He would often play at the pub and was always welcomed at parties. One Sunday morning, we were having a drink listening to Albert playing a medley of some fine tunes, such as 'Laura', 'Smoke gets in your eyes', 'Nancy' and many others. He was approached by one of the patrons we called 'Smiffy'. Smiffy always wore a black cheese cutter cap, a black suit and shirt with no collar, and the lapels of his jacket were always smothered in fag ash! Albert was in the middle of playing 'Laura' in his very stylish way. Smiffy, leaning up against the piano, extended his arm with a pint glass of beer across the top of the piano and said to Albert ''ere Albert, 'ow abaht playing 'Who's sorry now'?' In that one moment Smiffy destroyed the aura of the sophisticated music.

A few doors away from the Star of the East was a greengrocers, which Albert and some of the other boys knew as 'Fat Alice's'. Alice, the wife of the proprietor, was indeed a woman of large proportion with a nice pleasant face. Unbeknown to me, they would pay a visit to Alice when the husband wasn't there, and she would give them 'a levy and frank', Cockney rhyme for masturbation.

Franie was the shortest one of us, and of stocky build; he would call at my home early on Saturday evenings to find out what I was going to wear that night. His Father would stand outside their dining rooms with a snow-white starched apron worn very high, while his Mother worked like a Trojan inside. He would disappear down to the Cat & Mutton pub at the end of the Broadway leaving Mrs Evans to do just about everything. Franie was a porter in Convent Garden who, like several of the others in Covent Garden and Spitalfields, became a taxi driver.

Terry remained in the Merchant Navy until coming ashore to get married, knowing full well that he would be called up if he stepped down the gangway before he had reached the age of twenty-six. As expected, he spent his National Service in the Military Police. It was through this man's influence that my life turned around and he pointed me in the right direction.

Our dancing tentacles would reach out to the Royal in Tottenham in mid-week, the Lyceum in the Strand on Sunday nights, and the York Hall or Shoreditch Town Hall on most Saturdays. At the Royal we would dance to the Ray Ellington Quartet. At the Lyceum, it was the Oscar Rabin Band, and sometimes Vic Lewis at the Shoreditch Town Hall. The band leaders and the vocalists got to know us quite well because of our regular attendance. Outside the Lyceum was a coffee stall, no longer seen around London. We would have a coffee and a sausage sandwich, then start walking home. It was nothing for us to walk home from the Strand all the way back to Bethnal Green.

On Saturdays, in order to supplement my income, I got a job with a friend selling salt and vinegar from a horse and cart around Highbury. We would buy a gallon of ascetic acid and a large tin of caramel from a shop at the corner of Weymouth Terrace and Hackney Road. We would then ride to the end of Hoxton Market, where there was a stone horse trough. We used to place a wooden barrel with the acid and caramel under the water tap and fill it up, giving it a good stir, and 'presto' – vinegar. The salt would be in block form that we would saw off, as required. We would go knocking at doors around Highbury shouting, 'Salt and vinegar, salt and vinegar'. Housewives would come out with their jugs for us to fill up, and saw off a piece of salt from the block. We would have a slap-up meal at lunchtime and buy ourselves a packet of Royalty cigarettes. The Saturday income was nearly as much as I earned all week. I look back now and think 'However did I do that?', going through those streets shouting 'Salt and vinegar', but then I realised that the driving force was to earn more money, so embarrassment went out of the window.

Hoxton was considered rough, even by Bethnal Green standards. Nile Street, or 'the Nile,' as it was known, had a terrible reputation in my younger years, people were afraid to walk down it. So many stories abounded, that if you entered the Nile the chance of being robbed, beaten up or having your throat cut was more than likely to happen. Our Father often referred to the 'Jago', that was another place that brought fear and trepidation, even to East Enders, at the mere mention of the name. I never found out until later years where in Hoxton it actually was. It was, in fact, the Old Nichol Rookery, one of London's worst slums. A Reverend Osbourne Jay of the Holy Trinity persuaded the author Arthur Morrison to visit the area, resulting in a book being written by him, titled A *Child of the Jago*. This was a fictionalised account of the life of a child in the slum conditions in the Old Nichol, renaming the Old Nichol as 'The Jago'. The name Jago stuck, and the area was known as this thereafter. In 1886 practically 6,000 people were packed into this area. The mortality rate was twice that of Bethnal Green, and four times that of London as a whole. One in four children died before they reached one year of age. In 1844, the concentration was eight people to a small house, and there were 1,400 houses in an area less than 400 yards long. John Hollingshead, of the *Morning Post*, wrote *Ragged London* in 1861, and noted that the Jago had grown even more neglected in the last twenty years as old houses decayed and bona-fide trades became a cover up for thieves and prostitutes. *The Builder* in 1863 noted the numbers living in unfit basement cellars, the lack of sanitation, and that fresh running water was only available for ten to twelve minutes each day, excepting Sundays.

Society demanded a change for the clearance of the Old Nichol Street Rookery; which resulted in a forceful demonstration led by the Reverend Osbourne Jay. Charles Booth had already seen at first hand and noted the extreme poverty. Demolition actually began before Arthur Morrison's book was published. The campaign was such a success that the Prince of Wales officially opened the new estate in 1900, saying, 'Few indeed will forget this site, who had read Mr Morrison's A *Child of the Jago*'.

While new flats replaced the existing slums, many still lived in appalling conditions. The original inhabitants were moved, creating new overcrowding and more slums, in Dalston and Bethnal Green. At this time assistance was unavailable for the displaced, and this only added to the suffering and misery of the slums' former residents.

During the 1930s the reputation of Hoxton and its infamous areas remained, and we would only venture into the area during the daylight, most certainly not in darkness. Hoxton has now become the 'in' place to be, with its smart restaurants and celebrity residents. Yet even now, I would still not walk around there in the wee small hours.

In 1947 I realised that it would not be too long before I was called up for National Service. To fill out the time, I got a job at Wren's Shaped Ply Veneers in Fuller Street. The money was good, but oh so boring! I literally stood at a machine all day long drilling holes into squares of shaped veneered ply; while I was drilling I was daydreaming. One day, I was daydreaming so intently that the drill went straight through my left hand index finger. I pulled my finger away and tore it in two. Off I went under escort to the Mildmay Mission Hospital for treatment, having my arm in a sling for two months or more. In this factory one of the staff was deaf and dumb, know to every one as 'Dummy'. At home one day whilst Grandmother was sitting there, the telephone rang. I answered the call, and after a brief conversation put the telephone receiver down. Grandmother asked me who had called. I replied, 'Dummy from work'. She sat there for a full five minutes before the penny dropped. 'You silly daft sod, how could Dummy ring you?'. Such was my sense of humour! On another occasion she was telling me about her wedding at the Red Church in Bethnal Green Road. I said to her, 'Didn't we have a lovely time?' Once again with some delay she replied, 'How did you know, you weren't there!'

A film came out in 1947, *It always rains on Sunday* with John McCallum and Googie Withers. It depicted Bethnal Green. Many Bethnal Green residents protested at being portrayed as crooks, 'chancers' and murderers. The Cinematograph Exhibitors Association's reviewer declared it 'an unsavoury film…with an appeal only to the broad minded'. One particular line in the film by Googie Withers was, 'I wish there was no place like Bethnal Green'. Some thirty-odd years later I was with this lovely couple on board a ship. I brought the subject up with Miss Withers of the line she used, and we laughed about it! John McCallum, who is an Australian, told me that to get the East End accent right for the film, he went to Eddie Phillips, the boxer, who had a pub, the Rising Sun, in Globe Road, Bethnal Green.

Parties in the East End for our age group were a regular feature, and were very well conducted; I cannot recall any incident where there was any disruption. Records had taken over from the piano, though if one still had a piano and someone who could play, so much the better. The 'Knees up Mother Brown' era had gone. One party I attended in Stepney, reminded me of a Laurel and Hardy scene! A bungalow bath was turned upside down, resting on the backs of two chairs, with a table cloth placed over it, and this served as a bar. It goes to show how innovative people were!

Clothing became the number one item in our lives, it was suits, suits, suits. The boys would have tailor-made drape suits, the girls tailor-made drape costumes. The material had to be birds eye, pinhead, diagonal, hopsack or barathea. The back of the suit could only be seamless, wide shouldered and single breasted. Our tailors were Levine's in Green Street and Hoxton, Solomon's & Temples in Hackney Road, and Alfred Myers in Old Street.

When entering a dance hall, several of the boys would walk with the right arm held straight down the side, hand held part open, with the fingers curled as though the whole limb was paralysed. One of the boys had a suit with shoulder padding which was too wide for his shoulders, so he would keep bouncing his shoulders up and down to prevent his jacket slipping off. It was almost as though he had a nervous affliction! Our shirts had cut-away collars, spear point collars, and spread collars. Most of us wore Stetson hats, worn squarely on the head. We were influenced a very great deal by Hollywood gangster and tough guy films in the way we dressed.

Haircuts were also of great importance to us. We would go to Dave's in Hackney Road for a 'DA' (Duck's Arse), a Tony Curtis hairstyle, having a singe, or a Prashana hair friction. Prashana was a heavily scented hair lotion that we thought was wonderful. Looking back, it smelt like something out of a Turkish brothel. Sometimes, I would rub my hair vigorously with a towel in front of the fire until I made it frizzy. I thought that I had developed a new hairstyle!

Most of us would gather outside Pellicci's Café in Bethnal Green Road; the Pellicci's have been there as long as I can remember, and the interior of the café has remained exactly the same, even after all these years. Their parents hailed from Lucca in Tuscany;

many years ago they settled in the East End and opened the café in 1900. They had two cafés in my teenage years, the original, that is still there facing the Red Church, and the other was on the corner of Mape Street. The Pellicci brothers were all nice boys; Terry, Jeep, Pete and Nev. Jeep, whose name was Elio, was given this unusual nickname by his brothers; it derives from Popeye's son in the cartoons. Today Nev, as we know him, his real name is Nevio, is the only surviving brother, and with his daughter and son Nevio junior. He continue to run the business. Pellicci's has become quite famous and is frequented by many film celebrities. In fact the Pellicci's have attained a cult status. Rarely can you enter the establishment to find a table on any day of the week. The interior has remained the same for years with its wood-panelled Art Deco marquetry, and vivid yellow vitrolite paneling of the counter making it both unique and interesting.

Characters abounded in Bethnal Green, particularly around Pellicci's. A permanent fixture was Freddie Burrows, who worked in Spitalfields market as a porter. We gave him the name of 'Ruckie Boy'. He loved to use the word 'rucking' (a telling off) in his

Pellicci's Café, which has now become an icon. It was frequented by the Kray twins when they lived in Vallance Road.

The author with Nevio 'Nev' Pellicci, proprietor of the café. One of the old school still living in Bethnal Green.

vocabulary. 'I gave him a rucking', 'I gave her a rucking'… just about everyone got a rucking from Freddie at one time or another. Dear old Freddie, with his cheese cutter worn flat on his head and knotted scarf, had an affinity with cart horses and behaved in a manner that made him appear twenty years older than his years. Another character was 'Arthur the Suss'. Arthur looked more like a villain than a villain, which he never was. But unfortunately for him, he was always being picked up by the police on suspicion of some crime or another, hence he became known around 'the Green' as 'Arthur the Suss'. We had 'Trini', whose Christian name was Patsy! He acquired the nickname from a song by Trini Lopez, 'If I had a hammer', as he would use a hammer to smash a shop window for an article, specifically ordered by one of his clients. We all knew Harry Herbert who was lithe and slim, and a boxer at one time, although his walk was strangely feminine! Those who didn't know him, and might have thought otherwise, would have made a grave misjudgement! On one occasion we lined up at the cooked meat shop in Bethnal Green Road, for meat for his greyhound; we stood in the long queue that took ages, and by the time he got home the greyhound was dead! Then there were the Smith brothers, the Treseden brothers, and Charlie Bins. Charlie got his name from the glasses he wore. Glasses were always referred to as bins. He passed a remark to Ronnie Kray on one occasion asking him about his wife, namely referring to his homosexuality. Charlie knew something that I was completely unaware of – consequently it was to have repercussions. Charlie was paid a visit and worked over. The Brown twins, George and Jimmy, and

Teddy and Checker Berry were all colourful personalities, and very often, the Kray twins, and their brother Charlie, would congregate outside Pellicci's café. Bethnal Green was referred to as 'the Green', the locality 'the Manor'. A good-looking girl was known as 'a brahma' and a prostitute was known as 'a brass', not that we had any dealings with the latter! The girls would arrive with their hair in curlers, hidden by a turban, and wearing no make up as meeting altogether like this led to finding out where everyone was going that evening!

On Sunday mornings if it was dry, we would take a walk through to the flower market in Columbia Road, just two streets away from where we lived. We walked on through to Brick Lane, then Petticoat Lane into Bell Lane. Close by was a record stall, where we would stand and listen to all the latest record releases. This was our regular Sunday morning rendezvous, meeting up with some of the boys and chatting about the previous night's events.

We acquired a second-hand record player from a radio shop next to the Red Church in Bethnal Green road. I would buy a record of my choice one week, and my sister the next. Quite naturally, the type of music we chose was not of our Grandparent's taste. Now and then, to arouse their interest, we would buy a record that they would like. We purchased 'The Laughing Policeman', it was bought for a particular reason so that if either Grandparent was in a grumpy mood, I could play it. Before long, one of them would start laughing then the other who would find it difficult to keep a straight face! It was a great way of breaking the ice and maintaining a more harmonious atmosphere in the home! One of the other records was called 'The Box'. It started off with:

> As I was walking on the beach one day,
> Much to my surprise,
> When I discovered (at this point),
> A boomp, boomp; (noise),
> Right before my eyes…

This drove my Grandmother absolutely spare, she wanted to know what was in the box, which of course the song never revealed. It gave us a great kick seeing her trying to fathom out what it was. If we happened to have any records of an Irish nature, we would play them to see our Grandfather 'turn the taps on' at the drop of a hat!

As we were nearly eighteen and on the verge of being called up for National Service, we started to visit the pubs, both in Hackney and Bethnal Green. In those days, they had more or less taken over the music halls. We would only go to those where there was entertainment! They would have an MC, most of them gay, and they certainly made those places popular; they sang, told jokes and were excellent in returning any wisecracks made with the rapidity of a machine gun! Many of the patrons would go up on stage with just the accompaniment of a piano, and render a song or two. Some were quite talented, others were not. Nevertheless it was usually a good Saturday night out. If one particular pub was not 'humming', we would visit another. We had the Green Gate in Bethnal Green Road, the Basin House in Kingsland High Street, the Nelson in Morning

Lane, Hackney and the Dew Dragon in Homerton. We never drank to excess, mainly brown ales, graduating to light ales, rarely drinking spirits of any description. If we were dancing at Barry's we would use a small pub next door, the Mermaid, for the interval between dancing. Little did I know at the time but this pub was to play a very significant part in my life.

Saturday night was when we really dressed 'up to the nines'! Great care and attention was paid to how we looked before we set foot out onto the street. Apart from the women, the men were always eyeing each other up to see how each other dressed, or if anyone was wearing a new suit. The drape suit, the Stetson hat placed dead centre, rarely worn at an angle, was adopted from the film *The Killers* with Burt Lancaster who had a great influence on us at that time in what we wore, and even the facial expressions of trying to look hard and serious! If only I had known then that I would be in the company of Burt Lancaster in later years, sailing from Thailand to Australia, I would have never had thought this possible! One guy, who I thought really looked more menacing than any other, was Bobby Ramsey. He was a boxer, a real tough hombre, who looked every inch a gangster, although of course he wasn't. In the winter, the guards back overcoats, in either grey or navy, together with a silk paisley scarf, would be worn. If ever you stood in the Green Gate in Bethnal Green Road on a Saturday night, you would think you were in the company of gangsters and hoodlums. It was like a scene out of a movie in Chicago! Appearances, however, can be very deceptive; most were all gainfully employed.

If we were at Barry's at the closing of a dance and we were not taking a girl home, we would make for 'Smithy's' next to the bus garage, just off of London Fields for steak and chips. At other times we would go to a restaurant in Bethnal Green Road on the corner of Mansford Street.

There was this wonderful story of one of the boys whose relative dropped dead with a heart attack in Southend. The family could not afford for the services of an undertaker to bring him back to London, so they arranged to have the body brought back in a friend's van. Picking up the corpse in Southend they stopped off for a cup of tea on the way back. When they vacated the roadside café they discovered to their horror that the van had been stolen. The van and the corpse were never recovered to this day.

In summertime, we would make for Larkswood in Chingford. Larkswood was an open air lido swimming pool. Several of the boys took up weight-lifting, developing their bodies in an attempt to resemble Charles Atlas, strutting around the pool being admired by the girls. One character very well-known at this time was a fellow called Arthur Mason. Arthur had a beautiful physique, quite tanned and used to wear white trunks, so he stood out more than anyone in Larkswood! We would often see him at the Royal in Tottenham, with a blonde actress, Vera Day. Arthur was always very pleasant to talk to. We were most surprised when we went to see *Mr Roberts* at the Coliseum starring Tyrone Power. Arthur was in the cast playing a US sailor!

During this period, all the big names were coming over from America. The London Casino in Soho and the London Palladium were the Mecca for all these Hollywood stars. Father took my sister to see the Ink Spots – he was a very great fan and I was quite irked at not being asked.

One hot summer's evening we had a milkshake and other edibles I should never have eaten, at the Black and White Milk Bar in Charing Cross Road. We managed to get tickets to a performance at the London Casino where Sophie Tucker was appearing. We were seated up in 'the God's', the seats practically touching the theatre ceiling, you couldn't get any higher. The whole theatre was sweltering under the heat – air conditioned theatres were never heard of, and I think, even to this day, there are still many that are without it. I began to feel quite nauseous, but determined not to miss the star of the show, I held out as long as I could, before I made a mad dash to the fire exit stairs and was as sick as a dog!

Seeing the film *Up in Arms* starring Danny Kaye, I became an instant fan. His sophisticated style as a comedian was quite different to anything I had ever seen. When it became known that he was coming to London, I was determined to get theatre tickets. I immediately applied and acquired two tickets for his show at the Palladium. Danny Kaye

had taken London by storm; he was sold out for every performance. I invited a girl along who at the time, I was very keen on, dear little June Rudgely. My sister was very upset that I had not taken her! I reminded her that she had seen the Ink Spots and I hadn't! I borrowed a maroon coloured v-necked sweater from her, turned it back to front, and pinned it with a small safely pin, to make it appear like a crew neck sweater. This was something that we did quite often since we never possessed more than one sweater at a time.

I took dear June home after the show to say goodnight. When having a small kiss and cuddle, the safety pin holding my sweater became unfastened, the pin digging into the back of my neck each time I went to embrace her. The discomfort got the better of me, and it became about the quickest 'goodnight' I ever had with a girl! How could I tell her that I had a sweater turned back to front?

The author in Naples after National Service.

With my arm still in a sling from my accident at work, I ventured one Saturday evening into the Bethnal Green Road restaurant, on the corner of Mansford Street, I knew practically everyone dining there. There was a boy very well-known to us, who had a beautiful scarf that everyone was admiring; it was striped in browns, beiges and golds of different tones. He hung the scarf on a coat rack. While everyone was deep in conversation, I removed the scarf in fun. Regretfully, hours later I had forgotten all about it still being inside my sling, and I went home. The following morning, there was a knock at the door. Georgie Walker was standing there. ''Ere Derek, 'ave you got Leslie Pummel's scarf?' I told him that I had and how I had forgotten all about it until I got home the previous evening. Poor George said to me, 'You're a right bastard you are! I got nicked last night and 'ave to appear at Old Street!' George then explained that after the loss of the scarf, Leslie had accused everyone of taking it. Outside the restaurant, there was a dreadful commotion which resulted in dear old George being arrested and charged, for using abusive language to a police officer and disorderly conduct!

I accompanied George to Old Street Police Court to hear the charge; I stood in the public gallery as George stood before the magistrate. The charge was read out and George, in his flat monotone voice, pleaded guilty. The magistrate fined him 5s. He replied to the magistrate, 'That's my bleeding dinner money your honour, 'ow am I supposed to get my lunch?' At this point the whole thing became quite hilarious, I had to stifle my laughter at the court comedy, and tears ran down my cheeks! The whole episode was so funny that the London evening newspaper *The Evening News*, which had a column 'Courts Day by Day', written in a humorous style, included George in the column. The columnist made it sound even funnier! How I wish I had saved that article! Might I add, that I was not the flavour of the month with dear George!

Some months later, I took George to a dance in Kensington, somewhere a little more upmarket than the East End! We were standing there, eyeing up the girls. George had just had a new suit made, and turning round to me he said in that flat monotone voice of his, 'What do ya reckon Derek? I'm only the best dressed geyser 'ere in this room tonight!' George just couldn't help being full of self-esteem! He, and many others like him, were porters in Covent Garden or Spitalfields. When those markets closed down, most of them became taxi drivers. A few years later I was taking a girl out and hailed a taxi in Hackney Road, when who should the taxi driver be, but none other than dear old George! I could see George looking into the cab mirror, looking at the girl I was with; he hadn't changed one bit! Some years later, I was discussing George with one of his fellow taxi drivers, and apparently the other taxi drivers called him 'Georgie Buckall'. On asking why, he explained that George, who had had all his teeth extracted, had difficulty in his pronunciation, hence, instead of saying 'fuck all', he could only pronounce 'buck all'.

9

'IN THE KATE'

*T*o be in the 'Kate' is a cockney expression for being in the army; it derives from Kate Carney, a music hall star. Her name somehow found its way into the cockney vocabulary, Kate Carney rhyming with army.

Opening up the post one morning I received a letter requesting me to register at the labour exchange in Kingsland Road for National Service. Duly reporting at the appointed time and date, I was asked what arm of the service I wished to go into. Initially, I requested the Royal Navy, until I was informed that in the army one served the shortest time, so consequently I opted for the army.

A few weeks later, I received another letter, asking me to report for a medical in Burdett Road, Bow. Arriving at the centre in Burdett Road, I found it was packed with National Service fodder, many in a state of undress, arched over having their 'jacksies' looked up, being prodded and poked by doctors in white coats with their badges of office, their stethoscopes around their necks. I went through this conveyor belt procedure of medical examiners, along with all the others, and was pronounced 'A1'.

In early December I was on a troop train to Barnard Castle in County Durham. Fortunately, one of my old school classmates from Teesdale Street School was joining the same regiment; George Brown, one of the Brown twins, who lived in Peabody Buildings, Old Bethnal Green Road. Both twins were market porters at Covent Garden, following in their Father's footsteps, and were always beautifully dressed. Their brother Jimmy had been called up at the same time to the 3rd Carabiniers, another regiment of the Armoured Corps. We changed trains at Darlington, then on to Barnard Castle and were transported to the camp of the Royal Armoured Corps. The training regiment was the Prince of Wales Own 12th Royal Lancers.

We were transported from Barnard Castle Station to the barracks that held both regiment and trainee soldiers. The barracks comprised single brick buildings and Nissen huts. We were ushered into a brick building that accommodated roughly forty soldiers. A single combustion stove, situated in the centre of the room, was our only source of heating. We were a mixture of young men from all walks of life, and from all parts of the country. Here we had the extroverts, introverts, the brash, timid and the shy. Public school accents, Cockney, Geordie, Scottish; accents that you had never heard before, and some you had difficulty in understanding.

The whole day was spent being kitted out with kitbag, groundsheet, battledress, greatcoat, beret, tank suits, denim fatigue suits, boots, underwear, cutlery, jackknife and all your webbing that made up for FSMO (full service marching order). Gathering all this kit together and taking it to our barracks, we made for the dining hall and were given cards with the meals and days printed on it for a whole month; the dining hall orderly would punch a hole in our card for the meal taken on that specific day. As we trundled through this vast dining area for our very first army meal, a shout went up from the troops already dining, 'You'll be sorry!' This was done with every new intake as a welcoming gesture, as we later found ourselves doing the same thing when the next new intake arrived. If ever one can remember a meal, that army meal was unforgettable. Two semi-warm sausage rolls, not flaky pastry, not shortcrust, just hardened baked flour, cold boiled potatoes and carrots swimming in tepid gravy. It was revolting but being hungry from leaving London. we had no choice other than to eat it.

Because of the goings on, running here and there, and being bestowed the rank of Trooper, with the Army No. 22091632, I hadn't sighted George until I got to the dining hall. George, who had arrived at the barracks in a smart tailored suit, was now wearing army denims; it was a terrible transformation seeing this very smart man in such awful-looking clothing! Poor old George looked so forlorn and dejected! I really felt sorry for him, not realising that I must have looked like it too!

That very first night at lights out, I lay in bed listening to some of those boys sobbing; initially I could not make out why they were crying, not realising that some had never ever been away from home before. It must have been my experience as an evacuee and living away from home that had hardened me, as no tears came forth like some of the others.

The following day we were marched to the medical centre for our vaccinations and inoculations, having four injections in all, two in each arm, one in the upper and one in the lower. We were lined up in single file, and to my amazement, some of the boys started fainting before they even got to the doctor! I really thought that this was only something they did in the movies! Amongst groups of young men brought together, there are always those who are much brighter, and those not so bright. We had one boy we called 'Nig-Nog'. He had a north country accent you could cut with a knife and we had difficulty understanding him. Dear old Nig-Nog was always dropping off to sleep. One night we came back from the NAAFI to our barracks to find Nig-Nog fast asleep in bed. It was bitterly cold with snow on the ground. We lifted Nig Nog, still fast asleep in his bed, and carried him out on to the pathway outside the barracks and left him there. It was two hours or more after that he finally awoke to his very odd surroundings!

Our next few weeks were spent in 'square bashing' and kit-cleaning. The boots issued were brown ex-Australian army, and these had to be blackened and spit and polished. To get them totally black was no easy effort, as the brown leather shone through time and time again. It took a while to gain the 'spit and polish' technique – through perseverance it gradually paid off and we were able to make those toecaps and heels really shine. Our webbing brass had never seen a polish! Hours were spent rubbing the coarse metal to a smooth finish until it was shining. All the webbing had to be 'blanco'd', and low and behold if any 'blanco' was found on your brass! Our complete kit had to be laid out on our beds a million times over for inspection.

We drilled and drilled and drilled, marching up and down, rifle drill, shoulder arms, present arms, and pistol drill. It never seemed to come to an end! At any unannounced time of the evening, an NCO, with his riding crop under his arm, would order us to wear our FSMO, rifle and pistol and report to the drill sheds. This could be at ten o'clock in the evening or sometimes even later and we would drill for an hour or two. Marching drill, rifle drill and pistol drill, arriving back at our barrack room absolutely exhausted. At times you were ordered to lay your complete kit out on your bed. An NCO would come in to inspect, and seeing something not to his liking, he would pick up a boot and throw it right to the other end of the room, swearing and cussing at the poor unfortunate whose piece of equipment had not been up to standard! Whenever an NCO entered late in the evening, we knew we were in for a hard time. Reveille was sounded at 6a.m., our toilets and washhouses were 200yds away. It was a particularly cold winter, and often you would arrive for your ablutions to find the water hardly tepid. There was a bank of WC's with concrete flooring. Behind each toilet door, you would find someone had written a poem, or something crude. One I will always remember was:

> Be careful how you close this door
> For there's many an unborn trooper
> Who is fast asleep upon this floor!

We would muster on the vast drill square each morning in our various troops. The regimental band would be playing. The RSM, wee Georgie Day, was about the smartest soldier I ever saw. He was most noticeable by his glistening brown boots! I never quite fathomed out why he could wear brown boots, when we were issued with brown boots and had to make them black! Whenever he gave an order on the square it became a high pitched screech.

Army jargon is like no other. I do not know how this particular accent came about. We would be lined up as a troop on early morning parade. A squadron sergeant would come behind you and say something like, 'Am I hurting you? No? I should be, I'm standing on your bloody hair, get a bloody haircut!', even if you had your haircut the day before! 'Did you shave this morning? You forgot to take the paper off the razor blade'. At times you got the impression that they were deliberately trying to humiliate you. There were some NCOs who delighted in this, and I'm convinced that some had a sadistic streak that went unchecked.

Going to the dining hall on one particular lunchtime, we could not believe our eyes. The menu was the best we had seen on camp, everything was beautifully displayed and the choice much greater than we normally had. All the cooks were in snow-white aprons, all the equipment was gleaming. It did not take too long for the penny to drop that the regiment was having a high ranking officer visit the camp. The following day, and thereafter, we were back to normal.

One morning I received a freshly laundered tank suit. Not bothering to examine it, I put it on. The garment zipped from the ankle upwards on each leg to the shoulders. Standing to attention I felt a riding crop across my leg. 'Did you know your tank suit is torn?' I replied, 'No sir'. 'Another fucking liar in the regiment, double the troop around the square twelve times at the double'. We doubled that vast square as ordered and all the way down to the gunnery wing, finally coming to a halt. The Squadron Sergeant shouted 'Whose the c**t who said he never knew his tank suit was torn?' 'Me Sergeant', I replied. 'B-o-l-l-ocks!' he yelled back at the top of his voice. Fortunately, I had no repercussions from the rest of the boys of our Gunnery Troop.

The commanding officer of the regiment was Lt. Colonel Horsberry-Porter. The only time we ever saw him was when he was riding through the camp on horseback, a very tall man always wearing a winter fur coat. Only on one occasion did we have to see him personally in his office. We were briefed by the Squadron Sergeant Major to address the Lt. Colonel as 'Colonel.' To make quite sure that we said 'Colonel' at the end of every sentence, the SSMS gave you a prod with his riding crop. All NCOs carried a riding crop 'blanco'd' white with a silver top embossed with the 12th Royal Lancers Crest, great for prodding and poking.

The 'breaking us in' period from 'rookie' to 'soldier' was quite arduous, with all the physical exercises, drilling, boring fatigues and the actual gunnery training. The fatigues were assigned to the back of the cookhouse, with a mountain of potatoes to be peeled with hand-peelers. Nothing could be more soul-destroying than sitting there, peeling potatoes which never ever seemed to come to an end! We had the occasional film, shown in the regimental theatre, and sometimes a concert. It's funny how certain tunes remind you of a place or a person. At this particular time, '12th Street Rag' was all the rage – each time I hear it played now my thoughts immediately return to my training days with the 12th Royal Lancers.

We were given the task of carrying green wooden ammunition boxes on a particular rainy day, and were wearing greatcoats. Somehow the green dye from the boxes stained them. George and I were charged with this demeanour. We were individually marched into the Squadron Major's office. I was asked to give my account and the charge was dismissed. I waited for George to come out. 'What did you get George?', 'Five days jankers' said George. He then asked me what I got, I replied 'Nothing.' 'How the fucking hell did you get nothing?' I could not really explain to George why I got nothing and he got five days CB! This meant he had been 'confined to barracks' and had to report to the guardhouse in full service marching order (FMSO) for inspection every hour until midnight.

We had our first guard duty parade. The Duty Officer inspected us, and I was quite amazed that I was chosen as 'Stick Man'. The Stick Man is the smartest man on parade, selected by the duty officer. I had not the slightest idea what this meant, only that at the end of the inspection, I had to 'fall out'. The following morning, George and the rest of the guard returned to the barracks. 'What was it like George?' I asked, 'I nearly shit myself, guarding the perimeters of the camp in the dead of night', he replied. One patrolled the perimeters for two hours, then rested in all your kit for the next four, sleeping if you could on beds with just the wire springs to lie on. Weekend guard was always dreaded, having to do guard duties for forty-eight hours without taking off your uniform. At the end of the duty, you came away feeling an absolute mess.

The winter of 1948 was bitterly cold, particularly in the north, with such vast open spaces surrounding us. We were taken by truck very late at night into the middle of nowhere and dumped, given a map and a compass, and were instructed to find our way back to camp. There were about six of us in our party. I'm sure, like many others at that time, I had not a clue about map reading. We walked and walked across the countryside, absolutely frozen, finding a barn where we rested for a few hours, out of the cold. Eventually, through sheer luck, we found our way back to camp, arriving at the barracks with my hands so frozen I could not unbutton my greatcoat until I warmed them close to the combustion stove for several minutes when they thawed out.

We were given Christmas leave bang in the middle of our training. Arriving back at Bethnal Green in uniform, I felt rather proud of our Royal Armoured Corps red and yellow shoulder flashes, the red and yellow denoting 'Death before Dishonour' and the silver cap badge of the Mailed Fist and Crown. One attempted to pack in as much as you possibly could during those few days, before returning to Barnard Castle. We visited Barry's, where most of us then were all in uniform, as well as having plenty of Christmas parties to attend.

To return to camp was always a wrench, travelling back north on a crowded troop train. I don't think I ever got a seat returning from leave in the whole time I was in England. From Barnard Castle Station, we had a shortcut across the fields to the camp; there was hardly any time left before drawing your kit out, and your hands and face were filthy from the grime and soot of the train. We then had to get washed and changed for early morning parade which was always a race against time.

It was then back to the gunnery wing, learning more about the armament of our Daimler armoured cars and the ammunition that the two-pounders and 7.92 Besa machine guns would fire. We were also trained to judge distances, study range-finding and map reading, all of which was to turn us into first-class crew members of an armoured car. Halfway through our training we were sent to Appleby in Northumberland for actual shooting on the firing ranges from armoured cars.

I was teamed up with another boy, Howard, who, strangely enough, had worked for Windsmoor in Old Street, where my sister was currently working. At least we had a little something in common. We were fairly cramped inside the turret of a Daimler armoured car, having only the breech of the gun separating us. Howard was designated to load the shells, and I was to do the firing. Placing the shell into the breach, I aimed at the target and pulled the trigger. Nothing happened. I cocked the gun again and fired again, nothing happened. At this stage, and it was becoming quite scary as the shell could explode in the breach, I suspected that we had a dud one. Should anything like this occur, you are to remove the shell and throw it out of the turret. I attempted this one more time, re-cocked and fired again but still nothing happened. My gun loader started shouting, 'Oh quick – Oh quick – Oh, quick'. Opening up the breech, I removed the shell and threw it out of the turret, with a great sighs of relief. This was our baptism into using live ammunition, a hair-raising first time experience!

Our quarters in Appleby were quite spartan. Sleeping in a Nissen hut with a single stove, it was a cold and desolate place to be in winter. We were pleased when our gunnery was over and we were able to return to camp. One morning the whole regiment was mustered at very short notice to the parade ground. We all thought that we were going to be shipped out to Korea. There were a thousand men on the square, waiting to be addressed by the colonel. He began his speech by saying, 'You call yourselves Englishmen, I am disgusted with you!' We had not the faintest idea what he was talking about. We all marched to the other side of the camp, and were ordered to pass through a shower unit where someone had crapped in a shower cubicle! The excitement of being posted overseas went out of the window.

Grandmother had sent me one of her homemade cakes. When I was at home I hardly ever touched her creations. This time it was most welcome. I shared it with several of the boys, without any complaint. We were forever hungry; most of our money was spent on food in the NAAFI during the evenings. Our pay during training was 10s one week, £1 the next. Pay parade was quite a performance. To collect your 10s or a £1 you marched to the pay desk; two paces forward, saluted, collected your money, about turned and marched off!

We were given forty-eight hours leave, with travel warrants. Prior to going on leave, an NCO would come to inspect us and the barracks. We would stand by our beds, blankets folded around the three biscuit mattresses, and if the NCO was satisfied with your appearance and bed layout, you were allowed to proceed on leave. George was facing me on the opposite side. I had been inspected and was OK, but poor old George had cut himself shaving, and had to remain in barracks for the weekend. I was asked to pass a message on to his girlfriend when I got home, to say he was sorry he couldn't make it.

Most of the boys I knew had been called up for National Service. It was amazing to find how many of them managed to get around prolonging a leave, and how the word spread as to how to do it! There was a doctor in Nichol Square known as Black Joe who, for a £1, would issue you with a certificate to state that you were too sick to return to your unit. There were times when I had been sorely tempted to pay Black Joe a visit, but never got around to doing so.

Arriving back in London, it seemed that no sooner were you there, than your forty-eight hours leave was over! I returned back to camp once again from Euston by troop train, sleeping in the corridor of a carriage, smoke-filled and grimy. Alighting from the train at Barnard Castle in the early hours of the morning and walking across the fields, I felt like nothing on earth, due to not having a proper night's sleep. I lined up with all the others to collect my kit and no sooner had I got back to my barracks, when the bugle sounded for parade. I had no time to wash, just spruced myself up as best as I could. My face and hands were still grimy from the train. So, on noting this, the inspecting NCO ordered me to the bathrooms under escort, after the parade was over. I had to strip, bathe in a bath tub of ice-cold water, with a scrubbing brush that was meant for the floor. It was a most degrading and humiliating experience and I never, ever, forgot it. At times the army could be downright stupid; there was no one you could address or turn to when you felt an injustice had been done in those days.

Passing Out Parade with the 12th Royal Lancers (Royal Armoured Corps). From far left: George, Jock, the author, and Mush.

On the finalization of our training we had to take all our kit up on to the parade ground and lay it out on ground sheets for inspection. Everything had to be boxed square, with cardboard placed inside; rather a fruitless task as, when the inspection was over, the cardboard was thrown away!

The final day came for the Passing Out Parade, the one that we had been drilling for all this time. The 12th Royal Lancers regimental band was on the square to play through the whole event. The regiment's Lt. Colonel took the salute on horseback, as, by this time, we were fully conditioned soldiers. There was a great sigh of relief when all the drilling, gunnery course, fatigues and being barked and shouted at, had come to an end. Four of us, George included, had our photograph taken at the end of the passing out parade. I made a casual remark saying, 'I wonder what we will look like?' I didn't realise that the Squadron Sergeant Major was standing behind me. He said 'I'll tell you what you bloody well look like!'

Our Gunnery Sergeant asked me if I would like to stay on to become a gunnery instructor with the 12th Royal Lancers. I felt quite flattered, I never recognized that I had the capability of becoming an instructor. However, since most of the postings after training were abroad, I declined. The urge to travel far out-weighed anything else. We were mustered outside HQ and addressed by the SSM who read out the regiments that we were assigned to. The majority of us were posted to the 13th/18th Hussars stationed in North Africa, and the 1st Royal Dragoons (The Royals) which were stationed in Germany. George and I were posted to occupied Germany.

It was all very exciting as I had never travelled abroad before. We travelled by train from the north of England to Harwich, crossing over to the Hook of Holland by sea, then by train to Brunswick in Germany. Everywhere was full of interest to me, passing through Holland to Aachen at the German border, and through several German cities which were still in ruins from the war. Deutschland had not quite got back on its feet at this time – there was still much rebuilding to be done.

The barracks of the 1ˢᵗ Royal Dragoons were based at Wolfenbutel, just a few kilometres from Braunschweig. They were the finest I had ever seen! Built for the German army, they put ours back home to shame, and were constructed in a square of grey stone, solid as a rock and made to last. The regiment was divided into three squadrons, 'HQ', 'B' and 'C'; 'A' Squadron was based in Berlin. We were assigned to 'C' Squadron, and were quartered in rooms of four. Centrally heated, with double windows, we could not believe our good fortune at the wonderful transformation from the austere living accommodation at Barnard Castle to this! The immediate front part of the square was a huge archway, above it the officer's quarters, and either side was HQ Squadron admin and 'MT' (motor transport). To the right of the square was 'C' Squadron and to the left 'B' Squadron. At the far end leading up a stone staircase was the recreation area comprising the NAAFI and the library. In the centre of the inner square was a very pleasant cultivated garden.

We were taken to the regimental tailor, chalked and pinned up, the surplus material in our uniforms taken out, making us much smarter soldiers than when we arrived. The dining arrangements of the regiment were excellent; we were served by German waitresses, such a far cry from our training days! The standards were very high, so high in fact, that one of the cooks who was in the army catering corps, got five days CB for burning the bacon!

Our immediate programme was drilling – rifle drill and pistol drill – for yet another Passing Out Parade as a 1ˢᵗ Royal Dragoon. It seemed child's play in comparison to what we had been through with the 12ᵗʰ Royal Lancers. Perhaps too, at this stage, we were more conditioned and disciplined. Our Lt. Colonel, Rodney Heathcote-Amory, took the salute, addressing us as Gentlemen Dragoons of the Royals. It was a fine regiment, you were made to feel you belonged, and I felt rather proud to

Trooper Houghton, 1ˢᵗ Royal Dragoons, Brunswick, British Sector Germany, 1949.

139

be part of it. The regiment was steeped in history; it was the first cavalry regiment formed by Charles I, and then known as the 'Tangier Horse', dating back to 1660.

We were taken to see the regimental silver, displayed on a very large, highly-polished refectory table, in the officer's mess. It was a most magnificent sight, I had never seen so many beautiful silver pieces put together under one roof, really intricate craftsmanship which had been donated to the regiment over the years. One piece that stood out above all others, was a blue enamelled silver cigarette case, with a circle of diamonds with the initial 'W' also in diamonds in the centre. My inquisitive nature led me to ask who had presented it to the regiment. It had apparently been donated by Kaiser Wilhelm, who was at one time an Honorary Colonel in Chief of the regiment.

Each Thursday was Colonel's night; trumpeters would come on to the balcony outside the officer's mess, to play a fanfare: officers would dine in mess kit, and the whole evening would be a very impressive affair. We would stand and watch the trumpeters play practically every time we were in barracks.

We began the second part of our training to become fully fledged gunner mechanics (gunner drivers) by initially driving fifteen cwt Bedford trucks up and down the autobahn, then on to the AFV's (armoured fighting vehicles) across rough terrain, putting us through our paces. The driving position in those vehicles was a centre steering, you were almost stretched out on the floor. In the summer, encased in steel armour, it became very hot. Driving miles on the autobahn, it was very easy to fall off to sleep. Fortunately, you had a car commander, who was able to jolt you back over the intercom system! On night manoeuvres we were not allowed to use any lights other than follow the rear small red light of the car in front of you. We were out on manoeuvres one night, with George in the car in front of me. His car commander was a Lieutenant Farraday, who could not pronounce his 'r's. Following a small red light for hours was not an easy task, and the Lieutenant was shouting at poor old George 'Bwown, Bwown, what the bloody hell are you doing?'. Quite apart from the difficulty in driving on these night schemes, it did have it's humorous side. George and I were in the turret of an armoured car one day, when he turned around and said to me, 'You know, if my mum saw me in one of these things she would cry her fucking eyes out'. Finally, on passing all our tests we were transferred to 'B' Squadron. We did further gunnery on the firing ranges at Belsen, a name that will never be forgotten. Most of the camp by now held displaced persons from all over Europe.

Barrack room life in 'B' Squadron was good. Sleeping only four to a room, the squadron held our interest in forever being involved in various activities, keeping us constantly on the alert. The time came for the efficiency tests, where we route marched in FSMO, then ran in FSMO. When you ran, the camouflage netting of your helmet resting against your forehead stung like hell, possibly from the preserving agent of the netting. With your full pack, rifle and stinging helmet, running behind a truck and being timed was quite an exhausting exercise.

Most evenings, when not on duty, were spent having a glass of beer in the NAAFI at the far end of the barracks. The German beer supplied to the regiment was very good, and on a hot summer's day it could be quite refreshing. Coming out of the NAAFI one evening with

A seasoned Dragoon cleaning his shoes for a weekend leave.

George, we stood on the stone steps of the terrace. There was a full moon. George said to me, 'You see that moon? They can see that moon back home! What would you be doing now if you were home?' I replied that I would most probably be at Barry's. George then said, 'I would be with my bird.' We stood there gazing up at the moon in silence, both wrapped up in our own thoughts of home. Although George would appear to be a hard nut, I came to the conclusion that deep down, he really was a softy and a romantic.

Sitting in our room one evening, I was reading the *Hackney Gazette* that my Grandmother used to send, along with a cake, on a regular basis. When one of the boys came in and observed what I was reading, he asked, 'Christ, you don't live there, do you?' He had noticed the front page of the *Gazette* with its crime articles. Up to this point, it had never struck me how other people viewed those of us who lived in the East End. I could not see anything untoward in the paper; it was something I was used to, but I re-read the front page, to see what he was so disturbed about. I then explained to him what life was like, and that it was not as bad as it appeared in print. To an outsider it must have looked horrendous.

Germany then was still recovering; cigarettes and coffee were the main trading commodities. A pound of coffee would go a long way – a maid could be hired for a week for the price of a jar of Nescafé! You would see men of the Control Commission (CCG) in their dark navy blue-dyed battledress and berets everywhere, trading with the locals. It was a black market paradise. We had a regimental dance on one occasion; half the local girls arrived from Wolfenbutel, wearing coats made from army blankets! Thank God we never froze!

We were never paid in Deutschmarks, but in 'BAFFS', army currency. However, by trading in little odds and ends, we were able to obtain the mark for our personal purchases. We were in the British Zone of Occupied Germany (BAOR). Overlooking us was the Russian Zone; they were in a position to turn off our water supply at the drop of a hat, but fortunately, they never did. The relationship between the Allies and the Russians at this particular time was not exactly cordial. Our purpose in being there was to patrol the Russian Zone border between Helmstedt and Bad Hartzburg in the Hartz Mountains. We would be away from camp for three to four days at a time under canvas.

On one of our patrols into the mountains, I did not feel too well and as time wore on I felt increasingly worse. I could hardly swallow and my head was aching. Lasting out until we got back to camp, I went to the mess. If there is one thing I hate, it is the smell of boiled fish. This happened to be on the menu, and the very smell of it made me feel worse. I left the mess hall fairly rapidly, returned to my room and went to bed. The following morning I felt so ill that I reported sick. The army had a wonderful system when you reported sick; you placed all your kit into storage. I hardly had the strength to lift up a boot lace, let alone my whole kit. However, I managed to do everything one should under such circumstances, but with great difficulty. Reporting to the medical centre, as it was Easter, I found the regimental doctor was away for the weekend, so a local German doctor was called in. I was sent to bed in the hospital immediately. When it came to mealtime, the orderly brought my food in and when I lifted up the chop cover, I found it was boiled fish! I could have died from the smell alone! The following morning, I was taken by military ambulance to the military hospital in Hanover, having been diagnosed, inaccurately, as having diphtheria.

I was placed in a ward all by myself and given penicillin injections in the behind by a huge, and not so gentle, German nurse. She looked more like a Hausefrau than a nurse! After a week of rest and regular injections in what was by then a very sore backside, I returned to camp, having recovered from a very nasty bout of tonsillitis. It was something in my younger years that I used to get quite frequently, but after my treatment in Germany, I never had a reoccurrence.

One day, looking at the regimental notice, I saw that a ration clerk was required. I applied and was interviewed by the regimental Quarter Master and got the job, a nice relief from soldiering! I struck up a friendship with our regimental German barber, and now and then, gave him some cocoa powder. One evening, on Colonel's night, when all the officers were out on the balcony, I passed, giving a very smart salute, but bringing my arm down with such a slam that it broke open the secreted packet of cocoa! However the powder fortunately dispersed over the side of my uniform, away from the officers who were looking down from the balcony. I narrowly escaped being placed on a 'fizzer' (a charge). We supplied all the married families in the area with rations, and everything had to be worked out by fractions. Some of the wives would become terribly flirtatious in order to acquire extra rations, and other wives would complain. I was not terribly good at working out allowances in fractions then, so it resulted in married soldiers' wives complaining to the QM. I really should have known better!

Come Armistice Day, the regiment held a parade, with the regimental band marching down to Wolfenbutel. Shortly before going on parade, I was filling a cigarette lighter from a gelatine capsule, when some of the petrol dropped on to the toe of my boot, leaving a small dull patch. The inspection came and I was duly charged with having dirty boots. Going through the procedure of left, right, left, right, I was marched in to the Squadron Major, where I explained my mishap and was given five days CB (jankers). CB entailed you reporting to the guardhouse, in FSMO (full service marching order) for inspection several times a day. I volunteered for the boxing team, and was consequently excused from reporting to the guardhouse, and in between training, was ordered to work in the officer's mess for the five days, which I did not object to in the slightest!

The regiment had a strange way of getting together a boxing team in a rapid spell of time, but was nevertheless most effective. The whole regiment of OR's was lined up in two single files; the soldier facing you was your opponent, no matter how big or small, large or lean. You would then enter the ring for three minutes, and knock the hell out of each other; I lasted for about three or four bouts, finally getting knocked out in the fifth session. The line would gradually be reduced, until you had enough candidates to form a regimental boxing team!

I was then shifted to Administration in HQ, to spend the rest of my army days in a very pleasant office working out the guard duties for the regiment. A very nice number and surprising how popular I became! Now and again, we were given various duties outside the normal routine. One day, right out of the blue, six of us in HQ were ordered to draw rifles and fifty rounds of ammunition, without any details given. We were told to muster at 22.00 hrs, still without any knowledge of what we were about to do. At the given time, we were picked up by a truck, and taken into the middle of nowhere, to a railwayman's hut at the side of a railway track.

Our NCO then briefed us. We were to pick up a train that was going to Berlin. It was our task to see that all blinds were drawn, the carriage doors locked throughout the journey, and that no Russians were to be allowed on the train. The relationship between the Allies and the Russians was extremely volatile. I asked the NCO what we should do if any Russians attempted to board the train. We were informed that we should hit them with the butt of the rifle, but not to shoot!

The train slowed down at our meeting point, we boarded and were stationed along the carriages, checking each compartment to see that the blinds were drawn, as it had been known for the Russians to shoot if they weren't. We arrived at the checkpoint with uniformed Russians very much in evidence. I stood between the carriages and could not believe my eyes as there were no bolts on the carriage door! A very tall Russian officer, with two soldiers, came along and attempted to open the door next to where I was standing. I held it with all the strength I could muster. I could not visualize myself hitting three Russians with the butt of my rifle! With good fortune, they realised I was not allowing them to board the train, and moved on. It was a nerve-wracking episode. The train was allowed to proceed through the Russian Zone to Berlin. At Magdeburg, it slowed down to a walking pace. The station was crowded with Russian soldiers, and it was evident that they had been enjoying the wee small hours! I fully expected, observing the condition that many of them were in, that some might take a pot shot if one of the train travellers was silly enough to raise their blind. It was with a great sigh of relief when we passed through unhindered. We arrived in Berlin very tired, but not too tired to see as much of Berlin as we could!

During the following month I was selected, with five others, to go by train to Oldenburg to pick up a new supply of armoured cars. We were given a guard's van with bunks, and a stove for cooking our meals. A journey by road to Oldenburg was only a matter of hours away, but this journey took us four days. We were shunted and shoved, moved into sidings in goods' yards, and took turns to cook the main meal of the day from the compo rations we were supplied with. I decided to make a stew, my very first attempt at cooking! Not being very experienced, I placed too much potato powder into my concoction which resulted in it being so thick, you could cut it like a cake! I gave it away to a German railway guard who was with us throughout; he thought it was very good! Those few days were very hot and sunny, and I climbed to the top of the guards van to sunbathe. On the roof, I saw something that drew my attention. It was a lady's pistol, wrapped in a handkerchief! I wondered what mysteries this gun held, and why had someone wrapped it in a handkerchief. I could only think that it must have had some sinister history. For a while, I decided to keep it, so I cleaned it up, and made it workable again. Returning with the armoured cars to the regiment, my conscience got the better of me, and I decided to hand it in to the armoury, thus relieving me of any complications!

It was not too long after picking up the armoured cars in Oldenburg that we were named yet again and placed on a religious course at Verden. The course entailed religious studies, towards becoming confirmed. However we had not the slightest inkling that we were to be confirmed until our arrival at the religious centre. This was a lovely country house, set in several wooded acres, very restful with an air of serenity about it. After a few days, the atmosphere of the place seemed to envelop me into a cocoon of theology. It had me thinking so deeply, I felt on the brink of taking up the priesthood. It was only the influence of the others from the regiment, who were not as affected as I, which brought me back down to earth, severing the spiritual feelings that had so engrossed me. Quite possibly, it must have been the ambience and tranquillity of the place that had made me feel this way. Come the day of the confirmation, it was a mass production service at a church in Verden, conducted by the Bishop of Croydon, chaplain to the army. We army personnel were lined up in double file. I knelt before the Bishop with an ATS girl alongside me to take the bread and wine. Of all the confirmations I had attended back home, I had never ever experienced one like this, on such a grand scale.

Returning to the regiment, I found that I was due to go on leave after ten months away – it was a strange feeling, knowing you were going home after so long. We had our new cap badge issued. It was, in fact, the original type but had been changed in wartime because it looked too much like the German eagle. It was rather odd as when I did arrive home in uniform, and I was walking down Old Bethnal Green Road, I heard a young boy say to his Mother 'Look Mum, a German!' To put on a civilian suit again felt like you had nothing on your back. It was virtually weightless! It was lovely to visit the old haunts, say hello to the neighbours, go to Barry's, and meet up with old friends.

To eke out my soldier's pay, and to have a little more money to spend during my leave, I got a casual labour job at Mann & Crossman's brewery in Mile End Road. It was back-breaking work, stacking beer crates a mile high, for £1 a day. There were occasions when you had to pass through the bottling department, staffed entirely by women who would whistle and shout at you! I literally raced through that department, as stories abounded whereby those brewery wenches would grab you, take your trousers down, and put boot blacking around your nether regions, as part of a little excitement in their daily lives, so giving you an initiating ceremony for venturing into their domain! Those ladies were hardly the sophisticated types. Each evening, I would arrive home with every bone in my body aching, it was about the hardest physical work I had ever done. Within the shadow of the Mann & Crossman brewery is the Blind Beggar public house which became the most famous, or infamous, when on the night of 9 March 1966, Ronnie Kray went in with one of his cohorts and shot George Cornell three times in the head. The public house is now a byword for the East End.

Who was the 'Blind Beggar'? The Blind Beggar of Bethnal Green was, and is, the symbol and legend of Bethnal Green. His story became clouded in myth. It was at a time long before Bethnal Green became a chaotic and overcrowded slum in the nineteenth century. It was first mentioned in an eighth-century deed. By the Middle Ages it was rather isolated from London, being just a small and rather grand little village. There were manor houses and mansions in the surrounding countryside and cottages clustered around the green itself. In the 1200s, one of those manor houses belonged to Simon de Montfort. The story of how he went from rich noble to a poor beggar was recounted in Percy's *Reliques of Ancient English Poetry*. The tale went on to become a popular part of folklore during Tudor times [5]. Simon was a soldier in the service of the King, and fought at the Battle of Evesham, in the West Country, in 1265. Legend has it that he fell at the battle and was found, blinded and wandering by a nobleman's daughter who nursed him back to health; during the course of his recovery, they fell in love and wed. In time they had a daughter and named her Besse. Besse was very beautiful but could not find a husband, the problem being her Father. Besse was courted by four suitors: a rich gentleman, a knight, a London merchant and an innkeeper's son. Most of them withdrew their suit when they met Montfort to ask for the old soldier's consent to marriage. Montfort's reduced circumstances were related through a popular song at the time:

> My Father, shee said, is soone to be seene,
> The siely, blind beggar of Bednall-greene,
> That daylye sits begging for charitie,
> He is the good Father of pretty Besse
> Hei makrs and tokens are known very well;
> He always is led with a dog and bell
> A seely old man, God knoweth is he,
> Yet he is the Father of pretty Besse

In a predictable medieval twist, the courtly knight was the only man who could see past the seeming lack of decent dowry to the woman he loved. He received his reward, as the couple were given a dowry of £3,000, plus £100 for Besse's wedding dress.

It was now May 1950 and I was due to return to the regiment from my leave. Grandfather insisted on coming to Liverpool Street station to see me off. Reluctantly, I agreed. Waiting for the train to Harwich, I was in conversation with him leaning up against a column. In the station, a Redcap (military police) came over and cautioned me for doing so. Grandfather took exception to this. 'Who the bleeding hell does he think he's talking to?' I had to calm him down, thinking that if he didn't behave, I would be returning to barracks and facing a charge!

Arriving back at the regiment in Germany, it was only a matter of weeks before we were due to be 'demobbed'. In fact, that was all our minds were focused on. At long last came the day when we were to say goodbye to the army. We were interviewed prior to our departure, and asked if we would like to sign on as regulars. I don't think any of us did. Looking back on the whole period, I have never, for one moment, resented it. It did more good than anything else; there were, of course, ugly periods but they were soon forgotten, and all in all, it instilled a sense of pride in one's self, and gave a person backbone and self-discipline.

Finally, returning to England on a train, racing across Germany and Holland, I sat in the railway carriage, my thoughts churning, wondering what on earth I was going to do with my life. I had not the slightest idea what career I would like follow. For the past year and a half, I had not needed to worry about myself, but was now faced with the dilemma of my future. The train and boat crossing to the demobilisation centre in Colchester seemed to take an eternity. Finally, we arrived to hand in all our kit, which was in a much better condition than when we received it! We were divested of all our insignia. Eventually arriving in Bethnal Green, I was back home at No. 74.

10

A RETURN TO CIVILIAN LIFE

t home there was now only Grandmother, Grandfather and myself. It took a little time to readjust after army life, but gradually, I began to settle back into the old lifestyle. Not knowing what to do with my life still persisted, and I was yet to find the answer. After a couple of weeks leave, I began searching for a job. Through acquaintances I found casual work that suited me fine until I decided on my future. The job was at Foster's in Queensbridge Road. They were mainly a transport firm that had contracts with the Times Furnishing Company, and a separate division for the government's Ministry of Works.

During the war the government had requisitioned numerous properties around London for offices, some in the most salubrious areas. New government buildings were now being built to replace those they had requisitioned, and in order to return them to the original owners most of the old office furniture had been removed and taken to a depot in Neasden for selling off. The new buildings were, in most cases, furnished with brand new office furniture.

Foster's Yard, as we knew it, engaged a body of casual labour, although not so casual when you think some of them had been with the firm for a number of years. If ever there was a bunch of loveable rogues, they were it! Most of them had been in the armed forces, although some were deserters. If the yard was paid an official visit by police or Redcaps, the ones on the run would scurry over the wall! Practically every one of them gambled; travelling to a job they would be in the back of the van playing cards, as well as at lunchtime, and going home! Racing papers would be read – whether it be dogs or horses. The conversation would always be the bets they had placed, the horses that lost by a nose, and the prices they came in on. Their whole world revolved around gambling and racing, it was all horses and dogs. By strange coincidence, one of the drivers was the boy, Lenny Ebbs, with whom I had been evacuated.

We were divided into two crews. Those in one building would deal with the outgoing furniture, and those at the other end who would receive the incoming furniture. If you were on the outgoing team, it meant that you were in a position to earn, but if you were unfortunate to be on the receiving team there would be angst. However, you took it all in your stride, accepting the good with the bad. The opposite crew could always detect if you had 'had it off'. They watched what you smoked and what you ate, and if the cigarettes or the meal was more expensive than the norm, you then received envious remarks.

The humour and banter were constant; it was real good old cockney humour! We had one character called 'Holly', which was an abbreviation of his surname. If we were in an office shifting filing cabinets, Holly would place a florin (2s piece) on the floor, and exclaim out loud in front of the clerical staff, 'Blimey, look what I found!' The staff would look up with an expression of 'I wonder if it was mine?'. On one occasion when he did this, it backfired – a woman claimed that it was hers! We had an awful job convincing her that it was all done in fun! One of the other boys, I refer to them as boys, they were in fact very mature men, Dick Kelly, did the chippying (carpentry). Dick could throw his voice like a ventriloquist; he would yell out 'Charlie' in the office, and everyone would look around. Dick was quite an amusing character to observe, blond to greying hair, a thin pencil moustache, with a very tiny hand-rolled cigarette in the corner of his mouth. He was not exactly eloquent but would make me smile at times, by some of the words he used! If he thought something was silly, he would say 'bleaten 'diculous', not 'bleeding ridiculous'.

Foster's of course was very good at furnishing our homes! Some of the office furniture, glass cabinets, arm chairs and settees not considered good enough for their new offices were discarded. They would fetch a beautiful price today! My Grandmother's house benefited greatly in having a settee for the parlour, top quality lino in the kitchen and a few other items which enhanced her home!

At every lunchbreak, the cards would come out for a game of rummy. I became quite adept at this game, learning, of course, from some very skilled players. Money was always on the table. If we were in the Westminster area, we would use a café dubbed 'Hell's Kitchen', a huge place where the food was good and the prices very reasonable.

Our work took us all over London. On one occasion, when we were working quite close to St James theatre, Orson Welles came walking past. I could not think of his name at the time, he was dressed exactly as he was in *The Third Man*. I shouted out 'Look there's Harry Lime!' He was appearing at the St James in Othello. Sadly, that theatre is no longer there. Another time, we were working behind Victoria Palace and noticed Sally Ann Howells and other stars going into the rear entrance of the theatre. I followed in, quite sneakily, and was privileged to watch the rehearsals of the Royal Command Variety Performance, managing to see and hear Gracie Fields singing! Patricia Morrison was also there, she was appearing in *Kiss Me Kate*. I said to her, 'I haven't got an autograph book, so kiss me Kate.' She replied 'You've got something there.' They must have thought that I was one of the stage hands.

Once, we were on a job in Old Street, in a typing pool. It had been raining for days. One afternoon, water was seen coming through the ceiling quite heavily. Typists were sitting there with rainwater dripping on to them! We went above to investigate, and found that there was a flat roof, that had been completely stripped of its lead covering. We never found out who did it, but lead at this time was at a premium – it was a very sought-after commodity that fetched a very good price. It was known in the East End as 'blue'. At another job in Whitehall, facing Downing Street, I was moving furniture down a stone staircase that had lead runners. After a couple of times moving up and down the stairs, I noticed the lead runners had gone. 'The phantom has struck again!'

On Fridays after work, some of us would make for the York Hall Baths to take a bath. It was the usual performance of requesting a towel and that wretched little piece of soap that hardly ever lathered. I look back now, and recall with horror of having to put on the same work clothes to go home in! I always felt dirty immediately as I got dressed. However, it was a much better option than facing a bath in the scullery at home!

If I decided not to go out on a Saturday night, I would stay at home in the company of my Grandmother. On Saturday nights, she would lay all the cutlery out on the dinner table, it was never referred to as the dining table, and proceed to 'bluebell' polish and emery cloth the tableware. By this time, she had changed from keeping canaries to having budgerigars. The bird would be hopping around on the table and was able to speak, sounding very much like her! She would call him 'pretty Joey' and he would reply, 'pretty Joey'. I would give Grandmother a treat by going to Gosset Street to Annie's for fish and chips, and buy a bottle of stout for her as well. If, after the meal there was music on the wireless, I would dance her around the kitchen!

Our social life was centred around dancing and the cinema. Barry's would be frequented at least two to three times a week. The Royal in Tottenham mid-week, one of the town halls on Saturday nights, and Sunday nights it would be the Lyceum in the Strand, or on occasions, Oxford House in Bethnal Green. One night, a group of us were travelling back from the Lyceum in The Strand, not being rowdy by any means, just being generally humorous. At this particular time, there was a radio show called *PC.49* with Brian Reece. His favourite saying was, 'Evening all'. On reaching Liverpool Street station, a very big City of London policeman got on to our bus, and stood on the platform. Amongst our group were the two Stanleys, one big, one small. Both were weightlifters, had fine physiques and shared the same Christian name. I was sitting at the lower front end of the bus, and using the Dick Kelly technique of voice throwing, I shouted 'Off you go 49!' The constable, on hearing this, promptly grabbed big Stanley and made him get off the bus with him when it stopped at Great Eastern Street! I never got around to asking Stanley what that PC did to him!

The family had a funeral to attend. It was my Aunt Phyllis's, Grandfather's sister-in-law. She lived in Somerford Street, a street that always appeared so miserable and drab. Grandmother approached me, asking me if I would lend my Grandfather my pair of black shoes to attend the funeral. It resulted in my having to grace the funeral wearing brown shoes. It reminded me of the song by Stanley Holloway, 'Brown boots, I ask yer'! Come the day of the funeral, all the relatives had gathered in Aunt Phyllis's small terraced house. There were bottles of beer on the table, which resulted in my Aunt Marie's face looking like the Idris advert; being a Salvationist she looked on such things with disdain! The coffin was being led out of the house, relatives were sobbing and weeping, when suddenly my Grandmother's voice was heard. Stopping the procession of the relatives, she told them that they were walking out in the wrong order. The sobbing and weeping stopped immediately. The coffin and relatives returned to their original positions, regrouped and started off again, in the correct order, much to Grandmother's satisfaction! The sobbing and the weeping commenced again, almost to order! The funeral over with, all the family gathered in a pub in Brady Street. Two detectives in the bar approached me, and questioned me about the tie I was wearing. They thought it was one of the Guards regiments, until I convinced them that the dimensions of the red and blue stripes were narrower than the regimental tie. I do believe they would have arrested me for posing as a Guardsman! During this time, the conversation amongst my relatives had become very heated. I could not fathom out for a while what it was all about, until my Grandfather arose from his seat, as mad as hell. The relatives were already dividing up what Aunt Phyllis had left behind, even before she had been laid to rest. Grandfather had really lost his rag, calling them 'a lot of vultures'. We left the pub in total silence. It was a long time before things were cordial again. I wonder how many families have relatives, hovering like vultures ready to swoop, directly the departed have left this earth, to get their hands on the spoils.

Walking down Bethnal Green Road one evening, I noticed several people entering Wilmot Street. Curiosity getting the better of me, and I found that they were all going to Wilmot Street School. A political meeting was being held there with Sir Oswald Moseley speaking. I had not seen this man since the outbreak of war when he had held an enormous rally in Ridley Road market. I went in and sat down for the entire meeting, listening to what he and other speakers had to say. It was no longer anti-Semitic, they had shifted their agenda to the blacks and immigration. There was no question about it, Moseley was a brilliant politician and orator who had served in both the Conservative and Labour Parties, but who became disillusioned with party policies, and founded the British Union of Fascists. The man had both charisma and an oratorical skill that was capable of mesmerising the masses to have them eating out of the palm of his hand. Although I admired in him the way in which he could sway his audience, I could not agree or admire his political agenda. In the whole of the audience, there was only one black man. He asked Sir Oswald what he intended doing with the blacks, if his party obtained power. Moseley replied that he would compensate them, and request them to leave the country. I could not help but feel sorry for this lone coloured person, addressing this powerful personality on a very sensitive issue, but admired him for having the courage to face up to him directly, in a sea of white faces. At the conclusion of this meeting, I re-entered Bethnal Green Road towards the Salmon & Ball where there was a small public house, The Ship, where I decided to have a quiet glass of ale. Who should enter the pub but Moseley with his henchman. Somehow or the other, they thought that I was with their group, and rounds of drinks were bought that I had not the slightest objection to! I had the opportunity to speak briefly to Moseley about non-political matters and began listening more intently to the general conversation that followed. I realised that they had placed 'planters' in the audience, which made me aware for the very first time how corrupt politics can be.

One morning I received a letter marked OHMS. On opening it, I found that I had been called back into the army as a 'Z Reservist' with the 1st County of London Yeomanry

'Called up' a year after being demobbed with the 'Z call up' to the 1st County of London Yeomanry, 'The Rough Riders'.

(The Rough Riders) for further training. Reporting to Colchester, I was surprised to see an old East End associate, taking photographs of those who had been called up and back in uniform. Nosher Mason was now a 'smudger' (photographer) and had wasted no time in seeing an opportunity; he very kindly took my picture and sent me a complimentary photograph.

We were kitted out, assembled and transported to Thetford in Norfolk to be quartered under canvas for two weeks training. With typical army efficiency, I had been posted to a tank regiment, having been trained in armoured cars. Someone in Whitehall had done their work well! There were several other men with similar backgrounds, which resulted in our being sent to the transport section of the regiment. It was very spartan, living under canvas. Our ablutions were out in the open, and only with cold water taps. Our 'messing' was under marquees with field kitchens to cook the meals. Dining one day, I used a Dick Kelly technique from Foster's, of throwing the voice, and said in a very army officer clipped accent, 'Now just a few words chaps!' Everyone under the marquee put down their knives and forks, looked up and awaited the forthcoming speech that never occurred! It was my cockney sense of humour coming out I guess!

Men were stationed along the roadside on guard. On one occasion a visiting brigadier stopped his staff car, and asked one of the soldiers what he was guarding. 'Don't know, Sir', came the reply. So much for the Z call-up! We partook in night manoeuvres, and were stuck in a wood with live ammunition being used on us, feeding off dehydrated rations, those awful powdered and dried vegetables that you submerged into boiling water! I was more than pleased to see the end of that exercise!

Our tent was infested with earwigs. They were everywhere, each time you picked up an article of clothing, you would see them running out! Some nights we managed to go into Thetford to have a drink at one of the local pubs. It was not unusual to place your hand in your pocket to buy a round of drinks, to find the little buggers running around in the palm of your hand amongst the coins!

Returning to civilian life after two weeks of wasting the tax payer's money, it was back to Foster's, for how long I knew not. We had a very big job at newly-built offices in Kensington, Charles House. Every piece of furniture installed was brand spanking new. Carrying up some huge tables to the top floor, I suddenly felt a sharp pain in my groin. The pain lasted for a few days, then gradually went away. I thought no more of it.

Two to three times a week, my evenings were spent going dancing at Barry's. He introduced my friend Terry and me to a couple of middle-aged, wealthy Americans, and asked us if we would like to show them around the sights in the East End. The Americans had the most beautiful American car that they had brought over with them. An American vehicle was a rarity in the East End at this time; the car was an absolute show stopper. Its' cream bodywork sparkled, and its' chrome fittings gleamed. Whenever the car was parked, it automatically drew people like a magnet. Terry and I felt like the 'bee's knees', sitting in the backseat on upholstered white leather, being driven around the East End. We took these Americans to all the popular pubs where there was entertainment. As the evening progressed it became apparent to us that these men were gay. We realised during the course of the evening that Barry had set us up, since neither of us was that way inclined. We conveniently bid our adieus rather abruptly before the night had ended. We were forever weary of Barry after this episode, but continued being regular attendees to his establishment.

One of the boys who frequented Barry's at this time was Dennis Stafford. I knew him as Dennis Seigenberg. He was a shy, reticent, good-looking young man, softly spoken, polite and always impeccably dressed. On odd occasions we dated the same girl. Lovely, slender, blue-eyed Rose, who lived just off of Dalston Junction. Dennis was a natural born entrepreneur, who became a millionaire three times over. He somehow seemed to finish up on the wrong side of the law at various times of his life. I feel sure that if he had chosen the right path, he could well have been a captain of industry. Dennis had led an amazing life. Many beautiful women, and associations with the famous and infamous.

His Mother was greatly instrumental in sowing the seeds of his life into crime. She started by buying him a dinghy to use on the Regents Canal, relieving some the canal barges of their sugar cargo! He gradually developed his skills into becoming a housebreaker of large country houses! As time progressed, he was involved in all sorts of outrageous scams and fiddles. Homosexuality was illegal, at a time when he was part owner of gay night clubs in the West End of London, Dennis, I might add, was firmly heterosexual. Like many of us, he liked the good things in life. He made several earnest attempts to go straight. His first offence was for having a pistol in his car. Dennis claimed that it was placed there by a police informer; for this he was sentenced to seven years imprisonment. He escaped from prison with an accomplice, and made his way to Newcastle. Starting a textile business with his fellow escapee within two days of arriving in Newcastle, under assumed names and knowing absolutely nothing about textiles, but his colleague did. Amazingly, the textile business thrived, even having contracts with the local police. Regretfully, he was recognised and had to leave Newcastle post-haste. Making for Southampton, he boarded a liner to the West Indies, and established yet another business! Through a girlfriend sending him a telegram, it was intercepted by the police; Scotland Yard arrived in Trinidad shortly after. That ended Dennis's idyllic life in the tropics. He was returned to England and sentenced to a further eighteen months in High-Security in Dartmoor Prison. He escaped yet again from Dartmoor with a fellow prisoner; his co-conspirator drowned in the freezing waters of a reservoir during that very daring escape. He was one of the very few prisoners to escape from Dartmoor successfully.

I had forgotten all about Dennis, only hearing from time to time that he was doing quite well running night clubs and in the slot machine business in the North East of England.

Reading a newspaper one morning, I sat bolt upright, seeing Dennis's photograph splashed across the front page. He had was been charged with the murder of an Angus Sibbet, together with a business associate named Michael Luvaglio. It became known as the 'One-Armed Bandit Murder'. I read the article in disbelief; an Angus Sibbett had been shot dead in his Mark X Jaguar car in the mining village of South Hetton, County Durham.

He was up to everything in the book, where there was money to be made, but I could never in a million years envisage Dennis having murdered anyone. This was at a time when the Krays and the Richardsons were rounded up and imprisoned. The strong iron fist of the law that came down was red-hot. The establishment wanted results, and managed to add another feather to its cap. He had only ever met Angus Sibbett on two occasions. No real concrete evidence, forensic evidence, or motive was ever submitted by the prosecution. Both men were confident that they would be found not guilty. They were found guilty of this crime and sentenced to life imprisonment. Whilst in prison, Dennis compiled a fifty page dossier of his case protesting his innocence; it was smuggled out to his Father, who had hundreds of copies made. The dossier was sent to Members of Parliament, and people of influence who might be able to help. One was sent to an ex-girlfriend, the actress Jill Bennett, with whom he had had an affair. During their liaison, he found her to be unpredictable and highly strung. In Dennis's words, 'You would certainly not take her out on a full moon!'

By this time she had married John Osborne, the playwright. Jill became influential in passing the dossier on to a writer, and Dennis's story was made into a book and a film; 'Get Carter' Carter, was the name of an old partner of Dennis's, Ken Carter. Michael Caine played Dennis in the film. Dennis was to serve twelve years in prison with his alleged accomplice; they were released on licence. He has spent forty years proclaiming his innocence and fighting for justice. Quite naturally, he has become embittered with the justice system. 'I don't want sympathy, that's something between shit and syphilis'. Dennis has since co-authored a book, 'The Autobiography of a Gentleman Gangster' entitled *Fun Loving Criminal*.

Leaving Barry's dance hall on a pleasant warm evening, I decided to walk back home to Bethnal Green rather than take a bus. It was a walk that took me past the Hackney Empire and the Hackney Town Hall, cutting through London Fields into The Broadway, across Hackney road and into St Peter's Avenue. This is something one would never dream of doing in the age that we are now living in, for fear of being mugged or attacked. Approaching Woolworths, in Mare Street, I encountered a well-known East End figure, Tommy Smithson. We stopped and chatted for a while. I looked for a cigarette and discovered that I had run out of them. Tommy pulled out a packet of Players that held a solitary cigarette and gave it to me. He had been a former fairground prizefighter, a merchant seaman, and somehow in his short-lived and chequered career, became a gangster. He was known in the underworld as 'Mr Loser'. He became a minder, working for some of the most notorious names in the criminal world, Billy Hill, Jack Coma (aka Jack Spot), and also protecting numerous Maltese club owners in the West End of London. Through his undesirable line of work it was not unusual to find his name mentioned in a newspaper for being involved in some fracas with rivals. One notable fight was with Frederick 'Slim' Sullivan, resulting in Tommy slashing Slims throat and arms. He had a girlfriend, Fay Richardson, a prostitute, who was on remand for passing fraudulent cheques. Her three former boyfriends were all murdered. This should have been an omen for Tommy. He attempted to raise money for her defence by calling on several of the club owners he protected. Retaliation came his way when a meeting was arranged for him at the Black Cap pub in Camden Town. It was a set up! His enemies were waiting for him, and, at a given signal, the stubbing out of a cigar, he was attacked! He was slashed in the face, arms, and body, in the shape of large 'V's, for vengeance; his face required forty seven stitches. He was pushed over a wall in Regent's Park and left for dead! However, the hard, resilient Tommy pulled through, and it was not long before he was again back in business. On 25 June 1950, he went to call on George Caruana, a Maltese club owner. A pedestrian found him lying in the gutter; he had been shot in the neck and arms. He looked up at the man and said, 'Good morning, I'm dying!' Tommy was thirty-six years old. On many occasions, it has been put to me, how did I associate with these people? I grew up with them, and knew them, as I did any other ordinary boy or girl in the locality. They were completely at ease in my company, because knowing me most of my life, I was never a threat, nor did they have to look over their shoulder in my presence. East Enders have always held an admiration for the gangster and the villain. The Kray twins became icons, but one thing must be said; they never killed or maimed innocent people. It was with their own kind and everything was kept 'in house'. What I found intriguing with the Kray twins, Dennis Stafford and Tommy Smithson, with the exception of Dennis who I never heard use an obscene word, was that the others could swear like troopers, yet, in the presence of elderly people, they would never allow anyone to use a bad word. They held a great respect for the aged!

From Barry's, I met up with one of the boys in the Merchant Navy. He used to come home, and tell me about his trips to Hong Kong which intrigued me. He had a very lovely sister who looked like Juliet Prowse and before long we started dating. Her brother, Derek, often suggested I should join the Merchant Navy; my other friend, Terry,

A Hackney Town Hall wedding of cousins Mavis and Gordon. The author and his ex-wife are in the back row far right, sister Dawn third row far right, Aunt May second row far right and cousin Shelia and Aunt 'Noona' second row far left.

kept mentioning the same thing. At that stage in life, it still concerned me that I did not know where I was going. I had no solid plans for the future and felt that I was in limbo. Thinking over my Merchant Navy friends' suggestions of joining. Initially felt a little scared that I would not be suitable. All sorts of things were racing through my mind, until I finally decided to take the plunge and apply.

The romance with this lovely girl continued and I really cared for her, but thoughts of settling down without any prospects started to give me doubts, and I became more confused, trying to work out what I really wanted in life. Should I settle into a fairly ordinary humdrum existence, remaining in the East End, or take up the opportunity to see the world? I decided to place my thoughts on hold, and see what transpired.

I applied by letter to the Peninsular & Oriental Steamship Company, 122 Leadenhall Street, in the City of London. To my surprise, I had a reply within days, asking me along for an interview and a medical. I managed to leave early in the afternoon, and raced straight from the building in which we were working in Kensington, directly to P & O's city offices. The interview went well until the medical; dropping my trousers I discovered,

Sister Dawn's wedding. The author is the Best Man, standing alongside Grandmother, brother-in-law Don and parents outside St Peter's Church.

to my horror, that the dust and dirt from the work had penetrated them, so my legs had more dust on them than the furniture we had been shifting! I was terribly embarrassed, but with good grace, the doctor chose to ignore my discomfort. However, he discovered that I had a hernia. I practically flew off the examination table on hearing this, 'No, no, it can't be me!', but it was. I was told to have an operation, then reapply to the company three months after surgery. I started cursing Foster's for all that heavy furniture we had carried up those floors at Charles House. I recalled how I used to come home with a great pain in my groin, having my Grandfather to check it for me, but he had found nothing of consequence. I chose, therefore, to forget about it, when the pain wasn't so bad.

Making all the necessary arrangements via doctors and the London Hospital, I was sent to the London Hospital Annexes in Brentwood for surgery. This was to be my baptism into having 'the knife'. Techniques then were quite different to now, as surgery has advanced enormously. To be shaved in the nether regions by a pretty young nurse prior to surgery, I found most embarrassing! However, after a little while, you became accustomed to those procedures and took it all in your stride! During my hospital stay, the King died. It quite saddened me, hearing the news of the loss of our monarch. The other patients in the ward were affected in the same way as I; the ward suddenly developed an air of gloom for a day or so.

My girlfriend came to the hospital to visit me, she was a very caring girl. Indeed, she had also visited my Grandparents, unbeknown to me. I began to feel the pressure of the situation, and the knot was beginning to tighten. I had become intrigued with one of the nurses, not romantically, of course, but she had the loveliest voice which I found absolutely enchanting. When she asked me what I would like to eat, it was as though she was singing it! Her pronunciation of the word 'pudding' was like music to my ears! I became enraptured with her voice. It was even a pleasure having her take my stitches out and to listen to her speak. It was not the everyday voice you heard in the East End but I never knew where she came from. My total stay in hospital was ten days; nowadays, you would have been up and out the day following surgery.

Returning to London, I began to suffer from what I think was post-operational depression, though at the time I was completely unaware of what was happening to me. I was no longer interested in having a romantic relationship, neither did I feel amorous towards my girlfriend, and I could not understand the reasons for my 'out of character behavior'. Gradually, I began to ease out of the relationship, regretting to this day that I had been unable to express myself clearly to her and the reasons why I was distancing myself. I know that she was deeply hurt by my actions; it is something I have always wished I could have made amends for, but regretfully, at that time, I was not capable, and never knew how to explain my irrational behaviour.

With surgery preventing me from lifting anything, I was in no position to return to Foster's. I had to lead a fairly quiet existence for the next three months, until it was time to reapply to the P & O Shipping Company. Meanwhile, not being able to afford to be out of work, I started scanning the situations vacant columns in the London evening papers and the *Hackney Gazette* for a suitable position. As good fortune would have it, I saw a job that suited me 'down to the ground'. It was for a clerical position with the Royal Engineers Territorials in Victoria Park Square, advertising for a temporary 'Z' call-up clerk. As I had already experienced a 'Z' call-up, I applied for the position and was successful.

It was a nice place to work, within easy walking distance from home, and of course being ex-army, all the army terminology was familiar to me. There were two of us in the office, plus an adjutant with his own office, who was a regular serving soldier. The hours were quite civilised and the work enjoyable in that, as I was a civilian working within a military framework, I was holding a position where I could not be disciplined for any reason! This I found encouraging, and after my army days of regimentation, very gratifying.

Our days were spent programming and sending out notices to ex-army personnel, who were subject to a 'Z' call-up, which was to take place at Perranporth in Cornwall. The day arrived when we were all transported to an army barracks in Perranporth, for a glorious few weeks of a wonderful summer. I was given NCO Sergeant status, both in living accommodation and messing; also the salary had all kinds of additions and perks that made it a good financial working holiday. The evenings were spent in the Sergeant's mess, with a glass in your hand, and a sing-song around a piano. Some nights we went dancing at the Blue Lagoon in Newquay. There was an RAF camp close by. Lots of service people would be in Newquay at the weekend. I recall meeting a delightful Royal Air Force 'WAAF'. Its funny how some names never escape you. She had the lovely name of Jean de Gruchy. We walked and talked along the sands of Newquay, sitting on the rocks, getting drenched exploring a cave, a lovely pleasant, innocent interlude. After frequently meeting on those beautiful summer evenings, we exchanged addresses and telephone numbers but our very brief encounter never developed into anything further.

Life in the barracks for that short period was great fun, working and meeting people from all walks of life, and the general camaraderie of it all. Being back in a military atmosphere, I never realised until then how much the army had indoctrinated me. Walking along the side of a road one day in the confines of the camp, a squad of soldiers came marching past, accompanied by a military band. As it was passing and without my being aware, I immediately found myself standing to attention, arms placed firmly at my side. I suddenly become conscious of my posture, and felt rather stupid! I further found that whenever a military band played, I would automatically stand shoulders back, chest out, stomach in, almost marching in step to the music! The days in Perranporth waltzed by, and before we knew it, we were back in the Territorials office in Bethnal Green. The remaining weeks were spent ironing out a million and one discrepancies over non-payments and allowances that army personnel should have obtained, but hadn't up until then. The authorities concerned in providing money to families were very slow to act. This resulted in a lot of anger and frustrations, and we were left to make the apologies and attempt, as best we could, to pacify the several visits per day, mainly from wives questioning the payments that were due to them. One morning, after interviewing a host of angry people, a man walked into our office. I immediately thought it was another complaint over non-payment, but I was wrong. He introduced himself as representing Sir Alexander Korda, the filmmaker. Immediately, I became interested, and found that he was keen for the unit to provide soldiers for a film about to be made, called *Folly to be Wise* starring Alistair Sim, Elizabeth Allen and Matita Hunt. What a beautiful diversion, I thought, from handling complaints!

Approaching the adjutant concerning Sir Alexandr Korda's request, the matter was discussed and duly approved, subject to the nod from the individuals, whom I firmly believed we would have no problem with. I was correct, and every person we contacted was more than willing to participate in becoming a film extra. The pay at that time was £10 per day. This was as much as people were getting for a week's work, so quite naturally, everyone jumped at the chance, including me! I obtained permission from the adjutant to go filming along with the others.

Filming as an extra was a whole new exciting experience: being on a film lot, seeing and speaking to the stars. Alistair Sim was a pleasant man who spent some time talking with us. He was brilliant in his acting, rarely did they have to do a retake when he was before a camera. As extras, we were required to be in a small army garrison theatre, shouting and applauding at a panel of dignitaries on the stage, played by the three main stars, as well some other unknowns.

The takes and retakes went on for a few days, so we were quite delighted! Getting £10 per day was rather nice, and we wished it would never end! They were also filming

With the TA's (Territorial Army) Royal Engineers in a temporary position shortly before going to sea.

on another set, *Gilbert & Sullivan*. It was rather odd seeing people walking around the studios in wigs and gowns, smoking. It seemed so out of place! Eventually, with sorrow, the filming ended and it was back to the office in Victoria Park Square. The termination of my appointment was also coming to an end, as it was almost three months since I had had the operation.

I reapplied to Peninsular & Oriental Shipping Company who, in return, requested another medical. Going though the medical examination procedures yet again, I was over the moon and jubilant to find that I had been passed fit for service! I was engaged as a 'U/S' (Utility Steward) and placed on 'stand-by' for the SS *Strathmore*. P & O sent me along to the Shipping Federation in Dock Street, Stepney to be registered, become a member of the National Union of Seaman, and receive a Seaman's Ration Card. In 1952 we were still on rationing, the seaman's allowance being somewhat better however, than the ordinary civilians allowance.

A week or so passed by before I received a telegram, asking me to join the S.S. *Maloja* in King George V Dock. I packed my suitcase and bade my adieus to my grandparents; to them it was like I was going to the ends of the earth! I walked up the ship's gangway into a career that would span the next four decades. At long last, I had found my vocation; it was the sea.

That little old lady, Emma, who had helped in my Mother's café and read my fortune from the tea leaves in my teacup so many years before, had been absolutely correct in her predictions. I was to travel the world many times over, and in doing so, it was to give me the greatest social education of my entire life.

Endnotes

1 institutions.org.uk/workhouses/england/lon/bethnal_green_workhouse.htm
  www.aim25.ac.uk
2 http://en.wikipedia.org/wiki/Spitalfield_Riots
3 http://www.airpower.maxwell.af.mil/airchronicles/apj/apj89/sum89/hillson.html#
4 http://www.bbc.co.uk/ww2peopleswar/stories/09/a795909.shtml
5 http://en.wikipedia.org/wiki/The_Blind_Beggar

Printed in Great Britain
by Amazon